Lecture Notes in Computer Science 14701

Founding Editors

Gerhard Goos
Juris Hartmanis

Editorial Board Members

Elisa Bertino, *Purdue University, West Lafayette, IN, USA*
Wen Gao, *Peking University, Beijing, China*
Bernhard Steffen, *TU Dortmund University, Dortmund, Germany*
Moti Yung, *Columbia University, New York, NY, USA*

The series Lecture Notes in Computer Science (LNCS), including its subseries Lecture Notes in Artificial Intelligence (LNAI) and Lecture Notes in Bioinformatics (LNBI), has established itself as a medium for the publication of new developments in computer science and information technology research, teaching, and education.

LNCS enjoys close cooperation with the computer science R & D community, the series counts many renowned academics among its volume editors and paper authors, and collaborates with prestigious societies. Its mission is to serve this international community by providing an invaluable service, mainly focused on the publication of conference and workshop proceedings and postproceedings. LNCS commenced publication in 1973.

Pei-Luen Patrick Rau
Editor

Cross-Cultural Design

16th International Conference, CCD 2024
Held as Part of the 26th HCI International Conference, HCII 2024
Washington, DC, USA, June 29 – July 4, 2024
Proceedings, Part III

 Springer

Editor
Pei-Luen Patrick Rau
Tsinghua University
Beijing, China

ISSN 0302-9743   ISSN 1611-3349 (electronic)
Lecture Notes in Computer Science
ISBN 978-3-031-60903-9   ISBN 978-3-031-60904-6 (eBook)
https://doi.org/10.1007/978-3-031-60904-6

This Springer imprint is published by the registered company Springer Nature Switzerland AG
The registered company address is: Gewerbestrasse 11, 6330 Cham, Switzerland

If disposing of this product, please recycle the paper.

Foreword

This year we celebrate 40 years since the establishment of the HCI International (HCII) Conference, which has been a hub for presenting groundbreaking research and novel ideas and collaboration for people from all over the world.

The HCII conference was founded in 1984 by Prof. Gavriel Salvendy (Purdue University, USA, Tsinghua University, P.R. China, and University of Central Florida, USA) and the first event of the series, "1st USA-Japan Conference on Human-Computer Interaction", was held in Honolulu, Hawaii, USA, 18–20 August. Since then, HCI International is held jointly with several Thematic Areas and Affiliated Conferences, with each one under the auspices of a distinguished international Program Board and under one management and one registration. Twenty-six HCI International Conferences have been organized so far (every two years until 2013, and annually thereafter).

Over the years, this conference has served as a platform for scholars, researchers, industry experts and students to exchange ideas, connect, and address challenges in the ever-evolving HCI field. Throughout these 40 years, the conference has evolved itself, adapting to new technologies and emerging trends, while staying committed to its core mission of advancing knowledge and driving change.

As we celebrate this milestone anniversary, we reflect on the contributions of its founding members and appreciate the commitment of its current and past Affiliated Conference Program Board Chairs and members. We are also thankful to all past conference attendees who have shaped this community into what it is today.

The 26th International Conference on Human-Computer Interaction, HCI International 2024 (HCII 2024), was held as a 'hybrid' event at the Washington Hilton Hotel, Washington, DC, USA, during 29 June – 4 July 2024. It incorporated the 21 thematic areas and affiliated conferences listed below.

A total of 5108 individuals from academia, research institutes, industry, and government agencies from 85 countries submitted contributions, and 1271 papers and 309 posters were included in the volumes of the proceedings that were published just before the start of the conference, these are listed below. The contributions thoroughly cover the entire field of human-computer interaction, addressing major advances in knowledge and effective use of computers in a variety of application areas. These papers provide academics, researchers, engineers, scientists, practitioners and students with state-of-the-art information on the most recent advances in HCI.

The HCI International (HCII) conference also offers the option of presenting 'Late Breaking Work', and this applies both for papers and posters, with corresponding volumes of proceedings that will be published after the conference. Full papers will be included in the 'HCII 2024 - Late Breaking Papers' volumes of the proceedings to be published in the Springer LNCS series, while 'Poster Extended Abstracts' will be included as short research papers in the 'HCII 2024 - Late Breaking Posters' volumes to be published in the Springer CCIS series.

I would like to thank the Program Board Chairs and the members of the Program Boards of all thematic areas and affiliated conferences for their contribution towards the high scientific quality and overall success of the HCI International 2024 conference. Their manifold support in terms of paper reviewing (single-blind review process, with a minimum of two reviews per submission), session organization and their willingness to act as goodwill ambassadors for the conference is most highly appreciated.

This conference would not have been possible without the continuous and unwavering support and advice of Gavriel Salvendy, founder, General Chair Emeritus, and Scientific Advisor. For his outstanding efforts, I would like to express my sincere appreciation to Abbas Moallem, Communications Chair and Editor of HCI International News.

July 2024   Constantine Stephanidis

HCI International 2024 Thematic Areas
and Affiliated Conferences

- HCI: Human-Computer Interaction Thematic Area
- HIMI: Human Interface and the Management of Information Thematic Area
- EPCE: 21st International Conference on Engineering Psychology and Cognitive Ergonomics
- AC: 18th International Conference on Augmented Cognition
- UAHCI: 18th International Conference on Universal Access in Human-Computer Interaction
- CCD: 16th International Conference on Cross-Cultural Design
- SCSM: 16th International Conference on Social Computing and Social Media
- VAMR: 16th International Conference on Virtual, Augmented and Mixed Reality
- DHM: 15th International Conference on Digital Human Modeling & Applications in Health, Safety, Ergonomics & Risk Management
- DUXU: 13th International Conference on Design, User Experience and Usability
- C&C: 12th International Conference on Culture and Computing
- DAPI: 12th International Conference on Distributed, Ambient and Pervasive Interactions
- HCIBGO: 11th International Conference on HCI in Business, Government and Organizations
- LCT: 11th International Conference on Learning and Collaboration Technologies
- ITAP: 10th International Conference on Human Aspects of IT for the Aged Population
- AIS: 6th International Conference on Adaptive Instructional Systems
- HCI-CPT: 6th International Conference on HCI for Cybersecurity, Privacy and Trust
- HCI-Games: 6th International Conference on HCI in Games
- MobiTAS: 6th International Conference on HCI in Mobility, Transport and Automotive Systems
- AI-HCI: 5th International Conference on Artificial Intelligence in HCI
- MOBILE: 5th International Conference on Human-Centered Design, Operation and Evaluation of Mobile Communications

List of Conference Proceedings Volumes Appearing Before the Conference

1. LNCS 14684, Human-Computer Interaction: Part I, edited by Masaaki Kurosu and Ayako Hashizume
2. LNCS 14685, Human-Computer Interaction: Part II, edited by Masaaki Kurosu and Ayako Hashizume
3. LNCS 14686, Human-Computer Interaction: Part III, edited by Masaaki Kurosu and Ayako Hashizume
4. LNCS 14687, Human-Computer Interaction: Part IV, edited by Masaaki Kurosu and Ayako Hashizume
5. LNCS 14688, Human-Computer Interaction: Part V, edited by Masaaki Kurosu and Ayako Hashizume
6. LNCS 14689, Human Interface and the Management of Information: Part I, edited by Hirohiko Mori and Yumi Asahi
7. LNCS 14690, Human Interface and the Management of Information: Part II, edited by Hirohiko Mori and Yumi Asahi
8. LNCS 14691, Human Interface and the Management of Information: Part III, edited by Hirohiko Mori and Yumi Asahi
9. LNAI 14692, Engineering Psychology and Cognitive Ergonomics: Part I, edited by Don Harris and Wen-Chin Li
10. LNAI 14693, Engineering Psychology and Cognitive Ergonomics: Part II, edited by Don Harris and Wen-Chin Li
11. LNAI 14694, Augmented Cognition, Part I, edited by Dylan D. Schmorrow and Cali M. Fidopiastis
12. LNAI 14695, Augmented Cognition, Part II, edited by Dylan D. Schmorrow and Cali M. Fidopiastis
13. LNCS 14696, Universal Access in Human-Computer Interaction: Part I, edited by Margherita Antona and Constantine Stephanidis
14. LNCS 14697, Universal Access in Human-Computer Interaction: Part II, edited by Margherita Antona and Constantine Stephanidis
15. LNCS 14698, Universal Access in Human-Computer Interaction: Part III, edited by Margherita Antona and Constantine Stephanidis
16. LNCS 14699, Cross-Cultural Design: Part I, edited by Pei-Luen Patrick Rau
17. LNCS 14700, Cross-Cultural Design: Part II, edited by Pei-Luen Patrick Rau
18. LNCS 14701, Cross-Cultural Design: Part III, edited by Pei-Luen Patrick Rau
19. LNCS 14702, Cross-Cultural Design: Part IV, edited by Pei-Luen Patrick Rau
20. LNCS 14703, Social Computing and Social Media: Part I, edited by Adela Coman and Simona Vasilache
21. LNCS 14704, Social Computing and Social Media: Part II, edited by Adela Coman and Simona Vasilache
22. LNCS 14705, Social Computing and Social Media: Part III, edited by Adela Coman and Simona Vasilache

47. LNCS 14730, HCI in Games: Part I, edited by Xiaowen Fang
48. LNCS 14731, HCI in Games: Part II, edited by Xiaowen Fang
49. LNCS 14732, HCI in Mobility, Transport and Automotive Systems: Part I, edited by Heidi Krömker
50. LNCS 14733, HCI in Mobility, Transport and Automotive Systems: Part II, edited by Heidi Krömker
51. LNAI 14734, Artificial Intelligence in HCI: Part I, edited by Helmut Degen and Stavroula Ntoa
52. LNAI 14735, Artificial Intelligence in HCI: Part II, edited by Helmut Degen and Stavroula Ntoa
53. LNAI 14736, Artificial Intelligence in HCI: Part III, edited by Helmut Degen and Stavroula Ntoa
54. LNCS 14737, Design, Operation and Evaluation of Mobile Communications: Part I, edited by June Wei and George Margetis
55. LNCS 14738, Design, Operation and Evaluation of Mobile Communications: Part II, edited by June Wei and George Margetis
56. CCIS 2114, HCI International 2024 Posters - Part I, edited by Constantine Stephanidis, Margherita Antona, Stavroula Ntoa and Gavriel Salvendy
57. CCIS 2115, HCI International 2024 Posters - Part II, edited by Constantine Stephanidis, Margherita Antona, Stavroula Ntoa and Gavriel Salvendy
58. CCIS 2116, HCI International 2024 Posters - Part III, edited by Constantine Stephanidis, Margherita Antona, Stavroula Ntoa and Gavriel Salvendy
59. CCIS 2117, HCI International 2024 Posters - Part IV, edited by Constantine Stephanidis, Margherita Antona, Stavroula Ntoa and Gavriel Salvendy
60. CCIS 2118, HCI International 2024 Posters - Part V, edited by Constantine Stephanidis, Margherita Antona, Stavroula Ntoa and Gavriel Salvendy
61. CCIS 2119, HCI International 2024 Posters - Part VI, edited by Constantine Stephanidis, Margherita Antona, Stavroula Ntoa and Gavriel Salvendy
62. CCIS 2120, HCI International 2024 Posters - Part VII, edited by Constantine Stephanidis, Margherita Antona, Stavroula Ntoa and Gavriel Salvendy

https://2024.hci.international/proceedings

Preface

The increasing internationalization and globalization of communication, business and industry is leading to a wide cultural diversification of individuals and groups of users who access information, services and products. If interactive systems are to be usable, useful and appealing to such a wide range of users, culture becomes an important HCI issue. Therefore, HCI practitioners and designers face the challenges of designing across different cultures, and need to elaborate and adopt design approaches which take into account cultural models, factors, expectations and preferences, and allow development of cross-cultural user experiences that accommodate global users.

The 16th Cross-Cultural Design (CCD) Conference, an affiliated conference of the HCI International Conference, encouraged the submission of papers from academics, researchers, industry and professionals, on a broad range of theoretical and applied issues related to Cross-Cultural Design and its applications.

A considerable number of papers were accepted to this year's CCD conference addressing diverse topics, which spanned a wide variety of domains. A notable theme addressed by several contributions was that of user experience and product design from a cross-cultural point of view, offering insights into design, user interaction, and evaluation across different domains and how cultural contexts shape user preferences, expectations, and behaviors. Furthermore, a considerable number of papers explore how individuals perceive, attend to, and process information within cultural contexts. Furthermore, the impact of culture across different application domains is addressed, examining technologies for communication, cultural heritage, and digital transformation and bringing together cutting-edge research, innovative practices, and insightful studies. Finally, the influence of culture on emerging technologies is a prominent theme, with contributions discussing extended reality, aviation and transportation, as well as artificial intelligence, addressing a multitude of aspects such as narrative design, interaction design, evaluation of user experience and performance, artificial empathy, and ethical aspects.

Four volumes of the HCII 2024 proceedings are dedicated to this year's edition of the CCD conference:

- Part I addresses topics related to Cross-Cultural Design and User Experience, and Cross-Cultural Product Design;
- Part II addresses topics related to Cross-Cultural Communication and Interaction, and Cultural Perception, Attention and Information Processing;
- Part III addresses topics related to Cross-Cultural Tangible and Intangible Heritage and Cross-Cultural Digital Transformation;
- Part IV addresses topics related to Cross-Cultural Extended Reality, Cross-Cultural Design in Aviation and Transportation, and Artificial Intelligence from a Cross-Cultural Perspective.

The papers in these volumes were accepted for publication after a minimum of two single-blind reviews from the members of the CCD Program Board or, in some cases, from members of the Program Boards of other affiliated conferences. I would like to thank all of them for their invaluable contribution, support and efforts.

July 2024   Pei-Luen Patrick Rau

16th International Conference on Cross-Cultural Design (CCD2024)

Program Board Chair: **Pei-Luen Patrick Rau**, *Tsinghua University, China*

- Na Chen, *Beijing University of Chemical Technology, P.R. China*
- Zhe Chen, *Beihang University, P.R. China*
- Kuohsiang Chen, *National Cheng Kung University, Taiwan*
- Wen-Ko Chiou, *Chang Gung University, Taiwan*
- Zhiyong Fu, *Tsinghua University, P.R. China*
- Hanjing Huang, *Fuzhou University, P.R. China*
- Toshikazu Kato, *Chuo University, Japan*
- Xin Lei, *Zhejiang University of Technology, P.R. China*
- Sheau-Farn Max Liang, *National Taipei University of Technology, Taiwan*
- Dyi-Yih Michael Lin, *I-Shou University, Taiwan*
- Wei Lin, *Feng Chia University, Taiwan*
- Rungtai Lin, *National Taiwan University of Arts, Taiwan*
- Na Liu, *Beijing University of Posts and Telecommunications, P.R. China*
- Cheng-Hung Lo, *Xi'an Jiaotong-Liverpool University, P.R. China*
- Yongqi Lou, *Tongji University, P.R. China*
- Ta-Ping Lu, *Sichuan University, P.R. China*
- Liang Ma, *Tsinghua University, P.R. China*
- Huatong Sun, *University of Washington Tacoma, USA*
- Hao Tan, *Hunan University, P.R. China*
- Pei-Lee Teh, *Monash University Malaysia, Malaysia*
- Lin Wang, *Incheon National University, Korea*
- Hsiu-Ping Yueh, *National Taiwan University, Taiwan*
- Andong Zhang, *Shanghai Jiao Tong University, P.R. China*
- Runting Zhong, *Jiangnan University, P.R. China*
- Xingchen Zhou, *Beijing Normal University, P.R. China*

The full list with the Program Board Chairs and the members of the Program Boards of all thematic areas and affiliated conferences of HCII 2024 is available online at:

http://www.hci.international/board-members-2024.php

HCI International 2025 Conference

The 27th International Conference on Human-Computer Interaction, HCI International 2025, will be held jointly with the affiliated conferences at the Swedish Exhibition & Congress Centre and Gothia Towers Hotel, Gothenburg, Sweden, June 22–27, 2025. It will cover a broad spectrum of themes related to Human-Computer Interaction, including theoretical issues, methods, tools, processes, and case studies in HCI design, as well as novel interaction techniques, interfaces, and applications. The proceedings will be published by Springer. More information will become available on the conference website: https://2025.hci.international/.

General Chair
Prof. Constantine Stephanidis
University of Crete and ICS-FORTH
Heraklion, Crete, Greece
Email: general_chair@2025.hci.international

https://2025.hci.international/

Contents – Part III

Cross-Cultural Digital Transformation

Cross-Cultural Tangible and Intangible Heritage

Nature's Canvas: Exploring Landscape Through Cyanotype Assemblage Art

Zhonghao Chen[1]([✉]) [iD], André Krebber[2] [iD], and Yuehan Dou[1] [iD]

[1] Xi'an Jiangtong-Liverpool University, Suzhou, China
zhonghao.chen@xjtlu.edu.cn
[2] Faculty of Social Sciences, University of Kassel, Kassel, Germany

Abstract. The diverse manifestations of nature exhibit their own generative activities, intertwined with yet independent of human cultures. These challenges conventional narratives portraying nature as merely a passive resource for human use. Through an experiential methodology integrating field research and artistic practices, this interdisciplinary project aims to articulate nature's agentic voices. The field explorations enable first-hand experiential observations of the landscapes around Tai Lake in Suzhou, China. Cyanotype photography and assemblage techniques are then used to capture and reinterpret the environment's traces through subjective aesthetic impressions. The resulting images reflect philosophical perspectives from Adorno, Benjamin, and Chinese Shanshui painting on unveiling nature's affective essence through creative practices. This paper outlines the integrated process and presents preliminary artistic samples. It proposes that creative interdisciplinary research can move us beyond human-centred narratives toward more inclusive ecological co-creation and co-narration. Through artistic experimentation and open listening, the project facilitates deeper empathetic awareness of our embeddedness within lively, agentic nature.

Keywords: Nature-Inspired Art · Cyanotype · Creative Assemblage · Shanshui Painting

1 Introduction

"The most elemental process of modern times is the conquest of the world as images." - Martin Heidegger, Holzwege.

In recent years, images of nature as a passive resource and commodity have been widely challenged. The enormously diverse range of entities subsumed under the term is instead seen as a sphere of self-producing and self-willing activity, whose creatures are in myriad ways interwoven and interdependent with the activities of human cultures. Suppose we want to move towards a more sustainable future. In that case, this interdependence calls for considering nonhuman concerns and needs in our decision-making and actions accordingly, which then requires understanding these concerns. It requires urgently recognizing and listening to nonhuman entities and telling stories of multispecies origin.

P.-L. P. Rau (Ed.): HCII 2024, LNCS 14701, pp. 3–17, 2024.
https://doi.org/10.1007/978-3-031-60904-6_1

Forming a narrative is an important mechanism that curates, de-structures and re-structures the surrounding environment. It brings coherence to the fragmented diversity of our perceptions of experiences and events, both non-linearly and linearly. When we weave events and experiences into a narrative, we establish connections among them, highlighting specific meanings and attributes while sidelining others, thereby imbuing them with significance within our understanding of the world and history. Alongside frameworks, narrating emerges as a potent cultural technique, enabling us to grasp and navigate the transient nature of the environment and facilitating a space for crafting our worlds (Meretoja, 2014).

Among escalating ecological crises, the prevailing narratives regarding nature as articulated by modern Western culture are increasingly being scrutinized and deemed inadequate. Many of these narratives, rooted in Enlightenment ideals, need to be more suited to capture the complexities of our contemporary reality and often appear in direct contradiction to it. While the tangible shifts in our environment, such as ecological degradation, contribute to the inadequacy of these narratives, pre-existing inconsistencies have also vastly surfaced. Over recent decades, sustaining these conventional and linear narratives—such as portraying nature as passive and humans as solely active—has become challenging, revealing their inherent discordance with reality. Rather than serving as accurate depictions of our world, these narratives now resonate more as rallying cries.

A notable shift in the current historical context is the acknowledgement that humanity does not operate in isolation as the sole architect of the world. Despite the significant profile and detrimental impact on the environment as a young species, other beings, entities, particles, and matter play pivotal roles in shaping our shared reality. This evolving understanding underscores a collective co-creation of the world. After that, a co-fabrication and co-narrating throughout time, space and beyond. Increasing scholarly and artistic interest, accompanied by extensive research and practice focused on nonhuman agencies (Bowden, 2015), exemplifies this transformative realisation and underscores the multifaceted interactions and interdependencies that define our interconnected existence (Droz, 2021).

To navigate the complex narrative landscape, we sought the insights of cultural critics Theodor W. Adorno and Walter Benjamin, complemented by the traditions of Shanshui landscape painting and then rigorous examination from environment science. Adorno's Aesthetic Theory (2002: 68) seems prescient, resonating with our contemporary understanding of co-creation.

"Technique, which is said to have ravished nature, according to a schema borrowed ultimately from bourgeois sexual morality, under transformed relations of production would just as easily be able to assist nature and on this sad earth help it attain whereto perhaps it wants to head."-Adorno, Aesthetic Theory.

He argues that under altered production dynamics, the technique could collaborate with nature, aiding it in achieving its inherent aspirations on this living planet. Beyond merely portraying nature as an objectified entity, Adorno suggests that nature possesses its ambitions and hints at a mutual, perhaps symbiotic, relationship between culture and nature.

In light of this suggested cohesivity between human and nature, this interdisciplinary project employs cyanotype photography and assemblage art techniques to capture and translate the language of nonhuman entities in nature. Cyanotypes involve coating paper or canvas with a light-sensitive solution that turns vivid Prussian blue when exposed to UV rays. Placing these cyanotype materials out in the natural landscape allows the sun to imprint directly, with natural textures and forms blocking and filtering the light. The resulting images exhibit the indexical traces of flora, soil, insects, and other ecological elements. Additionally, found natural materials will be incorporated into the cyanotype canvases through assemblage art processes. This will allow the environment to actively transform the artwork over time.

Looking through the lens of Theodor W. Adorno's and Walter Benjamin's aesthetic theories (Repko & Szostak, 2020), we incorporate Cyanotypical Photography and Chinese Shanshui painting techniques to leverage natural processes in capturing the experiential spirit of the place as an alternative form of descriptive representation. We aim to examine how far creative image-making accompanied by technology offers the potential to access and translate the language and expression of nonhuman entities and narrate stories of the inter-ecological common.

2 Related Works

In a philosophical exploration, Adorno examines the intrinsic nature of beauty, mainly how it represents the natural world's inherent striving. He suggests that natural beauty is an authoritative yet enigmatic expression that binds and challenges human perception. Adorno asserts that moments of experiencing natural beauty allow humans to transcend their perspectives, perceiving nature on its terms (Adorno, 2002). This perception unveils nature's emotional and aspirational states as artworks fulfil what nature seemingly yearns for.

Diverging from Adorno's focus solely on natural beauty within aesthetic theory, Benjamin expands the discourse on language, suggesting that everything, animate or inanimate, possesses a communicative essence beyond human speech (Benjamin, 2004). Benjamin's perspective, resonating with Adorno's, emphasizes the inherent expressiveness of entities, emphasizing the need for understanding nature beyond mere instrumentalization. Benjamin's use of language aims to manifest things in their essence, making them recognizable and relatable. Both philosophers recognize the challenge in directly accessing nature's eloquence; it often requires artistic interpretation to comprehend nature's desires fully. Benjamin's exploration extends to Chinese literati paintings, which encapsulate an amalgamation of calligraphy, poetry, and painting (Benjamin, 2008). Benjamin captures nature's fluidity and ever-changing essence, acting as a medium between thought and image. Such art forms, characterized by their pursuit of the thought-image, offer avenues to understand and narrate nature's expressions more profoundly.

The art of image is a powerful instrument for interpreting and articulating narratives, significantly influencing our perceptions of the world. A reflective analysis of how Western society has employed visual media demonstrates a distinct human-centric and linear approach. Central to this perspective are notions of objectivity and linear perspective (Edgerton, 2009), which have profoundly shaped visual representation and cultural narratives. For example, historical depictions reflect societal viewpoints on land and ownership, as Cosgrove (1984) pointed out, and solidify specific cultural norms and values. Concurrently, the evolution of artistic methodologies provides avenues to capture the predominant cultural ideologies of different epochs. However, this historical evolution is multifaceted, sparking ongoing debates about emphasizing objectivity within these visual representations. Scholars such as Daston and Galison (2007) further illuminate these discussions, delving into questions surrounding the authenticity and reliability of narratives constructed visually.

Building upon the theoretical insights on mimesis by Gombrich (1960) and the evolution of optical imagery in Western discussions as outlined by Kemp (1990), our project delves into the concept of "likeness" as interpreted within Chinese Shanshui visual narratives, as presented by Sullivan (2008). Shanshui, translating to "Mountain and Water", is a cornerstone of traditional Chinese art (Clunas, 2004; Sullivan, 2008). This exploration occurs within today's digital and lens-based landscapes. To frame our investigation, we intertwine this concept with the broader idea of "expression," as articulated by Adorno and Benjamin. Benjamin's notion of the "language of things" (Ref) particularly emphasizes the intricate connection between the human and non-human realms. Through this viewpoint, we gain a richer understanding of the enduring significance of the Shanshui tradition and its ongoing relevance in contemporary visual culture.

Our artistic inquiry focuses on the creative pursuits of Shi Tao, a notable Chinese Buddhist monk, calligrapher, theorist, and artist from the early Qing dynasty, as highlighted by Clunas (2004). Shi Tao's artistic philosophy is concisely summarized by the idea of "drawing from the past to enlighten the present" (Han, 2013). This sentiment emphasizes Shi Tao's exceptional ability to blend historical inspirations with innovative approaches, enriching visual expression and our understanding of perception (Fig. 1).

Shi Tao's Shanshui paintings deeply connect with nature, echoing the subtle hints of a rhinoceros's essence as emphasized by Adorno (2002: 112). This deep connection grants Shanshui art a unique "validation" from nature, cultivating a genuine, reciprocal, and dynamic relationship that mirrors a conversation between humans and the non-human realm. Within Shanshui imagery, this bond is evident through four essential elements: perspective, non-space, the core of the Shanshui spirit, and action.

In contrast to Western techniques of image-making that often rely on optical tools and detailed precision (Hockney, 2001), Shanshui art confronts these conventions of objectified dimensionality, static, and linear visual depictions. For instance, Shi Tao's Shanshui creations move beyond fixed viewpoints, leading viewers on a seamless journey through the depicted terrains. This approach aligns with the literati concept of "wandering and contemplating" (Liu, 2017), prompting a more profound, reflective engagement with, within and beyond the image surface (Fig. 2).

Incorporating voids or non-spaces within Shanshui artworks, as highlighted by Hu (1995), holds profound meaning. These seemingly unfinished areas expose the limits of human understanding, revealing the enigmatic aspects of the universe emerging from a canvas of "emptiness." Such representations of non-space foster a fertile ground for imagination, offering limitless possibilities to depict and express the non-human and natural realms. Beyond mere image creation, Shanshui embodies a dynamic philosophy known as the Shanshui spirit (Gao, 2020)—a flexible and harmonious approach aligned

Fig. 1. A landscape painting by Shi Tao. Shi Tao 1698. Landscape, ink on paper, 136.0 x 58.2 cm. A landscape painting by Shi Tao depicting a serene natural configuration. Source: National Gallery of Viktoria, Melbourne, Australia. Retrieved from Wikimedia Commons (https://commons.wik imedia.org/wiki/File:Daoji_-_Landscape_-_Google_Art_Project.jpg).

with nature. This viewpoint acknowledges human predispositions, fosters interactions with the non-human world, and nurtures a profound understanding of one's role within the cosmos (Fig. 3).

Within traditional Shanshui art, crafting Shanshui images goes beyond simple portrayal. Literati artists emphasize Shanshui action, stressing a direct connection with

Nature as resource(reference)   Fixed perspective   Regulated Agency

Images of nature as a **passive resource and commodity** have been widely challenged in recent years.

Fig. 2. The relationship between the spectator, image, and depicted nature

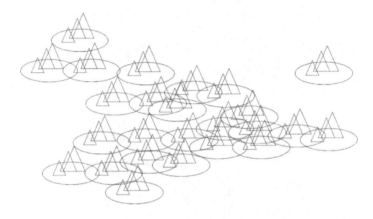

Images, practice and philosophies of Shanahui demonstrates an alternative paradigm of intract with nature that intertwines visuality, activity, technicality and narrativity

Fig. 3. This diagram indicates new perspectives of nature according to Shanshui philosophy.

nature, diverging from Adorno's view of a more passive engagement with nature in aesthetic encounters. This proactive stance, captured in Shi Tao's guidance: "exploring every unique peak to draft preliminary sketches" (Su & Hu, 2008), highlights an immersive and dynamic bond with nature. Actively immersing oneself in nature becomes integral to its artistic depiction, deeply interwoven with the creative process. Through such methods, as Shi Tao exemplifies, artists engage with expansive avenues of expression, establishing a harmonious bond where the artist and nature collaboratively work in creation.

Inspired by Shi Tao's sophisticated methods and frameworks, our reflective exploration aims to incorporate them into contemporary creative ventures. This evolution goes beyond simple replication, signifying a deliberate effort to integrate Shi Tao's insights into our artistic pursuits. Our objective is to illuminate the subtleties of nature's manifestations through a balanced fusion of traditional and modern approaches. In this transformative journey, age-old traditions harmoniously intersect with present-day contexts, providing a renewed lens to understand and engage with nature's complex nuances and languages.

3 Methods

This research utilized an exploratory fieldwork approach followed by artistic documentation methods to subjectively capture the vitality and essence of a landscape site. Initial experimental field research was conducted to immerse researchers in the location through observational data gathering, field mapping, documentation, and qualitative analysis. This inductive phase provided an experiential foundation for identifying salient themes and dynamics on the landscape. The researchers then leveraged cyanotype photographic printing techniques, employing the landscape as the exposure agent imprinting its traces. Additionally, assemblage practices incorporated naturally found artefacts into the cyanotype canvases, allowing the environment to transform the piece actively over time. These artistic techniques aimed to sustain the expressive spirit of place encountered through preliminary fieldwork. The cyanotype assemblage pieces were subjective visual documentation conveying ecological vitality through an evocative medium. This process exemplifies an interdisciplinary, experiential approach blending systematic field research with artistic methods for more intertwined landscape documentation (Fig. 4).

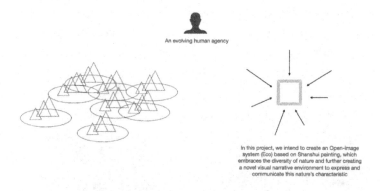

An evolving human agency

In this project, we intend to create an Open-image system (Eco) based on Shanshui painting, which embraces the diversity of nature and further creating a novel visual narrative environment to express and communicate this nature's characteristic

Shanshui legacy inspires an open being and further expose the limitation upon nature from the western visual narrative

Fig. 4. The three key aspects of this project.

The project was implemented at Tai Lake in Suzhou, China, an area noted for its considerable environmental and economic importance (Chen and Zhang, 2015). Additionally, moving away from Suzhou's renowned Garden heritage that highlights human artistry, the lake showcases a deep-rooted history emphasizing nature's central role in shaping Suzhou's landscape (Wang, 2018).

3.1 Exploratory Field Research

Following the principles of the Shanshui action philosophy, we explored the less-charted areas of Tai Lake using kayaks and sailboats. This hands-on approach deepened our connection with the environment, contrasting with typical modes of travel like road and air trips that can distance us from nature. Importantly, our expeditions revealed overlooked sections of Tai Lake—hidden behind the manicured portions of the lake's edge, reflecting aesthetic choices shaped by human activity. It is worth noting that these regions have not escaped human influence; instead, they remain less prioritized in human alteration. While human activities often focus on transforming visible parts of the lake near settlements, these quieter areas potentially serve as spaces where nature's voice can be more pronounced. As a result, these less-frequented areas become potential zones where nature's authentic voice can shine through, reacting to and resonating against human intervention. By leaving them untouched, we create spaces for nature to express its original character and push back against its marginalization (Figs. 5 and 6).

Fig. 5. Photograph capturing a field research expedition into Tai Lake

Fig. 6. Photograph capturing a researched field where cyanotype and assemblage activities were conducted during an expedition into Tai Lake

3.2 Cyanotype Photography and Assemblage

Cyanotypes (Ware, 1999) involve coating canvas or paper with a photosensitive solution that turns Prussian blue when exposed to UV light. Placing these prepared canvases and materials directly in the natural environment leverages sunlight as the exposure agent, with the landscape itself becoming the 'negative' as its features block and filter the light. Weathering, including the transformative effect of rain on cyanotypes, added an unexpected dimension where the environment participated in the artistic process with its own ink medium.

This thorough and time-intensive journey, often spanning multiple days, redefines the role of the image-maker. Prioritizing collaboration, flexibility, and interaction within a continuously evolving visual space highlights the importance of recognizing and respecting the influence of the entities encountered. This method contrasts sharply with conventional image-making narratives, where a single dominant figure usually dictates the visual narrative.

Upon perfecting the cyanotype technique, the canvas, having absorbed environmental influences, transitioned to the studio. Through rigorous scrutiny, we incorporated painterly interpretations, collectively weaving and deciphering stories embedded within the image's fabric. Following this, the canvas underwent painting, photography, and digital refinement phases, continuing the creative process using transmedia methods articulated by Jenkins (2006). By embracing techniques like layering and juxtaposition, intrinsic to Shanshui painting, we enhanced the myriad expressive facets of digital imagery. This method transcended conventional linear approaches, culminating in a hyperimage (Thürlemann, 2019) that captures the intricate narratives inherent to nature's expression.

4 Results and Discussion

The results of the cyanotype assemblage process conducted at the Tai Lake field site are shown in the samples presented in Figs. 7, 8 and 9. At first glimpse, the two cyanotype samples in Fig. 7 evoke majestic landscape vistas with rolling hills and a flowing river. The naturalistic compositions resemble traditional landscape paintings or photographs of scenic terrain. Yet upon closer inspection, these images emerged organically from the environment itself, not an artist's brush. The textures and impressions were generated through chance interactions between the cyanotype surface, ambient light, and the ecological elements of the field site. The cyanotypes contain a wealth of fine-grained detail from this serendipitous generative process. Grass blades, leaves, feathers, pebbles, sand, and other traces of flora and fauna add nuanced "brush strokes" analogous to Impressionist painters conveying a sense of motion using vivid dabs of colour. But in this case, the very specimens and substances of the Tai Lake terrain provided the pigments, filtered through the chemistry of cyanotype and the angle of the sun. The resulting compositions reflect the deep integration of artistic medium with the expressions of the landscape itself.

Figures 8 and 9 capture in-progress cyanotype assemblage pieces midway through their artistic evolution. Although retrieved at a midpoint, the work in Fig. 8 exemplifies a finished form from an aesthetic perspective. The hazy, muted tones evoke an atmospheric, smoldering mood, as if the environment emits a mysterious ethereal essence. While subdued, the organic shapes and stochastic textures vividly reflect the unpredictability and dynamism of the natural landscape. The cyanotype almost appears to breathe and

Fig. 7. Photograph displaying field samples of cyanotype

dissolve before our eyes. This transient quality highlights the intended co-fabrication with the environment itself as an active artistic collaborator. The piece also represents more profound questions about perception and knowing nature.

The work in Fig. 9 displays clashing yet mingling visual topologies that exhibit diverse impressions and documentation of the subject. This entangled, iterative and recursive pictoriality precisely indicates that our visual interpretations of the world are constrained by the limits of human sensation and cognition in representing the environment's complex material forms. The "actual" essence of nature remains elusive, obscured by our own incomplete modes of understanding. Yet the cyanotype nonetheless seems to resonate with our perceptual experience of nature's patterns, energies, and uncertainties. Through artistic insight, the work evokes the feeling of a living, agential landscape.

Through the perspectives offered by Adorno, Benjamin, and Shanshui practitioners, our approach exemplifies an effort to transcend our human-centered and human-caused viewpoints. However, using cyanotype as a medium for nature to articulate its intrinsic messages has limitations. While Adorno underscores nature's manifestation of beauty, this principle resonates more broadly, emphasizing our aesthetic encounters with nature as a whole. Yet, not all facets of nature are inherently beautiful or aesthetically communicative from a human perspective.

Fig. 8. An in-progress piece of the cyanotypical capturing and digital imaging

The vulnerability of human thought when confronted with natural beauty, coupled with the profound impact of this beauty, necessitates that art captures its elusive essence, according to Adorno. However, while artistic representations can echo indescribable nuances, they inevitably filter nature through a human lens. Our project aims to "hear" nature's language through iterative imaging, pushing back against anthropocentrism. But as Benjamin argues, mechanical reproduction inevitably strips away contextual nuances. So, while cyanotypes capture traces, they lose the multi-sensory richness of direct experience.

Adorno suggests that art, like Goethe's, translates nature's communication into human terms through co-narration (Adorno 2002: 73). However, this perspective presumes latent intentions within nature rather than a collaboration between separate entities with differing forms of agency. Our evolved abilities can consciously engage nature, but primarily in human terms. The persistent call across art to truly listen signifies the difficulty of embracing nature's radically different communication forms. While creative practices can foster empathy, we must remain aware of inherent limits in speaking for nature.

Fig. 9. An in-progress piece of the cyanotypical capturing and digital imaging

5 Conclusion

The study stands as a preliminary effort to apply Adorno and Benjamin's perspectives on discerning nature's expression through collaborative human creative faculties. It demonstrates the value of an interdisciplinary approach that blends fieldwork methodologies with artistic practices to capture the vitality and spirit of a landscape. The initial exploratory research provides an empirical foundation while the cyanotype assemblages translate that lived experience into a subjective visual medium. The resulting images evoke nature's dynamism through textural impressions and material traces of ecological processes.

The cyanotypes produced appear to resonate with the enigmatic essence described in their aesthetic theories. This suggests the potential of artistic methods to sustain nature's affective presence from embodied landscape encounters. While this study focused on a single locality at Tai Lake, the research team aims to expand the project across multiple field sites and seasons. Comparing cyanotypes and assemblages from diverse environments could reveal common patterns and unique variations, enriching the repository of nature's manifold voices.

This work attempts to cultivate a language and narrative where human and non-human contributions are impartially represented. It aspires to look past constructed dichotomies between culture and nature to appreciate their dynamic co-fabrication. The presented outcome offers a small step toward this goal of co-narration and deeper ecological awareness. Through creative effort and openness to alternate forms of expression, it aims to continue illuminating nature's perspectives in increasingly discernible ways.

References

1. Adorno, T.W.: Aesthetic Theory. Continuum, London; New York (2002)
2. Bowden, S.: Human and nonhuman agency in Deleuze. In: Deleuze and the non/human, 60–80. Palgrave Macmillan UK, London (2015)
3. Benjamin, W.: On language as such and on the language of man. In: Bullock, M.P., Jennings, M.W. (eds.) Walter Benjamin: Selected Writings, Volume 1, 1913–1926, pp. 62–74. The Belknap Press, Cambridge, MA; London (2004)
4. Benjamin, W.: Chinese paintings at the bibliotheque nationale. In: Jennings, M.W., Doherty, B., Levin, T.Y. (eds.) The Work of Art in the Age of Its Technological Reproducibility, and Other Writings on Media, pp. 257–261. The Belknap Press, Cambridge, MA; London (2008)
5. Chen, Y., Zhang, J.: Economic valuation of Tai lake wetlands: a case study in Jiangsu province China. J. Environ. Manage. **158**, 76–84 (2015)
6. Clunas, C.: Art in China. Oxford University Press, Oxford (2004)
7. Cosgrove, D.: Social Formation and Symbolic Landscape. Croom Helm, London (1984)
8. Droz, L.: The concept of milieu in environmental ethics: individual responsibility within an interconnected world. Routledge (2021)
9. Daston, L., Galison, P.: Objectivity. Zone Books (distributed by MIT Press), New York (2007)
10. Edgerton, S.Y.: The Mirror, the Window, and the Telescope: How Renaissance Linear Perspective Changed Our Vision of the Universe. Cornell University Press, Ithaca (2009)
11. Shiqiang, G.: Exploring a New Path: a teaching and research experiment between "Shanshui Spirit" and "Near Future." Art Contemporary **4**, 46–49 (2020)

12. Gombrich, E.H.: Art and Illusion: A Study in the Psychology of Pictorial Representation. Princeton University Press, Princeton (1960)
13. Gang, H.: Shi Tao's painting studies: "Innovation" and rectification — focusing on "Brush and ink should follow the times" and "Borrowing from the past to illuminate the present." Chin. Cultural Forum 1, 8–89 (2013)
14. Heidegger, M., von Herrmann, F.W.: Holzwege. v. Klostermann, Frankfurt am Main (1950)
15. Hockney, D.: Secret Knowledge: Rediscovering the Lost Techniques of the Old Masters. Thames & Hudson, London (2001)
16. Hu, D.: The philosophical origin of the black-white system of Chinese painting. Int. J. Polit., Culture Soc., 453–465 (1995)
17. Jenkins, H.: Convergence Culture: Where Old and New Media Collide. New York University Press, New York (2006)
18. Liu, L.: Path, place, and pace in mid-Ming Suzhou landscape painting. Res: Anthropol. Aesthetics 67(1), 207–224 (2017)
19. McEvilley, T.: The Exile's Return: Toward a Redefinition of Paintings for the Post-Modern Era. Cambridge University Press, Cambridge (1994)
20. Meretoja, H.: Narrative and Human Existence: ontology, epistemology, and ethics. New Literary History 45(1), 89–109 (2014). https://doi.org/10.1353/nlh.2014.0001
21. Reiss, J.H.: From Margin to Centre: The Spaces of Installation Art. MIT Press, Cambridge (2001)
22. Repko, A.F., Szostak, R.: Interdisciplinary Research: Process and Theory. Sage Publications (2020)
23. Sullivan, M.: The Arts of China. University of California Press, Berkeley (2008)
24. Jincheng, S., Yuanyuan, H.: Searching for all unique peak to create preliminary sketches: a preliminary study of Shi Tao's artistic creation thoughts in "Shi Tao's quotations on painting." Calligraphy and Painting World 3, 35–36 (2008)
25. Tao, S.: Landscape, ink on paper, 136.0 x 58.2 cm. National Gallery of Victoria, Melbourne, Australia. Wikimedia Commons. https://commons.wikimedia.org/wiki/File:Daoji_-_Landscape_-_Google_Art_Project.jpg (1698)
26. Shaw, J. K., Reeves-Evison, T. (Eds.): Fiction as Method. National Geographic Books (2017)
27. Thürlemann, F.: More Than One Picture: An Art History of the Hyperimage. Getty Publications (2019)
28. Wang, J.: Suzhou Gardens: Cultural Expressions and Ecological Interactions. Journal of Chinese Landscape Studies (2018)
29. Ware, M.: Cyanotype: The History, Science, and Art of Photographic Printing in Prussian Blue. Science Museum, London (1999)

Research on the Design of Art Derivatives from the Perspective of Digital Culture and Tourism: A Case Study of Works with Jiangsu Regional Themes

Xiaoli Chu[1] and Qing Liu[1,2(✉)]

[1] Jincheng College of Nanjing University of Aeronautics and Astronautics, Nanjing 210000, China
mollyliu0408@gmail.com
[2] Kyiv National University of Technologies and Design, Kyiv 01011, Ukraine

Abstract. Aim: To explore empowering methods and design approaches of digital intelligent design for art derivatives, especially propose innovative digital design solutions for Jiangsu regional theme painting art derivatives. **Methods:** Through analysis of the design theory underpinning Jiangsu regional theme art derivatives and digital innovation strategies, the paper investigates enhanced presentation techniques, expressive formats, and expanded creative directions enabled by digital technologies. A case study of the *Jingling Diagram Digital Art Exhibition* informs this exploration. **Conclusion:** It is hoped that digital innovative technologies can be utilized to further enhance the aesthetic effect, mark-et promotion and communication influence of Jiangsu regional theme art derivatives, to better exhibited characteristics and charm of regional culture. This provides new perspectives for continued exploration of digital cultural tourism, inheritance of regional culture, and artistic innovation, achieving multiple benefits in cultural shaping, urban tourism, and brand value.

Keywords: Digital technology · Art derivatives · Cultural tourism · City image

1 Introduction

As digital intelligent technologies rapidly develop and widespread adoption, cultural tourism is presented with new opportunities to promote the preservation and innovative evolution of urban regional cultural heritage. Within China's rich and storied artistic traditions, painting harbors profound cultural meaning and aesthetic merit, constituting a vital medium for inheriting culture, facilitating cultural exchange, and providing meaningful aesthetic experience. However, in this emergent era of digital economics, empowering the threshing of artistic derivatives through technological innovation remains an open question with great potential. This research takes as its subject matter the regional landscape paintings of Jiangsu, aiming to exhume their cultural underpinnings and artistic import. Jiangsu is a famous province in China, which owns rich cultural heritage.

P.-L. P. Rau (Ed.): HCII 2024, LNCS 14701, pp. 18–29, 2024.
https://doi.org/10.1007/978-3-031-60904-6_2

It discusses applying digital innovation to developing artistically derivative works as a means of disseminating and safeguarding Jiangsu's distinct cultural legacy. Simultaneously, elevating audience engagement with regional culture through technology promises to spur growth in cultural and creative industries while strengthening civic bonds to that heritage, unlocking a cascade of cultural, touristic, and brand value for Jiangsu. We contend that digitally inspired innovation will uncover new opportunities for Jiangsu's storied painting traditions to flourish amidst modernity, while catalyzing the cultured tourism industry's advancement.

2 Design Theory of Jiangsu Regional Theme Art Derivatives

2.1 Cultural Connotation and Artistic Characteristics

Jiangsu regional landscape painting constitutes a vital facet of Chinese artistic tradition, bearing a rich historical lineage and distinct stylistic motifs that unveil multifarious cultural connotations and aesthetic qualities. Firstly, by depicting the history, traditional culture, and folk customs native to Jiangsu, these regional works showcase profound cultural meaning. As a region steeped in antiquity, Jiangsu possesses abundant historical and cultural heritage. Artworks often adopt various locales' historical backdrop, endemic culture, and folk activities as their subject matter, inheriting and reinvigorating these cultural elements through the medium of painting. For instance, late-Ming artist Qiu Ying's famed painting *Prosperous Scenes of the Southern Capital* (see Fig. 1) vividly encapsulates Nanjing's economic vibrancy and societal vigor in the twilight of the Ming dynasty, garnering immense historical and artistic value that has earned it renown as a *Along the River During Qingming Festival* for Nanjing.

Fig. 1. Late-Ming artist Qiu Ying's famed painting *Prosperous Scenes of the Southern Capital.*

Additionally, Jiangsu regional art frequently depicts the province's natural scenery and cultural landmarks. With its signature waterways, lakes and rivers, Jiangsu's picturesque landscape offers rich inspiration. Works capture the beauty of gardens, quaint bridges and gentle streams through delicate brushwork and well-chosen colors, allowing audiences to appreciate the area's distinctive aesthetics. Historical buildings and cultural relic sites also feature prominently as key subjects, like in Huang Kekui's late Ming *Eight Scenes of Jinling* paintings which showcase top attractions in Nanjing, the former capital.

In terms of artistic style, Jiangsu regional paintings emphasize expressions of formal beauty and conceived imagery. Formal beauty manifests in techniques leveraging meticulous yet expressive Chinese painting methods, conveying native personalities and vistas through intricate, nuanced details. Meanwhile, conceived imagery underscores ambiance and emotions' role. Artists judiciously wield precise, full-bodied brushwork, contrasting palettes, ingenious composition, and signature techniques to imbue their works with a distinct atmosphere and resonant pathos full of creative tension and infectious appeal.

2.2   Design Strategy for Regional Themed Art Derivatives

As society develops economically and cultural consumption rises, demand increases for art derivatives - a new creative medium making fine art more relatable and obtainable for ordinary consumers. Art derivatives are a new medium for art to communicate with the public. It allows artworks to move from being 'shelf in a cabinet' in museums and other places into 'ordinary people's homes' [1].Therefore, developing derivatives based on regional landscape paintings could not only promote cultural heritage, but grant this traditional artform avenues to expand self-expression and innovation.

Screening and Positioning. When designing regional themed art derivatives, the first step is to screen and position the theme. According to the theme, style and cultural connotations of the painting works, sort out the elements and images that are suitable for transformation into derivatives. For different target consumer groups, conduct market research and analysis to determine the regional themed painting elements with the most market potential, thereby effectively positioning the product.

Creativity and Innovation. Innovative design is crucial when developing regional-themed art derivatives aimed at contemporary audiences. While staying true to their traditional artistic bases, designers can reimagine classic regional elements in freshly appealing ways. For instance, conventional symbols or patterns prominent in regional art movements can be stylized with bolder colors, integrated into geometric or minimalist renditions, or creatively blended with modern motifs. Beyond format adaptations, designers may also conceive engaging backstories and usage ideas that connect regional artworks to present-day contexts. Turning the featured painting or folk craft piece into a character with adventures relatable to modern cultural phenomena helps build an intriguing narrative around the product. Descriptions on the derivative's packaging or marketing materials can detail this character journey, enticing customers with the regional artwork's renewed life and meaning.

Regional artists themselves can additionally partner with designers to incorporate messages, perspectives, or creative influences that may previously have been marginalized, bringing innovative voice and representation. There are likely long-standing regional creative traditions still left to be tapped into as well. By thinking expansively about the range of cultural viewpoints and what inspiration past regional works could offer if translated to current mindsets, art derivatives can progress regional representation rather than just replicate it.

Cultural Promotion and Story Marketing. Effective design of regional art derivatives provides a powerful opportunity not just for commercial success, but for amplifying cultural impact. Packaging, product shapes, marketing materials and more can educate consumers on profound regional artistic traditions that may not be widely recognized today. For example, derivatives can excerpt brief historical narratives or artistic technique explanations, creatively formatted as a mini museum plaque or gallery guide passage. Designers can collaborate with local cultural experts to identify meaningful vignettes for sharing through these materials that illuminate the regional art form's importance. Gallery talks or digital animations led by such experts could also accompany product launches or be shared online to sustain engagement.

Moreover, the derivative products themselves become cultural design exhibits, from showcasing architectural ornamentation prevalent in the region to modeling pottery wares or figurines nodding to major artifacts. Embedding QR codes leading to detailed backgrounds and even artist biographies allows invested consumers to dig deeper. Yet for those drawn just visually or functionally, the works still suffuse regional foundations into everyday appreciation. Beyond intriguing form, captivating backstory seals consumer fascination - one spotlighting pivotal creators, turbulent eras, and artistic renaissances that magneticize cultural narratives. The derivatives become a portal bridging two worlds of meaning.

In summary, Jiangsu regional themed paintings fully demonstrate the combination of historical culture, natural landscapes and humanistic landscapes, allowing viewers to feel the unique charm and cultural heritage of Jiangsu regional culture and deeply experience the soft, tranquil and poetic atmosphere of Jiangsu regional culture. When designing Jiangsu regional themed art derivatives, these characteristics can be combined. Through digital technology innovation, the works show novel cultural connotations, achieve the unity of humanistic value and commercial value, and meet consumers' needs for product aesthetics, functions and experience [2], which can better promote the development of Jiangsu's cultural tourism industry.

3 Application of Digital Innovation Technologies in Art Derivative Design

The application of digital technology in art derivative design provides designers with extensive innovation space and rich expression. Making full use of digital technology can improve the service level of digital culture and tourism platforms. Through digital display, virtual reality, augmented reality and other technical means, a richer cultural tourism experience can be provided to tourists [3]. It can be seen from this that the extensive application of digital intelligent technology provides new opportunities and possibilities for cultural tourism.

3.1 Virtual Reality (VR) and Augmented Reality (AR) Technologies

Virtual reality unlock immersive derivative environments impossible to replicate physically while augmenting actual spaces with digital dimensionality. Designers can transport viewers across the vivid recreations of an artist's studio, a reimagined gallery showcasing interactive installations, or even fantastical lands inhabited by derivative characters.

Physically walking through these VR spaces brings graphic worlds alive with a presence mass prints or models cannot achieve.

Embedded stories captivate imagination as artifacts, animated figures, and hidden Easter eggs reveal tales of the artistic style's origins, celebrated creators, and more. Designers can collaborate with VR animation teams to envision how relics like an ancient regional architect's tools or a contemporary painter's splattered smock might spring to life, enriching cultural connections. Transitioning between VR spaces reflects progression in the art movement itself, educating as it engages. Augmented reality then seamlessly bridges these virtual experiences and physical products. Scanning derivative packaging, posters, clothing, and more unlocks 3D projections, animations, and even mini-games on mobile devices. Designers can integrate AR with social sharing for consumer participation. Blending these cutting-edge formats amplifies regional artform impact far beyond static appreciation, sparking personal adventures through cultural exploration.

3.2 Artificial Intelligence (AI) and Generative Art

AI expands derivative possibilities exponentially through generative art techniques like neural style transfer. Algorithms can analyze regional color palettes, textures, layouts and more from source works, then apply learned patterns onto 3D models, packaging graphics, textile prints at scale for infinite variations.

Designers set parameters like a flowing paint stroke or fragmented geometric mosaic to guide algorithmic remixing into novel iterations within the artistic vernacular. Batch outputs let designers curate selections reflecting consumer preferences and regional diversity. Campaigns showcase editions over time, spotlighting the range of one art form's expression through AI's emergent creativity. What's more, collaborative human and computer art Jewelry, apparel, housewares and beyond can embed NFC chips unlocking generative displays, environments or musical compositions activated through mobile apps. Consumers rediscover favorites as algorithms generate new interpretations, building an emotive connection through ever-evolving artwork.

Blending automation and human art direction amplifies regional creative traditions rather than replacing them. The tools liberate human designers to focus on nurturing cultural representation and meaning while machine partners handle technical production. It's a harmonious digital future that promises to propagate local craft far beyond physical limitations.

3.3 Digital Platforms and E-Commerce

With global digital connectivity, regional art derivative designers can transcend geographical and cultural barriers like never before. Sophisticated online platforms not only showcase products to exponentially more consumers, but provide insightful analytics on customer behavior and preferences that allow for highly tailored, dynamic promotion.

E-commerce empowers fine-grained targeting where compatible tastes signal demand despite physical distance—like a music service's algorithms inferring listeners open to crossover artistic fusion. Designers gain efficiency letting algorithms cluster niche consumer groups based on derived variables, enabling cost-effective digital advertising precisely when relevant. Machine learning recommends content and product variants more likely to compel engagement for each viewer over their buyer's journey rather than generic appeals. Social channels create two-way conversations with consumer communities interweaving derivative products themselves with the stirring narratives behind them for a lifestyle experience that ignites aspiration. Designers as culture ambassadors inviting audiences into the regional creative tradition through conversational story telling and participation in emerging works—much as artisans would exchange ideas face-to-face in traditional villages. Consumer co-creation and customization let individuals imprint identity on merchandise expressing their connections.

Freed from brick-and-mortar constraints, e-commerce liberates once localized or cost-prohibitive regional art forms to find economic sustainability through remote patrons. Global niches aggregate demand for continuity of endangered creative traditions or spotlight injustices to advocate solutions—building meaning far beyond monetary transactions. The digital facilitates cultural impact unbound by proximity.

The digital innovation approach plays an extremely important role in the design of art derivatives. Digital design has become a form of culture, living and thinking that is effective not only in the transfer of designs through digital interfaces, but also in the stage of cognitive and intellectual activities that are involved in the entire design process of designers [4]. Digital design not only enhances the artistic and commercial value of art derivatives, but also satisfies consumers' emotional needs for personalization, interactivity and novelty. It can be seen that digital innovation has become an important force to promote the development of art derivatives design, injecting new vitality and creativity into the design and development of art derivatives. Digital innovation approach plays an extremely important role in art derivatives design.

4   Case Study on the Design of Regional-Themed Art Derivatives in Jiangsu Province

4.1   Case Study of Jinling Diagram Digital Art Exhibition

In 2022, Nanjing Deki Art Museum launched an exhibition titled *Jinling Diagram Digital Art Exhibition* (see Fig. 2), which used digital technology means to use the Qing Dynasty court painter Feng Ning's *Jinling Diagram* (see Fig. 3) as a blueprint, and let the audience immersively experience the era of Nanjing in the Song Dynasty through an innovative display. This digitally innovative exhibition subverts people's impression of traditional art exhibitions.

Jinling Diagram is a scroll depicting the cityscape and folk customs of Jinling during the Southern Song Dynasty, showing the real and ordinary daily life of people in Nanjing during the Song Dynasty. The exhibition consists of five sections, including the entrance of the exhibition hall, the dynamic scroll of *Jinling Diagram*, the wall of figures, the cultural area of Jinling and the exit of the exhibition hall. At the entrance of the exhibition hall, the sculptures *Weifeng* and *Xiaoya*, which combine oriental aesthetics with trendy art, greet visitors, while 533 differently shaped *Jinling* IP figures made by 3D printing technology are also displayed at the entrance of the exhibition hall. At the entrance of the

Fig. 2. Jinling Diagram Digital Art Exhibition Hallspace-Deki Art Museum

Fig. 3. The Song Dynasty Moated City in Feng Ning's Imitation of the Song Dynasty Woodblock Edition Jinling Diagram from the Qing Dynasty

exhibition hall, there are 533 IP dolls of different shapes and sizes made by 3D printing technology; the Wall of Jinling Figures shows the images, identities and stories of the 533 figures in the Jinling Figures (see Fig. 4), and visitors can scan the QR code to learn more about the figures and their identities.

Fig. 4. Zheng Changfeng, the "Great Navigator" - One of the Character Roles in Jinling Diagrams.

Visitors can scan the QR code to learn the knowledge and interesting stories of the characters in the painting; the dynamic scroll of the Jinling Map is the core content of the exhibition, presented on the nearly 110-m-long, 3.6-m-high big screen, which is also the world's first dynamic interactive viewing mode. By wearing bracelets and headphones, visitors can choose their favorite characters and enter the painting to interact with the characters and feel the prosperous scene of Jinling in the Song Dynasty. The Jinling Map Cultural Zone displays cultural derivatives related to the Jinling Map, such as books, hand-made dolls, and peripheral products, and other cultural and creative products. Visitors can gain an in-depth understanding of the cultural connotation and artistic value of the Jinling Tu here; the exit of the exhibition hall is equipped with a viewing feedback area, allowing visitors to fill out a questionnaire or leave a message to make suggestions and comments on the exhibition. At the same time, the audience can also view their own behavioral data and achievement data in the exhibition hall.

Through innovative digital technology, this exhibition presents a brand new visiting experience for the audience to better understand and appreciate the artistic value of the Jinling Drawings. The technical principle of the exhibition Jinling Diagram Digital Art Exhibition mainly involves three parts, namely the indoor high-precision positioning system (UWB), the Unity engine and the intelligent management system, which is a centimeter-level positioning technology using ultra-wideband radio signals. Visitors wearing bracelets with UWB modules interact with the UWB base station in the exhibition hall to transmit real-time location information to the Intelligent Management System. The Unity engine is a cross-platform 3D engine widely used in game development and virtual reality, capable of high-quality graphic rendering and interactive development. The Unity engine transforms the traditional scroll of the Jinling Map into a 3D model and realizes the interactive behaviors of the characters on display. The display of character interaction behavior. By interacting with the 3D characters in the exhibition, the audience can more deeply feel the emotions and messages conveyed by the artworks. At the same time, the Unity engine also presented different scenes and effects based on the UWB position data obtained by the intelligent management system, enabling the audience to enjoy a brand new visual experience on the nearly 110-m-long and 3.6-m-high large screen (Table 1).

Jinling Diagram Digital Art Exhibition uses digital means to realize an innovative interactive exhibition mode. The application of digital technology allows the audience to gain a new visiting experience and better understand and appreciate the artistic value of *Jinling Diagram*. Through the UWB positioning system and intelligent management system, audience location information can be transmitted and managed in real time. The Unity engine converts the traditional *Jinling Diagram* scroll into a three-dimensional model to display the interactive behavior of characters. Virtual reality technology (VR) and augmented reality technology (AR) can immerse viewers into the world of artworks, enhancing their understanding and appreciation. Mixed reality technology (MR) combines real scenes and virtual elements to provide a more realistic and interactive exhibition experience. In addition to showing the original appearance of the *Jinling Diagram* scroll, the exhibition also incorporates a large number of knowledge points related to Nanjing's history and culture, such as the Eight Scenes of Jinling, the Four Famous Buildings of Jinling, the Twelve Hours of Jinling, etc., conveying more to the audience through the exhibition. Historical and cultural background. Audiences can gain more knowledge during the exhibition, which enhances the educational value and cultural connotation of the exhibition.

Table 1. Differences Between Different Types of Digital Technologies

Technology Type	Features	Application Scenario	Advantages/Application
USB	Centimeter-level positioning using ultra-wideband radio signals	Widely used for data transfer,High-accuracy positioning system	Transmit visitors' location information in real-time throughout the exhibition
Unity Engine	Cross-platform 3D engine for high-quality graphics rendering and interactive development	3D model conversion	Transform the traditional Jinling Map into an interactive 3D model
Intelligent management system	Real-time acquisition and management of location information, and realizes multi-scenario application	Data acquisition and management system	According to the acquired location information,different backgrounds and effects are switched
Augmented Reality(AR)	Superimposes a computer-generated image on a user's view of the real world,thus providing a composite view	Applied in navigation systems and on-site job assistance	Enhances real-world objects with computer-generated information
Virtual Reality (VR)	A simulated experience that can be similar to or completely different from the real world	Used for immersive experiences in gaming and training	Provides a fully immersive experience,visitors can immerse themselves in the virtual world of Jinling Maps using VR devices
Mixed Reality (MR)	A hybrid of real and virtual worlds to produce new environments and visualizations where physical and digital objects co-exist and interact in real time	Mixed reality devices Mixed reality applications	Through mixed reality devices and applications, visitors can interact with virtual elements in real world surroundings.

4.2 Digital Intelligence Technologies Empower Regional-Themed Art Derivatives

Diverse Presentation Methods. Digital intelligence technology provides more possibilities for the design and presentation of regional-themed art derivatives. Through the display of three-dimensional models, art derivatives can be presented in a more realistic and three-dimensional way, and consumers can more intuitively understand the appearance and structure of regional-themed art derivatives, enhancing the viewing effect and experience. Through the application of indoor positioning systems, audiences can move freely in the digital exhibition of regional-themed art derivatives, further enhancing the realism and freedom of the viewing experience. The application of virtual reality and augmented reality technology can give audiences a deeper understanding of regional culture. Through virtual reality helmets or applications running on mobile phones, you can immerse yourself in virtual regional scenes and feel the unique charm of regional culture; augmented reality technology combines digital regional-themed art derivatives with the real environment, through mobile phones or tablets The camera presents digital works of art in real scenes, allowing users to interact with virtual regional culture in reality, enhancing people's viewing experience and sense of participation.

Innovative Expressions. Digital innovation technology also gives more creative ideas to the design of regional-themed art derivatives. Designers take advantage of digital graphics rendering capabilities and the flexibility of interactive development to combine regional elements with artwork. For example, through virtual reality technology, audiences can experience realistic regional environments immersively; through augmented reality technology, regionally related information and stories can be displayed on derivatives. These digital innovative technologies have expanded the creative ideas for the design of regional-themed art derivatives, providing designers with more possibilities and room for creativity.

Widened Creative Perspectives. Digital innovation technology brings more possibilities and room for creativity to designers. Through digital technology, designers can combine traditional regional themes with modern technology to create artistic works with contemporary characteristics and innovative meaning. Digital innovation technology has expanded the creative ideas for the design of regional-themed art derivatives, bringing more creative inspiration and opportunities to designers.

It can be seen that digital intelligent innovation technology provides rich creative resources and expression forms for the design of art derivatives with regional themes in Jiangsu. With the maturity of digital intelligence technology and the convenience of integrated application, some technologies have gradually been applied to cultural and creative products, and have become an important driving force for product digital innovation [5]. Digital innovative technology provides more possibilities for the design of art derivatives, allowing the works to better convey the unique charm of Jiangsu regional culture. Technologies such as virtual reality and augmented reality allow the audience to experience the beauty and culture of Jiangsu region immersively. While bringing a more immersive viewing experience, it can also increase the audience's interest and recognition in art derivatives with regional themes in Jiangsu. In addition, digital innovation technology provides broader channels and platforms for the marketing and dissemination of art derivatives with regional themes in Jiangsu. Through channels such as digital platforms and social media, art derivatives can interact and disseminate more widely with audiences, expanding their influence and popularity. The application of digital innovation technology can promote the market development of Jiangsu regional theme art derivatives and promote them to a broader market.

5 Conclusion

In the future, with the continuous advancement of technology, the application of digital innovative technologies will become increasingly popular and mature, bringing more opportunities and challenges to the design of art derivatives and digital cultural tourism.

On the one hand, digital innovation technology will further change the consumption model of cultural tourism and art derivatives. With the popularization of smart devices and network technology, technologies such as virtual reality, augmented reality and artificial intelligence will be applied to richer and more diverse digital cultural tourism experiences, bringing users a more immersive and personalized cultural tourism experience. On the other hand, digital innovative technologies will further promote the integration of digital cultural tourism with other fields. The widespread application of digital technology will make the intersection between cultural tourism and education, entertainment, business and other fields closer, providing users with more comprehensive and diverse experiences and services. In addition, digital innovation technology will also promote the protection and inheritance of cultural heritage. Through digital technology, the digital protection and dissemination of cultural heritage will be more convenient and effective, allowing more people to access and understand excellent cultural heritage.

However, the application of digital innovation technologies also faces some challenges. The first is technical difficulties and cost issues. The development of digital innovation technology requires advanced hardware equipment and software systems, which may bring higher costs. At the same time, technological upgrading also requires designers and developers to continuously follow up and learn to maintain the ability to innovate with the times. Secondly, privacy and security issues are also one of the challenges faced by digital innovation technology. In the field of digital cultural tourism, users will involve personal information and payment information when using digital platforms, so protecting user privacy and data security is crucial. Relevant institutions and enterprises need to strengthen data security measures to prevent malicious attacks and data leaks.

In summary, the design of art derivatives from the perspective of digital cultural tourism needs to rely on the application of digital innovation technology to better express and convey the characteristics and charm of regional culture. Taking Jiangsu regional theme art derivatives as the research object, and through digital innovation and expression methods, its viewing effect, marketing and communication effect can be improved. Therefore, further research and exploration in the field of art derivative design research from the perspective of digital cultural tourism is still of great significance. Future development requires continued efforts in technology, marketing, user experience and information security to promote the widespread application and development of digital innovation technology in the fields of art derivatives design and digital cultural tourism. This will provide new ideas for digital cultural tourism, regional cultural inheritance and artistic innovation, and achieve multiple benefits in cultural shaping, urban tourism and brand value.

Acknowledgements. The authors acknowledge the contributions and support of the experts and team members in the writing process.

Foundations. 2023 General Project of Philosophy and Social Sciences Research in Jiangsu Universities: "Research on Urban Tourism Image Design from the Perspective of Cultural Heritage"(2023SJYB0669), Shaanxi Provincial Educational Science "14th Five-Year Plan" Project: "Integrating Silk Road Culture into the Teaching of Aesthetic Education Courses in Colleges and

Universities Innovation and practical research" (SGH23Y2315), Nanjing University of Aeronautics and Astronautics Jincheng College 2023 Excellent Aesthetic Education Course "Decoration Design" Construction Project.

References

1. Shi, X.Y.: Research on the development and design of Fengyang Phoenix painting art derivatives. J. Anhui Vocat. Tech. College **02**, 47–50 (2021)
2. Zhang, Y.J.: Research on the design method of derivatives of traditional Chinese calligraphy and painting art. Beauty Times (Part 1) (01), 20–21(2018)
3. Xu, L.J.: Research on the models and paths of integrated development of urban culture and tourism under the digital economy. Exhibit. Econ. **23**, 60–63 (2023)
4. Çakmakçıoğlu, B.A..: Effect of digital age on the transmission of cultural values in product design. Design J. **20**(sup 1), S3824-S3836 (2017)
5. Hu, Z.C.: Research on digital intelligent cultural and creative product design. Packag. Eng. **08**, 358–367 (2023)

Exploring Innovative Models of Guizhou Miao Embroidery from a Digital Perspective

Yiran Du[1]([⊠]) and Nan Jiang[2]([⊠])

[1] Nanjing Normal University, Nanjing, China
yirandu990722@gmail.com
[2] Nanjing University of the Arts, Nanjing, China

Abstract. Miao embroidery is not only a handcraft handed down from generation to generation by Miao women, but also an important carrier of Miao culture, known as "the history book worn on the body". In the current digital era, the effective integration of Guizhou Miao embroidery skills and teaching courses in universities is conducive to deepening the intrinsic value of digital product design courses. The establishment of the database is used to enhance the multi-faceted understanding and interpretation of Guizhou Miao embroidery culture, cultivate students to review and refine Miao embroidery elements from the perspective of design, and transform the national cultural factors contained in them into design materials. The database is applied in enterprises. Through the establishment of a large Miao embroidery craftsman database on the platform, design requirements are released online. According to the information shown in the database, orders can be distributed to craftsmen in a timely and accurate manner, further improving production efficiency and production capacity. The digital platform makes Miao embroidery products more easily accessible to global consumers, which helps to expand the market and increase sales channels.

Keywords: Miao embroidery · Database · Digitization · Intangible cultural heritage · Higher education · Enterprise production

1 Introduction

Miao embroidery is one of China's traditional intangible cultural heritages. When discussing Miao embroidery, it is essential to mention the Miao people, an ancient ethnic group among the 56 in China who have lost their written language for thousands of years. However, they have managed to preserve precious spiritual heritage such as myths and legends, historical stories, patriarchal systems, philosophical concepts, lifestyles, weddings, and funerals. Throughout the ages, Miao ancestors conveyed history through ancient songs, passed on civilization through embroidery techniques and expressed hope with batik patterns. Through songs and intricate needlework under wax knives, they created exquisite costumes known as "no words in heaven" by historians. These costumes not only embody the warmth of history but also represent a nation's rich heritage. The handicrafts of the Miao people reflect their firm beliefs and fearless spirit inherited

P.-L. P. Rau (Ed.): HCII 2024, LNCS 14701, pp. 30–47, 2024.
https://doi.org/10.1007/978-3-031-60904-6_3

from their ancestors; these cultural elements form their civilization system. Initially used for decorating clothes through embroidered paintings using natural dyes skillfully applied by Miao women onto cloth and thread according to their preferred colors and patterns; these colors and patterns hold great significance in analyzing and researching Miao embroidery today. The unique expression forms found within Miao embroidery patterns showcase the cultural spirit and national wisdom behind this art form. It is the interaction among modeling, subject matter, and content that produces the vivid artistic style of Guizhou Miao embroidery [1]. These intricate designs record both the tumultuous history of the Miao people while describing their mysterious myths.Utilization is the optimal form of inheritance. Only when tradition aligns with contemporary societal needs can the path of national art be preserved.

Currently, Miao embroidery has transitioned from tradition to fashion, spreading from Guizhou to a global scale and frequently gracing international stages. During the 2024 Spring/Summer Milan Fashion Week, Miao Embroidery from Guizhou was showcased in the Chinese Miao · Art Exhibition hosted by the Consulate General of China in Milan and the People's Government of Guizhou Province. The aesthetic essence of these traditional crafts can be translated into a fashionable language that resonates with more designers, thereby bringing this hand embroidery from mountainous regions to modern society. Consequently, determining an effective method for interpreting and documenting this code becomes paramount. To address this issue, Evan · China Handicraft Workshop organized and refined Miao embroidery patterns in 2017, establishing a comprehensive database along with an internet platform. To date, it has amassed over 4,000 distinct types of traditional Chinese aesthetic patterns as well as information on more than 8,000 inheritors of Miao embroidery handicrafts while also creating an online artisan database. Handicraft inheritors serve as vital carriers and transmitters of Miao embroidery; thus safeguarding their legacy remains central to protecting this cultural heritage through an established inheritance system based on these inheritors themselves. Inheritors possess expertise in crafting and preserving the intricate skills and cultural traditions associated with Miao embroidery projects; ultimately ensuring its intangible cultural heritage thrives through their continued efforts alongside designers specialized in Miao embroidery who contribute towards its evolution by integrating contemporary aesthetics styles along with new materials and technological advancements.

2 Establish the Gene Pool of Miao Embroidery Culture

2.1 The Function of Recording Patterns

Miao embroidery is a cultural heritage with a unique traditional inheritance mode that relies on oral transmission from mother to daughter, passing down not only the embroidery skills but also the stories and meanings behind the patterns. This makes Miao embroidery a "wordless history book" in Miao culture. Digitization can solve issues of popularization and enable creative transformation and innovative development while protecting, inheriting, and developing this intangible cultural heritage. The establishment of a digitized database for systematically collecting and sorting out various patterns is significant for its protection and inheritance.

The recording function of the database serves as its core component, enabling users to efficiently store, manage, and retrieve vast amounts of data. In the context of the Miao embroidery database, this recording function possesses several distinctive characteristics. Firstly, it allows for the comprehensive collection of Miao embroidery patterns from diverse regions and branches, encompassing images, descriptions, historical backgrounds, and other pertinent information. Secondly, it facilitates efficient classification of Miao embroidery based on geographical regions, branches, pattern types etc., empowering users to swiftly access specific information tailored to their needs. By leveraging digital technology capabilities, Miao embroidery patterns and associated information are transformed into electronic formats that ensure long-term preservation and effortless dissemination of data. The recorded contents within the database extend beyond visual representations of Miao embroidery; they also encompass cultural insights along with historical and technological details that provide users with a holistic understanding. This well-designed database empowers researchers, designers educators as well as the general public to effortlessly access and study materials related to Miao embroidery while fostering knowledge sharing and cultural diffusion. For instance, design research focused on integrating Miao embroidery patterns with modern demands has primarily relied on case analysis thus far, with most studies concentrating solely on graphical aspects , structural elements, connotations, and application methods pertaining to these patterns; few studies have delved into systematic organization or management strategies for handling extensive volumes of data concerning various Miao embroidery patterns. Designers currently lack a comprehensive database platform that enables rapid retrieval of Miao embroidery patterns and facilitates in-depth understanding of the associated knowledge. Therefore, the establishment of a database assumes paramount importance for efficient collection and analysis of Miao embroidery data.

With the continuous accumulation of new data, the database can be expanded continuously to incorporate novel Miao embroidery patterns and related information, thereby ensuring the currency and comprehensiveness of its content. The database is equipped with data analysis tools that facilitate researchers in analyzing popular trends and geographical distribution of Miao embroidery, thus providing valuable support for cultural research. In terms of digitized Miao embroidery patterns, the database can record copyright information to safeguard creators' rights and interests while serving as a legal foundation for authorized usage. Through these recording functions, the Miao embroidery database not only serves as an invaluable cultural resource library but also establishes a robust groundwork for protecting, researching, and innovating Miao embroidery. By collecting totems prevalent in numerous villages across Guizhou Province and establishing a comprehensive database, we not only document intricate patterns but also preserve the captivating legends passed down through generations.

2.2 Designers Connect to the Miao Embroidery Database

Guizhou Miao embroidery has the potential to gain global recognition and emerge as a leading fashion trend, owing to its seamless integration with designer databases. Designers can effortlessly extract exquisite design elements from the database and create fashionable products that epitomize elegance. The primary objective of establishing a connection between the Miao embroidery database and designers is to foster an interactive platform for artistic exchange, invigorate creative inspiration, and facilitate the contemporary application of traditional craftsmanship.

The Miao embroidery database encompasses a vast collection of patterns and techniques, serving as a valuable source of design inspiration for designers. By exploring this database, designers can gain insights into the historical, cultural, and technical aspects of Miao embroidery. This is particularly significant due to the mythical and auspicious meanings associated with Miao embroidery motifs. For instance, according to Miao beliefs, butterflies are considered ancestors who gave birth to the earliest humans. During the solemn ancestor worship ceremonies that occur once every 13 years, wizards chant the "Mother Butterfly Song". Moreover, butterfly patterns found in Miao embroidery and silver jewelry hold profound significance beyond mere adornments; they represent sacred and revered totems. In the perception of the Miao people, butterflies symbolize not only human ancestry but also serve as mothers to animals, gods, ghosts, and even all natural phenomena – representing the origin of all living beings. Consequently, by digitally understanding these cultural narratives and historical contexts behind such patterns while integrating them into their designs effectively enhances depth and emotional resonance within their work. Ultimately bridging traditional elements with modern design facilitates both cultural preservation and innovation.

As a comprehensive material database, the embroidery database offers designers an extensive collection of vector patterns that can be directly utilized in various product designs, including clothing, accessories, and household items. Traditional Guizhou Miao embroidery products have traditionally had limited applications primarily focused on clothing and daily necessities with a distinct national flavor. While possessing significant national artistic value, their practicality diminishes considerably once they leave the Miao village. Through design enhancements and improvements, the product range has slightly expanded; however, it remains predominantly centered around clothing such as garments, bags, accessories, and embroidered books. This narrow categorization combined with the vibrant colors of Miao embroidery and its strong national style sometimes appear incongruous within modern consumption scenarios where they fail to meet contemporary consumer demands effectively. Furthermore, given that Miao women constitute the primary practitioners of Guizhou Miao embroidery craftmanship today, most craftsmen adhere to traditional skills and aesthetics for production.

Due to the enclosed environment and limited exposure to the outside world, individuals involved in Miao embroidery have restricted access to cultural resources, resulting in a lack of opportunities for innovation. However, unlike designers within the cultural industry chain or creative companies, Miao embroidery possesses numerous elements that can be extended for design performance. The establishment of a comprehensive database can facilitate designers in utilizing digital means to create and enhance traditional cultural resources, thereby generating high-value products and delivering an emotionally evocative experience to users. For instance, by incorporating the various types and colors of embroidery from the database into modern designs, it is possible to produce contemporary works with a traditional essence. Consequently, establishing a Miao embroidery database serves as a catalyst for promoting Miao embroidery culture on a broader market scale. Designers worldwide can select craftsmen they prefer based on information provided in the database. By integrating Miao embroidery elements into modern designs, designers are able to capture both domestic and international consumers' attention while enhancing the market competitiveness of Miao embroidery products. Furthermore, this initiative also provides additional exhibition and sales platforms for inheritors of Miao embroidery techniques. As an example illustrating these concepts further: ZHUCHONGYUN recently showcased their "Miao" high-end series at their brand exhibition (see Fig. 1). Yang Ani—an intangible cultural heritage bearer of Miao embroidery—was invited to participate in this event where she demonstrated her artistic creation spanning thousands of years through various forms such as seed embroidery, braid embroidery, and broken thread embroidery techniques. ZHUCHONGYUN integrates the brand imagery of the white stork with the Miao ethnic group's butterfly totem, employing minimalist lines and three-dimensional silhouettes to accentuate the delicate essence of water and oriental grace within the silk texture.

Fig. 1. "Miao" high-end series

The establishment of the database represents a crucial milestone in the digital transformation of the Miao embroidery industry. Designers can leverage cutting-edge technologies, such as 3D printing and virtual reality, to present Miao embroidery patterns in innovative forms and infuse new vitality into this traditional art form. In 2019, Marni initiated the "Marni Miao Miao Cooperation Project" (see Fig. 2), where creative director Francesco Risso aimed to foster an intercultural dialogue between Eastern and Western aesthetics. Collaborating with over 400 skilled embroidery craftsmen, Marni successfully merged Italian traditions with Guizhou village culture, resulting in a plethora of distinctive creations that seamlessly blend ethnic customs with contemporary styles. Undoubtedly, the inherent "authenticity" embodied by handmade products played a pivotal role in driving the project's success. By constructing the comprehensive Miao embroidery database and actively involving designers, we can effectively promote the development of this industry while simultaneously generating increased employment opportunities for local artisans. Furthermore, these efforts will stimulate growth within related industrial sectors and contribute to overall economic advancement at a regional level. Serving as an invaluable resource platform for designers worldwide, the Miao embroidery database not only showcases traditional cultural heritage but also presents novel avenues for future generations of embroiderers and associated industries.

Fig. 2. Marni Miao Miao Cooperation Project

3   The Collection and Analysis of Miao Embroidery Craftsmen's Data

3.1   Handicraft Level

How to productize embroidery and connect craftsmen in the remote mountains with the outside world? According to the company's innovation, a "Miao embroidery craftsman database" has been built. Most Miao embroidery craftsmen have not undergone systematic learning and training, but have inherited this craft from their ancestors, which is non-standardized. Through organizing relevant training, we can learn what each craftsman can embroider and what he is good at, and transform the individual ability of each craftsman into the ability of a group. The database traces and records the history of Chinese aesthetics, builds a broader display platform for Miao embroidery craftsmen, attracts designers from around the world to participate in Miao embroidery creativity, and promotes the innovation and development of Miao embroidery traditional handicraft. The digital intelligent creativity platform also plays a main role in creativity stimulation and design creation in the design industry, which is conducive to gathering independent individuals in the industry and generating the main body cluster effect, innovating the industry format, and effectively improving the efficiency and quality of design creation [2]. The database contains the relevant information of each craftsman, such as the level of embroidery skills, the age of employment, and the embroidery method that he is good at, and puts this information into the database (Table 1). In the exploration of the reconstruction of intangible cultural heritage, many institutions have begun to use digital scanning, digital photography and database technology to digitally record, preserve and manage intangible cultural heritage [3].

Table 1. The database of embroiderers.

Name	Nationality	Age of embroidery	Level	Embroidery techniques they are good at
Xiufang Wang	Miao	30	Intermediate	The art of tin embroidery Dyeing and weaving
Wuhou Wangyi	Miao	31	Intermediate	The art of tin embroidery Dyeing and weaving
Laoge Long	Miao	5	Intermediate	The art of tin embroidery Dyeing and weaving
Laolao Long	Miao	30	Intermediate	The art of tin embroidery Dyeing and weaving
Yan Chen	Miao	39	Intermediate	The art of tin embroidery Dyeing and weaving
Liangmei Pan	Miao	26	Intermediate	Horsetail embroidery
Zhizhang Bai	Miao	17	Intermediate	Horsetail embroidery
Xiaouzi Lu	Miao	32	Intermediate	Horsetail embroidery
Yue Pan	Miao	40	Intermediate	Horsetail embroidery
Shixiang Wei	Miao	21	Intermediate	Horsetail embroidery
Lan Lu	Miao	24	Intermediate	Horsetail embroidery
Ri Lu	Miao	31	Intermediate	Horsetail embroidery
Xiao Wei	Miao	30	Intermediate	Horsetail embroidery
Yuezhi Jiang	Miao	52	Intermediate	Horsetail embroidery
Xiaoying Wei	Miao	27	Intermediate	Horsetail embroidery
Chun Chen	Miao	19	Intermediate	Horsetail embroidery
Yan Wei	Miao	50	Intermediate	Horsetail embroidery
Xiao Lu	Miao	26	Intermediate	Horsetail embroidery
Bo Pan	Miao	25	Intermediate	Horsetail embroidery
Cai Yang	Miao	36	Intermediate	Horsetail embroidery
Shiri Wei	Miao	09	Intermediate	Horsetail embroidery
Shifu Pan	Miao	71	Intermediate	Horsetail embroidery
Xie Yang	Miao	46	Intermediate	Horsetail embroidery
Xiuying Shi	Miao	38	Intermediate	Horsetail embroidery
Mingbo Pan	Miao	39	Intermediate	Horsetail embroidery
Guixiang Wei	Miao	54	Intermediate	Horsetail embroidery
Xiao Yang	Miao	53	Intermediate	Horsetail embroidery
Yuemei Pan	Miao	46	Intermediate	Horsetail embroidery
Yuemei Pan	Miao	44	Intermediate	Horsetail embroidery
Zhenlian Wu	Miao	51	Intermediate	Plain embroidery Multi-yarn embroidery Textile embroidery

According to the embroidery skill level of craftsmen, they can be divided into primary, intermediate, advanced and other levels. This is usually based on their work experience, the quality of the finished works and the certification or awards they have obtained. First of all, the enterprise company will record the skill level into the database, which can quickly match the appropriate craftsmen to participate in specific projects, ensure the efficient production process, reduce the production delay caused by skill mismatch, and help ensure the quality of the product, because high skill level craftsmen are usually able to produce more fine and higher quality Miao embroidery works. Secondly, for the consumer side, the establishment of the database of Evans Company can let consumers choose the corresponding skill level of craftsmen for personalized customization according to their requirements for product quality and process, to meet the consumer demand at different levels. Consumers can customize unique Miao embroidery works according to their preferences and needs, and this customized service can meet consumers' pursuit of uniqueness and personalization. It is necessary to consider shifting the focus from "things" to "people", and organically integrating certain cultural concepts into specific tangible items on the basis of fully analyzing user needs, preferences and behavior characteristics [4]. Personalized customization can let consumers participate in the product design process, make them feel more satisfied and invested, thus improving customer loyalty. Customized Miao embroidery works often have higher artistic value and collection value, which can add added value to the product and increase the sales price. At the same time, these classifications can help craftsmen and enterprises more accurately position the market, launch corresponding products for different consumer groups, and improve market competitiveness. Personalized customization reflects the importance enterprises attach to customer needs and their commitment to product quality, which helps to establish and improve the brand image, and improve consumers' trust and loyalty to the brand. Moreover, the record of skill levels provides a career development path for craftsmen. On the one hand, personalized customization often requires more craftsmen to participate, which helps to create more job opportunities for local communities and promote economic development. On the other hand, it encourages them to continuously improve their skills, and also provides a reference for their career planning. It can also be used as a basis for education and training, helping new artists understand industry standards, providing them with growth direction and goals, contributing to the inheritance of intangible cultural heritage, and ensuring that traditional skills can be accurately passed to the next generation. Finally, the optimal allocation of resources is something that every enterprise needs to consider. According to the skill level of craftsmen, enterprises can reasonably allocate resources, such as materials and tools, to ensure the optimal use of resources. In international exchanges, the recording of craftsmen's skill level is helpful for craftsmen to participate in international exchanges and cooperation, and enhance the international influence of Miao embroidery art. In a word, the recording of craftsmen's skill level in the enterprise database not only helps to improve the professional level of the entire Miao embroidery industry, but also promotes the personal growth of artists, enhances the market competitiveness of products, and promotes the inheritance and development of Miao embroidery culture.

3.2 Working Age

In the Miao embroidery database, craftsmen are classified according to their age. Human resource management: Understanding the number and distribution of craftsmen of different ages can help enterprises rationally plan human resources and ensure that artists of all ages can play their advantages in the production process. Through age classification, senior artists can be identified. They usually have rich experience and superb skills, and can serve as mentors for young artists to promote the inheritance of skills and knowledge. Different training and development plans can be designed for artists of different ages. Young artists may need more basic skills training, while senior artists may need to update their knowledge and learn new design concepts and technologies. Understanding the age distribution of artists can help enterprises better position the market. For example, young artists may be better at innovation and fashion design, while senior artists may be more suitable for traditional and high-end products. According to the age and physical condition of artists, work can be reasonably allocated to ensure production efficiency and artists' health. Understanding the age of artists can help enterprises develop incentive mechanisms, such as providing more career development opportunities for senior artists and providing growth space and learning resources for young artists. The age classification helps to show the diversity of the Miao embroidery industry, emphasize the contribution of artists of different ages to cultural heritage, and enhance the society's awareness and respect for the industry. The government and relevant institutions can formulate corresponding support policies according to the age distribution of artists, such as providing entrepreneurial support for young artists and retirement security for senior artists. Through the age classification, the sustainable development of the Miao embroidery industry can be ensured, and the skills gap caused by the imbalance of the age structure can be avoided. The age classification provides data support for cultural research, and helps to study the transmission and evolution of Miao embroidery art between different generations. Through this classification, the Miao embroidery database can not only better serve the management and development of the Miao embroidery industry, but also provide valuable information for cultural heritage and social research.

3.3 Good at Embroidery

The database collects the embroidery skills that craftsmen are good at, which is of great significance for the development and inheritance of the Miao embroidery industry. First of all, understanding the embroidery skills that artists are good at can help enterprises or customers accurately match project needs, and ensure that the quality and style of the work meet expectations. Enterprises can reasonably allocate work tasks according to the expertise of craftsmen, improve production efficiency, and reduce resource waste. For example, Evans connects the Miao embroidery craftsman database information with global designers, so that designers from around the world can understand embroidery craftsman database information with global designers, so that designers from around the world can understand and match the corresponding Miao embroidery craftsmen through the database, so as to realize innovative cooperation. The matching of embroidery stitches that Miao embroidery craftsmen are good at and designers is crucial to creating high-quality, innovative and culturally valuable Miao embroidery works. By cooperating with craftsmen who are good at specific stitches, designers can better learn and understand the traditional skills of Miao embroidery, and promote the inheritance of culture. Not only that, designers can design products with specific stitch characteristics according to the expertise of craftsmen, realize product differentiation, and meet the needs of different consumers. The collision of new ideas of designers and exquisite skills of craftsmen can inspire new ideas and promote the innovation and development of Miao embroidery art. In such a cooperation process, the cooperation between designers and craftsmen can form a unique brand style and enhance the brand recognition in the market. The technical information in the database can be used as a reference for education and training, helping new craftsmen learn and master a variety of embroidery techniques, and the collected technical information can provide data support for researchers to promote research and innovation in embroidery techniques. The collection of embroidery techniques that craftsmen are good at in the enterprise database not only helps to improve the overall level of the Miao embroidery industry, but also contributes to the protection, inheritance and development of Miao embroidery culture.

4   Construction of Miao Embroidery Pattern Database in Colleges and Universities

The effective integration of digitalization and teaching courses of Guizhou Miao embroidery skills in the School of Fine Arts and Design of Guizhou Kaili University is conducive to deepening the intrinsic value of digital product design courses. In the process of integrating traditional skills into digital product design courses, the rich historical and cultural heritage and exquisite handmade skills of Guizhou Miao embroidery are important content for development as teaching resources.After the basic completion of resource collection, Miao embroidered art experts should be a detailed screening of resources to ensure that the final storage of information authority and artistic value, and then review the data,Heavy, cataloging, editing, etc., making the data become scientific system [5].This model of integrating traditional arts and crafts resources into teaching has greatly improved the status quo of academic and technological emphasis in universities. The biggest advantage of the longitudinal research database of higher education is that it can provide various types of vertical section data for researchers to carry out rich longitudinal research topic analysis, such as understanding the development trend of the research subject with the change of time, excavating the mechanism and factors that contribute to the continuous change, and predicting future changes [6].

4.1   Needlework

The Database of Miao Embroidery in Southeast Guizhou of Kaili University Databases in universities can be used for a variety of purposes, such as supporting academic research and teaching resource management. By establishing and maintaining an efficient, safe and easy-to-use database, universities can improve the quality of teaching and research, and provide convenience for students and teachers. The Miao embroidery database in universities is mainly divided into three modules: embroidery stitch, pattern and color (Table 2). In this database, it can be seen that embroidery stitch is divided into seven categories, namely, ruffled embroidery, counted yarn embroidery, broken-line embroidery, flat embroidery, piled embroidery, braided embroidery and locked embroidery (see Fig. 3). There are 47 illustrations of ruffled embroidery, 38 illustrations of counted yarn embroidery, 158 illustrations of broken-line embroidery, 29 illustrations of flat embroidery, 24 illustrations of piled embroidery, 23 illustrations of braided embroidery and 138 illustrations of locked embroidery. It can be seen that embroidery, 24 illustrations of piled embroidery, 23 illustrations of braided embroidery and 138 illustrations of locked embroidery. It can be seen that broken-line embroidery is particularly common in Miao embroidery, while other stitches may be more popular in specific Miao areas or branches.

In the data charts of each embroidery stitch, the size, region, style, main pattern and main color of each Miao embroidery work are marked in detail. It can provide scholars with rich data to help them study the history and development of Miao embroidery and its relationship with different regional cultures.

Table 2. Classification of university databases

Fig. 3. Classification of Miao Embroidery Database in Colleges and Universities -- Embroidery Needlework

4.2 Patterns

Patterns in the database are classified into 8 dimensions: plants, figures, birds, dragons, geometry, butterflies, flowers and animals (see Fig. 4). There are 53 kinds of botanical patterns, 109 kinds of figure patterns, 138 kinds of bird patterns, 136 kinds of dragon patterns, 7 kinds of geometric patterns, 105 kinds of butterfly patterns, 158 kinds of flower patterns and 83 kinds of animal patterns. It can be seen that figures, birds, dragons, butterflies and flowers are the majority in Miao embroidery.Among various patterns of Miao embroidery, the most popular embroidery pattern is various images, concrete and abstract butterfly patterns. They have different images and various poses. The Miao craftsmen take butterflies as the eternal theme of embroidery.

Fig. 4. Classification of Miao Embroidery Database in Colleges and Universities -- Pattern

If you ask how many kinds of butterfly patterns are in Miao nationality clothing? It can be said that the butterfly patterns are so varied that it is difficult to estimate. The butterfly patterns embroidered by different regions, different schools and different craftsmen are very different. If you pursue the inspiration of craftsmen, you will find that these lifelike butterfly patterns are not only the Miao people's inheritance of their ancestors' crafts, but also their aesthetic intuition. Whereas decorative patterns covering their surface have meanings [7], Different from traditional Western painting, artists need to think deeply and arrange carefully before painting, but the craftsmen of Miao embroidery completely break such a way of painting. They are used to repeatedly sketching a line on the cloth with their thumb that only they can understand. Once they draw the first line, it is like finding out the source of inspiration. In terms of composition, Miao embroidery pursues full composition and emphasizes completeness. In the embroidery of butterfly patterns, butterflies are usually arranged symmetrically or appear in an asymmetric way. As the main body of the pattern, butterflies are also blended with fish, insects and beasts in Miao embroidery patterns to form the image of butterflies in the imagination of the Miao people. It can be said that there are various forms, and they can switch freely between realism, freehand brushwork and abstraction. Butterfly patterns usually do not appear alone, but mostly in combination with other patterns [8]. The collection and classification of patterns in the database is helpful to trace the historical development of Miao embroidery. By comparing the patterns of different periods, we can understand the historical changes and cultural evolution of Miao society. At the same time, the classified Miao embroidery data can be used for the study of artistic style and techniques, and analyze the influence of different techniques on artistic expression.

Regional traditional patterns should not be limited to transformation, but also to development and innovation, giving them a brand new carrier [9]. With the support of digital technology, the research and development team has transformed the Miao embroidery into a production language that can be identified by computers through digital transformation (see Fig. 5), so that science and technology and intangible cultural heritage can be integrated with each other, which not only realizes the scientific production, but also adds fashion elements to the products, greatly saving the production cycle and cost of Miao embroidery products, and making Miao embroidery more competitive in the market. This not only improves the output value of Miao embroidery, but also releases production capacity, so that Miao embroidery craftsmen and inheritors have more energy to make higher-end Miao embroidery products.

Fig. 5. Production and processing of Miao embroidery by digital control machine

4.3   Color

The existing color records of the Miao embroidery database in universities are green, blue, red, black, orange and white (see Fig. 6), among which there are 74 green legends, 49 blue legends, 239 red legends, 62 black legends, 10 orange legends and 5 white legends. Embroidery is good at weaving together similar colors and a variety of high purity colors on a single background color. Most colors are in the range of high purity hue, and medium and low purity hue are less.

Fig. 6. Classification of Miao Embroidery Database in Colleges and Universities -- Color

The color of embroidery is also influenced by the spirit of freedom and happiness of the ancestors of the Miao nationality. The color purity of embroidery is high, and the color contrast is strong. The abundant and highly unified modeling language of the Miao nationality's embroidery pattern of southeast of Guizhou Province relates closely to modern painting and aesthetics theory modern times in form and content [11]. People can directly see from the color of embroidery that the color of embroidery is created by Miao people's subjective understanding of nature. Miao craftsmen, without receiving systematic color learning, form a unique color law of Miao clothing by relying on sensitive color perception and color extraction from nature [12]. This is consistent with the expression of some styles of Western modernism and post-modernism art. Of course, the color composition, aesthetic concepts and expression of color emotions of Miao embroidery also restrict and influence each other in cultural backgrounds such as religious customs and traditional concepts and special living environment.

For example in the Shidong area of Taijiang county, most of the colors in Split Line Stitch are red and blue, while brown and purple can also be found in some cloths made by elderly women. With the cognition of nature and society, people's aesthetic tendency is also changing. In the abstract sense, of course, people's aesthetic tendency is also enhanced.

5   Establishment of Chinese Patterns Online Museum Database--Wen Zang Website

The function of patterns is to "store" and "record" the form of patterns, which belongs to static storage [13]. In order to establish a pattern database, founder Huang Qingsui began to collect and organize traditional patterns consciously. She often went to the countryside to collect and create, and recorded traditional patterns with cameras when she encountered characteristic traditional patterns. Huang Qingsui believes that such down-to-earth work in the field is not only conducive to the preservation of traditional culture, but also provides a reference for Chinese designers to return to their cultural origins and find design inspiration in the future.

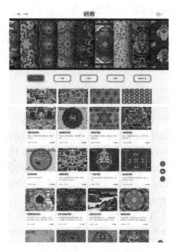

Fig. 7. Online museum database of Chinese patterns -- WenZang Website

The reason for the long cycle of pattern production is that the website is not only a simple record of patterns, but also a very complex process from input to output of pattern data. After the team gets the original image of the pattern, they will start to translate and digitize the image. In the process of design, creation, and display of the Miao embroidery patterns, it is easy to produce irreversible damage to the original works, which needs computer for indirect protection [14]. After the image is input into the professional software, the patterns are restored through thousands of lines and hundreds of millions of anchor points. However, the patterns are not simply copied from the traditional patterns, but the aesthetic theory is used to improve the color, shape, tension and other aspects of the patterns. The incomplete patterns, fuzzy patterns and patterns with chromatic aberration are restored and created into the final appearance. The vectorized patterns are input into the database, and a traditional pattern is thus preserved (see Fig. 7). The rational extraction and practical application of its characteristic design factors can further enrich the connotation of the design object, promote it to display more fully the unique charm of traditional culture, so as to make it more recognized by more people.

6 Digital Enabling to Open up "Online Market" for Miao Embroidery

6.1 Standardization of Production

Based on the industrial Internet, the traditional handicraft is digitally transformed to allow equipment and production data to interact with each other, and finally industrial embroidery is realized. The production efficiency of machine embroidery can be increased by 50 times, while the production cost is only one tenth of that of hand embroidery. With the development of the digital platform for Miao embroidery put into use, the designer team formed by the workshop can put the design samples into production immediately, although they are scattered all over the country. By introducing the digital management system, the production process of Miao embroidery can be optimized to ensure that each link has clear standards and specifications, and improve the production efficiency and product quality (Table 3). After the new patterns are efficiently generated by the digital system, more digital patterns can be further explored for application [15].

6.2 Product Scale

By introducing automated and intelligent equipment, such as numerical control embroidery machines, production efficiency can be greatly improved, and the time and labor cost required for manual embroidery can be reduced, so that Miao embroidery products can be produced at a faster speed and lower cost. Digital design software allows designers to quickly try different design elements and combinations, creating diversified Miao embroidery patterns to meet the needs of different consumers, thereby expanding product lines and market scale. By using big data analysis, enterprises can more accurately predict market trends and consumer preferences, timely adjust production plans, and build a situation for deep communication between the public and culture, so as to carry out cultural communication more quickly and deeply in the process of improving emotional experience [16], and ensure that product supply matches market demand.

Table 3. Digital Enabling of Intangible Cultural Heritage.

01 Craftsmen	02 Pattern database
Through the establishment of craftsman, the individual ability of craftsman is understood, and the individual ability of each craftsman is converted into the ability of a group.	Through the collection, application and redesign of patterns, the inheritance and innovation of traditional handicrafts are realized, and personalized services are customized.

Digital Enabling of Intangible Cultural Heritage

03 Production standardization	04 Product scale
Through the standardized training of craftsmen, professional designers participate, and the non-standardized craft is turned into a standardized product form.	Through the realization of intensive and scale production of products, the efficiency of man-hour and the maximization of economic benefits are realized, and the Miao embroidery industry is promoted to grow rapidly.

Through e-commerce platforms and social media, Miao embroidery products can more easily reach global consumers, establish brand image, expand international market, promote the value transformation of "design-product-industry", promote the formation of industrial value fission through digital technology, and promote the sharing and upgrading of industrial value [17]. The digital quality control system can ensure that each Miao embroidery product meets the unified quality standards, and improve the overall quality and market competitiveness of the product.To achieve the organic combination of traditional culture and modern market.

7 Conclusions

Digitalization can record and display the history, technology and cultural connotation of Miao embroidery, making this intangible cultural heritage able to transcend the limitations of time and space and be understood and learned by more people. At the same time, digital technology provides new possibilities for Miao embroidery design. Designers can use software tools to create new patterns and designs, while maintaining the traditional characteristics of Miao embroidery, promoting the innovation and development of Miao embroidery art. The mode of "university + enterprise" cooperation combines the traditional Miao embroidery industry with digitalization, and builds an interconnected digital Internet platform for Guizhou Miao embroidery industry. School-enterprise cooperation is an important step in optimizing resource allocation and promoting benefit sharing [18]. Looking at the field of education and research, the establishment of the Miao embroidery database provides abundant resources for scholars, designers and students to study the history, technology and culture of Miao embroidery, and promote academic exchanges and knowledge dissemination. In the creative production of enterprises, it builds a bridge between designers and Miao embroidery craftsmen. Designers can use the resources in the database, combined with modern design concepts, to create new Miao embroidery works, promoting the innovation and development of traditional art.

In addition, the digital platform makes Miao embroidery products more easily accessible to global consumers, helping to expand the market and increase sales channels. Through digital management, the production process can be optimized, production efficiency can be improved, costs can be reduced, and large-scale production can be realized. Digitization is an important direction for the integration of informationization and industrialization. The digital transformation of traditional embroidery is to establish a set of standardized production standards on the original cultural foundation, and to brand and symbolize Miao embroidery products, so as to better build the brand of Guizhou Miao embroidery.

References

1. Peng, Z., Deng, K., et al.: Study on the factors affecting the embroidery pattern style of Miao in Leishan. Asian Soc. Sci. **12**, 81 (2021)
2. Luo, S., Zhang, D.: Research on digital innovation model of design industry. Decoration (01), 17–21(2022)
3. Zhao, Y., Wu, X., Duo, T., et al.: Embracing the Cultural Digitalization Strategy: Review and Prospect of the Digitalization Practice of Intangible Cultural Heritage. Library Construction, pp. 1–10 (2023)
4. Liu, W., Huang, J.: Research on the confusion and solution of the smart inheritance of Miao embroidery in the digital age. Furniture Interior Decoration **01**, 68–74 (2023)
5. Long, Y.: Research on the establishment of Miao nationality embroidery database in western Hunan from the perspective of digitizing. In: Proceedings of 2017 4th International Conference on Education, Management and Computing Technology, pp. 970–973. Atlantis Press, China (2017)
6. Liu, H., Li, C., Huang, Z.: Empirical-based: construction of longitudinal research database of textile and garment higher education. Silk (05),76–85 (2021)
7. Han, D., Cong, L.: Miao traditional patterns: the origins and design transformation. Vis. Stud. (3–4), 425–432 (2023)
8. Cong, Y., Ning, J.: Research on the butterfly pattern and cultural connotation of Miao nationality costume in Southeast Guizhou. Art Observ. (02), 65–66 (2022)
9. Li, X.: Digital Extraction, Transformation and Development of Regional Traditional Patterns. Contemporary Literature (06), 14–15 (2023)
10. Hu, Q.: Character and Animal Patterns in Silver Jewelry Patterns of Miao Nationality in Southeast Guizhou. J. Nanjing Univ. Arts (Fine Arts and Design) (06), 121–125+238 (2015)
11. Zhang, Y., Liu, Y.: A modeling language and color application analysis of the Miao Nationality's embroidery pattern of southeast of Guizhou Province. Adv. Mater. Res. (1048), 285–289 (2014)
12. Zhao, X., Ning, J.: The color rules and characteristics of embroidery patterns in Miao nationality clothing in southeast Guizhou. J. Beijing Instit. Clothing Technol. (Natural Science Edition) (01), 21–28+34 (2021)
13. Tan, X., Xu, D.: Research on the generation and transformation of mother pattern of Shidong Miao Nationality. Decoration (09), 18–24 (2023)
14. Chen, Y.: Application research on computer modeling techniques in Miao embroidery. In: Proceedings of 2013 International Conference on Sport Science and Computer Science, pp. 308–316. WIT Press, HongKong (2013)
15. Tian, Y., Xue, K., Cui, Q., Xu, C., et al.: Research on digital generation of Miao embroidery patterns in Zunyi, Guizhou. J. Donghua Univ. (Social Science Edition) (02), 49–58 (2023)

16. Nie, H., Shi, M.: Digital cultural creative design of Miao embroidery pattern based on cultural translation. Design (18), 106–109 (2023)
17. Luo, S., Tian, X., et al.: Composition and innovation model of design industry network. Decoration (06), 64–68 (2021)
18. Li, L., Pan, S., Liu, Q.: Research on the mechanism of ethnic folk culture integration into school art education: a case study of Miao embroidery. Ethnic Educ. Res. (04), 130–136 (2017)

Exploring the Recognition of Illustration Styles in Marine Culture – "The Case of Fishermen's Painting in East Zhejiang Province as an Example"

Bai-Hui Du[✉] and Yi-Hang Lin[✉]

Graduate School of Creative Industry Design, National Taiwan University of Arts, New Taipei City 220307, Taiwan
baihuidu1@gmail.com, yh1206203323@163.com

Abstract. The Zhejiang East Fishermen's Painting is a unique form of artistic expression in the eastern part of Zhejiang Province, China. As part of intangible cultural heritage, this art form showcases the distinctive features of the local traditional maritime culture and holds potential cultural value. The style of Zhejiang East Fishermen's Painting typically features bold colors and delicate brushstrokes. The artworks primarily depict the daily lives of fishermen, marine scenes, worship of deities, and mythical legends, highlighting the significance of maritime culture to the local community. Fishermen's paintings face the inherent dilemma between "tradition" and "innovation". This study conducts preliminary cognitive research through three levels of cognitive progression: external perception, meaning cognition, and internal feelings. The aim is to explore the audience's preferences and assist creators in planning their works more effectively. The research focuses on understanding the perception of the style of fishermen's paintings. The research methods include case analysis of such artistic illustrations, questionnaire surveys, and MDS (multidimensional scaling) multiple regression analysis. Using cognitive communication theory, the study constructs nine categories of cognitive attributes related to painting styles. These attributes are classified into three creative cognitive models: "external appearance", "meaning cognition", and "internal feelings". The analysis examines how these attributes are interpreted and understood in the readers' cognition. Through the study of cognitive theory, the research establishes factors influencing audience preferences.

Keywords: Fishermen's painting · painting style · cognitive model · communication theory · multidimensional analysis

1 Introduction

1.1 Research Motivation

The coastal areas of East Zhejiang boast a rich maritime culture, which not only constitutes a vital part of the regional economy but is also intricately linked to the lives of residents. As one of the significant economic sources for the residents of East Zhejiang, fisheries play a crucial role. Fishermen's paintings, as a representative category

P.-L. P. Rau (Ed.): HCII 2024, LNCS 14701, pp. 48–65, 2024.
https://doi.org/10.1007/978-3-031-60904-6_4

of marine culture, bear the heritage of local traditional fishing culture. The scenes and themes depicted in these fishermen's paintings often reflect the cultural essence of the region, making these artworks not just expressions of art but vivid representations of the local traditional way of life and values.

On one hand, due to their deep roots in local maritime culture, fishermen's paintings have the potential to contribute to the preservation and inheritance of the local fishing culture. This artistic form not only enriches people's visual understanding of marine life but also serves to protect the fading traditions of the fishing industry. Through these artworks, people can catch a glimpse of past fishing village scenes, experiencing the profound cultural heritage of the marine environment. On the other hand, fishermen's paintings also provide an essential platform for local education and communication, allowing people from different regions to learn about the local maritime culture and fostering cultural exchange and understanding between different areas.

1.2 Research Purpose

The objectives of this research are as follows:

1. Analyze two categories of painting literature, one from artists with fishermen's experience and the other from artists without fishermen's experience.
2. Explore the cognitive communication theory of fishermen's painting creation, construct cognitive models, and provide an assessment foundation for subsequent questionnaire surveys.
3. Conduct a questionnaire survey on the differences between the two categories of paintings, understand respondents' variations in cognitive patterns and preference factors, and propose fishermen's painting recommendations that align with current identifications.

2 Literature Review

2.1 Literature Review on Fishermen's Paintings

Development History of Fishermen's Paintings. Fishermen's paintings along the coast of East Zhejiang belong to a form of artistic expression with a rich folk-art style, primarily focusing on the Zhoushan Archipelago region. There are various opinions on its specific historical origins, but according to the compilation by scholar Wang Yi-Qing, the academic community generally believes that it originated in the late 1970s and early 1980s. It went through an initial period of establishment in the early 1980s, a decline in the late 1990s, and a period of market development in the 21st century (He & Wang, 2011). According to the research by scholar Luo Jiang-Feng, in the early stages, the creators of fishermen's paintings were mainly individuals with fishermen's experience or from fishing village backgrounds. However, as the prosperity period began in the early 1990s, the backgrounds of the creators of fishermen's paintings became more diverse.

Themes for Fishermen Paintings. Themes for fishermen's paintings mainly revolve around the rich imagery of the sea, including fishermen's production activities, daily life scenes, mythological legends, and elements of faith. Early fishermen's paintings were inspired by the prevalent peasant art of the time. Peasant art was typically created and appreciated by farmers, constituting a form of popular art (Liao, 2015). Consequently, fishermen's paintings often employ bold, exaggerated, subjective, simple, and childlike techniques to interpret the rich cultural essence of folk traditions (Luo, 2009). Guided by this non-traditional, subjective flow of theory, regardless of the painting's theme, the artwork often exhibits large areas of color and distorted lines, creating a visually non-representational characteristic. This includes unique features such as indeterminate human forms and fish-like but not entirely fish-like expressions. For example, Lin Guo-fen's 'Ritual to the Sea God' swaps the roles of humans and fish, symbolizing the interdependence within the ecosystem. The distinctive expressive characteristics mentioned by Jin Tao in 1999 not only represent a technical experiment but also the artist's deep emotional expression within the composition.

Challenges and Development Suggestions for Fishermen's Paintings. The Development Process of Fishermen's Paintings: Compilation of Various Scholars' Perspectives on Current Status and Future Directions, as Summarized in Table 1: Research on Fishermen's Paintings.

Table 1. The Study of Fishermen's Paintings.

Researchers	Current Challenges	Future development recommendations
Jin, T (1999)	Generally well-regarded by experts but received a tepid response from the public Creative teams find it challenging to sustain Lack of a commercialization process	Maintaining the economic viability of the creative team Promoting the commercialization process
Luo, J. F.(2009)	The changing times constrain the creative space of original creators Evolution of artwork from within Lack of systematic academic research Lack of mechanisms, institutional deficiencies	Government support and guidance are prerequisites Academic theoretical research is a key pillar for development Establishing a support system for creative teams, streamlining profit-sharing, and nurturing new emerging artists Preserving the intrinsic marine culture of fishermen's paintings Promoting the trend of tourism-oriented development for fishermen's paintings

(*continued*)

Table 1. (*continued*)

Researchers	Current Challenges	Future development recommendations
Chen, Y. Y.(2014)	Contraction of creative teams, loss of talent Diminishing regional cultural identity	In the innovation process, it is crucial to emphasize the cultural essence of fishermen's paintings, finding a balance between innovation and tradition Prioritizing themes from folk culture and designing cultural and creative products that meet the needs of the public
Wang, Y. Q.(2022)	The creative team is facing a talent gap, lacking new emerging forces Insufficient creative bases and nurturing environments in society result in a lack of innovative thinking to adapt to changing times Difficulty in securing funding Monotony in peripheral cultural and creative products Lack of systematic academic theories and research In terms of feasibility studies, there is a lack of comparative research on various regions in Zhejiang Province, female and male creators, and creators from different historical periods, with insufficient statistical data support	The government should increase financial investment, supporting specific projects. Emphasize the quality of creators to enrich the content of creations Build a brand image, develop serialized products, and expand marketing channels. Actively promote digital protection research, facilitating the integrated development of industry, academia, and research

In summary, although different scholars may have some differences in their views on the current issues and future significance of fishermen's paintings, researchers generally focus on the challenges faced by creators. These challenges not only involve external factors but also delve into the cultural upbringing, artistic skills, and understanding of the local marine environment of the creators. The background of the creators, subtly and unconsciously, influences the choice of themes or the manner of expression in artistic creation.

In such a context, analyzing the differences in creators' backgrounds and exploring how these differences impact audience perceptions of their works becomes crucial. For instance, a creator with a background rooted in fishermen's experiences might express a profound understanding of the intrinsic marine culture through their work. Their creations may highlight vivid marine imagery, leading to a higher level of marine cultural awareness among the audience.

By elucidating the connection between the creator's background and their works, we may uncover how certain cultural elements are translated and presented, subsequently influencing the audience's perception.

Table 2. 10 Categories of Fishermen's Paintings.

Artwork	Author	Title of the Work	Author's Experience
	Sun Yue-Guo	Crab Deity	Fisherman, Fishing Industry Experience
	He Yue-Ming	One-year harvests one season, eat one fresh (world)	Fisherman, Over 40 Years of Fisherman and Fishermen's Experience
	Cai Cheng-Shi	Emergency Repair	Over 40 Years of Fisherman and Fishermen's Experience
	Zhu Son-Xiang	Bountiful Harvest	Fisherman, Fish Cargo Pier Worker
	Jiang De Ye	Zhoushan Ribbon Fish	Captain: Over 20 Years as a Fisherman
	Ma Shao-Hong	Ocean Marshal	Teacher
	Li Zhi-Qin	Around Happiness	Painter
	Zhou Man-Fei	Fishing Village	Art Teacher

(continued)

Table 2. (*continued*)

Artwork	Author	Title of the Work	Author's Experience
	Zhu Guo-An	Pants with Dragon Patterns	Professional Artist
	Yao Mei-Fei	Approaching Typhoon	Painter

Therefore, this study focuses on examining the differences in creators' backgrounds as the primary research objective. The aim is to investigate whether there are significant variations in audience perception regarding different aspects, such as the presentation of styles in fishermen's paintings, among various creators. In the later stages, the study will conduct a multivariate regression analysis. The research selected 10 fishermen's paintings, divided into two groups: one group includes 5 categories with creators having fishermen's experience, and the other group comprises 5 categories with creators lacking fishermen's experience.

Here, fishermen are defined as individuals whose livelihood involves fishing (Li, 1994). For the selection of fishermen's creators, we use fishermen's experience as the criterion, and detailed painting descriptions can be found in Table 2.

2.2 Exploration of Painting Styles

Theories Related to Visual Arts. Visual arts essentially refer to works where the primary focus of creation is visual, such as drawing, painting, photography, printmaking, lighting, and film (Shelley, 2023). Viewing artistic expression from a semiotic perspective, once a symbol (artwork) is created, its development and changes are no longer solely within the control of the creator (Shih, 2006). This suggests that the value of artwork lies not only in its formal aesthetic presentation but also in the emotions or speculative revelations it brings. Artworks serve as responses from artists to their own experiences and the socio-cultural environment. Simultaneously, they act as a medium for dialogue between the audience and art. This dialogue not only prompts people to interpret artworks but also provides viewers with the opportunity to express their own perspectives and emotions, thereby forming a personalized artistic.

Cognitive Theories and Communication Models experience. Norman (2005) proposed three levels of human Emotional design cognition: instinctive, behavioral, and reflective. This includes the audience's initial instinctive response, the behavior demonstrated in actual experience, and the emotional perception ultimately obtained through reflection. Through scholars like Chen Xi-Jing and others' research on "Poetry and

Painting," it is also understood that the cognitive levels for artistic works and the creative process include: external perception (whether the audience can see), meaning cognition (whether the audience can understand), and inner feelings (whether the audience can be moved) (Chen, Yan, Li, Lin, 2016; Lin, Chen, Lin, 2010). Based on the aforementioned "Poetry and Painting" communication matrix, this study establishes a communication matrix framework for fishermen's painting creation, as illustrated in Fig. 1.

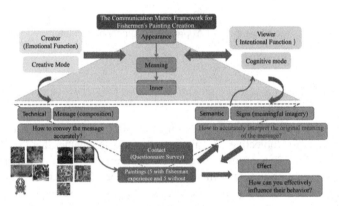

Fig. 1. The Communication Matrix Framework for Fishermen's Painting Creation.

The theoretical frameworks mentioned above exist in both the encoding process by the creator and the decoding process by the audience. In the realm of painting arts, how do we construct cognitive attributes? In the creation of paintings, there is a set of formal principles followed, including repetition, gradation, balance, harmony, contrast, proportion, rhythm, simplicity, and unity. Additionally, Jung Tsao categorizes the cognitive characteristics of painting into seven attributes: image design, color planning, uniqueness, functionality, expressiveness, thematic elements, and emotional meaning (Jung, 2009). The application of these principles contributes to effective communication between the creator and the audience in the construction of painting artworks. as shown in Fig. 1 below, this study integrates three cognitive levels, communication theories, and Jung Tsao's seven style cognitive attributes to derive nine cognitive attributes for fishermen's paintings: visual elements, composition, Painting themes, Style Features, atmosphere, emotional conveyance, Creating a Situation, Inner Expression, and Emotional resonance. The meanings of these nine cognitive attributes are further explained in Table 3.

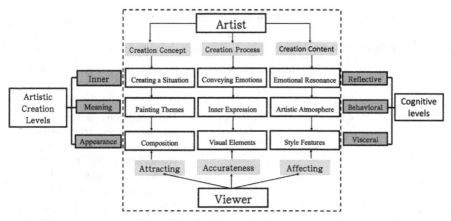

Fig. 2. The Communication Matrix Framework for Fishermen's Illustrative Painting Creation.

Table 3. The Definitions of 9 Cognitive Attributes.

Creation and cognitive aspects	Attributes	Definition
Appearance	Composition	The overall visual structure is formed through the arrangement of elements by an artist, as well as the organization and combination of these elements
	Visual Elements	The fundamental visual elements used in visual arts are typically the visible components in artworks or design pieces, such as points, lines, surfaces, color, shapes, etc
	Style Features	The distinctive artistic features expressed in an artwork, specifically manifested in aspects such as composition, utilization of visual elements, color selection, brushstroke techniques, etc., serve as points of individual creativity and artistic language formation
Meaning	Painting Themes	The specific content chosen by an artist in the creative process, such as landscapes, figures, abstract concepts, social issues, etc

(*continued*)

Table 3. (*continued*)

Creation and cognitive aspects	Attributes	Definition
	Inner Expression	Refers to the abstract or implied meanings, emotions, thoughts, or symbols contained in an artwork
	Artistic Atmosphere	The overall sense and emotional atmosphere presented in an artwork are created by a combination of visual elements, color usage, brushstroke techniques, lighting effects, and other factors in the composition
Inner	Creating a Situation	The artist consciously establishes a specific scene or environment through skillful use of visual elements, subject matter, composition, and other techniques
	Conveying Emotions	Artists typically use various means, such as composition, color usage, brushstroke techniques, and subject selection, to express and convey the emotional content behind their works
	Emotional Resonance	Artworks enable viewers to deeply understand, feel, and connect with the emotions conveyed in the artwork, creating a sense of empathy to some extent

3   Research Methodology

This study aims to investigate the cognitive perception of illustrative styles in fishermen's paintings. The research methodology encompasses case analysis, questionnaire surveys, and the application of MDS (multidimensional scaling) regression matrices. A cognitive theory-based analysis is conducted on the nine cognitive elements of illustrative perception, examining how they are interpreted and understood by the audience. Through the exploration of cognitive theories, the study constructs cognitive attributes for the illustration of fishermen's paintings to compare the creations of artists with and without fishermen's experience. MDS (multidimensional scaling) analysis is employed to understand the differences in audience preference factors. The goal is to propose illustrative styles in fishermen's paintings that resonate with current preferences and identities, based on the findings from the cognitive theory research.

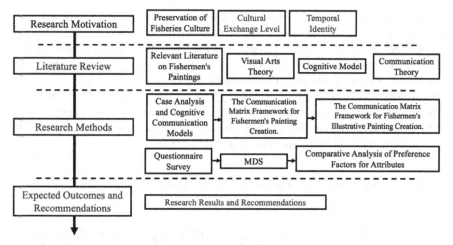

Fig. 3. The Research Framework for Fishermen's Painting.

4 Results and Discussion

4.1 MDS (Multidimensional Scaling) Analysis

After conducting the preliminary questionnaire survey, we received a total of 111 responses. We utilized SPSS for multidimensional scaling analysis (MDS), and the obtained stress coefficient and determination coefficient were Kruskal's Stress = 0.05994 and RSQ = 0.99153, respectively. Through this analysis, we derived the average audience identification data for the nine attributes, as summarized in Table 4 for fishermen's paintings. Items p1–p5 represent creations by artists with fishermen's experience, while items p6–p10 are creations by artists without fishermen's experience.

In Table 4, the researcher particularly focused on the average values for each attribute. Taking "Visual Elements" as an example, the average values for items p1–p5 all exceeded 4, indicating that the overall average was higher than items p6–p10. In these attributes, item p5 ("Zhoushan Ribbon Fish") not only received the highest score in Visual elements but also ranked high among creations by artists with fishermen's experience. Additionally, this item performed exceptionally well in the other six attributes, showing high audience recognition in terms of appearance, Inner expression, and emotional perception. In terms of Inner Expression and Creating a Situation, item p4 ("Bountiful Harvest ") had the highest average value, indicating that the audience easily comprehended meaning and Creating a Situation. It is noteworthy that among creations by artists without fishermen's experience (p6–p10), item p9 ("Pants with Dragon Patterns") stood out, particularly excelling in the "Composition" attribute. The arrangement and combination of elements in this category could express clear meanings. Comparing items p5 ("Zhoushan Ribbon Fish") and p9 ("Pants with Dragon Patterns"), both performed outstandingly in terms of appearance attributes. However, looking at the intrinsic feeling attribute, item p5 had a higher overall identification rate than item p9. This suggests that item p5 is more likely to be understood and resonated with by the audience, and both items achieved the highest score in the "Conveying Emotions" attribute, indicating high audience identification with emotional and cultural characteristics.

In summary, the highest attribute values for the top 10 fishermen's paintings are all in the realm of appearance attributes. This suggests that the audience is most perceptible to the aspect of visual perception. Creators with fishermen's experience tend to choose elements in the "Visual Elements" attribute to present a more concrete representation of marine culture, allowing the audience to have a clearer perception of marine imagery. On the other hand, creators without fishermen's experience are mostly recognized by the audience in terms of "Composition" and "Style Features".

Table 4. Average Values of 9 Categories of Style Attributes in Fishermen's Paintings.

		p1	p2	p3	p4	p5	p6	p7	p8	p9	p10
Appearance	F1 (Composition)	4.03	3.68	3.77	4.26	4.32	3.38	3.23	3.83	4.17	3.65
	F2 (Visual Elements)	4.26	4.38	4.20	4.40	4.53	3.29	3.22	4.02	4.09	3.60
	F3 (Style Features)	3.93	3.55	4.05	4.08	4.34	3.67	3.34	3.78	4.06	3.60
Meaning	F4 (Painting Themes)	3.88	3.63	3.68	4.14	4.23	3.23	3.09	3.75	4.01	3.58
	F5 (Inner Expression)	3.86	3.60	3.66	4.18	4.17	3.28	3.15	3.85	4.03	3.63
	F6 (Artistic Atmosphere)	4.09	3.62	3.91	4.08	4.29	3.88	3.35	3.76	4.05	3.73
Inner	F7 (Creating a Situation)	3.52	3.67	3.59	4.10	4.09	3.25	3.23	3.75	3.77	3.67
	F8 (Conveying Emotions)	3.86	3.72	3.70	4.05	4.23	3.46	3.34	3.68	4.00	3.64
	F9 (Emotional Resonance)	3.42	3.32	3.50	3.83	4.04	3.21	3.15	3.59	3.71	3.46

Applying the data from the above table to multidimensional scaling analysis, we obtained the cognitive spatial map of style attributes in three dimensions, as shown in the Fig. 4. The 10 fishermen's paintings exhibit four clustering patterns: [p1 (Crab Deity), p3 ("Emergency Repair"), p8 ("Fishing Village")], [p2"One-year harvests one season, eat one fresh (world)"], [p7 ("Around Happiness"), p6 ("Ocean Marshal"), p10 ("Approaching Typhoon")], and [p9 ("Pants with Dragon Patterns"), p4 ("Bountiful Harvest"), p5 ("Zhoushan Ribbon Fish")].

Excluding the four clusters in Fig. 4, it can be observed that the directions of "Visual Elements" and attributes such as "Emotional Resonance," "Atmosphere," and "Style Features" form an angle close to 90 degrees. This implies a very low correlation between these two categories of attributes, indicating a weak connection between "visual elements" and "Style Features," "Emotional resonance," and "Artistic Atmosphere." Additionally, it is worth noting that in the matrix structure of Fig. 2, the attributes of "Emotional resonance," "Artistic Atmosphere," and "Style Features" follow a progression in the creation context of the artists. Therefore, the attribute of "visual elements" has a significant impact on the core content of the creators. Except for "Visual Elements" positioned in the first quadrant, the remaining eight categories of attributes are in the fourth quadrant, indicating mutual correlations among these eight attributes.

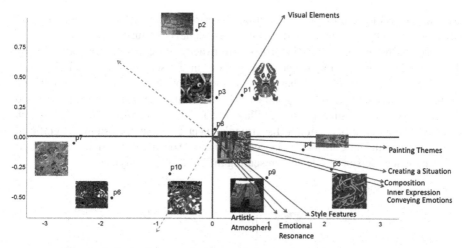

Fig. 4. Style Attributes and a Three-Dimensional Cognitive Space Map.

In the analysis, three clusters were formed: [p1 (Crab Deity), p3 ("Emergency Repair"), p8 ("Fishing Village")] in the first quadrant, showing the highest correlation with the "Visual Elements" attribute; the second quadrant included only one type, p2 ("One-year harvests one season, eat one fresh (world)"), which was relatively closer in the "Visual Elements" attribute but had low correlation with other content; the third quadrant included [p7 ("Around Happiness"), p6 ("Ocean Marshal"), p10 ("Approaching Typhoon")], and they performed lower in the characteristics of the 9 attributes, especially p7 ("Around Happiness"), which showed the most noticeable differences; the last cluster was [p9 ("Pants with Dragon Patterns"), p4 ("Bountiful Harvest"), p5 ("Zhoushan Ribbon Fish")], in the fourth quadrant, with the richest attribute features, and p5 ("Zhoushan Ribbon Fish") was the standout item。

Based on the above analysis, when dividing the paintings into those created by artists with and without fishermen's experience, a classification is obtained as shown in Fig. 5. Overall, paintings created by artists with fishermen's experience are generally in a position of high correlation with the nine attributes. However, p1 (Crab Deity), p2 ("One-year harvests one season, eat one fresh (world)"), and p3 ("Emergency Repair") lack in handling external appearance and meaning aspects, leading to a high correlation in the "Visual Elements" attribute. Nevertheless, it should be noted that, due to the lack of some external appearance and meaning aspects, these paintings may be less easily understood by the audience. p4 ("Bountiful Harvest") and p5 ("Zhoushan Ribbon Fish") show high correlation in external appearance, meaning, and internal content. Paintings created by artists without fishermen's experience, such as p8 ("Fishing Village"), show only low correlation in various attributes, lacking significant features. p9 ("Pants with Dragon Patterns") has a low correlation with marine elements in the "Visual Elements" attribute, but it still resonates with the audience due to its clear external appearance and strong meaning attributes. As for p7 ("Around Happiness"), p6 ("Ocean Marshal"), and p10 ("Approaching Typhoon"), they are in a position of extremely low correlation with the 9 attributes, possibly because the presentation of marine imagery in the "Visual Elements" attribute is too chaotic, making it difficult for the audience to further understand.

Through the above discussion, artists with fishermen's experience are affirmed by the respondents in the nine attributes, especially in the selection of visual elements. They tend to focus on themes related to fishermen's work and marine life, presenting a simpler and more unified style. In contrast, artists without fishermen's experience tend to depict diverse themes, such as fishing village life and deity worship, demonstrating rich diversity. Although artists without fishermen's experience may not show a significant performance in the nine attributes, they exhibit more flexibility in creativity, giving their works a distinct personal style and presenting different cultural styles.

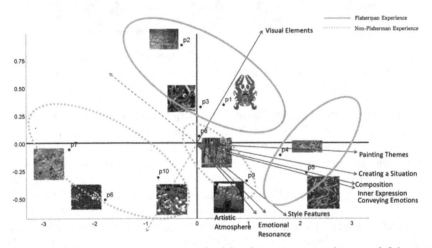

Fig. 5. The cognitive space map is categorized by the presence or absence of fishermen's experience.

Through the analysis of the "Preference" question data in the questionnaire survey, we compiled Table 5, which includes information about the average preference scores and rankings. According to the multiple regression analysis, the table shows that the top five ranked items all have certain correlations in the "Visual Elements" content. This indicates that when presenting clear and vivid marine imagery and related "visual elements," audiences are more likely to move from understanding to resonance. Additionally, the top three ranked items, p5 ("Zhoushan Ribbon Fish"), p4 ("Bountiful Harvest"), and p9 ("Pants with Dragon Patterns"), have higher levels of agreement on the three dimensions of semantic perception: "Painting Themes," "Artistic Atmosphere," and "Inner Expression." This not only signifies audience preferences for specific themes but also indicates that these paintings have meaningful expressions that align with the thematic nature. Through the high correlation of visual presentation and Inner Expression, these paintings evoke emotional resonance with the audience towards marine culture. This comprehensive advantage may contribute to attracting audience attention and eliciting positive responses.

Table 5. Average Preference Scores and Rankings.

	p5	p4	p9	p3	p1	p8	p10	p2	p6	p7
Ranking	1	2	3	4	5	6	7	8	9	10
Mean	4.18	3.85	3.82	3.71	3.65	3.63	3.41	3.39	3.20	3.14

4.2 Gender and Professional Background Layer Cognitive Analysis

In this section, we will discuss the impact of gender and professional background on the perception of fishermen's paintings. By analyzing the survey data, we divided the respondents into male (46 individuals) and female (65 individuals) groups, as well as those with an art and design background (39 individuals) and those without (72 individuals). Independent sample T-tests were conducted to delve into the differences in audience preferences for artworks and explore the specific degrees involved in the cognitive process of instinct, behavior, and reflection. We categorized these aspects into three layers: appearance, meaning, and internal. Additionally, we incorporated the preference level for each artwork to comprehensively understand the influence of gender and professional background differences on the cognitive three-layer aspects of fishermen's paintings, as shown in Fig. 3. The questionnaire items related to the 9 attributes were grouped into Appearance ("Composition", "Visual Elements", "Style Features"), Meaning ("Painting Themes", "Inner Expression", "Artistic Atmosphere"), Inner ("Creating a Situation", "Conveying Emotions", "Emotional Resonance"), and finally, the 10th question regarding the preference level for each artwork.

4.2.1 Gender

The independent sample t-test analysis for gender differences in Table 6 reveals significant variations in appearance, meaning, and internal aspects for p3 ("Emergency Repair") and p10 ("Approaching Typhoon"). Among them, p3 ("Emergency Repair") exhibits the most significant gender difference, particularly in Appearance (p = .000***), meaning (p = .000***), and Inner (p = .023***). This indicates that the female group has significantly higher identification with the appearance and meaning of p3 (Emergency Repair) compared to the male group. For p10 ("Approaching Typhoon"), the significant differences are observed in Appearance (p = .023*), meaning (p = .014*), and Inner (p = .017*). Additionally, in the overall preference ratings for the 10 items, p3 (Emergency Repair) also shows higher female identification than male identification. It suggests that p3 ("Emergency Repair") is more popular among females in terms of appearance selection, meaning definition, and internal resonance, while no significant differences are found in the other eight categories.

Table 6. Gender Differences in Style Perception Table.

Artwork	Evaluation criteria	t-test for Equality Means		
		T	df	Sig
	Appearance	−4.312***	109	.000
	Meaning	−3.594***	109	.000
	Inner	−2.302*	109	.023
	Appearance	−2.116*	109	.037
	Meaning	−2.501*	109	.014
	Inner	−2.416*	109	.017
	Artwork Preference	−3.623***	109	.000

* p < .05 *** p < .001

4.2.2 Professional Background

The investigation into participants' professional backgrounds allowed us to categorize them into two groups: those with an art and design background and those without. In Table 7 below, we identified significant differences between the two groups, especially in three items: p6 ("Ocean Marshal"), p7 ("Around Happiness"), and p10 ("Approaching Typhoon"). It shows that participants without an art background had significantly higher levels of identification with these items compared to those with an art background. In p6 ("Ocean Marshal"), significant differences were observed in Appearance (p = .017*), Meaning (p = .003**), and Inner (p = .005**). For p7 ("Around Happiness"), differences were found only in the meaning aspect (p = .039*), while for p10 ("Approaching Typhoon"), differences were present in Appearance (p = .021*), Meaning (p = .044*), and overall liking of the artwork (p = .021*).

Examining the visual characteristics of these items, we observed that the artworks presented complex visual effects composed of multiple elements, creating a rich and unconventional visual representation. Despite the complexity, the artworks retained clear distinctions between different elements, such as people, boats, and houses, allowing viewers to identify and differentiate these elements. This unique recognition factor contributed to the preference of participants without an art background. Simultaneously, this characteristic led to a somewhat ambiguous presentation of meaning and internal aspects. The differing perspectives on this stylistic distinction may stem from the emphasis on recognizability and functionality in visual artworks during the professional training of those with an art and design background.

Table 7. The table shows the stylistic perception differences between participants with and without design backgrounds.

Artwork	Evaluation criteria	t-test for Equality Means		
		T	df	Sig
	Appearance	−2.426*	109	.017
	Meaning	−3.026**	109	.003
	Inner	−2.834**	109	.005
	Meaning	−2.086*	109	.039
	Appearance	−2.343*	109	.021
	Meaning	−2.035*	109	.044
	Artwork Preference	−2.567*	109	.012

$* p < .05 ** p < .01$

5 Conclusion and Recommendations

This study investigates the stylistic differences between experienced fishermen and non-experienced fishermen creators, identifying audience preference factors for these two background groups of creators. The research conclusions will reveal relevant similarities and differences, offering recommendations for current fishermen's art creation.

In this study, the nine categories of cognitive attributes were brought into MDS multivariate regression analysis. Comparing the creations of two different background creators, the conclusion indicates that in the category of "Visual Perception" (including "Composition", "Visual Elements", and "Style Features"), all 10 paintings received acclaim from the audience. However, it is noteworthy that there are still distinctions in the performance of external attributes between the two background groups. For creators with fishermen's experience, the clarity of marine imagery in "Visual Elements" is recognized by the audience. For creators without fishermen's experience, their works in creative features ("Composition", "Style Features") align with audience preferences. This is also consistent with the conclusions of later independent sample T-tests, showing significant differences in artwork preference between male and female groups and groups with or without artistic backgrounds, particularly in non-experienced fishermen's creations. This suggests that certain audiences have specific preferences for this type of artwork.

The attribute "Visual Elements" influences the creation's content. In the MDS three-dimensional space, it is observed that there is a lack of correlation between "Visual elements" and three other attributes: "Style Features", "Artistic Atmosphere", and "Emotional resonance". In other words, if visual elements are too specifically presented, it may lead to issues of lacking creativity and audience understanding. This also has an impact on meaning recognition.

In the previous studies, fishermen's paintings faced the dilemma of "tradition" and "innovation". This study conducts preliminary cognitive research through the progression of external perception, meaning recognition, and internal feelings to assist creators in more effectively planning their works. The study explores how different audience groups can have a deeper understanding of Zhejiang the East China Sea culture. In general, external perception ("Composition", "Visual elements", "Style Features") is the first level of perception for the audience. At this level, the audience's first perception is the simplicity of the visual subject, evoking an immediate response to marine imagery (such as boats, marine life, fishing activities, etc.). These factors contribute to conveying strong cultural messages, making the audience feel the characteristics of marine culture. In terms of meaning recognition ("Painting Themes", "Inner Expression", "Artistic Atmosphere"), there needs to be a clear theme for easy understanding of the meaning and theme. This requires a focus on the traditional theme's Inner Expression, and the use of a single theme may lead to aesthetic fatigue. Therefore, it is also necessary to consider the applicable range of themes to create a diverse style expression, contributing to the richness of the work's content. Finally, in terms of internal inner ("Creating a Situation", Conveying Emotions", "Emotional Resonance"), the "Conveying Emotions" attribute received the most recognition from the audience in the research questionnaire, while "Emotional Resonance" received the least recognition. Although overall works can convey emotions and cultural characteristics, there is a significant challenge in evoking emotional resonance from the audience. As a forward-looking discussion, the research sample is limited to works by two background creators. Future research can further increase the number of samples, explore more diverse constitutive factors, and intricately integrate cultural elements into the creation, providing a more nuanced style experience.

References

1. Chen, Y.I.: The characteristics and developmental journey of Zhoushan fishermen paintings. China Arts 4(5), 119–123 (2014)
2. Chen, S.J., Yen, H.Y., Lee, S., Lin, L.C.: Applying design thinking in curating model a case study of the exhibition of turning poetry into painting. J. Design 21(4), 1–24 (2016)
3. He, L.F., Wang, Y.: Prospects and ideas for the industrialization of Zhoushan fishermen paintings. J. Zhejiang Ocean Univ. 28(1), 55–59 (2011)
4. Hsu, F.H.: A study on the signification of visual art communication (master's thesis). National Taiwan University of Arts (2008)
5. Huang, M.H.: Zhoushan Fishermen Paintings Born from Island Soil, Zhejiang Art News 11 (2019)

6. Jin, T.: A discourse on Zhoushan maritime art. J. Zhejiang Ocean Univ. **16**(1), 38–43 (1999)
7. Jung, T.: Study on the visual style of digital illustration design using vector skills. J. Bus. Design (14), 253–272 (2010). https://doi.org/10.29514/TJCD.201011.0015
8. Liao, K.M.: First Volume of Contemporary Chinese Folk Painting. Science Press, China (1994)
9. Li, X.: Revised Mandarin Chinese Dictionary. The Commercial Press, Ltd., Taiwan (1994)
10. Lin, C., Chen, S., Lin, R.: Efficacy of virtual reality in painting art exhibitions appreciation. Appl. Sci. **10**(9) (2020)
11. Luo, J.F.: Research on the inheritance and development of Zhoushan fishermen paintings. J. Zhejiang Normal Univ. **34**(1), 79–84 (2009)
12. Luo, J.F.: Maritime folk art: Zhoushan fishermen paintings. China Arts, 107–111 (2001)
13. Norman, D.A.: The Design of Everyday Things. Basic Books, USA (2013)
14. Shen, W.Q.: Portrait of the Sea God. Zhejiang People's Fine Arts Publishing House, China (2019)
15. Wen-Qian, S.: Fishermen Paintings Chronicle |Tianya New Publication, https://www.sohu.com/a/411864874_99953422. Accessed 17 Oct 2023
16. Shih, H.J.: Examining the inherent differences between performing arts and visual arts from the perspective of the 'Moment of Creation' in art. J. Aesthet. Arts Manage. **2**, 74–80 (2006)
17. Torossian, A.: A Guide to Aesthetics. Oxford University Press, London (1937)
18. Wang, Y.Q.: Review of the current research situation and problem analysis of fishermen's painting. Packaging Design **6**(2), 174–175 (2022)
19. Wang, Y.F., Fu, J.Q.: Research on inheritance and development of island folk culture. J. Baotou Vocational Tech. College **20**(3), 88–92 (2019)
20. What Are the Visual Arts? https://www.thoughtco.com/what-are-the-visual-arts-182706. Accessed 27 Oct 2023
21. Chanting Tides, Cherishing Memories: Xu Zhong-fang, the Spiritual Journey of Fishermen Painter. http://www.360doc.com/content/17/1120/18/42824938_705625024.shtml. Accessed 3 Nov 2023
22. Fishermen Paintings: Inspiration from the Sea. https://www.sohu.com/a/411864874_999 53422. Accessed 26 Oct 2023
23. Principles of Beauty. https://pedia.cloud.edu.tw/Entry/Detail/?title=%E7%BE%8E%E7%9A%84%E5%8E%9F%E7%90%86. Accessed 9 Oct 2023

Unveiling User Cognitive Ergonomics Excellence: Digitally Redesigning Traditional Chinese Textile Patterns

Dongze Huo[1,2]([✉]) [iD]

[1] Kyiv National University of Technologies and Design, Mala Shyianovska
(Nemyrovycha-Danchenka) Street 2, Kyiv 01011, Ukraine
`001823@peihua.edu.cn`
[2] Xi'an Peihua University, Changning Street 888, Chang'an District, Xi'an 710125, China

Abstract. The convergence of traditional craftsmanship and cutting-edge digital technologies has sparked a revolution in the realm of modern visual design, particularly in the context of traditional Chinese patterns. This essay explores the intersection of User Cognitive Ergonomics and digital methodologies, drawing inspiration from a wealth of research that spans speculative artefacts, body-to-pattern relationships, bespoke parametric blocks, global influences, and the evolution of pattern practices. The goal is to illuminate the transformative potential of User Cognitive Ergonomics considerations in the digital realm, emphasizing a harmonious blend of tradition and innovation.

Keywords: Cross-cultural interaction · User Cognitive Ergonomics · Digital redesign · Traditional pattern · Transformation

1 Introduction

In the transformative landscape of design, where the old is being re-imagined through the new, traditional Chinese textile patterns emerge as a profound canvas for exploration. These patterns, with their rich tapestry of historical, cultural, and artistic significance, are being re-envisioned in the digital age. This paper embarks on a journey that weaves together the intricate threads of heritage preservation and digital innovation, exploring how User Cognitive Ergonomics can enhance the digital methods employed in the redesign of these traditional patterns.

Grounded in a synthesis of diverse scholarly insights, this study draws upon the foundational work of R. K. J. De Silva, P. U. Navodhya & Simeon Gill (2023) and Simeon Gill, Hailah Al Houf, Steve Hayes & Jo Conlon (2023), who provide a modern understanding of the traditional crafting techniques and their adaptation to digital platforms. Their research offers a lens through which we can view the nuanced interplay between tangible craftsmanship and digital precision, ensuring that traditional patterns are not only preserved but also revitalized in the digital redesign process.

Sonika Soni Khar & Sanjeevani Manish Ayachit (2013) contribute to this narrative by reflecting on historical design methods, emphasizing the need to look backwards

P.-L. P. Rau (Ed.): HCII 2024, LNCS 14701, pp. 66–74, 2024.
https://doi.org/10.1007/978-3-031-60904-6_5

to move forward. Their insights into traditional Indian pattern making offer valuable parallels to the Chinese context, suggesting that an understanding of historical design principles is crucial for the development of contemporary digital methods that resonate on a global stage.

Robert W. Proctor, Shimon Y. Nof, Yuehwern Yih, Parasuram Balasubramanian, Jerome R. Busemeyer, Pascale Carayon, Chi-Yue Chiu, Fariborz Farahmand, Cleotilde Gonzalez, Jay Gore, Steven J. Landry, Mark Lehto, Pei-Luen Rau, William Rouse, Louis Tay, Kim-Phuong L. Vu, Sang Eun Woo & Gavriel Salvendy (2011) expands the scope by addressing the broader implications of cross-cultural decision making in the design and use of digital media. Their work informs this study's approach to digital redesign, ensuring that the transformation of patterns is not only aesthetically pleasing but also cognitively ergonomic, fostering a user experience that transcends cultural boundaries.

By anchoring our exploration in such extensive research, we aim to illuminate the transformative potential of User Cognitive Ergonomics considerations in the realm of digital design, emphasizing a harmonious blend of tradition and innovation.

2   Research Content

2.1   Aesthetic Innovation and User Cognitive Ergonomics

The digital redesign of traditional Chinese textile patterns presents a unique fusion of heritage and modernity, where aesthetic innovation plays a critical role. Ma Yu-Ming, Du He-min, and Yao Hao's (2023) work serves as a cornerstone for this exploration, emphasizing an innovative approach grounded in aesthetic experience and the mapping of product features space. It advocates for the digital redesign that not only translates traditional motifs into the digital realm but reimagines them to resonate with contemporary sensibilities while honoring their intrinsic cultural value.

In tandem with these principles, Siyi Wang (2018) provides an interdisciplinary framework that revolutionizes museum exhibition design. This approach is emblematic of the holistic design philosophy that this paper espouses, one that integrates touch, sound, smell, space, and memory to craft a sensory-rich experience that both captivates and educates. Siyi Wang (2018)'s methodology challenges conventional exhibition concepts, pushing the boundaries of how traditional patterns are presented and perceived in contemporary settings.

Building upon these foundational works, our research further explores the application of digital methodologies to traditional patterns. The intricate artistry of traditional Chinese textile patterns stands at the crossroads of tradition and innovation. Digital redesign efforts are not merely about transferring these patterns into a new medium; they are about re-envisioning them through technology while honoring their cultural and artistic integrity.

The pursuit of aesthetic innovation involves a careful balance between cultural heritage preservation and the advancement of digital design methodologies. It's a pursuit that demands respect for visual harmony and the cultural narratives embedded within each pattern. The extraction process of traditional pattern elements is a meticulous practice that involves deconstructing complex motifs into fundamental symbols. This process is not only technical but also interpretive, requiring an understanding of the historical and cultural context from which these patterns arise.

Once the core elements are extracted, the next step is the deformation design, where these symbols are reconfigured to create new patterns that resonate with contemporary aesthetics while maintaining their traditional significance. It interprets how symbols can be deconstructed and reformed, showing the potential for varied yet coherent designs that stem from a single traditional motif. The deformation process is emblematic of the digital redesign's transformative potential; it reflects how traditional elements can evolve into novel designs that remain cognizant of their origins.

In synthesizing the traditional with the digital, this research underscores the significance of User Cognitive Ergonomics. The redesign process is not just about visual appeal; it is about how users interact with and perceive these patterns in a digital context. The redesign process incorporates an intuitive understanding of user perception, ensuring that the patterns are not only visually harmonious but also cognitively ergonomic. Thus, the digital redesign of traditional Chinese textile patterns becomes a testament to the harmonious blend of heritage and innovation, as it navigates through the realms of aesthetics, user experience, and cultural respect.

2.2 The Interplay of Body and Pattern

The journey from traditional crafting to digital excellence in textile design is marked by the precision that technology affords and the human touch that tradition commands. R. K. J. De Silva, P. U. Navodhya & Simeon Gill (2023) provides insightful analysis into this transformative journey, shedding light on the nuanced interplay between the tactile craftsmanship of the past and the digital precision of the future. Their study delves into the implications of the body-to-pattern relationship, offering a pivotal understanding of how digital technologies can capture the essence of traditional techniques while enhancing user comfort and functionality.

The transition from conventional drafting methods to automated digital prototyping, as discussed by R. K. J. De Silva, P. U. Navodhya & Simeon Gill (2023), represents a significant advancement in the field. Their work is instrumental in demonstrating how User Cognitive Ergonomics can be woven into the fabric of digital redesign, ensuring that the resulting patterns are not only accurate representations of traditional motifs but also ergonomically optimized for the modern wearer. This consideration is crucial, as it acknowledges the wearer's comfort and the pattern's functionality as fundamental components of design excellence.

In this context, "precision" extends beyond the mere dimensions of a pattern; it encapsulates the meticulous consideration of how a pattern interacts with the body. R. K. J. De Silva, P. U. Navodhya & Simeon Gill (2023)'s approach underscores the importance of integrating ergonomic principles from the outset of the digital design process. It is through this lens that the digital redesign process becomes a harmonious blend of tradition and innovation, respecting the time-honored techniques of Chinese textile patterns while embracing the possibilities offered by modern digital tools.

2.3 Designing in the Metaverse

The realm of design is witnessing a paradigm shift with the advent of the Metaverse, where the traditional boundaries of creativity are being redefined. Ming-Hsiang Tsou and Christian Mejia (2023) stand at the forefront of this exploration, advocating for a role expansion of cartographers to user interface designers within these virtual spaces. Their work illuminates the potential of virtual reality (VR), augmented reality (AR), and mixed reality (MR) as tools that can profoundly enhance the User Cognitive Ergonomics of pattern redesign.

In their visionary approach, Ming-Hsiang Tsou & Christian Mejia (2023) propose a multi-dimensional understanding of design that leverages the immersive qualities of VR, AR, and MR. These technologies allow for a more intuitive and interactive experience, enabling users to engage with traditional patterns in a dynamic and responsive environment. This immersive interaction goes beyond mere visual appreciation, facilitating a deeper cognitive connection with the patterns that is informed by their cultural and historical contexts.

The Metaverse provides a unique platform for the manifestation of these traditional designs, transcending the limitations of the physical world. Designers are now able to create spaces where users can interact with patterns in a holistic manner, experiencing the texture, scale, and detail of traditional textiles in a fully immersive way. Ming-Hsiang Tsou & Christian Mejia (2023)'s contributions suggest that this level of engagement could revolutionize the way we perceive and understand traditional patterns, offering new insights into their significance and relevance in a digital age.

2.4 Data as a Medium for Creativity

In the quest to harmonize traditional artistry with innovative digital design, a data-driven approach emerges as a powerful medium for the inheritance and evolution of cultural motifs. Rong Han, Hong Zhang, Rui Li & Chunfa Sha (2019) present a compelling case for the data-driven creative design of ancient Chinese artefacts. Their research underscores the potential of data to act as a catalyst for the reinterpretation of traditional designs, imbuing them with new life and relevance in the digital age.

This section draws inspiration from their methodology to explore the digital revival of two exemplary brocade patterns: "A Pair of Deer Patterns in A String of Beads" and "Wan Shi Ru Yi". These brocade patterns, each with their own rich historical narratives and aesthetic complexities, are ripe for a digital renaissance that respects their legacy while propelling them into the future.

The "A Pair of Deer Patterns in A String of Beads" brocade, characterized by its intricate interplay of fauna and ornamentation, serves as a testament to the mastery of ancient weavers. By applying data analysis to this pattern, we can deconstruct its elements to understand the underlying structures and motifs that can be adapted and reimagined for contemporary design applications. (Example: Fig. 1 and Fig. 2).

Similarly, the "Wan Shi Ru Yi" brocade pattern, with its swirls of auspicious symbols and vibrant hues, presents a visual feast that is both timeless and deeply rooted in cultural symbolism. Through data-driven analysis, each curve and contour can be distilled into digital form, allowing for variations that retain the essence of the original while meeting modern aesthetic preferences. (Example: Figs. 3, 4, and 5).

Fig. 1. A pair of deer patterns in a string of beads Brocade

Fig. 2. Pattern extraction

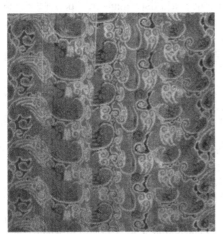

Fig. 3. "Wan Shi Ru Yi" brocade pattern

Fig. 4. Pattern extraction

In synthesizing tradition with data analytics, the project aims to elevate User Cognitive Ergonomics by ensuring that the redesigned patterns resonate on a cognitive level with contemporary audiences. The meticulous data-driven process does not simply translate traditional motifs into the digital language; it re-enchants them, ensuring that the cultural narratives they carry are understood and appreciated within the modern digital framework. In this research, the principles outlined by Rong Han, Hong Zhang, Rui Li, China Sha (2019) are not merely applied but are woven into the fabric of our methodology, forming a tapestry that stretches across time—linking the intricate handiwork of ancient weavers with the innovative spirit of today's digital artisans. Data serves as the golden thread in this endeavor, bridging heritage with modernity and allowing

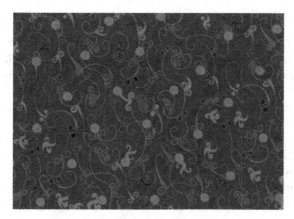

Fig. 5. Digital redesign

for a dialogue that honors tradition while embracing progress. Figures in this section depict the original brocade patterns alongside their data-driven reinterpretations, charting a course from the tactile elegance of traditional craftsmanship to the pixel-perfect precision of digital forms. These visual representations encapsulate the transformative journey of each pattern, illustrating how the essence of the past is being meticulously carried forward into the digital panorama of textile design.

3 Methods

3.1 User Experience Ecosystem Perspective

At the core of the digital redesign of traditional Chinese textile patterns lies the user experience, a domain that Wei Xu (2014) explores with remarkable insight. Xu's approach, emphasizing an enhanced ergonomics perspective within product design, suggests that the user experience ecosystem is not a singular entity but a complex network of interactions. This paper takes a leaf from Wei Xu (2014)'s comprehensive research to underline the importance of such an ecosystem in the digital realm, particularly in the context of User Cognitive Ergonomics.

Wei Xu (2014)'s research provides a vital framework for understanding how patterns are not just seen but experienced, and how these experiences can be mapped and optimized for a digital interface. By applying an ecosystem perspective, this study goes beyond aesthetics to consider the broader context in which patterns are engaged with, considering the cognitive load, emotional response, and cultural resonance.

This section delves into how an ecosystem approach can influence the redesign process, ensuring that patterns are not only digitally accurate but also resonant with the users' cognitive and emotional realms. Drawing on Wei Xu (2014)'s findings, the redesign efforts are oriented towards creating a seamless interaction between the pattern and the user, fostering an environment where tradition and technology coexist in a mutually enhancing relationship.

3.2 IPII Design Approach

In addressing the complexities of digital redesign within the realm of textile patterns, the Interaction, Process, Integration, and Intelligence (IPII) design approach, as elaborated by Wei Xu, Dov Furie, Manjunath Mahabhaleshwar, Bala Suresh, and Hardev Chouhan (2019), provides a comprehensive framework. This methodology is pivotal in structuring the redesign process to be user-centric, ensuring that each aspect of the user's interaction with the pattern is considered and enhanced.

The IPII approach champions a holistic view of design, one that encapsulates interaction, acknowledges the multiplicity of processes, seeks integration across different platforms, and applies intelligent solutions to design challenges. It is this nuanced approach that this paper adopts to ensure the digital redesign of traditional Chinese textile patterns is not only visually appealing but also ergonomically sound and cognitively engaging.

Applying the IPII framework, the study systematically examines the interaction between user and pattern, streamlines the process of design from concept to final product, integrates user feedback for continuous improvement, and employs intelligent algorithms to adapt patterns in a way that is both authentic to their heritage and functional in their new digital form. This method, rooted in the insights provided by Xu and his colleagues, enables the creation of designs that are as smart and user-friendly as they are beautiful. (Wei Xu, Dov Furie, Manjunath Mahabhaleshwar, Bala Suresh, and Hardev Chouhan, 2019).

3.3 Cognition in Traditional Versus Digital Media

The evolution of design cognition, particularly when transitioning from traditional media to digital platforms, has profound implications for how patterns are conceptualized and perceived. Zafer Bilda (2001) provides an in-depth analysis of this cognitive shift, offering invaluable insights into the designer's perspective during the conceptual design phase. Zafer Bilda (2001)'s work is integral to understanding the contrasts and continuities in cognitive strategies employed by designers as they navigate between the tactile world of traditional media and the virtual realm of digital interfaces.

Incorporating Zafer Bilda (2001)'s findings, this section explores how cognitive processes adapt and evolve in response to the tools and media used by designers. As we digitize traditional Chinese textile patterns, it's essential to recognize that the medium itself can influence design decisions, problem-solving approaches, and ultimately, the creative outcomes. Zafer Bilda (2001)'s research underlines the necessity of a cognitive approach that is attuned to the nuances of digital media without losing sight of the rich heritage embodied in traditional patterns.

This cognitive awareness is particularly significant as we consider User Cognitive Ergonomics in the digital redesign of patterns. By applying Zafer Bilda (2001)'s insights, the research aims to ensure that the transition of traditional patterns into the digital domain does not merely replicate but rather reinterprets these motifs in a way that is cognitively harmonious with contemporary user experiences. This approach champions a design philosophy that respects the cognitive aspects of both the creator and the end-user, fostering a digital environment where traditional patterns are not only seen but are understood and appreciated at a deeper cognitive level. (Zafer Bilda, 2001).

3.4 Interactive Exhibition Design

Interactive exhibition design has become a critical component in the presentation and interpretation of traditional patterns, particularly as we transition into more digitally oriented spaces. Jihong Li (2019) provides a comprehensive examination of this subject, using "Walking Memory" as a case study to showcase the effectiveness of multifaceted design approaches. Jihong Li (2019)'s research is instrumental in demonstrating how interactive elements can enhance User Cognitive Ergonomics, making traditional patterns more accessible and engaging for contemporary audiences.

In her work, Jihong Li (2019) illustrates that an interactive exhibition is not just about visual display; it's an orchestrated experience that activates various senses and cognitive pathways. Taking cues from this holistic approach, this section discusses the application of interactive design principles in the context of digital redesign. It's about creating a bridge between the viewer and the textile pattern display, one that facilitates an immersive experience by enabling the audience to interact with patterns in a manner that is both intuitive and informative. (Jihong Li, 2019).

The insights provided by Jihong Li (2019) inform the methods used in this research to create digital exhibitions that not only showcase the beauty of traditional Chinese patterns but also encourage the audience to engage with them on a deeper level. By integrating traditional designs with interactive technology, the patterns are presented in a way that is more than just aesthetically pleasing—they become stories told through the fabric, inviting exploration, and understanding.

4 Conclusion

This paper has embarked on a scholarly odyssey, charting the course of traditional Chinese textile patterns as they transition into the digital era under the guiding principles of User Cognitive Ergonomics. Throughout this journey, the transformative potential has been illuminated that such ergonomic considerations hold when thoughtfully integrated into the realm of digital redesign. Each chapter of the exploration, from aesthetic innovation to the data-driven intersection, has reinforced the symbiotic relationship between the enduring heritage of traditional patterns and the innovative possibilities afforded by modern technologies.

Beginning with examining how the digital redesign transcends aesthetic frontiers, marrying the intricacies of traditional craftsmanship with the boundless potential of digital methodologies. Further, It has been delved into the precision that technology brings to the time-honored practices of textile design, enhancing user comfort and pattern functionality. The foray into the Metaverse revealed new dimensions of creativity, where traditional designs are not merely replicated but re-imagined in immersive, interactive spaces. And at the intersection of data and tradition, It has been witnessed how analytical approaches breathe new life into ancient motifs, ensuring their relevance for future generations.

The methods section provided a deep dive into the User Experience Ecosystem, the IPII Design Approach, and the cognitive shifts from traditional to digital media—all through the lens of enhancing the user's interaction with these re-envisioned patterns.

Jihong Li (2019)'s insights on interactive exhibition design further highlighted the importance of engaging users in a dialogue with the past, one that is enriched by technology's touch.

In conclusion, as the threads of tradition and technology are woven together, the future of textile design is one of co-creation, where users, designers, and technologies collaborate in harmony. The rich tapestry of Chinese heritage, when interlaced with User Cognitive Ergonomics, promises not only a visual feast but also an intuitive, interactive experience that honors the past while embracing the future.

As this paper closes, it also opens a doorway to further inquiry. Future research may probe deeper into the practical application of these ergonomic principles, gathering user feedback from projects that have successfully merged the tradition with the avant-garde. Moreover, the exploration of augmented reality and virtual reality in textile design beckons, promising innovative pathways to enhance the user's cognitive and sensory engagement with patterns that have adorned human history for centuries.

References

De Silva, R.K.J., Navodhya, P.U., Gill, S.: Analysis of body-to-pattern relationship using traditional pattern drafting techniques: implications for automated digital prototyping. Int. J. Fashion Design Technol. Educ. 1–13 (2023)

Gill, S., Al Houf, H., Hayes, S., Conlon, J.: Evolving pattern practice, from traditional patterns to bespoke parametric blocks. Int. J. Fashion Design Technol. Educ. 1–18 (2023)

Khar, S.S., Ayachit, S.M.: Looking backwards to go forward – use of traditional Indian pattern making to develop contemporary methods for global fashion. Int. J. Fashion Design Technol. Educ. 6(3), 181–189 (2013)

Proctor, R.W., et al.: Understanding and improving cross-cultural decision making in design and use of digital media: a research agenda. Int. J. Hum.-Comput. Interact. 27(2), 151–190 (2011)

Ma, Y.-M., Du, H.-m.., Yao, H.: On innovative design of traditional Chinese patterns based on aesthetic experience to product features space mapping. Cogent Arts Human. 10(2) (2023)

Wang, S.: Multi-sensory museum: an interdisciplinary vision based on touch, sound, smell, space and memory - a new concept that breaks through the traditional exhibition design of museums. Sci. Educ. Museums 4(6), 437–438 (2018)

Tsou, M.-H., Mejia, C.: Beyond mapping: extend the role of cartographers to user interface designers in the Metaverse using virtual reality, augmented reality, and mixed reality. Cartograph. Geograph. Inf. Sci. 1–15 (2023)

Han, R.., Zhang, H., Li, R., Sha, C.: Data as a medium for inheritance and creativity of traditional design. A case study on data-driven modern creative design of ancient Chinese catering utensils. Design J. 22(1), 1117–1133 (2019)

Xu, W.: Enhanced ergonomics approaches for product design: a user experience ecosystem perspective and case studies. Ergonomics 57(1), 34–51 (2014)

Xu, W., Furie, D., Mahabhaleshwar, M., Suresh, B., Chouhan, H.: Applications of an interaction, process, integration and intelligence (IPII) design approach for ergonomics solutions. Ergonomics 62(7), 954–980 (2019)

Bilda, Z.: Designers' Cognition in Traditional Versus Digital Media During Conceptual Design. Bilkent Universitesi (Turkey), Diss (2001)

Li, J.: Research on the design of interactive exhibits for multiple communication purposes—taking "Walking Memory" as an example. Popul. Sci. Res. 14(4), 89–99 (2019)

A Study on the Audience's Perception Differences of the "New Culture" Animated Movie "A Journey of Thirty Thousand Kilometers in Chang'an"

Xueqing Li⑩, Xiuying Ling⑩, and Jun Wu^(✉) ⑩

School of Fine Arts and Design, Faculty of Arts, Shenzhen University, Shenzhen 518061, Guangdong, China
{2300505001,2020050153}@email.szu.edu.cn, junwu2006@hotmail.com

Abstract. With the burgeoning progress of the global economy, animated films steeped in traditional cultural themes, as a distinctive genre, predominantly orbit around authentic or fanciful myths, legends, or allusions entrenched in traditional heritage. Delving into the cognitive variances discerned among audiences engaging with these animated embodiments of cultural legacy not only serves the purpose of preserving and propelling traditional ethos but also augments viewers' cultural assurance and gratification derived from an enchanting cinematic sojourn, thereby proffering novel insights for the cinematic artisans. This investigation focalizes on the Chinese audience, employing the inaugural opus of the "New Culture Series" animated film, titled "A Journey of Thirty Thousand Kilometers in Chang'an," as an exemplar to scrutinize cognitive differentials among diverse spectators. The research yields the following revelations: (1) male spectators exhibit heightened emotional discernment of adverse sentiments compared to their female counterparts; (2) adolescents and those in the throes of middle age express resounding approval of the film, coupled with an intricate spectrum of emotional cognition; (3) audiences from assorted professional domains, notably those in film and animation, design, arts, history, philosophy, and scientific pursuits, evince markedly elevated ratings in both film evaluation and emotional acumen; (4) audiences endowed with higher educational attainments manifest a more profound cognitive appreciation of the film, while those with more modest educational backgrounds unveil a wealthier tapestry of emotional cognizance; (5) the mode of film consumption significantly influences audience appraisals and emotional acuity, with favorable online viewing experiences precipitating a more enriched emotional discernment in the spectatorship.

Keywords: "New Culture" · Animated Movie · Emotional Cognition · Tradition Culture · "New Culture"

1   Introduction

Since its inception, films as an independent art form have always been popular among people from all walks of life. Animated films, based on the general function of films, are able to entertain the public while breaking free from the constraints of the real world

P.-L. P. Rau (Ed.): HCII 2024, LNCS 14701, pp. 75–89, 2024.
https://doi.org/10.1007/978-3-031-60904-6_6

[1], and they are an important component of the cultural and creative industries [2]. Folk traditional culture possesses distinct national characteristics and artistic expressions, and its unique cultural implications have developed into animated styles with regional and national characteristics. Many characters and animal figures in national animation are mostly derived from myths, fables, folk legends, and other excellent traditional cultures of their own country or nation, displaying unique artistic charm [3]. The revival of culture and the enhancement of national soft power cannot be achieved without the inheritance and exploration of cultural works. Establishing a system for the inheritance and development of excellent traditional Chinese culture has risen to become a national strategic goal in the new era [4].Chinese animation has been exploring the path of nationalization, emphasizing the presentation of Chinese elements as much as possible. The main problem that has not been overcome is that Chinese animation focuses too much on form, neglecting content and cultural connotations, resulting in a simple expressive style and creating a form of hollow and uninspired language, which does not gain the audience's recognition [2]. The study of emotion in art and design has received widespread attention, and emotion has become an increasingly important object that needs to be satisfied in life [5]. Emotion is the emotional result of the interaction with the content of film and television during the viewing process [6]. How traditional cultural animated films can resonate with the audience and achieve a dual experience of body and mind through artistic creation is particularly important. The "New Culture" series of animated films breaks the narrative framework of the "New Gods List" series of animated films, boldly innovating on the basis of national style, and has a groundbreaking significance for Chinese animated films [7]. The animated film "A Journey of Thirty Thousand kilometers in Chang'an" is the first work in the "New Culture" series opened by Light Chasing Animation following the adaptation wave of the new myth series, with a final box office of 1.824 billion yuan, ranking second on the current Chinese film history's animated film box office.

This study takes the audience's experiences and preferences as the research object, uses quantitative research methods, and based on the relevant theories of communication, cognitive psychology, and film and television design principles, and the theory of goal achievement. Starting from the research on the joint influence of positive and negative emotions generated by different emotional cognition on animated films, the main purposes of this study are as follows:

a. To explore the cognitive differences of audiences with different backgrounds towards "new cultural" animated films.
b. To investigate the emotional cognitive conditions of audiences with different backgrounds watching "new cultural" animated films.
c. The impact of different ways of viewing on the audience's cognitive understanding of "new cultural" animated films.

2 Literature Review

2.1 The Significance of "New Culture"

Animated Films The use of films as "tools for living" has been studied within the academic traditions of textual analysis, audience effects research, cultural studies, and satisfaction research [8]. Animated films not only have a long history, but are also one of the most creative and diverse genres in today's world film industry [9]. With the construction of film industry aesthetics and the reform of technical images, domestic animated films in China have been continuously moving towards reform and revival. Building on existing films and literary works, they have continuously rewritten and subverted traditional emotional expressions and aesthetic styles of animated films in an attempt to break through. In recent years, there has been a positive trend in development [10]. When it comes to the creation of "Chinese-style" animated works, the "New Legend" and "New Gods" series have already accumulated a familiarity with the "Chinese-style" in terms of color, scenes, props, and character design [11]. The "New Culture series," on the other hand, demonstrates a unique aesthetic pursuit, embodying a shift from "Chinese-style" to "Chinese nature" and represents a comprehensive attempt to construct the peak of Chinese civilization history in the form of animation. It has taken a pioneering step for the future narrative of Chinese animated films on the history of Chinese civilization [12]. Meanwhile, film is an important medium and a reflection instrument for moral education [13]. Excellent animated films can help young people absorb the essence of national culture, guide them to form the correct outlook on life and values, and are of great significance in enriching the leisure cultural life of young people [14]. "New Culture" animated films contain rich cultural connotations and humanistic emotions, possessing certain cultural and educational value. As a brand-new series of animated films, they hold high research value. They are not only a response to national policies, but also a pressing need for the creative practice of animated films themselves [15]. Experience offers sensory, emotional, cognitive, behavioral, and relational values [16]. Existing studies have focused on the themes, visual effects, and storylines of animated films, but there are few studies discussing the audience's viewing behavior, film evaluation, and aesthetic preferences within a broader context, which to some extent limits a deeper understanding of audience viewing preferences. Therefore, exploring the new changes in the symbiotic and mutual beneficial relationship between "New Culture" animated film audiences and films will provide a reference for the future integration of traditional Chinese culture and film and television creation.

2.2 Emotional Perception of Film Viewers

Works of art have infectious power, i.e., the power to trigger emotions, feelings, and even actions in viewers through the forms and elements of the work, including film [17]. Cultural studies seek to understand the relationship between various human products and the larger social structures that produce and consume them [8]. As the world moves towards globalisation and market competition becomes increasingly fierce and complex, the development of film and television products cannot be separated from the influence of the audience, which is the fundamental driving force supporting the development of film and television and prompting its continuous progress [18]. The artistic value and commodity value of film and television works are realised through the cultural market [19]. Similar to the four dimensions of brand experience, i.e. emotional experience, behavioural experience, sensory experience and knowledge experience. These experiences stimulate emotional bonds and lasting impressions in consumers [20]. Films are "reflections of people's deeper inclinations" [21]. Emotion is often considered to be at the heart of media entertainment, whether it is films, novels, television programmes, music videos or computer games [22]. Audiences are at the centre of the emotional economy. From the perspective of the media industry, the affective economy is about ensuring that live events, programmes or formats have not only an economic value, but also an emotional value as an interactive experience integrated into people's lives [23]. Arts experiences can bring private and public benefits: intoxication, pleasure, increased empathy, cognitive growth, social bonding, and the expression of public meaning. Key factors in arts experiences and audience consumption are an awareness of the intrinsic needs of the audience and how audience participation can lead to repeat participation and therefore sustainability [24]. Satisfaction is the result of a comparison between prior expectations and perceived performance, and several empirical studies support the dependence of affective processes on cognitive processes [25]. Audience preferences and evaluations, to a large extent, determine the economic and artistic value of a film. Films have a stress-relieving and spiritual compensatory effect on human beings. Through films, audiences can release subconscious emotions [26]. Emotional experience plays an inescapable role in collective cultural memory, film viewing psychology, film viewing style, film viewing pleasure, and the audience's choice of film and understanding of narrative [27]. Film emotion can bring extraordinary satisfaction and pleasure [28]. Correct understanding of the audience's emotional needs and the corresponding experience and its feedback, and the integration of emotion and viewing experience are the key factors for the success of film and television works [29]. Empathy is a cognitive and emotional state, an emotional-affective response, and an ability. The ultimate goal of cultural communication is to produce cultural identity and cultural heritage, and the premise of cultural identity is the affirmation of attitude, and the affirmation of attitude depends on the emotional identity, thus creating short videos based on empathy can stimulate the audience's potential emotional motivation and link. In the process of "receiving information - integrating information - outputting information", the audience will produce "cultural resonance", and make the emotional response to the information expected by the communicator, thus continuously strengthening the awakening and cognition of traditional Chinese culture. The animation film as a means of empathy and sympathy As a medium of empathy and sympathy, animated films can generate emotional and psychological responses in the audience after watching them, so as to achieve cultural identity [30].

2.3 Audience Cognitive Differences in Animated Films with Traditional Cultural Themes

Behind the changes in the number of screens, box office, number of moviegoers, film production, etc., we can see the great changes in the Chinese film audience groups. On the one hand, the audience has a higher degree of recognition of Chinese films; on the other hand, due to different ages, genders, qualifications, classes, etc., the audience has different aesthetic interests in terms of film genres, themes, and styles, which affects more and more the creation of films and the development of the industry. Audiences pay more attention to the positive guidance of films on ideology and the inheritance of the spirit of traditional Chinese culture [31]. Cognitive bias refers to the systematic distortion of the representations produced by human cognition compared with certain aspects of objective reality. Different individuals have different cognitive differences [32]. Traditional cultural values have become the historical foundation and internal support for the development of Chinese animation films, and their modern expression in animation films needs to be reconstructed with the help of artistic expression forms that meet the aesthetic interests of contemporary audiences, and complete the modern transformation of traditional cultural values [33]. Nowadays, Chinese film audience groups have an increased demand for traditional culture, domestic animated films should integrate traditional culture with the spirit of the times, interpret traditional stories in a contemporary way, realise the "all-age" animated films, analyse the market preferences, and use the Internet and other new media communication modes to carry out a diversified media dissemination, which will expand the audience base of domestic animated films [34]. The audience of domestic animation film is expanded [34]. With the rapid development of media technology, it is difficult to unify the infinite requirements of the audience for the quality of content production with the limited attention of the audience. Through the refined and systematic analysis of different levels of audience groups in terms of age structure, content selection, viewing experience, willingness to preferences, etc., to accurately understand the audience's emotional needs, preferences, experience, feedback, "dynamic emotions into the experience of the audience of film and television dramas" [35], we can make clear the differences between the needs of different groups, so as to guide the Chinese traditional cultural excellence in animation films. The differences in the needs of different groups can be clarified, thus guiding the direction of the production of short video content of Chinese excellent traditional culture, in order to increase the audience's experience and sense of identity, realise the precise dissemination of Chinese traditional culture, and enhance the dissemination speed and effect of culture. Achieve the audience's identification, dissemination and inheritance of Chinese traditional culture [30].

3   Research Objects and Methods

3.1   Research Methods

This study, drawing upon antecedent research [36], meticulously crafted a bespoke questionnaire to probe the nuanced facets of audience perception surrounding the "New Culture" animated masterpiece, "A Journey of Thirty Thousand Kilometers in Chang'an." Anchored in the underpinnings of communication theory, cognitive studies, and the artistic principles governing film and television, the questionnaire delineated five pivotal independent variables: gender, age, professional pedigree, educational attainment, and viewing proclivities. Correspondingly, it encompassed an array of eleven dependent variables, encapsulating the exhibition of indigenous cultural nuances within the film, the eloquence in portraying the cultural tapestry of ancient poetry, the intensity of creative innovation embedded in the film, the film's capacity to fortify cultural identity, the commendation bestowed upon its adaptational prowess, the aesthetic acclaim for the film's stylistic finesse, the personal proclivity towards the film, the willingness to advocate its merits to familial and social circles, the eagerness to delve deeper into the cultural expanse of ancient poetry, the anticipations associated with forthcoming "New Culture" animated cinematic endeavors, and the cherished characters within the narrative (as delineated in Table 1). Ratings were meticulously solicited through a refined five-point scale (1 = vehemently dissent, 5 = unequivocally assent).

For this research, an online questionnaire was utilized and can be accessed via this link: https://www.wjx.cn/vm/PnjlhRv.aspx#1. A random sample of respondents who are viewers of the film "A Journey of Thirty Thousand kilometers in Chang'an" was selected. Prior to answering the questionnaire, the participants were briefed about the purpose of the study, the proper way of answering the questionnaire, and their consent to participate was obtained. They filled out the questionnaire thoughtfully.

Table 1. General assessment questions of the questionnaire and their corresponding numbers

number	General assessment issues
A1	The Functionality of the Film
A2	Representation of Ancient Poetry Culture in this Film
A3	Creative Strength of the Film
A4	Enhancement of Cultural Identity
A5	Your Approval of the Adaptation of the Film
A6	Acknowledgment of the Aesthetic Style of the Film
A7	Your preference for the film
A8	Your willingness to recommend the film to your friends and family
A9	The film will inspire you to further explore the culture of ancient poetry
A10	Your next expectation for a "new culture" animation film
A11	Your favorite character

3.2 Sample Collection of Questionnaires

A total of 326 questionnaires were collected in this study and 322 valid questionnaires were obtained after excluding invalid questionnaires. In terms of gender: 133 (40.8.8%) were male and 193 (59.2%) were female. As for age: 93 (28.53%) under 19 years old, 150 (46.01%) between 20–29 years old, 14 (4.29%) between 30–39 years old, 45 (13.8%) between 40–59 years old, and 24 (7.36%) over 50 years old. Professional background: 51 related to film and animation, 39 related to other design, 99 related to art, 27 related to literature, history and philosophy, 19 related to mathematics, science and chemistry, and 91 related to others. Education level: 36 people have high school/secondary school and below, 219 people have college/undergraduate degrees, 59 people have master's degrees, and 12 people have doctoral degrees. In terms of viewing methods: 189 people viewed movies online and 137 people viewed movies in theatres. The effective sample size of this study is 322, and the distribution of questions for each variable is reasonable.

4 Results

4.1 Reliability and Validity Analysis

The scrutiny of the reliability and validity of the amassed questionnaire data predominantly revolves around a meticulous examination of the quality inherent in survey questionnaire design and the harvested data, affirming the appropriateness of the data for subsequent empirical analysis.

Upon delving into an analysis of the reliability data gleaned from the questionnaire, it becomes apparent that the Cronbach's Alpha coefficient, residing within the spectrum of 0 to 1, assumes a heightened reliability as it approaches the zenith of this scale. The statistical dissection unveils a Cronbach's Alpha of 0.952, a testament to the questionnaire's outstanding reliability. The "post-deletion Cronbach's Alpha," spanning from 0.949 to 0.958, attests to a robust internal consistency across thematic domains, thereby validating the judicious selection of topics. Furthermore, the validity analysis discloses a Kaiser-Meyer-Olkin (KMO) value of 0.954, indicative of a markedly elevated numerical magnitude. The significance level (Sig) registers at 0.000, underscoring its utmost statistical significance.

4.2 Analysis of Gender Differences in Various Variables

Employing the subjects' gender as the independent variable and considering the 11 comprehensive evaluation queries pertaining to animated films as dependent variables, an independent samples T-test was deployed for discernment. The evaluations across the 11 facets, encompassing the portrayal of indigenous culture, creative profundity, cultural resonance, acknowledgment, and predilection within the animated masterpiece "A Journey of Thirty Thousand Kilometers in Chang'an," were consistently analogous. No substantive disparities surfaced among the audience concerning these facets. It is manifest that the ratings from spectators of diverse genders exhibit proximity, indicating a dearth of conspicuous distinctions. The animated opus "A Journey of Thirty Thousand Kilometers in Chang'an," orbiting around the cultural tapestry of Tang Dynasty poetry, artfully unfolds the zenith of the illustrious Tang Dynasty, thereby illuminating the profound opulence embedded in Chinese poetry. Enveloped in a distinctive thematic aura, the film stands as an inaugural foray into the precincts of the "New Culture" genre within the animated realm, eliciting emotional reverberations across gender lines and engendering a laudable diffusion of cultural impact.

4.3 Analysis of Age Differences in Various Variables

Utilizing the subjects' the subjects' age as the independent variable, a variance analysis was conducted on the 11 overall evaluation questions regarding animated films, and the

Table 2. Analysis of Significant Differences in Characteristics Evaluation Across Age Groups.

Issues	Source of variation	SS	Df	MS	F	Sig	Post-Hoc
A3	Between Groups Within Groups Total	9.141 191.214 200.355	4 316 320	2.285 .605	3.777**	.005	4>2
A5	Between Groups Within Groups Total	10.184 206.471 216.654	4 316 320	2.546 .653	3.896**	.004	1>2
A7	Between Groups Within Groups Total	7.747 232.720 240.467	4 316 320	1.937 .736	2.630*	.034	
A8	Between Groups Within Groups Total	9.007 245.841 254.847	4 316 320	2.252 .778	2.894*	.022	
A9	Between Groups Within Groups Total	9.252 229.970 239.221	4 316 320	2.313 .728	3.178*	.014	4>2

* $p < .05.$** $p < .01.$ *** $p < .001$ 1 = 19 and under; 2 = 19–29; 3 = 30–39; 4 = 40–49; 5 = 50 and over
A7 : 4(4.67) > 1(4.48) > 5(4.38) > 2(3.95) > 3(4.36) > 2(4.20) A8.:1(3.97) > 5(3.93) > 2(3.48) > 4(3.40) > 3(3.88) > 3(3.32)

results are presented in Table 2. Significantly divergent opinions among viewers were observed in the categories of creative strength of the film, approval of the adaptation, likability, willingness to recommend the film to your friends and family, and the inspire you to further explore the culture of ancient poetry. Notably, distinctions were particularly pronounced in the assessment of the film's creative strength and the approval of the adaptation. Upon scrutinizing the mean values about creative strength and the inclination to explore the culture of ancient poetry in the film, it becomes evident that viewers aged 40–49 exhibit higher levels of acceptance compared to their counterparts aged 20–29. Preference, respondents below 19 years old demonstrated a higher acceptance of the film's adaptation compared to those aged 20–29. Analyzing likability scores, it emerges that viewers aged 40–49 scored the highest, while those aged 20–29 scored the lowest. Interestingly, viewers below 19 years old expressed the highest willingness to recommend the film, while viewers aged 30–39 demonstrated the lowest inclination. The animated film "A Journey of Thirty Thousand kilometers in Chang'an" not only portrays distinct Chinese cultural features but also stands as a significant innovation in cultural themes. Considering China's encouragement of the "two-child policy," it is likely that viewers aged 40–49 are accompanying children to watch the film, aiming to instill an interest in Tang Dynasty poetry culture, providing a glimpse into the grandeur of the Great Tang Dynasty, showcasing the charisma of poets, and offering a deeper understanding of traditional culture. Leveraging the animated medium as a new platform, the film effectively serves educational purposes. Hence, viewers aged 40–49 express higher satisfaction levels regarding the film's creative intensity, likability, and their willingness to further explore ancient poetry and culture.

4.4 Analysis of Professional Differences in Various Variables

Utilizing the subjects' professional backgrounds as the independent variable, a variance analysis was conducted on the 11 overall evaluation questions pertaining to animated films, and the outcomes are delineated in Table 3. Noteworthy disparities were observed among viewers in terms of their willingness to recommend the film to your friends and family, and inspire you to further explore the culture of ancient poetry. In the context of the inclination to recommend the film, a discernible pattern emerges when contrasting the mean values: respondents from disciplines other than film and animation related and those affiliated with Arts related significantly higher scores compared to their counterparts in the animation field. This signifies a pronounced receptiveness among audiences from diverse professional backgrounds, particularly those unrelated to animation, demonstrating a higher level of endorsement for the "New Culture" animated film and, consequently, yielding elevated scores. Regarding the willingness to explore ancient poetry and culture, respondents from non-animation disciplines markedly outscore those in animation-related fields. The numerical values derived from these two questions collectively reveal a heightened acceptance level among audiences with diverse professional backgrounds, indicating a greater receptivity towards the "New Culture" animated film and eliciting higher overall scores. Audiences with backgrounds in Arts related easily resonate with the portrayal of Chinese traditional culture and historical themes, attesting to the film's ability to evoke a professional resonance. Conversely, viewers with expertise in film and animation related bring a wealth of creative experience and relevant knowledge, analyzing the film with a more discerning eye. Their assessments focus on technical applications, audio-visual presentations, narrative logic, and other aspects, resulting in lower scores. Their emotional engagement tends to be less pronounced, and their evaluations are characterized by a more rational thought process. This dichotomy in viewing perspectives and emotional experiences contributes to the lower scores attributed to audiences with a background in animation-related professions.

Table 3. Analysis of the number of significantly different variants of the professional background and characteristics rubrics.

Issues	Source of variation	SS	Df	MS	F	Sig	Post-Hoc
A8	Between Groups	9.191	5	1.838	2.357*	.040	
	Within Groups	245.656	315	.780			
	Total	254.847	320				
A9	Between Groups	13.341	5	2.668	3.721**	.003	6>1
	Within Groups	225.880	315	.717			
	Total	239.221	320				

* p < .05.** p < .01. *** p < .001 1 = Film and animation related; 2 = Design related; 3 = Art related; 4 = Arts related; 5 = Science and engineering related; 6 = Other
A8 : 6(4.58) > 4(4.48) > 5(4.39) > 3(4.36) > 2(4.13) > 1(4.00)

Table 4. Analysis of the number of significantly different variants of the professional background and characteristics rubrics

Issues	Source of variation	SS	Df	MS	F	Sig	Post-Hoc
A3	Between Groups	10.718	3	3.57	5.927**	.001	3>2
	Within Groups	189.637	317	3	*		
	Total	200.355	320	.598			
A5	Between Groups	14.847	3	4.94	7.774**	.000	1>3
	Within Groups	201.807	317	9	*		
	Total	216.654	320	.637			
A7	Between Groups	6.416	3	2.13	2.896*	.035	
	Within Groups	234.052	317	9			
	Total	240.467	320	.738			
A8	Between Groups	12.463	3	4.15	5.433**	.001	1>3
	Within Groups	242.384	317	4	*		
	Total	254.847	320	.765			
A9	Between Groups	11.703	3	3.90	5.435**	.001	2>3
	Within Groups	227.518	317	1	*		
	Total	239.221	320	.718			

* p < .05.** p < .01. *** p < .001 1 = High school and below; 2 = College/Undergraduate; 3 = Master's degree; 4 = Doctoral degree
A8 : 6(4.58) > 4(4.48) > 5(4.39) > 3(4.36) > 2(4.13) > 1(4.00)

4.5 Analysis of Educational Attainment Differences in Various Variables

Leveraging the subjects' educational attainment as the independent variable, an in-depth variance analysis was meticulously conducted on the 11 comprehensive evaluation queries germane to animated cinematic endeavors, with the outcomes meticulously delineated in Table 4. Among the discerned opinions within the audience, notable disparities emerged significantly across several dimensions, encompassing the film's creative potency, commendation of its adaptation, likability, propensity to recommend it to kin and kindred spirits, and the impetus to embark on further explorations into the cultural tapestry of ancient poetry. Notably, substantial disparities were manifest in the realms of adaptation approval, recommendations to friends and family, and the inspiration to delve into the cultural intricacies of ancient poetry (Sig = .000, Sig = .001). In the realm of the film's creative vigour, an intriguing pattern surfaces: viewers possessing a master's degree manifest notably elevated scores when contrasted with their counterparts holding a college or undergraduate degree. Conversely, concerning the recognition of the film's adaptation and the eagerness to endorse it, audiences with a high school diploma or vocational training, and those below, register markedly higher scores than their counterparts with a master's degree. In the assessment of the film's likability, a nuanced exploration of mean values divulges that audiences with a doctoral degree accrue significantly higher scores than those holding a high school diploma or vocational training, and below. Regarding the proclivity to delve into the realms of ancient poetry and culture, audiences with a college or undergraduate degree garner significantly higher scores than their counterparts with a master's degree. Audiences wielding a master's degree, endowed with robust logical reasoning and an embrace of innovative concepts, play a pivotal role in shaping the narrative of the animated film "A Journey of Thirty Thousand Kilometers in Chang'an." Its distinctive "dual male protagonist" structure unfolds a captivating panorama of the Great Tang Dynasty and the opulence of poetry and culture through the expressive medium of animation, rendering it an avant-garde masterpiece. Consequently, viewers possessing a master's degree express heightened satisfaction with the film's creative dynamism. Audiences with a high school diploma or vocational training, often younger and steeped in the purity of their internal world, exhibit a proclivity towards sharing and a keen focus on visual and narrative evolution. The film's artistic reinterpretation of historical content invokes admiration within this demographic, precipitating higher evaluations in terms of adaptation recognition and the willingness to advocate it to others. Audiences boasting a doctoral degree, characterized by acute observation skills and rigorous logical thinking, seek to fathom novel occurrences across diverse domains. The film "A Journey of Thirty Thousand Kilometers in Chang'an" assumes epochal significance in Chinese animation, earning the favor of this erudite demographic. The portrayal of Tang Dynasty poetry and historical anecdotes within the film galvanizes a desire to recommend it among audiences with a college or undergraduate degree, underscoring their fervor to elevate their cultural literacy and deepen their fascination with traditional Chinese culture.

4.6 Analysis of Viewing Methods Differences in Various Variables

Employing the subjects' viewing methods as the independent variable and the 11 overall evaluation questions regarding animated films as the dependent variables, independent samples T-tests were conducted to discern any significant differences. The analysis unveils a notable distinction in the recognition of the film's adaptation, where online streaming displays a considerably higher level of acceptance compared to traditional cinema viewing. The heightened recognition of film adaptation in online streaming can be attributed to the greater control it affords viewers. The online platform provides an environment where details can be revisited at will, fostering repeated viewing experiences. This, in turn, stimulates a profound understanding of the film, elevating the audience's appreciation for the adaptation. The inherent controllability and flexibility of online streaming contribute to a more pronounced acknowledgment of the film's adaptation when contrasted with the cinematic viewing experience (Table 5).

Table 5. T-test Analysis of Disparities in Characteristic Evaluations Based on Viewing Methods

Issues	ViewingmMethods	N	M	SD	T	Scheffe comparison
A5	Internet	185	4.41	.710	2.138*	Internet>cinema
	Cinema	136	4.21	.946		

5 Conclusion and Suggestions

Based on the aforementioned research findings, the emotional experiences of audiences with diverse backgrounds towards the animated film "A Journey of Thirty Thousand kilometers in Chang'an" are both similar and distinctive. The conclusions drawn from this study are as follows:

1. Viewers of disparate genders exhibit negligible disparities in their cognitive interpretation of animated films, affirming the film's commendable resonance across gender lines concerning its themes and narrative content. However, a notable contrast surfaces in emotional perception, wherein male audiences manifest notably superior scores. This suggests their adeptness at immersing themselves in the protagonist's tumultuous odyssey, evoking a profound emotional connection. This accentuates the universal allure of traditional cultural motifs, capable of evoking emotional experiences and disseminating cultural values.
2. Audiences spanning various age cohorts display marked variations in their appraisals of the film's creative vigor, adaptation endorsement, likability, proclivity to recommend, and the inclination to delve into ancient poetry and culture. Generally, middle and senior age cohorts evince heightened approval for films steeped in traditional cultural motifs. In contrast, teenage viewers showcase heightened interest in the animation's presentation format, securing the highest scores in adaptation approval and recommendation proclivity. Moreover, in the realm of emotional perception, both teenagers and the middle-aged to senior demographic exhibit a more nuanced understanding of the film's emotional resonance. Adolescents, propelled by curiosity and an explorative mindset, demonstrate heightened receptivity and possess an abundance of intuitive emotional experiences. Meanwhile, the middle-aged and senior audience, enriched by life experiences, demonstrate a diverse array of emotional responses post-viewing. To ensure the sustained success of traditional cultural films, innovation in their creation, a precise analysis of the emotional needs across age demographics, and content tailored to diverse sensibilities become imperative.

3. Audiences hailing from diverse professional backgrounds display significant contrasts in their inclination to recommend the film and explore ancient poetry and culture. Those outside the realm of animation exhibit heightened receptivity, surpassing their counterparts within the animation field. Professionals in film and animation, attuned to the technical facets, consequently score lower. Emotionally, audiences outside the animation domain tend to be more expressive, their sentiments swayed by the narrative's evolution, leading to a more enriched emotional journey. Conversely, audiences from STEM fields or humanities showcase strong logical reasoning, attentiveness to nuanced expressions, and distinctive emotional sensibilities. Those with backgrounds in film, animation, and design-related fields, shaped by artistic training, place greater emphasis on visual aesthetics, resulting in a diminished emotional resonance during viewing.

4. Audiences with varying educational attainments showcase significant disparities in their assessments of the film's creative intensity, adaptation endorsement, likability, recommendation proclivity, and the inclination to explore ancient poetry and culture. Viewers with advanced degrees demonstrate keen observational skills and meticulous logical thinking, leading to an enhanced recognition of the film's innovative elements. Conversely, audiences with lower educational backgrounds exhibit a more intuitive cognition, with higher approval rates and a greater inclination to share. In terms of emotional perception, audiences across educational backgrounds exhibit significant differences in the 18 emotional experiences related to animated films. College or undergraduate degree holders tend to undergo more emotionally rich experiences compared to those with a high school diploma or vocational training and below. Master's and doctoral degree holders display a heightened sensitivity to the cultural nuances depicted in the film. Future film endeavors should prioritize profound content and the dissemination of cultural depth, tailoring designs to engage audiences with varying educational backgrounds.

5. Divergent viewing methods reveal noteworthy distinctions in the recognition of the film's adaptation and emotional perception, with online streaming eclipsing cinema viewing. The convenience and broader accessibility inherent in online streaming contribute to an elevated emotional perception among audiences.

By delving into audience viewing behaviors, evaluations, and aesthetic preferences, a deeper understanding of audience preferences can be attained, providing valuable insights for the continued development of the "New Culture" animated film series. This research delves into a pivotal facet of audience emotional perception, particularly within the ambit of the "New Culture" film series. While concentrating solely on Chinese audiences and the animated film "A Journey of Thirty Thousand Kilometers in Chang'an" from the "New Culture" series, future investigations can traverse regional differences and subsequent releases within the series. By dissecting audience viewing behaviors, evaluations, and aesthetic inclinations, a nuanced comprehension of audience preferences can be achieved, offering invaluable insights for the ongoing evolution of the "New Culture" animated film series.

Funding. This work was supported by the General Projects in Social Science Planning of Guangdong Province, NO. GD22CYS12; and the General Projects in Philosophy Social Science Planning of Anhui Province, NO. AHSKQ2020D145.

References

1. Feng, T.T., Fan, K.K.: A brief analysis of Chinese and Western cultural differences in animated films featuring Chinese elements. In: 2016 International Conference on Advanced Materials for Science and Engineering (ICAMSE), pp. 113–115. IEEE (2016)
2. Fan, K.K., Feng, T.T.: Sustainable development strategy of Chinese animation industry. Sustainability **13**(13), 7235 (2021)
3. Wang, J.: Analysis on setting of animated characters modeling in accordance with national traditional culture. In: 1st International Conference on Arts, Design and Contemporary Education (ICADCE 2015), pp. 433–436. Atlantis Press (2015)
4. Zhang, J.: Traditional cultural expression and marketable construction of "Chasing Light Animation" films. Contemp. Cinema **12**, 148–151 (2019)
5. Turner, J.C., Hogg, M.A., Oakes, P.J., Reicher, S.D., Wetherell, M.S.: Rediscovering the Social Group: A Self-Categorization Theory. Basil Blackwell (1987)
6. Sun, J.: Thirty thousand leagues in Chang'an: the universe of tang poetry illuminates the modern civilisation of the Chinese people. Film Arts **04**, 62–65 (2023)
7. Lu, K.: How films stimulate the audience's emotions-a review of Karl Plantinga's cognitive perceptual theory. J. Beijing Film Acad. **36**(06), 12–21 (2020)
8. Young, S.D.: Movies as equipment for living: a developmental analysis of the importance of film in everyday life. Crit. Stud. Media Commun. **17**(4), 447–468 (2000)
9. Sun, Y.: Historical traceability, morphological changes and current analysis of international animation film festivals. Contemp. Animat. **04**, 19–28 (2023)
10. Liu, D.: Emotional deconstruction and aesthetic style in domestic animation films. Film Literat. **06**, 78–80 (2022)
11. Tu, Y., Yan, H.: Thirty thousand leagues in Chang'an: a perspective on chinese sexuality. Contemp. Animat. **04**, 29–32 (2023)
12. Wang, Y.: An animated configuration of the peak weather of Chinese civilization history - after the viewing of 30,000 leagues of Chang'an. Contemp. Cinema **08**, 31–37 (2023)
13. Wang, H., Fu, L.: The influence of Chinese animated films on the moral education of Chinese teenagers. In: Proceedings of the 7th International Conference on Contemporary Education, Social Sciences and Humanities (Philosophy of Being Human as the Core of Interdisciplinary Research) (ICCESSH 2022), pp. 188–195. Atlantis Press SARL, Paris (2023)
14. Wang, H., Meng, F.: The role of film and television works in adolescent self-education. Movie Rev. **20**, 72–75 (2010). (in Chinese)
15. Yang, X., Su, W.: A theory of film narrative in the Chinese school of new animation. Stud. Ethnic Arts **05**, 47–55 (2023)
16. Schmitt, B.: Experiential marketing. J. Mark. Manag. **15**(1–3), 53–67 (1999)
17. Zhang, D.: An analysis of the levels of artistic impact of the eight hundred. Film Literat. **767**(02), 85–87 (2021)
18. Huang, H., Yu, H., Han, P., Chen, K.: Audience and film and television brand strategy development: an analysis of Beijing film and television audience survey. Mod. Commun. **01**, 36–41 (2004)
19. Huang, H.: Audience Theory of Film and Television. Beijing Normal University Press, Beijing (2007)
20. Kim, Y.K., Sullivan, P.: Emotional branding speaks to consumers' heart: the case of fashion brands. Fashion Textiles **6**(1), 1–16 (2019)

21. Kracauer, S.: From Caligari to Hitler: A Psychological History of the German Film. Princeton University Press (2019)
22. Bartsch, A.: Emotional gratification in entertainment experience. Media Psychol. **15**(3), 267–302 (2012)
23. Pine, B.J., Gilmore, J.H.: The Experience Economy. Harvard Business Press (2011)
24. Radbourne, J.: The impact of the arts experience on audiences. In: The Routledge Companion to Arts Marketing, pp. 204–213. Routledge (2013)
25. Ladhari, R.: The movie experience: a revised approach to determinants of satisfaction. J. Bus. Res. **60**(5), 454–462 (2007)
26. Jia, Y., Li, X.: Interactivity of film and viewers' psychology of film viewing. Film Rev. **15**, 66–70 (2018)
27. Zheng, J.: Controlling audience emotions - a review of moving the audience: American Cinema and the audience experience. Film Art **54**(01), 150 (2010)
28. Wiley, N.: Emotion and film theory. In: Studies in Symbolic Interaction, pp. 169–187. Emerald Group Publishing Limited (2003)
29. Lu, K.: A brief history of Chinese film audience studies. Film New Works **41**(2), 94 (2020)
30. Zhao, Y., Yuan, G., Wang, J.: Optimization of Chinese traditional culture short video communication strategy from the perspective of audience demand. Media **19**, 93–95 (2022)
31. Xue, N., Li, L.: Audience composition and aesthetic preferences: an analysis based on the Chinese film audience satisfaction survey. Contemporary Cinema **03**, 4–16 (2022)
32. Haselton, M.G., Nettle, D., Murray, D.R.: The evolution of cognitive bias. In: Buss, D.M. (ed.) The Handbook of Evolutionary Psychology, pp. 1–20. Wiley (2015)
33. Yu, M.: Modern expression of traditional cultural values in Chinese animation films. Contemp. Cinema **09**, 168–170 (2018)
34. Ge, S.: Analysis on traditional cultural communication strategies of domestic animated films a case study of domestic animated films after 2015. China Press **04**, 68–69 (2022)
35. Lu, K.: How films stimulate the audience's emotions–a review of Karl Plantinga's cognitive-perceptual theory. J. Beijing Film Acad. **36**(06), 12–21 (2020)
36. Wu, J., Qian, F., Gao, Y.: Emotional cognition: a study of audience differences between microfilm and sand animation. Cult. Indust. Res. **03**, 260–274 (2019)

Cross-Media Digital Form Design and Comparative Measurement of Intangible Cultural Heritage in Zhuhai: Promoting Cultural Exchange and Global Communication

Yudan Shen[1,2]([✉]) [ID]

[1] Beijing Institute of Technology, Zhuhai 519088, China
303727037@qq.com
[2] National Yang Ming Chiao Tung University, Hsinchu City 300, Taiwan

Abstract. Background: In the context of globalization today, cultural diversity and modern media communication are particularly important for preserving and inheriting intangible cultural heritage. With the continuous development of media technology and innovative design, digital media forms have become increasingly diverse. It is necessary to further study how different digital media forms can contribute to the dissemination of intangible cultural heritage.

Research Methodology: Through the research methods of focus groups, experimental methods, and in-depth interviews, this study conducted comparative measurements of four media forms: text and image reports, visual media, information visualization, and interactive media. Evaluation was based on audience appeal, information conveyance effectiveness, and cultural emotion transmission, exploring how these cross-media forms facilitate cultural exchange and globalized modern communication.

Research Findings: Our research reveals the strengths and limitations of different design forms in conveying intangible cultural heritage information and cultural emotions. Specifically, text and image reports can present the details of intangible skills through text and images, visual media conveys cultural emotions through visual narratives, information visualizations provide clear information presentation, and interactive media design can stimulate audience engagement and in-depth cultural understanding. This emphasizes the importance of media design forms in the exchange and dissemination of intangible cultural heritage.

Conclusion: The conclusions of this study emphasize the pivotal role of media design forms in regional cultural presentation and global dissemination, offering practical guidance for future design endeavors.

Keywords: Intangible cultural heritage · Cross-media digital form design · Cultural exchange

1 Research Background

In the current wave of globalization, the preservation of cultural diversity and the inheritance of intangible cultural heritage have become increasingly prominent issues. Cultural diversity is a vital component of human society, reflecting the unique traditions, beliefs,

P.-L. P. Rau (Ed.): HCII 2024, LNCS 14701, pp. 90–104, 2024.
https://doi.org/10.1007/978-3-031-60904-6_7

and ways of life of different communities. As the carriers of cultural diversity, intangible cultural heritage embodies the skills, rituals, and knowledge passed down through generations. These heritages not only symbolize the identity of a community but also serve as a link between the past and present, tradition and modernity. In the tide of globalization, protecting intangible cultural heritage has become a crucial means of maintaining cultural diversity, ensuring the continued inheritance of unique cultural traditions in various regions.

As a coastal city in southern China, Zhuhai possesses abundant intangible cultural heritage such as Mudfish Trapping, Waterborne Weddings, and Lion Dance. These elements bear the rich history, culture, and traditions of the Zhuhai region. However, with the rapid advancement of modernization and globalization, Zhuhai's intangible cultural heritage is facing the risk of gradual disappearance and oblivion. The swift urbanization has led to the decline of traditional craftsmanship, diminished interest among the younger generation in traditional culture, and increasingly challenging circumstances for inheritance. Moreover, the cultural impact of globalization has subjected Zhuhai's intangible cultural heritage to competition and pressures from foreign cultures. Against this backdrop, effective preservation and inheritance of intangible cultural heritage in Zhuhai have become pressing issues in need of resolution.

To address this challenge, the rise of digital media technology has emerged as an innovative means of protection and inheritance. With the diversification of digital media forms such as social media, online videos, interactive projections, etc., there are more possibilities for the display and dissemination of intangible cultural heritage. The characteristic of digital media lies in its ability to transcend geographical and temporal constraints, disseminating cultural elements globally, thereby providing new opportunities for the preservation and inheritance of intangible cultural heritage.

In the increasingly diverse landscape of digital media forms today, how different digital media forms contribute to the dissemination of Zhuhai's intangible cultural heritage and their effectiveness in promoting cultural information dissemination have become key questions in this study. Through the methods of cross-media form design and comparative measurement, we aim to delve into this issue, intending to provide innovative ideas and practical solutions for the protection and inheritance of intangible cultural heritage.

2 Literature Review

2.1 Communication of Intangible Cultural Heritage (ICH) and Digital Media Forms

With the continuous development of digital technology, utilizing digital means to enhance the protection and communication of cultural heritage has become a global concern. The digital technology system of ICH primarily utilizes existing information technology to digitally preserve and present ICH through methods such as pictures, audio, videos, and interactive displays [1].

The emergence of digital technology has changed the mode of recording ICH, playing an increasingly important role in its dissemination. Research has begun to focus on the transformation of information forms during the digitization process of intangible cultural heritage. More and more ICH dissemination is no longer limited to traditional textual descriptions but extends cultural expressions through cross-media design methods such as graphic design, digital films, animation, interactive applications, and more.

These digital technologies not only enrich the dissemination of ICH but also enhance the public's experience of encountering and understanding traditional culture [2, 3].

Some researchers have pointed out that in digital presentations of intangible cultural heritage, it is not only essential to facilitate effective cultural communication but also to consider the experiential enjoyment [4], that is, the experience of "edutainment" [5]. Therefore, when evaluating the effectiveness of disseminating information about intangible cultural heritage, equal importance should be placed on audience appeal, cultural emotion transmission, and information conveyance effectiveness. Audience appeal has been commonly used in past research to evaluate important aspects of the user experience [6]. Lin and Gregor (2006), in their study on website design in museum experiences, considered enjoyment as a sub-dimension that includes a sense of engagement [7]. In researching how curiosity promotes digital content related to cultural heritage, Abraham (2015) regarded curiosity as an intrinsic mechanism that encourages individuals to seek information [8]. This desire to know, see, and experience sparks exploratory behavior to obtain new information [9]. In a study assessing the communication effects of ICH, researchers conducted two rounds of in-depth interviews with expert groups to gather initial factors that may influence the digital dissemination of ICH. They found that the perceived technical level of ICH digital information communication plays a role [1], including perceptions of content integrity, richness, interface simplicity, and other aspects among audiences. Meanwhile, as the inheritance and continuation of a certain ethnic or regional culture, intangible cultural heritage significantly represents people's genuine acceptance and affection for this culture through its cultural identification and emotional depth. Therefore, this study will evaluate the effectiveness of digital dissemination of intangible cultural heritage from three aspects: audience engagement, information dissemination effects, and cultural emotional transmission.

2.2   The Discrepancy in Communication Effectiveness of Media Forms

Paivio (1986) proposed the Dual-Coding Theory (DCT) [10], which suggests that presenting information in different forms simultaneously, such as verbal codes combined with non-verbal information, can better capture the attention of the audience. Later, Mayer (1997) further developed the Multimedia Learning Cognitive Theory based on the Dual-Coding Theory, arguing that in a multimedia environment, the more diverse sensory stimuli there are, the higher the level of information reception by the audience.

Researchers have conducted comparisons of communication effectiveness under different media forms, such as comparing information exchange and socioemotional relations in communication activities involving face-to-face, telephone, meetings, desktop video and videoconferencing, voice mail, text, and electronic mail [12]. They found that different media forms have varying communication effects.

Some researchers have found that compared to pure text content, static information graphics with charts and graphs can enhance the understanding and engagement of participants [13]. Additionally, designs combining text and graphics can further stimulate audience thinking about the content [14]. In contrast to static information graphics, the conveyance of messages through audio-visual dynamics is more effective [15]. Interactive information can enhance the audience's experiential perception [16]. According to the above research results, interactive and dynamic media design forms have better information dissemination effects than static text or image designs.

However, other studies have found that there is no significant difference in knowledge absorption between static pictures and computer animations [17]. One study, reviewing research on the use of pictures and animations across various fields, also indicated that animations do not have a better effect on knowledge absorption than static pictures [18]. Interaction may impose a burden on the audience's information reception and interfere with their overall understanding of the message [19].

Researchers have found that through comparing three forms of information representation - static, dynamic, and interactive, different media design forms have their respective advantages. Static and dynamic visualizations provide better reading experiences for the audience, while pure text and interactive visualizations enhance their reading comprehension [20]. Through a meta-analysis evaluating the effect of using animations compared to static visualizations in instructional material, researchers found that animation was more effective when learning with iconic visualizations. Learning was enhanced with animation when no accompanying text was provided [21]. This study confirms the impact of media format differences on cultural information dissemination and learning outcomes.

Regarding the comparison of media digital form for traditional culture, Kim and Hong (2020) focused on investigating the impact of 2D and 3D presentation modes on visitor communication and enjoyment in exhibitions [4]. The researchers found that 2D presentations were more effective for intuitive communication compared to 3D. The 2D display method engaged visitors in exploring exhibition content while also showing interest in information acquisition, whereas 3D visitors preferred exploring virtual environments.

In addition, other researchers have found that factors influencing the effectiveness of media information dissemination include the cultural experiences of the audience [1], as well as motivational factors [22].

In summary, previous research results regarding the differences in communication effects caused by media design formats have been inconsistent, especially in the context of ICH information dissemination, where the effects of different media design formats have not been systematically examined. The relationship between audience cultural experiences, positioning, and the selection of digital media formats also remains unclear. Therefore, based on the literature review and identified gaps in the academic field, this study poses the following two research questions:

Q1: What are the differences in the communication effects among different digital media forms?

Q2: What is the relationship between the cultural experiences and motivational needs of audiences and the selection of digital media forms?

3 Research Methodology

3.1 Focus Groups

In order to identify the most common and popular cultural presentation forms on digital media platforms among young people, the researchers utilized focus group methodology. Seven university students were invited to participate in offline focus group discussions, consisting of 4 females and 3 males, organized and facilitated by the researchers. The focus groups centered around the digital cultural presentation forms of intangible cultural heritage. Participants were invited to share their preferences, perceptions, and cultural experiences with digital media to better understand their acceptance of different forms on digital media, focusing on their views on the presentation of Zhuhai's intangible cultural heritage, thereby providing targeted guidance for subsequent experimental designs.

The main discussion topics in the focus groups included two aspects:

1. Regarding intangible heritage information, what are the most commonly encountered and most popular digital media forms of intangible cultural heritage among young people?
2. In the dissemination of intangible heritage information, what are the typical representatives of four digital media forms: ① text-based with supplementary images, ② image-based with supplementary text, ③ dynamic video-based, and ④ interactive digital media forms?

The focus group discussions lasted for 120 minutes, and ultimately, participants voted to select four of the most representative digital media forms they deemed: online text and image report, short video, information visualization, and interactive projection. Online text and image reports were identified as the most common media form for Zhuhai's intangible heritage dissemination, also considered relatively "old-fashioned" by young people. The other three digital media forms are relatively new but have been increasingly popular among young people. The results of the focus group discussions helped determine the experimental stimulus forms for subsequent experimental designs.

3.2 Experimental Methods

Experimental Design. Through quantitative research methods, specifically experimental methodology, this study conducted comparative measurements of online text and image reports, visual media, information visualizations, and interactive projections in terms of audience appeal (including engagement and curiosity), information conveyance effectiveness (including specificity, vividness, clarity, intuitiveness, and conciseness of information dissemination), and cultural emotion transmission (including cultural identification and emotional depth).

This experiment involved comparing four different digital media design forms. Based on the results of the focus groups, this study used relatively traditional online text and image reports as the control group, and short video, information visualizations, and interactive projections as the experimental groups (see figure). Following the research framework, the four different media forms served as the independent variables, while audience appeal, information conveyance effectiveness, and cultural emotion transmission served as the dependent variables. The questionnaire utilized a 5-point scale, with 1 indicating strongly disagree and 5 indicating strongly agree.

Experimental Materials. To eliminate potential influences from differences in intangible cultural heritage projects, we selected the same representative and widely recognized intangible cultural heritage project in Zhuhai – Lion Dance. Information related to Lion Dance was presented in the forms of text and image reports (see Fig. 1), short video clips, information visualizations, and interactive projections.

This study produced short video, information visualization, and interactive projection themed around Lion Dance. The short video clips primarily depicted the rigorous training process and splendid performance of lion dancing through narrative storytelling (see Fig. 2). Information visualizations mainly illustrated the performance process and props of lion dancing using illustrated graphics (see Fig. 3). The interactive projections allowed the audience to change the light and shadow on lion dance props through drumming and touching, implying the performance process of lion dancing through changes in projection and music (see Fig. 4).

Fig. 1. Control Group: Text and Image Reports (Sourced from Zhuhai Intangible Cultural Heritage Database)

Experimental Process. This study invited 62 participants to take part in the experiment, recruited from two universities in southern China. They mainly came from 13 different cities in China, with a gender ratio of 10:21 (male: female) and varying degrees of experience with and exposure to intangible cultural heritage.

The experiment employed a within-group design, where all 62 participants viewed and experienced four media forms depicting the Zhuhai Lion Dance intangible cultural heritage: text and image reports, visual media, information visualization, and interactive media. To avoid potential learning effects from the same sequence, the presentation

Fig. 2. Experimental Group 1: Short Video (Filmed by the Research Team)

order of the four media forms was randomly assigned to each participant. Before the experiment began, researchers explained the purpose and procedures to the participants. Each media form was viewed for approximately 5 min. After viewing all forms, participants completed measurement questionnaires, with the entire experiment lasting about 40 min.

3.3   In-Depth Interviews

To gain a comprehensive understanding of the impact of different media forms on the dissemination of intangible cultural heritage (ICH) from Zhuhai, researchers conducted in-depth interviews with three participants from the experiment and two scholars specializing in ICH dissemination studies. Each interview, focusing on the development and application of ICH dissemination media, lasted approximately 30 min per participant.

Through these in-depth interviews, researchers collected individual experiences, perspectives, and sentiments regarding the presentation forms of ICH. The participation of expert scholars provided a more professional perspective, aiding in a deeper understanding of the influence of media design forms on ICH dissemination from both academic and practical viewpoints. Analysis of the interview content will enrich and deepen the interpretation of research findings.

By integrating the above research methods, the researchers aim to comprehensively and systematically explore the effects and influences of different media forms in presenting Zhuhai's intangible cultural heritage on digital media platforms.

Fig. 3. Experimental Group 2: Information Visualization (Designed by the Research Team)

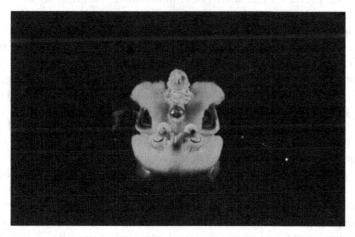

Fig. 4. Experimental Group 3: Interactive Projection (Designed by the Research Team)

4 Analysis of Results

The data analysis in this study proceeded in two stages. Firstly, quantitative statistics were conducted on the experimental data. Secondly, the content of the interviews was analyzed.

4.1 Experimental Data Analysis

In this study, the comparison test of the four digital media forms was conducted using SPSS's General Linear Model – Repeated Measures function.

The data results indicate significant differences among the four digital media forms in terms of audience engagement, curiosity, specificity, vividness, clarity, intuitiveness, conciseness, cultural identification, and emotional depth.

In terms of audience engagement, there were significant differences among the four digital media forms ($F = 31.604$, $p < .01$). Post hoc comparisons revealed that interactive projection ($M = 4.58$, $SD = .49$) and short video ($M = 4.23$, $SD = .48$) had significantly higher audience engagement than text and image reports ($M = 4.10$, $SD = .42$), while information visualization ($M = 4.01$, $SD = .52$) had significantly lower engagement than text and image reports.

Regarding curiosity, significant differences were found among the four digital media forms ($F = 62.166$, $p < .05$). Post hoc comparisons indicated that interactive projection ($M = 4.76$, $SD = .42$) and short video ($M = 4.25$, $SD = .48$) elicited significantly higher levels of curiosity than text and image reports ($M = 4.06$, $SD = .47$), while curiosity levels for information visualization ($M = 4.04$, $SD = .46$) did not significantly differ from those for text and image reports.

In terms of the specificity of heritage information dissemination, there were significant differences among the four digital media forms ($F = 17.701$, $p < .01$). Post hoc comparisons revealed that short video, information visualization, and interactive projection all had significantly lower specificity than text and image reports.

Regarding the perceived vividness of heritage information dissemination, significant differences were found among the four digital media forms ($F = 3.414$, $p < .05$). Post hoc comparisons showed that interactive projection ($M = 4.05$, $SD = .28$) and short video ($M = 4.03$, $SD = .25$) were significantly more vivid than text and image reports ($M = 3.94$, $SD = .36$), while information visualization ($M = 4.0$, $SD = .31$) did not significantly differ from text and image reports.

In terms of the perceived clarity of heritage information dissemination, there were significant differences among the four digital media forms ($F = 7.002$, $p < .05$). Post hoc comparisons indicated that information visualization ($M = 4.06$, $SD = .40$) was significantly clearer than text and image reports ($M = 3.92$, $SD = .33$), while short video ($M = 3.92$, $SD = .36$) and interactive projection ($M = 3.81$, $SD = .60$) did not significantly differ from text and image reports.

Regarding the perceived intuitiveness of heritage information dissemination, significant differences were found among the four digital media forms ($F = 7.487$, $p < .05$). Post hoc comparisons revealed that information visualization ($M = 4.18$, $SD = .29$) was significantly more intuitive than text and image reports ($M = 4.00$, $SD = .26$), while short video (M = 4.06, SD = .29) and interactive projection (M = 3.94, SD = .54) did not significantly differ from text and image reports.

In terms of the perceived conciseness of heritage information dissemination, there were significant differences among the four digital media forms (F = 22.668, p < .01). Post hoc comparisons showed that information visualization (M = 4.24, SD = .43) was significantly more concise than text and image reports (M = 3.62, SD = .70), while short video (M = 3.97, SD = .25) and interactive projection (M = 3.89, SD = .32) did not significantly differ from text and image reports.

Regarding cultural identification, significant differences were found among the four digital media forms (F = 11.773, p < .01). Post hoc comparisons indicated that short video (M = 4.15, SD = .54) elicited significantly higher cultural identification than text and image reports (M = 4.02, SD = .38), while information visualization (M = 3.83, SD = .53) and interactive projection (M = 3.90, SD = .56) elicited significantly lower cultural identification than text and image reports.

In terms of emotional depth, significant differences were found among the four digital media forms (F = 26.927, p < .01). Post hoc comparisons showed that short video (M = 4.10, SD = .59) elicited significantly deeper emotional responses than text and image reports (M = 3.88, SD = .48), while information visualization (M = 3.52, SD = .77) and interactive projection (M = 3.65, SD = .65) elicited significantly shallower emotional responses than text and image reports (see Table 1).

Table 1. Comparison of mean values for control group and experimental groups

Group	Control group	Experimental groups		
Digital Form	text and image reports	short video	information visualization	interactive projection
Engagement	4.10	4.23**	4.01*	4.58***
Curiosity	4.06	4.25***	4.03	4.76***
Specificity	4.03	3.77***	3.69***	3.65***
Vividness	3.93	4.03*	4.00	4.05*
Clarity	3.92	3.92	4.06**	3.81
Intuitiveness	4.00	4.06	4.18***	3.94
Conciseness	3.62	3.97***	4.24***	3.89**
Cultural identification	4.02	4.15*	3.83**	3.90*
Emotional depth	3.88	4.10***	3.52***	3.65***

Note: * indicates p < = .05, ** indicates p < = .01, and *** indicates p < = .001

4.2 Interview Data Analysis

Through in-depth interviews, researchers found that the differences in the effectiveness of the four digital media forms in disseminating cultural heritage were influenced not only by design elements but also by the cultural background and preferences of the audience. Factors such as the audience's understanding of cultural heritage, interest in traditional craftsmanship, and preference for interactive experiences all influenced their feedback under different design formats. These findings provide a deeper understanding of the role of digital media forms in disseminating cultural heritage.

Regarding the audience's cultural background, the study indicated that audiences with higher cultural literacy tended to have a deeper understanding of the history and cultural connotations of cultural heritage and were more eager for new experiences. Many of them had previously seen more text and image reports on cultural heritage, thus having a certain understanding of it, and they showed a preference for interactive media designs. Some interviewees expressed, "The interactive process can explore the diversity of culture," "Dynamic forms provide a richer experience," "Interactivity seems much more interesting." These audiences may be more willing to participate in virtual exhibitions, interactive applications, or multimedia displays to gain a richer cultural heritage experience.

Conversely, audiences with less understanding of cultural heritage may prefer media forms such as text and image reports and information visualization to quickly obtain basic information. They pointed out that images and interactions often require more time to watch, while information visualization can quickly and clearly understand the outline through a single image.

In terms of demand positioning, some audiences focus more on emotional resonance with cultural heritage, and they tend to choose visual media. Some interviewees said, "The immersive feeling of images is strong, and inspirational protagonists make me emotionally uplifted," "I am really proud of our traditional culture, I think it is very powerful." On the other hand, some audiences focused more on knowledge learning and preferred information provided in text and image reports.

5   Discussion

5.1   Effectiveness Evaluation of Digital Media Form Designs

Based on the measurement and comparison of experimental data, significant differences exist among the four digital media forms in terms of audience appeal, information conveyance effectiveness, and cultural emotion transmission, each with its own advantages.

Firstly, in terms of audience appeal, interactive media design performs the best. Audiences are more likely to engage and feel curious under interactive media design, willing to spend more time delving into intangible cultural heritage (ICH). However, text and image reports, as well as information visualization, show relatively weaker appeal, possibly because they are more traditional and static in presentation, making it difficult to capture the audience's attention. Image media falls in the middle.

Secondly, regarding information conveyance effectiveness, information visualization excels in clarity, intuitiveness, and conciseness of information conveyance. Audiences can quickly obtain basic information about ICH through this design format. However, text and image reports excel in specificity of information delivery, presenting detailed aspects of ICH, allowing audiences to comprehensively understand its history, craftsmanship, and production methods. Interactive media and image media forms are more likely to make audiences feel vivid and lively, but sometimes information conveyance may not be comprehensive enough. While interactive media design encourages deeper exploration by the audience, it may be relatively complex in information integration, requiring more careful balance.

Lastly, in terms of cultural emotion transmission, image media design, with its vivid visual narrative, can better evoke emotional resonance among the audience. The emotional conveyance of images can foster strong cultural identification and emotional depth. Text and image reports, through in-depth interpretation, can also to some extent evoke emotional connections to ICH. Information visualization and interactive media are relatively lacking in this aspect, making it difficult to deeply move the audience emotionally.

In conclusion, different design formats have their own advantages and limitations in cultural communication. Therefore, when designing digital media forms, designers should comprehensively consider the strengths and limitations of various design formats according to the communication objectives to achieve the best cultural exchange and dissemination effects. Through the effective use of these design formats, intangible cultural heritage can be more widely inherited and protected in the digital age.

5.2 The Relationship Between Audience Cultural Background and Choice of Digital Media Forms

Through the analysis of interview data, this study found that the dissemination effects of different digital media forms are not only influenced by design elements but also by the audience's cultural background and demand positioning. This emphasizes the personalized needs and diverse responses of media design forms in the dissemination of intangible cultural heritage (ICH).

Audiences with higher cultural literacy and deeper understanding of ICH tend to choose digital media forms that provide richer and more in-depth information, such as text and image reports and interactive media design. They may prefer to further understand the history, inheritance methods, and craftsmanship of ICH through in-depth textual descriptions, detailed image displays, and interactive experiences. Conversely, audiences with shallower understanding of ICH may prefer digital media forms that provide basic information, such as information visualization or image media, to quickly obtain basic information in an intuitive manner.

Audience cultural background and demand positioning also affect their emotional resonance and cultural identification with ICH. Some audiences place more emphasis on emotional resonance with ICH, and they tend to choose image media design. These audiences may be more easily moved by visual, auditory, and emotional stimuli, so designers can use video, audio, and image media to arouse their interest and resonance with ICH. On the other hand, some audiences who prioritize participation and closeness may prefer interactive media design. They hope to actively participate in the inheritance and experience of ICH, so designers can develop interactive applications, virtual experiences, or on-site interactive activities to meet the needs of this audience group.

Therefore, in practical design, designers need to consider not only the differences in digital media forms but also the cultural backgrounds and knowledge levels of different audience groups to ensure effective content dissemination and acceptance. In the context of global cultural communication, the cultural backgrounds and demand differences of audiences from different regions and ethnicities around the world may be even greater. In the face of multiculturalism, cultural expression requires diverse media forms design based on respect for tradition to meet the needs of people with different cultural experiences, carefully balance output forms with individual receiver factors, and achieve better dissemination effects.

5.3 The Key Role of Cross-Media Form Design in Cultural Communication and Preservation

In previous studies on cross-cultural communication, much emphasis has been placed on the diversity of cultural content, with relatively less attention paid to the importance of communication forms. The results of this study emphasize the crucial role of media design forms in regional cultural display and global dissemination, indicating that cross-media design influences cultural communication effects at different levels.

Cross-media form design allows information to be presented in various forms and media, including static text and images, dynamic videos, and interactive applications. Therefore, cross-media form design offers a promising vision of meeting the needs and preferences of different audience groups through diverse communication forms, enhancing the coverage and effectiveness of cultural communication.

Cross-media form design can fully utilize the expressive means and characteristics of different media to present rich and diverse cultural content. For example, image media can convey cultural emotions through visual narrative, while interactive media design can enhance audience participation and provide opportunities for in-depth exploration through gamification elements, attracting more attention and interest from audiences, and promoting cultural communication and understanding. Information visualization has advantages in conveying clarity, intuitiveness, and conciseness. Text and image reports are more suitable for presenting specific detailed information. These findings will help designers make correct judgments based on communication purposes, effectively combining traditional culture with modern digital technology, enabling traditional culture to be inherited and developed in the digital age.

In summary, cross-media form design plays an indispensable and crucial role in cultural communication and preservation. It enriches the forms of cultural communication with its respective advantages, enhances the possibilities of cultural exchange and dissemination, promotes the inheritance and development of traditional culture, and provides effective approaches and means for cultural protection and sustainable development.

6 Conclusions

Through empirical research on the dissemination of intangible cultural heritage (ICH) through text and image reports, video media, information visualization, and interactive media design, this study provides an in-depth analysis of their performance in attracting audiences, conveying information, and transmitting cultural emotions.

The research findings reveal that in the dissemination of intangible cultural heritage information in Zhuhai, different digital media forms play different roles in cultural exchange and global dissemination, each leveraging its unique advantages. Text and image reports present the details of intangible cultural heritage through a combination of text and images, while video media conveys cultural emotions through visual narratives. Information visualization provides clear information presentation, and interactive media design stimulates audience engagement, encouraging them to delve deeper into understanding intangible cultural heritage. It is important to note that these differences are influenced by audience cultural experiences and demand positioning, and the choice of design forms should be carefully balanced.

Based on the strengths and limitations of different digital media forms in conveying information and cultural emotions of intangible cultural heritage, we can see that cross-media form design plays a crucial role in the dissemination and protection of Zhuhai's intangible cultural heritage. Different media forms promote cultural exchange and global modern communication at different levels, contributing not only to the inheritance and protection of cultural heritage but also to fostering audience interest in intangible cultural heritage, promoting cultural diversity, sustainable development, and providing reference for designers' subsequent work. In future design work, we suggest that designers choose media forms adaptively and according to needs. First, consider the advantages and disadvantages of different digital media forms, and then flexibly apply different forms in combination with audience cultural backgrounds and needs to achieve effective cultural communication and dissemination. Through the comprehensive use of these media forms, we hope to showcase China's intangible cultural heritage more creatively and attractively on digital media platforms globally.

This study provides empirical evidence for the selection of media design forms in the dissemination of intangible cultural heritage but there are still aspects that can be further explored in future research. For example, further consideration could be given to the different reactions of audiences of different ages to media design, or delve deeper into the mechanisms and influencing factors of media design forms in the dissemination of intangible cultural heritage. This will contribute to a more comprehensive understanding of the role of media design forms in the dissemination of intangible cultural heritage and provide more specific and practical guiding principles.

Acknowledgments. This study was funded by the Philosophy and Social Science Planning Project of Guangdong Province in 2024, "Research on Digital Creative Design and Dissemination of Intangible Cultural Heritage of Cantonese Cuisine" (GD24CYS32), as well as by the Philosophy and Social Science Planning Project of Zhuhai City, "Research on Digital Collection, Digital Creative Design, and Dissemination of Intangible Cultural Heritage in Zhuhai" (2021YBA048).

References

1. Xue, K., Li, Y., Meng, X.: An evaluation model to assess the communication effects of intangible cultural heritage. J. Cult. Herit. **40**, 124–132 (2019)
2. Jin, S., Fan, M., Wang, Y., Liu, Q.: Reconstructing traditional Chinese paintings with immersive virtual reality. In: Extended Abstracts of the 2020 CHI Conference on Human Factors in Computing Systems, pp. 1–8 (2020)

3. Ji, Y., Tan, P., Hills, D.: Chinese traditional handicraft education using AR content. Leonardo **53**(2), 199–200 (2020)
4. Kim, S., Hong, S.: How virtual exhibition presentation affects visitor communication and enjoyment: an exploration of 2D versus 3D. Des. J. **23**(5), 677–696 (2020)
5. Boskovic, D., Rizvic, S., Okanovic, V., Sljivo, S., Sinanovic, N., Measuring immersion and edutainment in multimedia cultural heritage applications. In: 2017 XXVI International Conference on Information, Communication and Automation Technologies (ICAT), pp. 1–6. IEEE (2017)
6. Wanta, W., Gao, D.: Young readers and the newspaper: information recall and perceived enjoyment, readability, and attractiveness. J. Quart. **71**(4), 926–936 (1994)
7. Lin, A.C., Gregor, S.D.: Designing websites for learning and enjoyment: a study of museum experiences. Int. Rev. Res. Open Distrib. Learn. **7**(3), 1–21 (2006)
8. Abraham, J.: The role of curiosity in making up digital content promoting cultural heritage. Procedia Soc. Behav. Sci. **184**, 259–265 (2015)
9. Litman, J.: Curiosity and the pleasures of learning: wanting and liking new information. Cogn. Emot. **19**(6), 793–814 (2005)
10. Paivio, A.: Mental Representations: A Dual Coding Approach. Oxford University Press, New York (1986)
11. Mayer, R.E.: Multimedia learning: are we asking the right questions? Educ. Psychol. **32**(1), 1–19 (1997)
12. Rice, R.E.: Media appropriateness: using social presence theory to compare traditional and new organizational media. Hum. Commun. Res. **19**(4), 451–484 (1993)
13. Colombo, L., Landoni, M., Rubegni, E., Understanding reading experience to inform the design of eBooks for children. In: H. Schelhowe (ed.) Proceedings of IDC 2012: The 11th International Conference on Interaction Design and Children, pp. 272–275. ACM, New York (2012)
14. Larson, L.C.: E-books and audiobooks: extending the digital reading experience. Read. Teach. **69**(2), 169–177 (2015)
15. Occa, A., Suggs, L.S.: Communicating breast cancer screening with young women: an experimental test of didactic and narrative messages using video and infographics. J. Health Commun. **21**(1), 1–11 (2016)
16. Locoro, A., Cabitza, F., Actis-Grosso, R., Batini, C.: Static and interactive infographics in daily tasks: a value-in-use and quality of interaction user study. Comput. Hum. Behav. **71**, 240–257 (2017)
17. Rieber, L.P., Hannafin, M.J.: Effects of textual and animated orienting activities and practice on learning from computer-based instruction. Comput. Schools **5**(1–2), 77–89 (1988)
18. Tversky, B., Morrison, J.B., Betrancourt, M.: Animation: can it facilitate? Int. J. Hum.-Comput. Stud. **57**(4), 247–262 (2002)
19. Lee, E.-J., Kim, Y.W.: Effects of infographics on news elaboration, acquisition, and evaluation: prior knowledge and issue involvement as moderators. New Media Soc. **18**(8), 1579–1598 (2016)
20. Huang, Z.Y., Huang, H.P.: The influence of information visualization on readers' reading experience and reading comprehension of scientific issues. Chinese J. Sci. Educ. **26**(3), 197–218(2018)
21. Berney, S., Bétrancourt, M.: Does animation enhance learning? A meta-analysis. Comput. Educ. **101**, 150–167 (2016)
22. Khan, M.L.: Social media engagement: what motivates user participation and consumption on YouTube? Comput. Hum. Behav. **66**, 236–247 (2017)

Information Visualization Expression of Cultural Heritage and Innovation of Communication Paradigm Paths - The Overseas Communication of "The Compendium of Materia Medica" as an Example

ZiYuan Sun(✉)

Wuhan University of Technology, 122 Luoshi Road, Wuhan, Hubei, People's Republic of China
2637437177@qq.com

Abstract. Between the 17th and 20th centuries, the Chinese medical work Ben Cao Gang Mu (本草纲目), a representative of China's outstanding canonical works, was mainly disseminated overseas through the paper-based medium, and the related editions and language translations became an important research topic, but one of the most noteworthy is the "pictorialization" of Ben Cao Gang Mu (本草纲目), which was also an early example of visualizing and promoting the dissemination of Ben Cao Gang Mu based on drawings. This is also an early example of visualizing and promoting the dissemination of the Materia Medica based on drawings. After entering the 21st century, the medium and structure of cultural communication have undergone great changes, and the domestic and overseas communication of the Materia Medica has shown the trend of digitization. From the current research and practice, it can be seen that, on the one hand, the digital communication of the Materia Medica is communicated in the form of information visualization and knowledge mapping, but from the view of the existing research results, the mining of information of the Materia Medica is too partial, and the interactivity is weak. Interactivity is weak and other problems. On the other hand, the dissemination of Materia Medica by means of film and video works, video games and other forms has shown a trend of entertainment, and this kind of practice and research also has the same problems of one-sided information mining and lack of experience as mentioned above. As a representative of China's outstanding cultural texts, it is difficult to show the cultural charm it really contains.

In order to solve the problems of formality and superficiality that exist in the current digital design of cultural heritage, this study focuses on the innovation of cultural heritage digital products and dissemination paradigms, taking the Compendium of Materia Medica as an example, aiming to make the dissemination of the multiple connotations of the excellent cultural heritage represented by the Compendium of Materia Medica more profound, with a stronger vitality and sustainability. The main academic contributions of this study are reflected in the following aspects: first, the dissemination of the digital products of the Compendium of Materia Medica makes full use of the advantages of digital interactive media in terms of its strong timeliness, wide scope of dissemination, and variety of dissemination modes, which allows users to actively participate, share, comment,

P.-L. P. Rau (Ed.): HCII 2024, LNCS 14701, pp. 105–112, 2024.
https://doi.org/10.1007/978-3-031-60904-6_8

and interact with the content, and can directly receive user feedback; it allows for the content to be continuously updated, and contains rich media content such as moving images, animations, games, knowledge maps, etc., and users can directly receive user feedback. It allows the content to be continuously updated and contains rich media content such as dynamic images, animations, games, knowledge maps, etc., so that users can often share the content with each other and get pleasure from it; it allows users to actively create various forms of content, so that users can share it with others through non-network and get feedbacks, and maximize the effect of dissemination with the help of these advantages; secondly, from the angle of informatization of Materia Medica, based on the theory of "Cultural Gene Secondly", from the perspective of informatization of the Materia Medica, based on the theory of "cultural genes" and the use of information visualization, knowledge mapping and other technologies and means, it summarizes and summarizes the knowledge of the Materia Medica, the process of inheritance and evolution of the cultural system, and records it in an orderly manner, so as to systematically and clearly excavate the cultural genes contained therein, and ultimately to form a visualized and interactive cultural gene map of the Materia Medica. Finally, following the trend of entertainment in cultural communication, research is conducted on the RPG game themed on "Materia Medica", which has stronger narrative and interactivity than other entertainment means, and is more capable of carrying a complete story and rich emotions. Through the innovation of the above modes, a multimodal and multi-channel cultural content dissemination paradigm of cultural heritage will be constructed in the end.

This study adopts the research perspective of cross-fusion of disciplines based on design to conduct cross-cultural communication research, enhances the innovation and creativity of the subject research through design thinking and innovative thinking, provides more diversified and creative programs and strategies, and increases the attractiveness and influence of digital cross-cultural communication. The digital design of cultural heritage is to use digital and information technology to explore the sustainable development path of cultural heritage revitalization and utilization, and to form a new pattern of diversified protection and inheritance. From the cultural resources end, cultural heritage digitization can promote the transformation of massive cultural heritage resources from data to assets, and promote the sustainable development of social and economic benefits by meeting the ever-changing cultural communication needs of the market.

Keywords: Cultural heritage preservation and development · Information visualization · Diffusion Paradigm Pathway Innovation

1 Historical Value of the Materia Medica and the Current Status of Its Dissemination

The Compendium of Materia Medica, the heirloom work of Li Shizhen, a medical doctor of the Ming Dynasty in China, is not only the most comprehensive, rich and systematic book on Chinese medicine among ancient Chinese works, but also a worldwide work on museum science. The Compendium of Materia Medica encompasses knowledge of astronomy, geography, biology, chemistry, geology, mining, and even history, elevating Chinese medical science to a new level, and is a bright pearl in the history of China's outstanding traditional culture. Since the publication of the Jinling text in 1596, the Materia Medica has been widely disseminated in East Asia, Europe and the United States in the way of "East Learning and West Progressing", which has had a far-reaching influence, and during the period from the 17th century to the 20th century, the relevant editions and language translations of the Materia Medica have been disseminated overseas mainly through the medium of paper. In the 21st century, the medium, logic and context of information dissemination have changed dramatically, and the medium of communication represented by paper books can no longer satisfy the ever-increasing demand for cultural dissemination. From the existing results, it can be seen that the digital dissemination of "Materia Medica" presents a significant digital trend, which is mainly realized by information visualization. The principle is to transform traditional Chinese medicine knowledge into the form of graphics, charts, images, illustrations, games and interactive applications to convey to the public, which has the advantages of being easy to disseminate and easy to accept, and at the same time, there are still practical problems such as lack of objectivity in information mining and weak quality of user experience, which make it difficult to show the true meaning of traditional Chinese medicine. At the same time, there are still practical problems such as lack of objectivity in information mining and weak quality of user experience, which make it difficult to show the cultural charm it really contains. It can be found that it is urgent to explore the strategies and paths of how to effectively combine art and science and technology to realize the digital information visualization and dissemination of the Materia Medica. In order to solve the problems of heavy form and superficiality that exist in the current digital design of cultural heritage, this paper will take the practice of digital information dissemination art design of Materia Medica as an example to explore the digital information visualization expression of Chinese excellent traditional culture and the specific path innovation of the dissemination paradigm, aiming at letting the multiple connotations of excellent cultural heritage represented by Materia Medica disseminate more profoundly and have stronger vitality and sustainability.

2   Research Perspectives

2.1   Cross-disciplinary Based Research Perspectives

The development of science and technology has pushed the cross-fertilization of disciplines into an inevitable trend. China carried out a major disciplinary development adjustment in August 2020, formally incorporating cross-disciplines into disciplinary categories and becoming the 14th disciplinary category. This change reflects the fact that today's scientific research and the solution of practical problems increasingly require the support of interdisciplinary knowledge systems and research resources. Considering that the study of the dissemination paradigm of the digital interactive exhibits of the Materia Medica in overseas Asia involves various aspects of society, culture, technology, etc., its research perspective inevitably needs to be based on the perspectives of multiple disciplines, such as culture, communication, design, etc., in order to realize a more comprehensive and integrated study.

2.2 Perspectives Based on User Research

By conducting an in-depth study of the dissemination of the digital interactive exhibits of the Compendium of Materia Medica in overseas regions based on the perspective of user research, we are able to gain a more comprehensive understanding of the needs and feedbacks of overseas populations on digital exhibits related to Chinese medicine. This study will focus on the user behaviors, preferences, and psychology of people in overseas regions to help better understand the cultural and social background of the audience. Through this understanding, we will be able to tailor the content and format of the digital interactive exhibits to better meet the needs and expectations of the audience and achieve a targeted communication strategy.

2.3 Research Perspectives Based on the Integration of Science and Art

Adhering to the research concept of cross-fertilization of science and art, we will give full play to the design and expression advantages in the field of art, and create a series of communication exhibits with both sense of form and sense of experience by extracting the unique cultural genes embedded in the Materia Medica and transforming them into a rational art using interactive information technology. With the aid of technology, we will organically integrate interactive information technology into the design of the digital interactive exhibits of the Compendium of Materia Medica and the process of knowledge and culture dissemination, so as to significantly enhance the diversity, interactivity, and sense of immersion of the exhibits, solve the problems of poor interactivity, single aesthetics, and weak experiential experience of the traditional dissemination works, and promote the transformation of the dissemination of knowledge and culture from one-way dissemination to multi-directional interaction.

2.4 Research Perspective Based on Theory to Practice

Researching the dissemination paradigm of the digitized exhibits of the Materia Medica in overseas regions from the perspective of theory-to-practice research helps to better understand the dissemination environment and characteristics of the digitized exhibits in overseas regions. It provides scientific theoretical support for the promotion and dissemination of digital exhibits by gaining an in-depth understanding of the dissemination laws and trends of digital exhibits in overseas regions on the basis of theoretical research. At the same time, based on the actual development trend of digital design informatization and entertaining, we will conduct in-depth research on user needs, communication strategies and other aspects, so as to provide practical suggestions and methods for the dissemination of the digitized interactive exhibits of the Materia Medica.

3 Object and Main Content of the Study

First, re-arranging and Database Establishment of Materia Medica in the Context of Multi-disciplinary Integration In the context of multi-disciplinary cross-fertilization, digital technology is utilized to digitize ancient books by re-reading, summarizing and organizing Materia Medica, initially establishing and designing a database of Materia Medica, carrying out intelligent processing and analysis, and providing more convenient and efficient retrieval methods. Give full play to the advantages of various disciplines, improve the efficiency and accuracy of the work, and make greater contributions to the inheritance of Chinese excellent traditional culture.

Second,research on the design of visualized, interactive and perceptible cultural gene map of Materia Medica Starting from the perspective of informatization of Materia Medica, based on the theory of "cultural gene", and applying the technology and means of information visualization and knowledge mapping, we will summarize and summarize the knowledge of Materia Medica, the process of inheritance and evolution of the cultural system, and record the information of the Materia Medica in order, so that the knowledge and culture of the Materia Medica will be recorded and the information of the Materia Medica will be transmitted to the public. Record the content, history, version change and dissemination history of the Materia Medica through attribute categorization, logical analysis, arrangement and deconstruction, and systematically and clearly excavate the cultural genes contained therein, and ultimately form a visualized and interactive cultural gene map of the Materia Medica.

Thirdly, design of Entertaining, Experiencing and Immersive RPGs on the Theme of "Compendium of Materia Medica" Following the trend of entertaining cultural communication, we are going to study the RPGs on the theme of "Compendium of Materia Medica", which has stronger narrativity and interactivity than other means of entertainment, and it is more capable of carrying a complete story and rich emotions; the RPG on the theme of "Compendium of Materia Medica" also breaks the seriousness and formality of traditional knowledge dissemination. The seriousness and formality of traditional knowledge dissemination and adopt a more relaxed and interesting way to present knowledge.

4 The Specific Path of Informatization Expression of the Materia Medica

To do a good job in the digital dissemination of Chinese excellent traditional culture in the information age, it is necessary to give full play to the advantages of information technology and the characteristics of new media dissemination by utilizing the cross-disciplinary information technology, and to highly integrate and refine culture, dissemination, media, and art, so as to create digital interactive exhibits in line with the needs of the times, and to guide the expression of high-quality information and artistic meanings. General Secretary Xi Jinping has repeatedly used the theory of "cultural genes" to explain the excellent traditional Chinese culture, and gradually constructed a systematic theory of the connection between traditional culture and socialism with Chinese characteristics, with "Chinese cultural genes" as the core. The theory of "Chinese cultural gene" carries the ideological elements and spiritual codes of Chinese culture, which carries the splendid civilization, inherits the history and culture, and maintains the national spirit. In order to solve the outstanding problems of emphasizing form but not connotation in the current overseas dissemination of excellent Chinese culture, this paper, based on the theory of cultural genes, carries out an orderly exploration of the artistic expression strategies and paths in the overseas dissemination of "Materia Medica"; makes full use of the advantages of the digital interactive media, and starts from the "cultural genes map" and the "role-playing interactive game" to the "cultural genes map". Taking full advantage of digital interactive media, this paper explores a new path for the excavation, protection and dissemination of Chinese outstanding traditional culture that adapts to the evolution of the digital era and meets the needs of digital media communication, starting from the two directions of "cultural gene mapping" and "role-playing interactive game".

4.1   Visualization Design of Cultural Gene Mapping of Materia Medica

The visualization design of cultural gene mapping refers to the use of informatization technology to structure and store a series of related cultural knowledge, and to orient the interactive multimodal cultural gene mapping information expression. Based on the theory of cultural genes, this paper firstly characterizes and quantitatively extracts a large number of entity pictures and semantic relations covered in the Compendium of Materia Medica, records the inheritance and evolution process of the cultural system in an orderly manner, and tries to scientifically and reasonably excavate the embedded cultural elements; after standardizing and artificially revising the collected data, it constructs the entity and relation models, and then integrates the related picture resources to build a multimodal and structured cultural gene map of the Compendium of Materia Medica. After the collected data are standardized and manually revised, the entity and relationship models are constructed, and the related picture resources are integrated together to construct a multimodal and structured resource database of Materia Medica. After that, this paper expresses the unique cultural elements and knowledge data of Materia Medica artistically through effective information interaction technology. Fully utilizing the technical means of information visualization and knowledge mapping, and giving full play to the advantages of visual communication design unique to the art field, a series of multimodal cultural genealogical maps with a sense of form, a sense of experience and professionalism are designed (Fig. 1). The cultural gene map of Materia Medica can accurately and intuitively display the knowledge system of Materia Medica with the characteristics of accuracy, interactivity and sense of immersion, which promotes the transformation of the communication of Materia Medica from one-way communication to multi-directional interaction, and at the same time, facilitates the preservation and sustainable utilization of the relevant knowledge, with a stronger vitality.

Fig. 1. Cultural genealogical mapping of the sixteen parts and editions of the Materia Medica

4.2 Role-Playing Game Design of "Compendium of Materia Medica"

Following the trend of experientialization of cultural communication, this paper explores the design of a role-playing game based on the theme of "Compendium of Materia Medica", specifically using the elements of "Compendium of Materia Medica" as the cultural kernel of the game, and using the story of Li Shizhen's story of tasting all kinds of herbs when he was writing his books as the prototype for the game's characters, and the narrative journey of collecting and discovering the secrets of herbs by means of explorations, battles, and quests, to help players immerse themselves in the game in a gamified way (Fig. 2). The game integrates exploration, narrative, combat, collection and solution into one, combining the ink and wash style of the Northern Song Dynasty's "Thousands of Miles of Rivers and Mountains" with modern game art to form a relaxing, lively, and trendy colorful atmosphere, which brings fun to users while initially constructing an "immersive experience" of excellent Chinese cultural elements. In the design of the game mechanism, in addition to the basic functions of sharing, commenting, and simple interaction, it also sets up interesting science, user feedback, and self-created content mechanisms to maximize the dissemination effect of the cultural knowledge related to "Materia Medica" in the form of game interaction. Compared with other traditional communication methods, role-playing games have stronger narrativity and interactivity, and are more capable of carrying complete stories and rich emotions, so that users can fully feel the cultural connotations in the process of experiencing the game of "Materia Medica", and help gamers to fully experience the great charm of "Materia Medica".

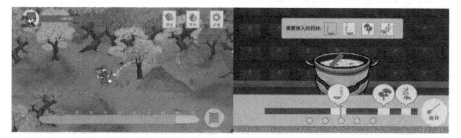

Fig. 2. Combat and Pharmaceutical Interface of the Materia Medica Role-Playing Game

5 Conclusion

The research significance of the digital dissemination of the Compendium of Materia Medica lies firstly in the fact that it can promote the conversion of excellent Chinese classics to digitalization, realize the modern revitalization of cultural heritage, and form a new pattern of diversified protection and inheritance. Secondly, the study of the artistic expression of the digital interactive exhibits of the Compendium of Materia Medica is a new perspective for the study of the dissemination and mutual appreciation of the excellent traditional Chinese culture, which provides a new way of thinking for solving the "theory of clash of civilizations". Finally, from the perspective of cultural resources, the digital dissemination of Chinese excellent traditional culture calls for a huge amount of excellent cultural resources to be transformed from data to assets, and the cultural digital assets constructed through the theory of cultural genes will become an important resource guarantee for our country in the competition of the world cultural market.

References

1. Li, G., Xu, Q., Wu, Y., et al.: Research on the construction of multimodal knowledge graph based on Materia Medica. Mod. Comput. **28**(13), 10–17+24 (2022)
2. Zhang, Y., Yin, N.: The translation and dissemination of Materia Medica in Europe and America. J. North China Univ. Sci. Technol. (Soc. Sci. Edn.) **22**(05), 126–133 (2022)
3. Jiang, S., Lu, X.: The interactivity of display communication in cultural heritage digitization and its application–the contemporary communication of Dunhuang culture as an example. Mod. Commun. (J. Commun. Univ. China) **35**(08), 19–23 (2013)
4. Sun, X.: A review of the development of olfactory informatization products and its design research. Packag. Eng. **43**(06), 24–31 (2022)
5. Zhao, W.-J., Liu, J.-Y., Lu, X.: Multimodal discourse analysis in the visual grammar perspective-taking China in the Canonical Books-Ben Cao Gang Mu as an example. Sci. Technol. Commun. **15**(08), 42–44 (2023)
6. Yu, G., Yang, Y.: Participation, immersion, feedback: three elements of effective communication in the surplus era-a theoretical discussion on the game paradigm as the mainstream paradigm of future communication. China Publishing **433**(08), 16–22 (2018)
7. Yang, Y., Ji, T., Zhang, D.: Design and application of cultural heritage in serious games. Packag. Eng. **41**(04), 312–317 (2020)
8. Zhang, M.: Presence and empathy: a study of game experience design from the perspective of narrative transmission. J. Nanjing Arts Inst. (Art Design) **196**(04), 82–87 (2021)
9. Li, H.: Trends and strategies of gamification in knowledge dissemination. Young Journalist **742**(02), 94–96 (2023)
10. Li, S.Z.: Introduction to Information Visualization Design, p. 05. Tsinghua University Press, Beijing (2021)
11. Chen, H.: Introduction to Knowledge Graph, p. 02. Electronic Industry Press, Beijing (2021)
12. Chen, D., Zhu, H.E., Zhou, L., Guan, J.Z.: Construction and Dissemination of Chinese Medicine Cultural Discourse System, p. 08. Sichuan University Press, Chengdu (2021)
13. Li, N.: A deep-learning-based approach for multi modal educational knowledge graph construction. Information **13**(2), 91 (2022)
14. Baumgartner, M., Rossetto, L., Bernstein, A.: Towards using semantic-web technologies for multi-modal knowledge graph construction. The 28th ACM International Conference on Multimedia (MM 2020). ACM (2020). https://doi.org/10.1145/3394171.3416292

Digital Interactive Experience Design Based on Guangxi Yao Ethnic Embroidery Patterns

Meirong Sun and Xing Yuan[✉]

School of Culture and Media, Hezhou University, Hezhou 542899, China
37741657@qq.com

Abstract. This study takes Guangxi Yao ethnic embroidery patterns as the practical object. Through literature review both domestically and internationally, as well as comparisons with traditional culture, a comprehensive database is constructed to analyze the composition of Guangxi Yao ethnic embroidery patterns and explore their significance in Yao culture. The challenges and opportunities of digitalization in the preservation of Guangxi Yao embroidery culture are discussed. By identifying patterns and optimizing strategies, traditional Yao ethnic embroidery patterns are combined with digital interactive technology to leverage emerging technologies as a catalyst for the development of intangible cultural heritage. This approach creates new forms of experience, enhances user engagement, conveys the unique charm of Yao ethnic embroidery culture, and provides strategies, recommendations, and avenues for the digital preservation, promotion, and communication of intangible cultural heritage.

Keywords: Guangxi Yao Ethnic Group · Embroidery Patterns · Digitalization · Interactive Experience Design

1 Introduction

The "Opinions on Promoting the Implementation of the National Cultural Digitalization Strategy" issued by the Central Committee of the Communist Party of China and the General Office of the State Council points out that by 2035, the long-term task of constructing a national cultural big data system will be completed to achieve rapid development of digital cultural productivity and enable the whole nation to share the digital achievements of Chinese civilization. The digital technology has brought about a new transformation in the configuration system of elements, and with the advancement of technologies such as the Internet of Things, artificial intelligence, and cloud computing, the cultural industry has entered a period of explosive growth in digital culture, ushering in a new era of digitalization. Both domestically and internationally, there is a full recognition of the importance of protecting and developing ethnic cultures. The "14th Five-Year Plan" period is an important strategic opportunity for the modern development of China's cultural industry. In the era of economic globalization, digital technology plays a strong driving role in optimizing and upgrading cultural products

P.-L. P. Rau (Ed.): HCII 2024, LNCS 14701, pp. 113–127, 2024.
https://doi.org/10.1007/978-3-031-60904-6_9

and services, intensifying the competition for international cultural soft power. Digitizing ethnic cultures is beneficial for unleashing the dual value of cultural industries. Therefore, seizing the opportunities of digital technology and economic development, leveraging the advantages of data algorithms and the linkage of the digital economy, and achieving multidimensional interaction and integrated development between ethnic cultures and other industries are of great value and significance for the development of China's digital economy.

Cultural digitalization provides new scenarios for cultural life. For example, from online literature, online videos, live streaming, digital libraries, virtual museums, and e-sports, to cloud performances, cloud viewing, and cloud tourism, new forms of cultural formats have emerged. Digital technology enriches the types of cultural products and services. With deepening digitization, cultural consumption experiences will transition from "online" to "real-time." New digital experiences can create virtual and real-world integrated consumer scenes, providing an effective path for the creative transformation and innovative development of outstanding traditional Chinese culture in the digital world. Cultural databases need a top-level design to meet the active demands of market entities. Culture has always been the deepest and most enduring force driving the development of human society, and the rapid development of diverse digital technologies highlights the eternal charm of Chinese culture. By infusing digital elements into cultural preservation and inheritance, Chinese ethnic cultures will shine even brighter in the digital age.

China has a long history and profound cultural heritage, giving rise to numerous valuable intangible cultural heritages among the people. The Yao ethnic group is a large ethnic group that has endured the changes of thousands of years. With a population of approximately 2.85 million people in China, the Yao people have diverse branches and complex lineages, with some residing in foreign countries. Over thousands of years, the Yao ethnic group has undergone cultural evolution, creating a splendid and colorful ancient Chinese culture and developing many distinctive achievements of Yao culture. The Yao people are mainly distributed in regions such as Guizhou, Hunan, and the Guangxi Zhuang Autonomous Region in China, with Guangxi being the province with the largest population of Yao people in China. Due to differences in origin legends, production methods, places of residence, and clothing, more than 30 different appellations have emerged, such as Pan Yao, Guoshan Yao, Bai Ku Yao, Cha Shan Yao, Hong Tou Yao, Huang Hua Yao, Hua Lan Yao, Pingdi Yao, and so on. The multitude of appellations within the Yao ethnic group is relatively rare among Chinese ethnic minorities.

Guangxi Yao ethnic embroidery has a long and rich history and is an important part of the national cultural digital preservation. Effective inheritance and innovative development of Yao ethnic embroidery contribute to the enrichment of ethnic cultural connotations and are the responsibilities of the nation and researchers today. Within Yao culture, Yao embroidery patterns are diverse and serve as iconic symbols of Yao clothing culture, showcasing the ethnic characteristics. These patterns are also important artistic forms, embodying the wisdom, aesthetic concepts, and cultural heritage of the Yao people.

2   Regional Culture of the Yao Ethnic Group

The Yao ethnic group in China is one of the minority ethnic groups and is mainly distributed in Guangxi Zhuang Autonomous Region, Hunan, Yunnan, and Guizhou, with Guangxi being the most concentrated. This ethnic group has a long history, and it can be inferred from the three ethnic myths of "Changgu," "Panhu," and "Du Hai" that they originated from ancient times in China. "There is no mountain in Lingnan without Yao." The Yao people are mainly distributed in the mountainous areas of the southern and northern parts of the Five Ridges. The Yao ethnic group is divided into four major branches: Panyao, Bunuyao, Chashanyao, and Pingdiyao, with a wide distribution, and each branch has different customs and habits. Each branch retains its own language but does not have its own writing system. They record and inherit their culture through artistic forms such as songs, dances, dramas, and pictorial records. The patterns on their costumes are like a "wordless book," preserving the special deeds and stories of their ethnicity. Each pattern has different meanings and symbols, interpreting the development history of their ethnicity and narrating the evolution of Yao costume culture, carrying the Yao people's pursuit and longing for a better life.

Yao ethnic culture is particularly prominent in their belief system and totem. They believe that all things have spirits and worship multiple gods. According to the "Guoshanbang" records, the ancestor, Panwang (Panhu), was a colorful dog. He earned merit in a battle between the "Pingwang" and the "Gaowang," and was highly regarded by the "Pingwang." He married the Pingwang's third princess and gave birth to six sons and six daughters, who became the twelve Yao clans. Therefore, the Pan Yao men and women often wear colorful clothes to worship their ancestors. The book "Records of the Southern Barbarians" in Chinese history has early records of Yao people's clothing and costumes, making it the earliest documentation of Yao costume. Yao costumes are known for their vibrant colors, intricate patterns, and exquisite craftsmanship. According to historical records, in Changsha Commandery, there were Yi people called Moyao, and their female descendants wore blue cloth shirts and patchwork skirts without shoes. The Pan Wang seal is a symbol of their faith engraved in their hearts. On the 16th day of the tenth lunar month, the whole Yao ethnic group wears the most solemn clothes to participate in worship activities.

The Yao people have achieved considerable accomplishments in the field of embroidery craftsmanship, which has become an indispensable part of their production and daily life from ancient times to the present. There is a saying among the Yao people that "Yao girls love to embroider flowers; if they can't embroider, they won't find a husband." This saying indicates that embroidery is the foundation of their lives and holds a significant position, showcasing the Yao people's embroidery skills. According to the Yao folklore about the origin of embroidery, they only use colors other than red, blue, yellow, white, and black to commemorate their ancestor, Panhu. In the book "Guangdong Xin Yu," it is recorded, "Panhu's fur is colorful, making Yao girls dress in a patchy manner." In ancient China, red, blue, yellow, white, and black were called "zhengse", symbolizing inviolable authority [1].

The Yao ethnic group is mainly distributed in the northwest, northeast, and southern mountainous regions of Guangxi. Depending on the different main settlement areas, different branches have formed, including the Landian Yao in Baise Lingyun, the Hong

Yao in Longsheng, Guilin, the Pan Yao in Guiping, Guigang, and the Bai Ku Yao in Nandan, Hechi. Due to differences in natural environment, geographical conditions, and ethnic aesthetics, the Yao ethnic group has developed its unique Yao costume culture, which was included in the first batch of national intangible cultural heritage list in 2006. Current research on Yao costumes mainly focuses on the changes in costume culture, research on historical and cultural connotations, aesthetic and artistic analysis of costume patterns, and innovative redesign and application of patterns. However, research and application of digitalization of Yao embroidery patterns are relatively scarce. This study combines Yao embroidery pattern art with modern science and technology, conducts research on Yao patterns, and applies digital processing methods to establish a digital interactive experience design system based on Yao embroidery patterns in Guangxi.

3   Significance of Yao Ethnic Embroidery in Guangxi

3.1   Characteristics of Yao Ethnic Embroidery Patterns

Yao ethnic embroidery patterns possess both explicit elements that convey ethnic features and implicit elements that reflect the cultural significance within the patterns. Stemming from ancient worship of deities, Yao embroidery patterns are often associated with religious beliefs. They extract elements from the natural world and modify them for application in everyday clothing, with the intention of blessing oneself and family with peace and prosperity. Yao embroidery encompasses a variety of motifs, including geometric patterns, animal motifs, plant motifs, celestial and landscape motifs, as well as wan motifs.

Pan Yao Sun Pattern (Fig. 1). According to ancient texts, "with the morning sun, there is the way, and the shaman mixes with it." Combined with the teachings of Buddhism, the religious nature of the Yao people is intensified, and their worship of ancestors and deities is strengthened. The "eight-pointed star," also known as the "sunburst," is believed to symbolize the worship of the "sun god." Some also believe that the "eight-pointed star" evolved from eight chrysanthemum flowers or lotus flowers. Living deep in the mountains all year round, experiencing frequent rainy seasons, and working in the fields, the sun shines with warm tones, providing ample sunlight. The eight-pointed star pattern resembles the radiance of the sun, spreading in all directions.

Pan Wang Seal (Fig. 2). Pan Wang is the ancestor of the Yao ethnic group, and the seal of Pan Wang's authority is called the "Pan Wang Seal." There is a rich folklore and image inheritance related to the Pan Wang Seal in Yao folklore, forming a cultural phenomenon of the Pan Wang Seal. To express reverence for their ancestors, the Pan Wang Seal often appears in Yao embroidery works. When embroidered on clothing, the Yao people wear it as a token of gratitude and to remember the great benevolence of Pan Wang. It also symbolizes their right to cultivate and manage the mountains, exempting them from grain taxes, corvée labor, and oppression by evil spirits, thus ensuring their safety.

The composition of the "Pan Wang Seal" pattern is rigorous and naturally simple, with a combination of vivid and rich graphic patterns that form a unique cultural language. From the types of patterns, they can generally be divided into five categories:

Fig. 1. Sun Pattern.

symbolic patterns, humanoid patterns, floral patterns, plant patterns, and animal patterns. Humans, plants, and animals are interdependent and interconnected, forming the foundation of the natural ecological system of the Yao ethnic group. Therefore, the "Pan Wang Seal" pattern includes humanoid patterns, floral patterns, and dragon-dog patterns, which respectively represent humans, plants, and animals. There are more than 20 common combinations of graphic patterns, including humanoid patterns, deer patterns, octagonal flower patterns, spider flower patterns, star patterns, pine cone patterns, boundary patterns, fishbone patterns, flower cluster patterns, floral patterns, bird patterns, swastika patterns, zigzag patterns, hoof print patterns, Pan Wang seal patterns, tofu grid patterns, flower bud patterns, lotus flower bud patterns, nut patterns, and more. Although these patterns are designed in a simple manner, they succinctly capture the beautiful characteristics and vivid imagery of the objects. For example, the octagonal flower pattern is created by rotating and mirroring two parallelograms along the central axis, making the graphic pattern lively and rich [2].

Fig. 2. Pan Wang Pattern.

Animal Patterns (Fig. 3). Common animal patterns include dog patterns (dragon-dog patterns), butterfly patterns, dragon and snake patterns, rooster patterns, spider patterns, and more. The worship of the ancestor "Pan Hu" associates the "dog" as the ancestral symbol. They are often depicted in pairs, connected back to back, appearing on the collar, hemline, or headscarf. Butterfly patterns also appear in pairs, symbolizing prosperity of offspring and the well-being of the household. White pants worn by the Bai Ku Yao people feature spider pattern embroidery, as they believe that the spider goddess can protect them, likening the spider to the mother of creation. Rooster patterns are considered auspicious by the Yao people, as the rooster crows while chasing the sun, symbolizing a bright and positive meaning.

Fig. 3. Animal Patterns.

Plant Patterns (Fig. 4). These include patterns of the Tree of Life, Divine Rod, grain seedlings, grass, and various other floral patterns. Plant patterns are often derived from observations and imaginations of natural elements. They abstract and summarize the shapes of plants, creating embroidered patterns that are playful and whimsical. The symbolism of these patterns is then incorporated into clothing. The Tree of Life pattern is commonly found on the pant legs of Bai Se Tianlin Pan Yao women's attire. The Yao people imbue this tree with the function of connecting with celestial beings. They believe it symbolizes continuous growth, upward progress, and the struggle against destiny. The pattern is typically embroidered on sleeves, pant legs, and headscarves, arranged in rows or groups. The grain seedling pattern represents abundant harvests and is often embroidered on the collar and pant legs, symbolizing the prosperous growth of crops and the people.

Geometric Patterns (Fig. 5). Common geometric patterns include thunder patterns, circle patterns, swastika patterns, spiral patterns, cloud patterns, and more. The structure of these patterns often involves continuous squares or continuous quadrilaterals. These geometric patterns are composed of simple elements such as dots, lines, and shapes like triangles, squares, circles, and diamonds. Through rotation or movement, they form vibrant totemic designs. The structure of these patterns is carefully designed and should not be altered randomly. They are often found on the collar, headscarf, hemline, and back of women's clothing.

Fig. 4. Plant Patterns.

Fig. 5. Geometric Patterns.

3.2 Extraction of Stylistic Features of Embroidery Patterns in Various Yao Subgroups in Guangxi

Guangxi is a region where the Han majority and various ethnic minorities coexist. They mutually influence and promote each other in terms of aesthetics and choice of themes. The worship of the Pan Hu, the Yao King, runs deep in the Yao people's blood. The stolen Pan Hu Seal, they embroider it on their clothing and suspenders as a way to remember the shame and to motivate their ethnic group to strive forward! Clothing is an external manifestation of ethnic beliefs. By observing their attire, one can understand their hearts [3].

(1) **Guangxi Jinxiu - Octagonal Flower Pattern, Hualan Yao Embroidered Suspenders.** In the Dayoutai area of Jinxiu, Guangxi, there are five Yao subgroups living

together, namely the Chashan Yao, Hualan Yao, Pan Yao, Shanzi Yao, and Aoyao. Among them, the Hualan Yao embroidery has the most intricate patterns, covering the sleeves from the head to the shoulders. The women's attire of the Hualan Yao is embroidered with exquisite and vibrant patterns, including blue flowers, gold and silver flowers, cornflowers, camellias, and octagonal flowers, all depicted vividly. "Hualan" means colorful or vibrant, hence the name "Hualan Yao." The Hualan Yao clothing is elegant and beautiful, and entering a Hualan Yao village feels like stepping into a garden.

The suspenders of various ethnic groups in Guangxi showcase a rich variety of patterns, each with its own unique expression. Generally, the patterns on the suspenders adopt symmetrical and balanced compositions, with similar or approximate patterns arranged symmetrically above and below the central line or center point, maintaining a strong sense of symmetrical beauty (Fig. 6).

Fig. 6. Symmetrical Patterns.

(2) **Jinxiu, Guangxi-Pan Yao Headscarf.** The Pan Yao clothing in Dayoutai consists of three types: red head attire, white head attire, and pointed head attire. The men's headscarf is 1 foot wide and 15 feet long, with 420 dogtooth flowers embroidered on both ends using red, yellow, and green silk threads. The headscarf is then folded into three layers and wrapped around the head in a crossed manner. In the southern part of Dayoutai, men wear headbands or headscarves mainly made of checkered gauze. In the central and northern parts of Dayoutai, the Pan Yao men's "pa" (headscarf) is

not made of checkered gauze but instead uses two black fabrics, with one end of one fabric embroidered with flowers. When wrapping the head, the unembroidered "pa" is opened and placed on the top of the head, while the unopened "pa" is wrapped around the head from right to left in a parallel manner. After the first fabric is wrapped, the end of the embroidered fabric is caught and wrapped around the head, with the embroidered end on the outer layer. Finally, it is secured with a "bottle thread," and the trailing end of the "bottle thread" is tucked into the layers of the "pa" at the back of the head (Fig. 7).

Fig. 7. Jinxiu Pan Yao Patterns.

(3) **Nandan, Guangxi-Wax-dyed Flower Patterns on the Back of Bai Ku Yao Women's Clothing.** There is an ancient ethnic group in Nandan County, Hechi, that has traversed through time and space, singing and drinking while cultivating their own land. They possess a deep understanding of joy and sorrow through their own dyeing and weaving. Their distinctive clothing style and diverse folk customs make them an intriguing group. They mainly reside in Bawu and Lihu Yao Ethnic Town in Nandan County. This ethnic group is the fascinating Bai Ku Yao (Fig. 8) that continuously captivates people's curiosity.

Due to historical and environmental factors, the clothing art of the Bai Ku Yao retains its precious originality, vivid historical significance, and rich, complete artistic expression.

(4) **Nandan, Guangxi-Lihu Bai Ku Yao Suspenders Heart (Fig. 9).** "Knee-length white trousers with embroidered large seals on the back" is a summary of Bai Ku Yao clothing. Bai Ku Yao **women's** attire can be divided into two types: ceremonial attire and casual attire. The ceremonial attire consists of four overlapping jackets and a pleated skirt, while the casual attire consists of a single jacket or a black top with a skirt. One distinctive feature is the jacket, which is composed of symmetrical square-shaped panels that are connected in the front and back. The central part is left open to expose the chest, and the front panel is black, while the back panel is dyed with a blue base. It is embroidered with the character "田" (tian), which represents the Yao King's seal.

Fig. 8. Nandan Yao Ethnic Patterns.

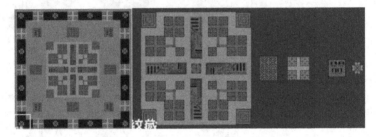

Fig. 9. Bai Ku Yao Suspenders Patterns.

(5) **Du'an, Guangxi-Qilin Pattern Dish-shaped Embroidered Suspenders Heart (Fig. 10).** Du'an Yao Autonomous County is located in Hechi City, Guangxi Zhuang Autonomous Region. In 2023, the traditional clothing production techniques of the Yao ethnic group in Du'an were included in the ninth batch of Guangxi Intangible Cultural Heritage list. The essence of the Yao ethnic group lies in their respect for the universe and all living things. They believe that everything in nature has its own life and deserves reverence, including wheat ears, flying birds, rivers, and even horses.

The Qilin pattern on the dish-shaped embroidered suspenders heart in Du'an represents the flourishing and prosperity of the ethnic group's lineage.

Fig. 10. Du'an Yao Ethnic Patterns.

4 The Significance of Yao Ethnic Embroidery Patterns in Yao Culture in Guangxi

4.1 The Relationship Between Yao Ethnic Embroidery Patterns and Traditional Yao Culture

The embroidery patterns of the Yao ethnic group in Guangxi are inseparable from their traditional culture. The inheritance of Yao ethnic embroidery patterns represents the continuation and development of their cultural traditions. Yao ethnic embroidery is considered a precious traditional craft, and the Yao people pass down their cultural wisdom and technical expertise to the younger generations. This inheritance goes beyond the transmission of techniques; it includes the transmission of traditional knowledge, aesthetic concepts, and values inherent in Yao culture. Yao ethnic embroidery has become an integral part of their culture.

The patterns and designs in Yao ethnic embroidery carry rich ethnic memories and cultural symbols, embodying the wisdom and emotions of the Yao people. It serves as an important carrier of Yao culture. Through the inheritance and display of embroidery patterns, the Yao people express their respect and appreciation for their cultural traditions, deepening their sense of identity and cultural roots.

4.2 Symbolic Significance and Social Functions of Yao Ethnic Embroidery Patterns in Guangxi

The Yao women often gather together during their leisure time to engage in embroidery. This practice serves as an important means of socializing, exchanging ideas, and learning skills. The exquisite craftsmanship and unique designs of embroidery works often represent the skill level and social status of the embroiderers.

The Yao ethnic embroidery, with its exquisite craftsmanship and distinctive design style, showcases the unique understanding and aesthetic pursuit of the Yao people towards nature and life. Embroidery patterns carry rich symbolic meanings, often representing the beliefs, values, and way of life of the Yao people. Elements such as flowers, animals, and geometric shapes in the patterns, conveyed through delicate lines and rich colors, convey the Yao people's pursuit of beauty and love for life.

Furthermore, Yao ethnic embroidery is widely used in the daily life of the Yao people. Embroidery decorations can be seen on Yao clothing, bedding, curtains, shoes, and hats, among other items. It is an important way for Yao women to showcase their skills and identity. Embroidery patterns are not only visually pleasing but also carry unique symbolic meanings. For example, floral patterns represent prosperity and happiness, while animal patterns represent auspiciousness and blessings. Therefore, Yao ethnic embroidery has become a significant symbol of Yao culture, representing the identity, honor, and traditional values of the Yao people, with profound historical and cultural significance.

4.3 Social Interaction and Ritual Activities of Yao Ethnic Embroidery Patterns in Guangxi

The Yao ethnic embroidery patterns play an important role in various ceremonies and events within Yao society, such as wedding ceremonies, festive celebrations, and religious rituals. Embroidery works are often considered essential items for weddings and important festivals, and they serve as significant gifts during Yao women's marriage and coming-of-age ceremonies.

The unique symbolic meanings carried by different embroidery patterns not only serve decorative and aesthetic purposes but also hold important functions in social life. The selection and use of embroidery patterns can convey different social messages and cultural connotations, deepening the emotional connections among the Yao people and promoting social cohesion and a sense of belonging.

4.4 Economic Income and Ethnic Industry of Yao Ethnic Embroidery in Guangxi

The Yao ethnic embroidery, as a traditional handicraft, not only has widespread applications within Yao communities but has also become an important ethnic industry in the Yao regions. Through the production and sale of embroidery, many Yao women are able to generate economic income, improve their living conditions, and contribute to the local economic development and the preservation of Yao culture.

In summary, Yao ethnic embroidery patterns hold a significant position in Yao culture and play multiple roles. They serve as a medium for artistic expression and aesthetic pursuit, symbolize cultural identity and traditional values of the Yao people, and also play an important role in social interaction and economic development. Preserving and inheriting the unique charm of Yao ethnic embroidery patterns and promoting the transmission and innovation of embroidery skills are of great significance in maintaining the diversity and richness of Yao culture.

5 Designing Digital Interactive Experiences for Yao Ethnic Embroidery Patterns in Guangxi

The goal of digital interactive experiences is to bring Yao ethnic embroidery art into the era of modern technology and provide participants with a unique way to explore the culture. Through digital platforms, the exquisite beauty of Yao embroidery is presented, allowing people to immerse themselves in the unique charm of Yao culture [4].

5.1 Digital Creation of Yao Ethnic Embroidery Patterns in Guangxi

Digital processing methods for Yao ethnic embroidery patterns in Guangxi involve techniques such as image scanning and vectorization to preserve the details and textures of the patterns. A digital creation tool is provided to allow users to design Yao embroidery patterns based on their own creativity and ideas. This tool may include basic drawing and pattern editing functions, allowing users to select different pattern elements, colors, and line styles for creation and adjustment.

5.2 Digital Exhibition of Yao Ethnic Embroidery Patterns in Guangxi

An online platform or mobile application can be developed to showcase high-definition images and detailed information about Yao ethnic embroidery patterns in Guangxi. This platform aims to demonstrate the rich diversity and unique characteristics of Yao embroidery patterns. Users can browse through a variety of embroidery patterns on the platform, while also learning about the cultural significance, historical background, and embroidery techniques associated with each pattern. The platform can also provide search functionality, allowing users to filter and search for patterns based on different themes, pattern types, or regions.

5.3 Community Interaction and Interactive Learning Module

Establishing a community feature and interactive learning module on the exhibition platform will provide functions for online learning, communication, and discussion. Through multimedia formats such as text, audio, and video, users will be introduced to the basic techniques, pattern design, and creative process of Yao embroidery patterns, enriching the educational resources and tutorials for Yao ethnic embroidery in Guangxi. The online communication and discussion features will enable enthusiasts of Guangxi Yao ethnic embroidery to share their creations, experiences, and stories with each other. Users can engage in virtual practice to learn basic embroidery skills, such as thread selection and embroidery needle techniques. They can also publish their own Yao embroidery works, exchange embroidery techniques, participate in embroidery competitions, and promote interaction and communication among users. The platform can also provide opportunities for collaborative projects, allowing users to participate together in embroidery design and production, thereby promoting diversity and innovation in embroidery pattern content.

5.4 Customization Services for Yao Ethnic Embroidery Patterns in Guangxi

Providing users with customized services for Yao ethnic embroidery patterns, users can choose specific patterns and product types (such as clothing, home decor, etc.) based on their preferences and needs. They can then communicate with Yao embroidery artisans to create personalized Yao embroidery pieces that are unique to them.

5.5 Virtual Reality Interactive Experience of Yao Ethnic Embroidery Patterns in Guangxi

Utilizing virtual reality technology, a design proposal is presented for a digitized interactive experience based on Yao ethnic embroidery patterns in Guangxi. The proposal involves creating a virtual environment that offers users a virtual try-on feature, allowing them to apply Yao embroidery patterns to virtual clothing models to gain a more intuitive understanding of how the patterns look on garments [5]. Users can select different clothing styles and Yao embroidery patterns to try on and mix and match. They can also interact with the embroidery patterns, combining digital technology to create new experiential forms. This immersive experience enables users to appreciate and experience the unique charm of Yao ethnic embroidery patterns in Guangxi.

The proposed digitized interactive experience includes learning embroidery techniques, creating personalized patterns, virtual try-on of Yao ethnic clothing, and participation in community interactions. It aims to provide more people with opportunities for learning, appreciation, and engagement by combining Yao embroidery patterns with digital technology. The goal is to offer users a comprehensive digitized interactive experience with Yao embroidery patterns, allowing them to gain a deeper understanding and experience of the unique charm of Yao ethnic culture. By arousing people's interest and love for Yao embroidery, the proposal aims to continue the heritage of Yao ethnic culture, encouraging active participation rather than mere observation. Users can infuse their creativity and passion into this traditional art form, allowing Yao embroidery, a precious cultural heritage, to be widely disseminated and recognized. Additionally, this proposal serves as a tribute to Yao ethnic culture, revitalizing it with new vitality and charm in the modern society.

6 Conclusion

This research aims to explore the design of digitized interactive experiences based on Yao ethnic embroidery patterns in Guangxi to promote cultural heritage and innovation. By combining traditional Yao ethnic embroidery patterns with digital interactive technology, new experiential forms are created to enhance user engagement and convey the unique charm of Yao ethnic culture. This study employs methods such as literature review, field research, and design experiments to systematically investigate the history, characteristics of Yao ethnic embroidery patterns in Guangxi, as well as the theories and technologies of digitized interactive experiences.

Throughout the design process, we have endeavored to preserve the traditional aesthetic beauty of Yao ethnic embroidery patterns while integrating virtual exhibitions, interactive games, and mobile applications to design various digitized interactive experience solutions. The research findings indicate that the design of digitized interactive experiences based on Yao ethnic embroidery patterns in Guangxi has the potential to promote cultural heritage and enhance user experiences. However, the study also has limitations that require further in-depth research and improvement. In the future, we will continue to explore the application of digitized interactive experiences in the field of Yao ethnic embroidery patterns in Guangxi and contribute to the development of cultural innovation and heritage preservation.

Foundations. Guangxi Educational Science Planning Project (China): "Research on the Integration Path of 'Art Education + Political Education' Design Education Based on Guangxi's Intangible Cultural Heritage Resources" (Program Code: 2021C360).

References

1. Yu, S.J.: The cultural connotation of Yao ethnic clothing patterns. J. Guangxi Minzu Univ. (Philos. Soc. Sci. Edn. (01), 38–41 (1994)
2. Yu, S.J.: Cultural Transformation of the Yao Ethnic Group. Ethnic Publishing House, Beijing (2005)

3. Chen, L.H.: Analysis of octagonal patterns in traditional Yao ethnic clothing in Northern Guangxi region. Artistic Spectacle **04**, 93–94 (2020)
4. Li, R.Y., Ma, H.: Digital application and dissemination of the Yao ethnic Panhu totem in clothing. Chem. Fiber Textile Technol. **51**(06), 75–77 (2022)
5. Wang, H.: Research on clothing design of Guangxi Yao ethnic group embroidery patterns from the perspective of regional culture. Western Leather **45**(09), 108–110 (2023)

Engaging Children in Cultural Heritage Through Book Craft: An Interaction Design Approach

Yunpeng Xiang and Cheng-Hung Lo[✉]

Xi'an Jiaotong-Liverpool University, 111 Renai Road, Suzhou, China
ChengHung.Lo@xjtlu.edu.cn

Abstract. From a trans-disciplinary perspective, this paper presents a child-centered cultural heritage interpretation project that incorporates interaction design techniques into the development of a physical lapbook. We engaged 74 primary school students aged 9–10 from Suzhou, China in the co-design process. This involved understanding users and their needs, framing information architecture, designing interactive elements, testing and refinements, and implementing the final design. The process resulted in the collaborative creation of a lapbook introducing Suzhou food heritages. Observation and questionnaire survey were carried out to evaluate participants' engagement and heritage comprehension. The finding showed the project has positively impacted users' knowledge acquisition, comprehension, willingness to share, and overall satisfaction. Interaction design techniques also effectively transferred into crafting the physical storybook. The project demonstrates the value of a co-design process and interaction design principles for engaging audience in heritage interpretations and developing non-digital media such as books.

Keywords: Cultural Heritage · Interaction Design · Lapbook · Heritage Interpretation

1 Introduction

Engaging children in the exploration of intangible cultural heritages is an ongoing subject of interest for multiple countries, with UNESCO (2003) emphasizing the significance of both formal and informal heritage education in transmitting these cultural heritages. Tilden (1977) had early discussed the heritage interpretation for children is never a simplified copy of the one for adults. It needs to produce inner connect between the children through creating immersive experience with multi adoptable medium, inspiring the children to think rather than just being taught, and finally forming their own comprehension of cultural heritages. Currently, numerous heritage interpreting projects have been implemented to actively involve children, wherein researchers strive to create engaging and playful environments that align with children's psychological characteristics. Examples includes the heritage educational activities with new high-techs like VR/AR in museums, schools and communities (Köse and Akmehmet, 2023; Pérez-Guilarte et al.

2023), the digital games, picture books, and teaching aids toys with bright colors and vivid forms (He 2020; Tang 2020). In light of these interpretation works, the children's books play a vital role to enable children to perceive, immerse and nourish themselves in the rich traditional cultural expressions and ecological spaces. Books combine rich graphic, lively storyline, and intuitive uses and thus is an appropriate medium for the early cognitive development stage (Wang and Cheng 2021).

In the current era populated with digital or integrated forms of multiple media, traditional children's books are facing challenges from behavioral and habitual changes of readers. Crafts or techniques were thus developed or innovated to make reading physical books a multidimensional and interactive experience (Zhou 2012; Jiang 2019). Design of interactive books has become a subject of intense interest and is a well-adopted format in promoting cultural heritages (Zhang and Zhang 2021). Especially for intangible cultural heritages, interactive books have distinct advantages in illustrating vividly the craft process while retaining other sensory experiences such as touch and physical embodiment (Qian and Wang, 2023). However, majority of these previous studies and practices have their focus on the user experience during reading the completed books. The users (children) received the information passively, following pre-fixed reading flows. Our project aims to investigate the feasibility of incorporating users into the book design process and framing their participation as part of the whole experience, thereby granting users initiative to acquire the conveyed knowledge through active engagements.

In this study, we engaged with 74 primary school students aged 9–10 from Suzhou, China in collaboratively creating a lapbook focusing on the cultural heritage of Suzhou food. Specifically, we structured the design process with interactive design techniques, which were commonly practiced for developing digitally based interactive systems. Observations and user feedback were also gathered to examine the approach's impact on users' knowledge acquisition, comprehension, willingness to share, and overall satisfaction with the experience.

2 Related Work

Cultural heritages, being integral components of traditional culture, play a pivotal role in the preservation and transmission of national cultures. Extensive research has been conducted to explore strategies for revitalizing both tangible and intangible cultural heritages within contemporary society, and the consensus is that the fulfilment need the public participation and awareness of cultural heritages as much as possible (Pirkovič 2023). Interpreting cultural heritage through diverse media becomes crucial for safeguarding and enhancing public awareness of heritages. Particularly when targeting children, it is essential to exercise caution and ensure a wide range of media options are available, and the interpretation is not a mere transmission and enumeration of information to children, but aims to connect the heritages with their personalities and experience and provokes their further discussion and thinking (Tilden 1977). The rather popular media devoting to the cultural heritage interpretation for children is the children's books (Vrcić-Mataija 2023), and in China, there are plenty practices of children's book to introduce national cultural heritages, e.g., 'Chinese intangible cultural heritage' series published by Hunan Children's Publishing House (Tang 2023). Meanwhile, the further researches explored the possible development of children's books interpreting heritages through combining multi techniques, like emerging materials and crafts and VR/AR techniques, to accommodate children's changing psychological needs and reading habits, as well as enhancing their reading experience (Jiang 2019; Polyzou et al. 2023). Treating reading activities as a user experience, the interactive design techniques may be adaptable in developing the children's books interpreting cultural heritages.

Interaction design draws on psychological principles to shape user experiences. This includes Fitts's Law for clear information delivery (MacKenzie 1992), flow theory for immersive engagement (Wang and Pan 2021), and Gestalt theory for intuitive interfaces (Kapllani and Elmimouni 2020). Incorporating these would support creating children's books that foster deeper understanding through immersive reading experiences (Hou and Lien 2022). Lapbooks uniquely integrate interactivity through movable elements. This enables designing engaging content structures, task flows, and user behaviors. The multi-sensory interactions in lapbooks can heighten emotional connection, interest, and learning for young readers (Samrin et al. 2023). Therefore, grounding lapbook creation in interaction design provides a potent approach to crafting captivating heritage interpretation tools.

3   Methods

The project aimed to engage children in local food heritages by inviting them to co-create a lapbook on the chosen theme. To enhance their curiosity, enthusiasm, and comprehension, interactive design techniques were employed for developing this project. Additionally, observation and questionnaires were utilized during the co-creation process to assess the children's engagement and gather feedback. In collaboration with a local primary school, we invited 74 Grade 3 students to participate in the project. To facilitate active engagement and simulate real-world collaboration, our project utilized role-play by having students imagine working in an editorial office. At the start of the co-design process, primary school students were introduced to the conceptual framework of an editorial team tasked with creating a storybook. The students, divided into 3 groups, were given three sub-topics: Suzhou traditional dish, flour food, and sticky rice cake. The subsequent sections will elaborate on how we conducted an interactive and collaborative designing experience that introduced Suzhou's local food heritages to the children.

3.1   Stage 1: Understanding Users and Their Needs

In this project, the students are both co-designers and users of the lapbook. Their active involvement in the design process helps gain a clear understanding of their thoughts, preferences and requirements of this project (Maguire 2001). We gave the students two tasks to complete. After that, we obtained a general understanding of their prior knowledge, and they also knew the exact information on local food heritages they preferred to receive.

To assess students' familiarity with local Suzhou food heritage, we firstly designed a BINGO activity using traditional Suzhou dishes and hometown foods. Students were instructed to sign their name in boxes next to dishes they recognized. Linking 5 signature boxes in a line would yield a "BINGO." Figs. 1 and 2 show the BINGO card design and gameplay. None achieved BINGO, indicating low familiarity with Suzhou cuisine. Only 2 dishes were widely recognized - Qingtuan sticky rice cakes and Haitang cakes. This reflected students' limited knowledge of Suzhou food heritage. However, it was observed that the activity sparked curiosity and willingness to learn more. Students expressed enthusiasm for garnering greater knowledge about Suzhou's culinary traditions. This positive engagement provided a promising start for the heritage interpretation project.

Fig. 1. Sample image of the 'BINGO' game of Suzhou traditional food

Fig. 2. Students playing the 'BINGO' game

A follow-up study list task (Fig. 3) encouraged students to interview peers and gather impressions, interests, and questions about Suzhou food heritage. Their initial impressions centered on unrelated cuisines like ramen and pasta, highlighting insufficient background knowledge of Suzhou traditions (Fig. 4). However, building on the BINGO activity, students demonstrated curiosity by brainstorming questions including:

- What is the meaning behind dish names?
- What are the flavors and textures?
- When are dishes consumed?
- How are they cooked?
- Who invented them?
- What are the stories behind them?
- How do they differ from other cuisines?

These insights established design goals for the lapbook - answering the students' questions while presenting information that stimulates ongoing interest and curiosity about Suzhou culinary heritage. The study list offered promising indicators, despite limited initial knowledge. We observed that students were eager to fill knowledge gaps and engage more deeply with Suzhou's food traditions through tailored heritage interpretation.

Fig. 3. Image of the study list

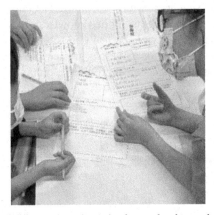

Fig. 4. Students interviewing each other and to complete the study list

3.2   Stage 2: Framing the Information Architecture

The second stage focused on framing the lapbook's information architecture to address students' questions from stage one. Organizing information can be tedious for young students. To promote ongoing engagement, we applied flow theory principles - balancing skill and challenge to yield satisfaction and participation (Csikszentmihalyi and LeFevre 1989). We adjusted difficulty by simplifying and pre-gathering information on Suzhou cuisine. Simplified text and visuals were pinned randomly around the classroom. Through group discussion, students identified relevant links to match 6 foods. The research team guided classification into logical categories like ingredients, cooking, flavors and anecdotes - mapping to earlier questions. This achievable yet challenging task allowed students to take ownership over structuring the information architecture (Figs. 5 and 6). Flow theory informed the design to maintain active participation in assembling framework components. Students experienced satisfaction through their efforts to logically organize accessible heritage content. This co-design process enabled them to actively shape the lapbook's information architecture aligned to their knowledge interests.

3.3   Stage 3: Designing Interactive Elements

We adopted interaction design techniques considering each book page as an interactive interface. As Moggridge (2007) described, interaction design involves shaping user behavior, task flow, and information structure. Stage 3 leveraged the established information architecture to design page layouts and reading sequences. Students organized ingredient lists, cooking methods, flavor profiles, and anecdotes logically within each page spread (Figs. 7 and 8). The research team provided guidance on interface and layout

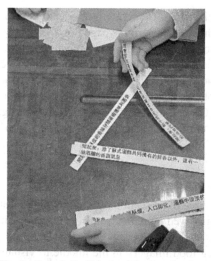

Fig. 5. Descriptive labels of Suzhou food heritages

Fig. 6. Students discussing how to arrange the descriptive information

principles for presenting different information types clearly. For example, bulleted lists for concise ingredients, paragraph text for anecdotal stories, and visual diagrams for cooking steps. This application of interaction design facilitated intuitive page layouts with logical reading flow. Students gained hands-on experience tailoring information presentation and reading guidance for target users. The iterative refinement of page templates enabled them to actively shape the lapbook's look, feel, and narrative experience from a reader's perspective.

Fig. 7. Students discussing about the page layout

Fig. 8. Students arranging the layout

We provided design guidance grounded in interaction principles. Students grouped related content in proximity and separated unrelated information, following Gestalt psychology layout rules (Li and Cao 2019). We advised labeling distinct information types with consistent colors for easy identification per interaction design conventions

134 Y. Xiang and C.-H. Lo

(Kumar and Goundar 2019; Mokhtar and Aziz 2022). Centering user-friendly experiences, students considered their own reading habits to determine page flow. Most opted to foreground captivating graphics over text. To boost engagement, we suggested playful "flip-up" questions to reveal answers underneath, inspired by conversational interfaces (McTear, 2016). For example, "What is Aozao?" invites flipping the flap to read about the noodle's origin. This interactive format blends attractive visuals, intuitive layouts, and engaging reveals to prompt participation. Grounding decisions in interaction design principles equipped students to intentionally craft page experiences from the reader's perspective.

3.4 Stage 4: Testing and Refinement

The students' draft lapbook pages contained three main sections aligning with the categorized food information (Fig. 9). The top displayed ingredients upfront with cooking methods revealed in a flippable interaction, as students felt seeing ingredients logically precedes cooking. They centered eye-catching food imagery in the middle to visually represent flavors. Attractive questions were placed at the bottom to encourage flipping up the flap to uncover origin stories and anecdotes. This considered layout grounded page regions in the four information types. The ingredient-cooking sections provided utility. Vibrant food images created appeal. Compelling questions enabled discovery. The students intuitively aligned layout with reading priorities and interactive patterns. Their designs demonstrated assimilation of interaction design techniques to guide information presentation. The modular page system effectively integrated text, visuals and interactions based on user perspective.

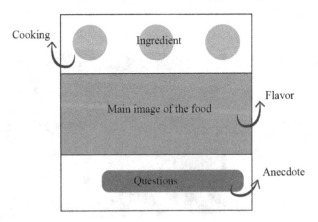

Fig. 9. The content structure of the book page

3.5 Stage 5: Implementing the Final Design

To finish the design process, the research team created display boards showcasing page layouts, information types, and interactive flaps (Fig. 10). We held a mini exhibition inviting students to view pages with friends (Fig. 11). This shared the outcomes broadly after collaborative ideation. We also selected several students' designs to recreate as a physical lapbook (Fig. 12). Producing this final prototype provided closure by materializing their visions. The celebratory exhibition and sample lapbook enabled students to see their work transformed from concepts to completed artifacts. The polished lapbooks offered an engaging endpoint to the co-design journey. Students took pride in their creations being valued, displayed, and produced in final form. This exhibition brought satisfying closure while propagating their work.

Fig. 10. Display boards of book pages

Fig. 11. Students reading the display boards

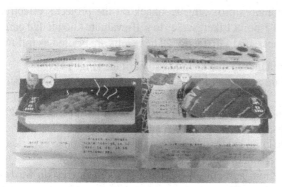

Fig. 12. Photo of the polished lapbooks

Fig. 13. Students sharing their understandings on local food heritages

4   Results and Discussion

We conducted a reflective session to have students summarized their understanding of Suzhou's culinary heritage and culture (Fig. 13). Their writings highlighted characteristics like "sweet taste," "fine shapes," and "fresh" ingredients (Table 1). Most appropriately captured local flavors, cooking methods, and seasonal diets. Compared to their initial knowledge, students demonstrated enriched comprehension of Suzhou's food traditions. Where previously they lacked exposure, they now grasped defining traits like seasonal freshness and delicate flavors. The concluding reflections evidenced growth in applying knowledge gained through the co-design process. Students progressed from unfamiliarity to outlining emblematic qualities of Suzhou cuisine. This displayed enhanced learning and engagement with the local intangible cultural heritage.

Table 1. Samples of students' understanding on local food heritages

Key phrases extracted from student writings	Matching characteristics of local food heritage and cuisine culture
Taste sweet	Typical flavor in sweet and fresh
Very fresh	
Funny and nice-looking shapes	Local cooking style with rich details in process and meaningful well-display in name and shapes
Complex cooking process	
Many details hidden	
Many strange names of food	
Many ingredients from water	Seasonal diet blessed with a moderate climate of distinctive seasons and rich produce
Eat different in seasons	

Students completed questionnaires providing feedback on the project's effectiveness. The 7-question survey used 5-point Likert scales to self-evaluate knowledge gains, comprehension, sharing willingness, and satisfaction. The results are briefed as follows:

- 78% felt they achieved understanding of Suzhou food heritage (Fig. 14).
- 79% appreciated acquiring and analyzing knowledge through the co-design process (Fig. 15).
- Self-reported comprehension of heritage cuisine was also high, with less than 20% responding explicitly with disagreements (Figs. 16 and 17).
- However, willingness to share knowledge (64%) exceeded taking action to experience foods learned (26%) by project's end (Figs. 18 and 19).
- Over 60% expressed satisfaction, agreeing the project sparked interest in Suzhou cuisine versus other activities (Fig. 20).

In summary, the questionnaire revealed students believed they expanded knowledge and comprehension of Suzhou's culinary traditions through active participation. While many were willing to share insights, fewer had already put new knowledge into practice. Nonetheless, strong majorities conveyed enjoyment and interest in the heritage theme.

We conducted comparative analysis between the three student groups focusing on different topics - Suzhou dishes, flour foods, and sticky rice cakes. ANOVA results (Table 2) showed statistically significant group differences across the 7 questionnaire items and 4 dimensions - knowledge, comprehension, sharing willingness, and satisfaction ($p < 0.005$). Table 3 summarizes the mean scores, with Class 1, 2, and 3 representing

'After the courses, I have known the secrets of Suzhou food heritage,
including its ingredients and cooking process.'

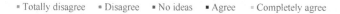

■ Totally disagree   ■ Disagree   ■ No ideas   ■ Agree   ▪ Completely agree

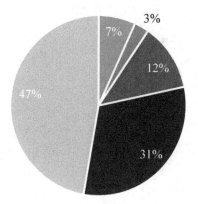

Fig. 14. Perceived knowledge acquisition on Suzhou food heritages

'I have learned how to collect, select, identify and integrate
information of Suzhou-style food heritage.'

■ Totally disagree   ■ Disagree   ▪ No ideas   ■ Agree   ▪ Completely agree

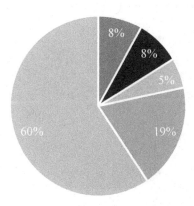

Fig. 15. Perceived learning on the information collection and analysis

the groups for dishes, flour foods, and cakes respectively. Class 1 scores were markedly lower than the other two groups, while Class 3 provided the most positive responses. This aligns with Stage 1, where students showed greater baseline familiarity with sticky rice cakes. Students gained more knowledge, understanding, willingness to share, and satisfaction when building on pre-existing heritage awareness. This suggests future projects

'I can understand and enjoy the stories of Suzhou food heritages.'

■ Totally disagree   ■ Disagree   ■ No ideas   ■ Agree   ■ Completely agree

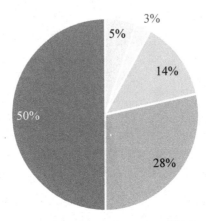

Fig. 16. Perceived understanding on the stories of Suzhou food heritages

'I can understand some local traditional culture through learning the food heritages in this project.'

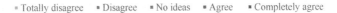

■ Totally disagree   ■ Disagree   ■ No ideas   ■ Agree   ■ Completely agree

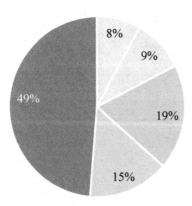

Fig. 17. Perceived cultural understanding of the local cuisine

should leverage familiar entry points before expanding to less known areas. Starting from familiar ground can boost engagement.

'I would like to share the knowledge from this project with my family and friends.'

▪ Totally disagree   ▪ Disagree   ▪ No ideas   ▪ Agree   ▪ Completely agree

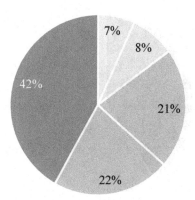

Fig. 18. Preference on sharing the apprehended knowledge

'After the course, I have invited my family to taste the food we learned in the class.'

▪ Yes   ▪ No

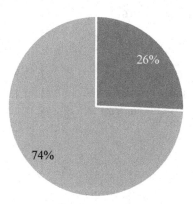

Fig. 19. Achieved sharings

'Different with other food-related projects, it made me feel more enjoyable and Suzhou-style food more interesting and attractive.'

· Totally disagree   · Disagree   ▪ No ideas   ▪ Agree   ▪ Completely agree

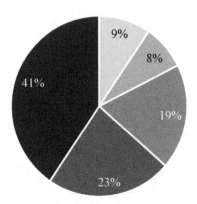

Fig. 20. Overall satisfaction of the experience

Table 2. ANOVA results

		Sum of Squares	df	Mean Square	F	Sig
After the project, I have invited my family to taste the food we learned in the class	Between Groups	4.503	2	2.251	16.619	.000
	Within Groups	9.619	71	.135		
	Total	14.122	73			
After the project, I have known what is Suzhou food heritages, including its ingredient and cooking	Between Groups	15.612	2	7.806	6.866	.002
	Within Groups	80.726	71	1.137		
	Total	96.338	73			

(continued)

Table 2. (*continued*)

		Sum of Squares	df	Mean Square	F	Sig
I would like to share the knowledge from this project with my family and friends	Between Groups	32.658	2	16.329	14.244	.000
	Within Groups	81.396	71	1.146		
	Total	114.054	73			
I have learned how to collect, select, identify and integrate information of Suzhou food heritages	Between Groups	34.976	2	17.488	13.847	.000
	Within Groups	89.673	71	1.263		
	Total	124.649	73			
I can understand and enjoy the stories of Suzhou food heritages	Between Groups	15.636	2	7.818	7.529	.001
	Within Groups	73.729	71	1.038		
	Total	89.365	73			
I can know some local traditional culture through learning the food heritages in this project	Between Groups	34.110	2	17.055	12.543	.000
	Within Groups	96.538	71	1.360		
	Total	130.649	73			
Different with other food-related course, it made me feel more enjoyable and Suzhou-style food more interesting and attractive	Between Groups	102.416	2	51.208	147.325	.000
	Within Groups	24.679	71	.348		
	Total	127.095	73			

Table 3. Means Plots of 7 questions

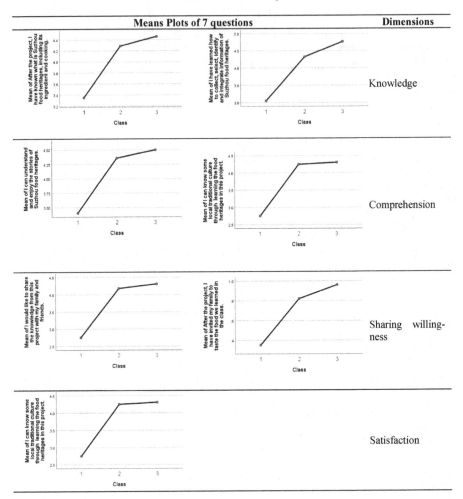

5 Conclusion

This project developed a cultural heritage interpretation co-design process for primary students focused on Suzhou's food traditions. We adapted the interaction design process and applied corresponding techniques to guide the creation of a lapbook. Starting with playful tasks identifying the students' needs, we set goals to address their curiosity about Suzhou cuisine. They were then engaged in shaping information architecture, designing interactive elements embodied in page content, prototype testing and refinement, and implementing the final design. Observations of the process and analysis of final feedback showed the value of this participatory and interaction design-led approach for heritage learning. Students displayed strong outcome across knowledge, comprehension, sharing willingness, and satisfaction regarding Suzhou food. Further comparisons between cuisine themes revealed the importance of leveraging familiar and connectable entry points before expanding to less known areas. The co-design process allows youth to shape experiences that educate through discovery. This fusion of participation, cultural learning, and interaction design holds meaningful potential for engaging intangible cultural heritage.

While this project provides an initial model for youth co-design of heritage lapbooks, future work could apply the process to more intangible cultural topics, conduct longitudinal assessments of impact, quantitatively evaluate knowledge gains, and integrate external heritage knowledge through partnerships. There are also opportunties to iteratively refine, expand, and enhance this participatory approach to elevate youth engagement with intangible cultural heritage across an array of themes, formats, and knowledge-building collaborations.

References

UNESCO. Text of the Convention for the Safeguarding of the Intangible Cultural Heritage (2003). https://ich.unesco.org/en/convention

Tilden, F.: Interpreting Our Heritage Third Edition (1977)

Köse, F., Akmehmet, K.T.: The examination of the educational activities for intangible cultural heritage of toy museum in Türkiye. J. Int. Museum Educ. 5, 1–14 (2023). https://doi.org/10.51637/jimuseumed.1220313

Pérez-Guilarte, Y., Gusman, I., Lois González, R.C.: Understanding the significance of cultural heritage in society from preschool: an educational practice with student teachers. Heritage 6(9), 6172–6188 (2023). https://doi.org/10.3390/heritage6090324

Vrcić-Mataija, S.: Transfer of oral fairy tales into the medium of picture books – (Re) interpretation of cultural heritage in croatian native picture books (2023)

He, R.: Innovative design research on the localization of children's playing teaching aids under the view of intangible cultural heritage. Innov. Des. 6, 35–39 (2020). https://doi.org/10.3969/J.ISSN.1674-4187.2020.06.005

Tang, T.: Children's intangible cultural heritage game design based on serious game theory. China Pack. 40(11), 3 (2020)

Wang, M., Cheng, G.: The practical path of intangible cultural heritage picture book. China Publ. J. (2), 36–39 (2021). https://doi.org/10.3969/j.issn.1002-4166.2021.02.007

Zhou, Z.: Study on book design in the context of multimedia era. China Acad. Art (2012). https://doi.org/10.7666/d.Y2200366

Jiang, L.: Dimensional space of book design: exploration on interactive-experience-designed education through printed books under the background of new media age. Des. Educ. (6), 85–90 (2019). https://doi.org/10.3969/J.ISSN.1674-4187.2019.06.013

Zhang, Z., Zhang, T.: Design of interactive experience books from the perspective of cultural innovation. Packa. Eng. 42(20), 267–275, 282 (2021). https://doi.org/10.19554/j.cnki.1001-3563.2021.20.030

Qian, J., Wang, X.: Design of interactive experience book: su deng based on cultural heritage protection. Packa. Eng. 44(14), 297–305 (2023). https://doi.org/10.19554/j.cnki.1001-3563.2023.14.032

Pirkovič, J.: Model of heritage interpretation tailored to public co-participation. Ars & Humanitas: Revija Za Umetnost in Humanistiko 17(1), 251–270 (2023). https://doi.org/10.4312/ars.17.1.251-270

Tang, S.: Using picture books to empower China's intangible cultural heritages. Democracy monthly (2023). https://www.mj.org.cn/zsjg/mzzzs/mzzxyd/yj/202303/t20230303_275 052.htm

Polyzou, S., Botsoglou, K., Zygouris, N.C., Stamoulis, G.: Interactive books for preschool children: from traditional interactive paper books to augmented reality books: listening to children's voices through mosaic approach. Education 3–13 **51**(6), 881–892–892 (2023). https://doi.org/10.1080/03004279.2021.2025131

MacKenzie, I.S.: Fitts' law as a research and design tool in human-computer interaction. Human-Comput. Interact. **7**(1), 91 (1992). https://doi.org/10.1207/s15327051hci0701_3

Wang, C., Pan, Y.: Research on interactive picture book design of children's education based on flow theory. Jpn. J. Ergon. **57**(Supplement-2), K10 (2021). https://doi.org/10.5100/jje.57.K10

Kapllani, L., Elmimouni, H.: Gestalt principles in web design: a study of the usage of similarity, symmetry and closure in today's websites. Proc. Assoc. Inf. Sci. Technol. **57**(1), e340 (2020). https://doi.org/10.1002/pra2.340

Hou, H.-I., Lien, W.-C.: Students' critical thinking skills in an interactive EMI learning context: combining experiential learning and reflective practices. IUP J. Engl. Stud. **17**(2) (2022)

Samrin, S., Riansyah, F., Patih, T., Tarty, I.P., Nastiti, D.K.: Enhancing mathematical interest and learning outcomes: the lift-the-flap book incorporating tolaki local wisdom and islamic values. Tadris: Jurnal Keguruan Dan Ilmu Tarbiyah **8**(1), 33–47 (2023). https://doi.org/10.24042/tad ris.v8i1.14206

Maguire, M.: Methods to support human-centred design. Int. J. Hum Comput Stud. **55**(4), 587–634 (2001). https://doi.org/10.1006/ijhc.2001.0503

Csikszentmihalyi, M., LeFevre, J.: Optimal Experiencein Work and Leisure (1989)

Moggridge, B.: Designing Interactions. The MIT Press, Cambridge (2007)

Li, B., Cao, Y.: Research on layout design of main interface of stadium monitoring system based on gestalt psychology. In: Yamamoto, Sakae, Mori, H. (eds.) HCII 2019. LNCS, vol. 11569, pp. 44–55. Springer, Cham (2019). https://doi.org/10.1007/978-3-030-22660-2_4

Kumar, B.A., Goundar, M.S.: Usability heuristics for mobile learning applications. Educ. Inf. Technol. Off. J. IFIP Tech. Committee Educ. **24**(2), 1819–1833 (2019). https://doi.org/10.1007/s10639-019-09860-z

Mokhtar, E.S., Omar, A.C., Aziz, N.: Expert consensus on formation of design principles for malay sign language mobile application based on Nielsen's and Molich's design guidelines. TEM J. **11**(2), 585–593 (2022). https://doi.org/10.18421/TEM112-12

McTear, M.: The conversational interface. In: Callejas, Z., Griol, D. (eds.) Talking to Smart Devices. Springer, Heidleberg (2016)

Application of Motion Capture Technology in Ethnic Costume Cultural and Creative Products: Taking Guangxi Zhuang Ethnic Culture as an Example

Yue Yan[✉]

School of Art and Design, Xiangsihu College of Guangxi Minzu University, Nanning 530225, China
2249171251@qq.com

Abstract. Aim: Motion capture technology is a digital means that has been widely applied in fields such as film animation, gaming entertainment, and virtual reality. Any artwork is a combination of material and spiritual elements, and ethnic costumes are no exception. With industrial development, traditional skills related to ethnic costumes have gradually been replaced by machines, making the protection and promotion of ethnic cultural connotations even more important. In the digital age, utilizing digital means to promote the cultural connotations of ethnic costumes is a question worth considering. **Methods:** By employing a three-level model of emotion-based design, the digital cultural and creative design of ethnic costumes can be analyzed. While protecting and inheriting intangible cultural heritage, emotion-based design can guide the design process from cultural, interactive, and transformative perspectives, promoting the simultaneous development of the cultural connotations and traditional craftsmanship of ethnic costumes. **Results:** By focusing on the cultural content of ethnic costumes, designing visual and auditory elements, and incorporating interactive features, the application of motion capture technology in the emotion-based cultural and creative design of ethnic costumes can enhance production efficiency and strengthen presentation effects, thereby facilitating the digital dissemination and development of ethnic culture. Taking the culture of the Zhuang ethnic group in Guangxi as an example, the application of digital methods such as motion capture technology in the design of digital cultural and creative products related to ethnic costumes can drive the digital dissemination of ethnic costume culture. **Conclusion:** This paper guided by emotion-based design, discusses the multi-level design of digital cultural and creative products, including cultural, interactive, and transformative aspects. It explores the application of motion capture technology to assist in the design of cultural and creative products related to ethnic costumes. By exploring relevant design methods and practices, this paper enriches the theoretical research on ethnic costume cultural and creative products and provides some references.

Keywords: Motion Capture Technology · Ethnic Costumes Ethnic Culture · Digital Cultural and Creative · Emotion-Based Design

P.-L. P. Rau (Ed.): HCII 2024, LNCS 14701, pp. 145–160, 2024.
https://doi.org/10.1007/978-3-031-60904-6_11

1 Instruction

In traditional cultural creative communication, the dissemination speed of materialized forms is limited and easily influenced by various external factors, such as the price of cultural and creative products and physical damage. Good design concepts are necessary to effectively convey cultural stories. By employing digital means such as images, videos, games, etc., cultural stories can be told more easily and intuitively. Digital means can reduce the cost of cultural dissemination, increase the replicability of cultural content, and enhance the speed of dissemination. In the digital environment, the rich variety of expressive modes provides limitless narrative possibilities.

Different regional cultures nurture unique ethnic identities, and strengthening ethnic cultural identity and external recognition is an important issue. By exploring the transformation and development of ethnic costume cultural and creative products in the digital age through digital technology and expressive modes, the diversification of ethnic culture can be promoted.

On November 18, 2020, the Ministry of Culture and Tourism of China issued an opinion on promoting the high-quality development of the digital cultural industry, which emphasized the importance of "promoting the digitization of excellent cultural resources." The opinion encourages the utilization of local distinctive cultural resources to develop digital cultural products with distinct regional and ethnic characteristics, in support of poverty alleviation and development [1]. China is home to 56 ethnic groups, each with unique cultural features. In the era of active digital transformation across various industries worldwide, organizing outstanding local cultural content and utilizing digital means to promote traditional Chinese culture and Chinese ethnic culture can create digital cultural products that are more easily disseminated and consumed. This, in turn, can facilitate both online and offline sales of related ethnic cultural and creative products, thereby contributing to the creation of more employment opportunities.

Products are ubiquitous consumer goods in people's daily lives and can be categorized into material products (physical goods) and non-material products (services). Cultural and creative products refer to products that, while meeting people's usage needs, emphasize cultural services through creative design. China possesses abundant ethnic cultural resources, and the rapid and intuitive differentiation of different ethnic groups is often achieved through clothing and other visual means. Each ethnic group has multiple branches with distinct languages and clothing characteristics, making it crucial to conduct cultural classification research for each ethnic group and its branches. In the academic research field, there has been extensive research on ethnic minorities, and cultural and creative products serve as important tools for effectively disseminating and popularizing ethnic minority cultures.

2   Development Opportunities for Ethnic Costume Cultural and Creative Products in the Digital Era

2.1   Enhancing the Dissemination Speed of Ethnic Culture Through the Digital Transformation of Creative Products

The dissemination of cultural information in material form is limited in speed and susceptible to external factors, necessitating the use of effective design concepts to convey cultural stories. The design of cultural and creative products can be categorized into three levels: cultural image, cultural content, and cultural connotation. The integration of digital tools, such as images, videos, games, VR/AR, with material cultural and creative products, enables a more intuitive narration of cultural stories, reduces dissemination costs, increases content replicability, and enhances the speed of cultural transmission. In the digital era, advancing the digital transformation of cultural and creative products not only satisfies the growing demand for spiritual enrichment but also accelerates cultural dissemination, while expanding the social and economic benefits of the digital industry.

2.2   Enriched Digital Creative Presentations Promote the Diversified Development of Ethnic Culture

Material cultural and creative products are often associated with practical items such as stationery, clothing, and figurines. In the material realm, the expression of culture is confined to specific forms and spaces, posing challenges for designers to effectively convey cultural stories. However, in the digital environment, diverse digital presentation methods offer unlimited narrative possibilities.

Zhang Chong classified material cultural and creative products into categories such as office and daily supplies, decorative souvenirs, and collaboration items, while digital forms include graphic and textual content, short videos, film and television, virtual reality, programming (H5 mini-programs, apps), games, NFTs, and expression skins [2]. Material-based cultural creation and dissemination combine cultural content with practical and tangible objects, integrating cultural transmission into the daily lives of the masses. Digital forms allow for the reorganization and integration of cultural content, providing expandability and technological richness, enriching the spiritual lives of the general public. Exploring the successful combination of material and digital aspects of cultural and creative products facilitates the effective dissemination of cultural connotations on both material and spiritual levels.

Lu Rui categorized the digital presentation methods of cultural and creative products as follows: ① Radar induction - individual cultural and creative products, ② Online apps - dynamic presentation of graphic images, ③Sensory interactive systems - consumer participatory design, ④ Projection fusion technology - immersive experience, ⑤ Installation art experiential spaces - promotion and dissemination of cultural and creative products [3]. Different types of digital technologies inject infinite possibilities into cultural creativity. By employing digital technologies to assist in the design of existing cultural and creative product forms through the integration of "material + digital," or by constructing digital systems around cultural themes such as websites, apps, mini-programs, H5 pages, VR, AR, games, and audiovisual libraries, a "digital universe" is created, enhancing individual interactivity and engagement with cultural creative content. The use of digital technology and installations expands offline exhibition forms of cultural and creative products, creating immersive cultural experiential spaces at the collective level.

In the past, different regional cultures have given rise to diverse ethnicities, each with its unique cultural images and connotations. Today, the development of information technology has eliminated temporal boundaries in regional exchanges, while spatial obstacles have diminished due to high-speed transportation. How to strengthen the sense of cultural identity and external recognition of various ethnic cultures in an era characterized by technological advancement, networking, information dissemination, and homogenization is a thought-provoking question. By embracing the richness of digital technology and expressive means, exploring the transformation and development of ethnic costume cultural creative products in the digital age, we can enhance the speed of ethnic cultural dissemination and promote the diversified development of ethnic culture.

3 The Application Value of Motion Capture Technology in Fashion Cultural Creative Products

3.1 Promoting the Digitization of Ethnic Fashion Products

As of November 26, 2023, a total of 51 relevant literature on "ethnic fashion cultural creative products" were retrieved from the CNKI platform in China. The number of literatures is relatively small, mainly focusing on the design application of ethnic elements in cultural creative products. Among them, the top 10 most cited topics include "Yao ethnic clothing patterns" (2 papers), "She ethnic clothing" (2 papers), "Miao embroidery in Southeast Guizhou," "traditional handicrafts of Guizhou," "Yugu ethnic clothing in Sunan," "Manchu patterns," "Hezhe ethnic group," "Yugu ethnic clothing patterns," "Zhuang ethnic auspicious patterns in clothing," "Yi ethnic clothing elements," "Miao embroidery art," "Gansu Longnan Bai Ma Tibetan tourism cultural creative brand 'Meizuo,'" "She ethnic cultural creative clothing products," "Yunnan Dai ethnic waistcloth art," "Sun Drum Miao-Dong clothing museum in Southeast Guizhou," "Buyi ethnic clothing patterns," "Yi ethnic clothing patterns," "Longsheng Hong Yao ethnic group," "Qiang ethnic clothing patterns," "Color perception of Jinxiu Ao Yao ethnic clothing in Guangxi," "Characteristics of ethnic minorities in northern Guangxi," "Tibetan jewelry," and "Miao ethnic clothing patterns." It can be observed that there is a relatively high number of literatures on the research directions of Yao, Miao, She, Yugu, Tibetan, and Yi ethnic groups. However, there is limited creative thinking from the perspective of "digitization" in this literature.

Among the retrieved literature, Dan Junjun conducted in-depth research and interpretation on the Miao ethnic totem culture as the research object, exploring its formation, composition, cultural connotations, and discussing the relationship between human emotions and cultural creative products in the field of art and crafts [4]. Jin Peiyao et al. proposed a design methodology for Mongolian cultural creative products based on the theory of emotionalization in three levels [5].

Meanwhile, a total of 132 relevant literature on "emotionalized cultural creative products" were retrieved from CNKI, with an increasing number of publications since

2016. Among them, the top 10 most cited topics include "theory and practice," "university campuses," "levels of reflection," "Qingyang sachets," "museums," "humanization and emotionalization," "campus cultural creativity and business models," "Suzhou gardens," "Shanghai red cultural creativity," "red cultural and museum creative products," and "emotional experience." It can be observed that there is a significant amount of literature on the research directions of theory, university campuses, museums, red culture, and regional aspects in the context of emotionalized cultural creative products. Most of the cases discussed in the literature are related to material forms of cultural creative products, with very few discussions on the combination of digital forms of cultural creative products.

Taking the example of the Yao ethnic clothing (Nandan County) as a national-level intangible cultural heritage project in China, the exhibition area of the Bai Ku Yao ethnic clothing showcases mainly physical displays of ethnic clothing, traditional instruments, textual introductions, and cultural creative products (Fig. 1 and Fig. 2). The cultural creative products mainly include physical items such as pillows, scarves, and earrings. Based on the current research and development status of Chinese ethnic clothing and cultural creative products, exploring the design of ethnic clothing cultural creative products through digitization and emotionalization can enrich the theoretical exploration of ethnic clothing cultural creative products and provide reference for relevant design methods and practical applications.

Fig. 1. The Intangible Cultural Heritage Exhibition Hall of Bai Ku Yao Village.

3.2 Classification and Characteristics of Motion Capture Technology

Motion Capture (MoCap), abbreviated as MoCap, refers to the process of recognizing and extracting human movements using specialized equipment. MoCap technology is a digital method that has been widely applied in various fields, including film animation,

Fig. 2. The Exhibition Area of Original Ecological Indigo Wax Dye Workshop in Nandan County Yao Village.

gaming and entertainment, virtual reality, simulation training, medical assistance, and industrial simulation. The classification of motion capture technology can be approached from different perspectives, such as the specific body parts being captured and the types of capture devices used.

Regarding the specific body parts being captured, motion capture can focus on capturing movements of the body, face, hands, and other body parts. Optical, inertial, and video-based motion capture systems are utilized to capture data on head movements, torso movements, limb movements, etc. Additionally, mobile applications with features like Live Link Face can utilize smartphone cameras to capture facial expressions, while virtual reality data gloves can capture precise hand movements.

In terms of capture device types, there are currently three commonly used technologies in the market: optical motion capture, inertial motion capture, and video-based motion capture:

Optical Motion Capture. Taking Shenzhen RuiLiShi as an example of a domestic company with independent research and development capabilities in motion capture, their optical motion capture products are divided into active and passive optical motion capture systems. The active optical motion capture system uses LED markers that emit light, while the passive system uses high-brightness reflective markers. These optical markers are attached to key body parts and the motion data is captured by a high-speed camera array, which is then processed by motion capture software.

The advantages of optical motion capture include suitability for high-speed motion capture and high precision. However, it has some limitations such as high cost and requirements for a controlled environment.

Inertial Motion Capture. Taking Beijing Noitom as an example of a domestic company with international competitiveness in motion capture, their inertial motion capture products are categorized into entry-level, advanced, and professional-grade wireless inertial motion capture systems. Inertial motion capture is achieved through the use of inertial sensors integrated with gyroscopes, accelerometers, magnetometers, etc., which are worn on key body parts to capture motion data.

The advantages of inertial motion capture include minimal environmental impact and moderate pricing. However, it has limitations such as limited battery life and potential data drift issues.

Video-based Motion Capture. Taking Microsoft's motion sensing device Kinect and the 2D animation software Adobe Character Animator as examples, video-based motion capture is the closest form of motion capture technology to everyday life. It enables human-computer interaction through peripherals and does not require wearable devices. Video motion capture utilizes techniques such as motion capture and voice recognition. Although Kinect has been discontinued, it marked the application of video motion capture products in people's daily lives. Adobe Character Animator has even lower entry barriers, as it only requires a computer with a connected camera to capture full-body movements of 2D characters.

The drawbacks of video-based motion capture include the need for further technological advancements and relatively lower precision compared to other types of motion capture.

As of November 26, 2023, a total of over 1800 literature documents related to "motion capture" were retrieved on the Chinese CNKI platform. These documents are abundant in quantity and primarily focus on disciplines such as computer software and applications, automation technology, sports, drama, film and television arts, music and dance, education theory and management, fine arts, calligraphy, sculpture and photography, telecommunications technology, aerospace science and engineering, and journalism and media. Against the backdrop of the increasingly mature development of motion capture technology, the integration of different technological advantages and applications in artistic and media disciplines, such as drama, film and television arts, music and dance, fine arts, calligraphy, sculpture and photography, journalism and media, can explore the digital development of traditional and ethnic cultures.

Every piece of artwork is a combination of material and spiritual elements in a specific era, and ethnic costumes are no exception. In the context of the booming development of industry in the new era, the craftsmanship of ethnic costumes is gradually being replaced by cost-effective industrial machines. In this situation, the protection and promotion of the cultural connotation of ethnic cultures have become more urgent. In the background of easier material development in modern society, we can consider how to promote the spiritual essence of ethnic costumes from the perspective of digital means.

3.3 Enhancing the Cross-Platform and In-Depth Dissemination of Ethnic Costume Culture

Donald Arthur Norman summarized the three levels of brain processing information as "visceral, behavioral, and reflective" to form the theory of emotional design [6]. In previous research, the author transformed the theory of emotional design into a three-level model of emotional design for virtual tourism, namely "culture, interaction, and transformation" [7]. Guided by the three-level model of emotional design for virtual tourism, an analysis of digital creative design of ethnic costumes is conducted.

At the "culture" level, traditional and exquisite elements of ethnic costumes are used to attract the audience's attention. Relevant cultural elements such as ethnic costume craftsmanship, minority languages, mythological legends, and historical stories can be incorporated. At the "interaction" level, based on the specific content of ethnic costume elements or related cultural elements, a perspective shift is employed: What type of interaction do the audience desire with ethnic costumes? How do the preferred forms of interaction differ among different age groups? This information helps in selecting the best approach for designing various types of interactions. At the "transformation" level, the results of "culture" and "interaction" are transformed into memorable elements for the audience, thereby elevating their emotional connection with these ethnic costume-related elements.

In the process of using the three-level model of emotional design for virtual tourism in the creative design of ethnic costume cultural products, it is essential to actively combine digital technologies and presentation formats with the material foundation.

At The "Culture" Level. Ethnic costume elements or related cultural elements are showcased using various means such as images, audio-visual libraries, and VR/AR. The display should emphasize not only the visual and technical aspects but also provide detailed information about the cultural elements, including their names and characteristics.

At The "Interaction" Level. Various forms of interaction are employed around ethnic costumes. This includes physical interactions such as designing simple and understandable hands-on projects and interactive games, as well as digital interactions such as screen interactions, motion interactions, and installation interactions. This approach brings the ethnic culture to life and encourages audience engagement. The interactive projects should be closely tied to cultural content customization to enhance participants' understanding of the cultural elements through practical interactions.

At the "Transformation" Level. Combining the basic cultural memory from the "culture" level with the advanced practical memory from the "interaction" level, the aim is to strengthen the audience's memory of the characteristics of ethnic costumes during the experience. This enables the audience to gain spiritual experiences and cultural memories through the creative content of ethnic costume culture. this process promotes the in-depth dissemination of ethnic costume craftsmanship and cultural formation with rich layers.

In the current context where intangible cultural heritage of ethnic costume craftsmanship is receiving attention and protection, emotionally guided digital creative design, incorporating the multiple levels of "culture," "interaction," and "transformation," can facilitate the dissemination of the cultural essence of ethnic costumes, allowing it to develop in tandem with traditional craftsmanship. This approach contributes to the integration of the "memory" and "craftsmanship" aspects of ethnic costumes.

4 Application of Motion Capture Technology in Cultural and Creative Products Featuring Ethnic Costumes

4.1 Design Planning for Digital Creative Products Featuring Ethnic Costumes

Emotionally-guided design in virtual tourism employs a three-level framework of "culture," "interaction," and "transformation" to guide the design of digital creative products with ethnic costumes as the theme. This article briefly discusses the application of motion capture technology in the design of cultural and creative products featuring ethnic costumes. The design process begins with the "culture" level, which involves gathering information on ethnic costume types, pattern colors, craftsmanship, traditional customs, production, and daily life to plan a series of emotionally-driven digital product designs at the "culture" level, centered around ethnic costume culture. These designs can be classified based on platforms and project categories:

Using Platforms. ① Computer-based: Detailed web pages that include text, images, tables, videos, animations, VR/AR scenes, and mini-games. Designed for browsing and interaction on computers, these pages can comprehensively showcase cultural content related to ethnic costumes. ② Mobile-based: Selected content in the form of articles or H5 pages on public accounts, featuring text, videos, animations, VR mini-interactions, and mini-games. Designed for mobile devices, such as smartphones and tablets, these formats consider the browsing habits and interaction patterns of mobile users, providing interactive audiovisual presentations. ③ Installation-based: Physical interactive projects with ethnic costumes as the cultural backdrop, integrating concepts of VR/AR/MR. These projects combine technologies such as holographic projection, radar sensing, and motion capture to create installations that blend digital technology with artistic expression.

Project Categories. ① Video Category: Cultural narrative films or educational documentaries about ethnic costume culture created through animation, filming, or other video production techniques. ② VR/AR Project Category: Virtual simulation educational projects or VR/AR animations with ethnic costumes as the cultural backdrop. ③ Game Category: Development of functional games, including 3D, 2D, and motion-sensing games, with ethnic costumes as the cultural backdrop.

At the "interactive" level, design the physical and digital interactive components. In the realm of material cultural and creative forms, besides physical products, there is an emphasis on the development of handmade physical products. For example, creating cross-stitch handbags featuring individual patterns or five-color patterns of ethnic costumes, and developing parent-child series products such as "ethnic costume pattern coloring + paper cutting." Additionally, designing offline flash practices and promotional projects related to ethnic costumes to enhance online and offline interactions. By combining physical products and packaging with QR codes linking to digital products, for instance through activities like "cultural creative gift lottery," physical products can promote digital products, while digital products can connect to a wider range of physical products.

In the domain of digital formats, apart from the fundamental audiovisual library, interactive design is reinforced. For instance, designing web-based mini-games that involve searching for ethnic costume colors derived from natural dyes, constructing VR scenes and interactions related to ethnic costume festivals, and developing thematic games mentioned earlier. Through the integration of screen interaction, motion-sensing interaction, and installation-based interaction, among other digital interactive practices, the dissemination of cultural information about ethnic costumes is continually enhanced.

At the "transformation" level, by comprehensively showcasing cultural information on ethnic costumes at the "cultural" level and through the implementation of physical and digital interactive practices at the "interactive" level, the transformation of cultural memory points related to ethnic costumes is strengthened. This aims to enhance the audience's sense of accomplishment in creative cultural experiences with ethnic costumes and encourage each audience member to become a disseminator of ethnic costume craftsmanship and culture.

4.2 Application of Motion Capture Technology in Cultural and Creative Product Design for Ethnic Costumes

According to the design planning of digital cultural and creative products related to ethnic costumes, this study focuses on incorporating motion capture technology into the specific practice of designing emotionally-driven cultural and creative products. The study revolves around ethnic costume culture, with the story background set in the Guangxi Zhuang ethnic culture. It involves designing visually and auditorily engaging content with high recognition for Guangxi Zhuang culture, incorporating interactive hotspots.

Showcasing Highly Recognizable Cultural Content of the Guangxi Zhuang Ethnic Group. The Guangxi Zhuang ethnic group has a diverse and vibrant culture. When selecting specific cultural content for exhibition, the following elements can be considered, with reference to the Intangible Cultural Heritage List of Guangxi Zhuang Autonomous Region:

Rich Zhuang Cuisine Culture. In recent years, the "Rice Noodle Making Technique" (listed on the National Intangible Cultural Heritage List of China) represented by Liuzhou Luosifen, a famous dish from Guangxi, has gained significant recognition and popularity in China's culinary culture. The Liuzhou Luosifen brand was ranked 29th in China's brand value evaluation in 2023, with a brand value of 11.022 billion yuan [8]. Additionally, Guangxi's unique snacks, such as Wuzhou Guilin Gao (Tortoise Jelly) with its "Tortoise Jelly Preparation Technique" (listed on the National Intangible Cultural Heritage List of China), are popular both domestically and internationally as Chinese geographical indication products.

Splendid Zhuang Folk Culture. Guangxi is a region where multiple ethnic groups reside, with the Zhuang ethnic group comprising approximately 30% of the population. The Zhuang ethnic group's folk customs include the "San Yue San" festival (listed on the National Intangible Cultural Heritage List of China), which involves rituals, offering sacrifices, and preparing colorful sticky rice ("Zhuang Five-Color Sticky Rice Making Technique," listed on the Guangxi Zhuang Autonomous Region Intangible Cultural Heritage List), as well as activities such as firecracker throwing, duet singing, throwing embroidered balls, and "egg fights" [9].

Exquisite Zhuang Costume Culture. Guangxi has four items related to ethnic costume culture listed on the National Intangible Cultural Heritage List of China. These include the Zhuang brocade weaving technique, Yao costumes (Hezhou City), Yao costumes (Nandan County), and Longsheng Yao costumes.

The Zhuang brocade weaving technique is one of China's traditional handicrafts and is renowned as one of the four famous brocades in China. The Yao costumes in Hezhou City mainly include Gaoshan Yao (Panyao), Pingdi Yao, and Tuyao [10]. The patterns of the White Pants Yao costumes in Nandan County, Guangxi, record the history of struggle and migration of the White Pants people, showcasing the unique ethnic charm of a minority group [11]. The Longsheng Yao costume making technique specifically refers to the production of Red Yao costumes.

Cultural Design of Digital Cultural and Creative Products in Guangxi Zhuang Rural Areas. In the design of cultural and creative products centered around ethnic costumes, it is important not to limit the concept to clothing alone. It is also possible to link it with the culture of the selected subject in terms of food, housing, and transportation. This article takes Guangxi Zhuang culture as an example and selects specific Zhuang cultural elements from the Intangible Cultural Heritage List of Guangxi Zhuang Autonomous Region for design and exhibition.

Students and faculty from the Xiangsi Lake College of Guangxi University for Nationalities collaborated to design and create the animated IP "Na Xiao Chu" (Little Chef), along with a series of animations and cultural and creative products. In the character design of "Na Xiao Chu," the concept of "Beautiful Guangxi Zhuang" is used, and major characters such as Xiao Zhuang, Xiao Mei, Dr. Na, and Xiao Xi are introduced. Xiao Zhuang and Xiao Mei represent the young generation of Guangxi Zhuang and their costumes are designed by incorporating elements from Zhuang ethnic attire. Dr. Na and Xiao Xi, as future humans, have attire that combines ethnic costume characteristics to showcase a blend of traditional and futuristic elements.

In the "Na Xiao Chu" animated series, the first episode of the two-dimensional animation series focuses on the Guangxi regional intangible cultural heritage cuisine, "Five-Colored Glutinous Rice" (Fig. 3), while the second episode highlights the national-level intangible cultural heritage cuisine, "Liuzhou Luosifen" (River Snail Rice Noodles) (Fig. 4). The three-dimensional animated series of Guangxi intangible cultural heritage cuisine in "Na Xiao Chu" features four episodes: "Tortoise Jelly Preparation Technique," "Tea Customs (Yao Ethnic Oil Tea Customs)," "Wuming Lemon Duck Making Technique," and "Yulin Niuba Making Technique." Through the challenging process of "seeking, cooking, and tasting delicacies," the series showcases the diligence and bravery of the working people of Guangxi Zhuang rural areas, narrating unique stories that reflect the ethnic characteristics of Guangxi.

Interactive and Transformative Design of Digital Cultural and Creative Products in Guangxi Zhuang Rural Areas.

Non-real-time Application of Motion Capture Technology for Developers. In the production of 3D animations, 3D games, and VR/AR projects, optical and inertial motion capture devices are used to create animations for Guangxi Zhuang cultural characters.

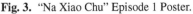

Fig. 3. "Na Xiao Chu" Episode 1 Poster.   **Fig. 4.** "Na Xiao Chu" Episode 2 Poster.

Motion capture technology significantly improves the efficiency of character animation production and reduces the barrier to entry for animation production. Traditional 2D animation techniques required frame-by-frame drawing of character movements, demanding high drawing skills. With the increase in professional animation software and its powerful features, the use of software tools for keyframe adjustments and tweening has simplified 2D animation production. In 3D animation production, creating character animations manually requires a good understanding of human and animal movements, which is challenging and time-consuming. The development and application of motion capture technology will further reduce the difficulty of character animation production. Utilizing motion capture technology to create realistic and natural character movements enhances the expressive ability of animated characters, enabling better storytelling and strengthening the portrayal of Guangxi Zhuang cultural imagery. Motion capture technology allows for easier integration of Guangxi Zhuang cultural customs, dances, and movements related to folk activities into the animation performance, enhancing the creation of a specific cultural atmosphere. For example, inviting inheritors of intangible cultural heritage or dance performers to record motion data. By accumulating a certain amount of data, a motion database of intangible cultural heritage projects can be formed, contributing to the digital preservation of intangible cultural heritage and providing valuable resources for future research.

Real-time Application of Motion Capture Technology for Users: In VR/AR projects, optical, inertial, and video-based motion capture devices, combined with facial capture smartphones and VR data gloves, can be used for real-time motion capture of users. In 3D, 2D, and motion-controlled games, motion capture devices capture natural body movements, transforming traditional human-computer interaction methods. By combining motion capture from a third-person perspective, users can experience the cultural life and activity scenes of Guangxi Zhuang region, enhancing the immersion of virtual scenes. Alternatively, from a first-person perspective, users can experience interactions between hand movements, characters, and scenes using VR goggles, data gloves, and other devices, enhancing the naturalness and realism of the interaction process. By highlighting Guangxi Zhuang cultural elements in the interaction process, the expression of cultural connotations is promoted, strengthening the transformation of Guangxi Zhuang cultural memory.

In the design of digital installations, physical scenes are built using elements of Guangxi Zhuang folk activities and ethnic costumes, combined with projected thematic images and radar sensing. Real-time interaction is achieved by integrating inertial or video motion capture devices, enhancing the user's sensory and interactive experience through "audio-visual + motion" in the realm of cultural creativity (Figs. 5, 6, 7 and 8)."

Fig. 5. "Na Xiao Chu" Episode 3 Poster.

Fig. 6. Oil Tea Production Scene of the Yao Ethnic Group in Gongcheng.

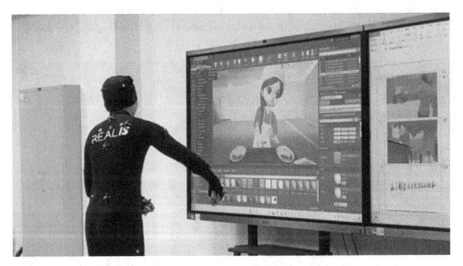

Fig. 7. Interactive Character Scenes of Lemon Duck in Wuming.

Fig. 8. AR Calligraphy Interaction Using VR Headset.

5 Conclusion

This study guided by emotion-driven design principles, examines the multi-level design of digital cultural creativity in virtual tourism. The article covers various aspects of digital cultural creativity design, including culture, interaction, and transformation. Specifically, it discusses the design considerations for different digital platforms, such as computer-based, mobile-based, and device-based platforms, based on their unique characteristics for presentation. Additionally, it explores effective cultural dissemination types and strategies based on project categories, such as video, VR/AR, and gaming.

Using Guangxi Zhuang Ethnic Culture Creative Digital Products as a case analysis, this research investigates the application of digitization methods, including motion capture technology, in the design of ethnic clothing digital cultural products, both in real-time and non-real-time contexts. These digitization methods provide support for the design of ethnic clothing cultural products, facilitating the digital dissemination of ethnic clothing culture. The findings of this study contribute valuable insights into relevant design methods and practical approaches.

Whether it is the creation of an ethnic cultural ambiance during the production process or the facilitation of ethnic cultural interaction in the experiential process, motion capture technology enhances production efficiency and strengthens presentation effects in storytelling related to ethnic culture. This serves as a significant catalyst for the digital dissemination and development of ethnic culture.

Foundations. Research Project for the Enhancement of Research Basic Competence of Young and Middle-aged Teachers in Guangxi Universities in 2023: "Emotion-Driven Design Research of Digital Cultural Creative Products for Guoshan Yao Clothing in Guangxi" (Program Code: 2023KY1648);Special Research Project on Digital Transformation in 2023 for Xiangsihu College, Guangxi University for Nationalities: "Exploration of Digital Transformation and Classroom Teaching Mode Reform Based on Motion Capture Laboratory" (Program Code:

2023SZHO41);Special Project on Experiential Education and Labor Education in the "14th Five-Year Plan" of Guangxi Education Science in 2022: "Research on the Construction of Research-oriented Education System for Intangible Cultural Heritage in Guangxi Universities" (Program Code: 2022ZJY1802);Guangxi Educational Science Planning Project(China): "Research on the Integra-tion Path of 'Art Education + Political Education' Design Education Based on GUangxi's Intan-gible Cultural Heritage Resources" (Program Code: 2021C360).

References

1. Opinion of the Ministry of Culture and Tourism on Promoting High-Quality Development of the Digital Culture Industry. https://www.gov.cn/zhengce/zhengceku/2020-11/27/content_5565316.htm. Accessed 25 Dec 2023
2. Zhang, C.: Exploration of the digital transformation of cultural and creative products. Culture Industry **16**, 128–130 (2022). (in Chinese)
3. Lu, R.: A brief analysis of the digital presentation and brand promotion of cultural and creative products. View Publ. **13**, 92–94 (2020). (in Chinese)
4. Dan, J.J.: Research on Emotion-Driven Design Methods for Creative Products Based on Miao Ethnic Totem Culture. Guizhou University (2018). (in Chinese)
5. Jin, P.Y., Zhang, X.H.: Emotional design study on Mongolian cultural and creative products. Furnit. Interior Des. **09**, 34–38 (2021). (in Chinese)
6. Norman, D.: Emotional Design: Why We Love (or Hate) Everyday Things. Basic Books, New York (2007)
7. Yan, Y.: Research on Emotion-Driven Design of Virtual Tourism Scenic Areas Based on PACT-P. Guangxi Normal University (2018)
8. 22 billion yuan! Latest Performance Report of Liuzhou Snail Rice Noodles Revealed. https://www.sohu.com/a/753310215_121123705. Accessed 25 Dec 2023
9. Zhuang Ethnic Group's Bronze Drum Custom. https://www.gxfybhw.cn/dir-21.html. Accessed 25 Dec 2023
10. Yuan, X.: Form and design transformation in the transmission of the costume culture of yao people in Hezhou, Guangxi. China Intangible Cult. Herit. (02), 81–89 (2023). (in Chinese)
11. Liu, S.J., Jiang, Z.L.: On craftsmanship of baikuyao clothing and its cultural connotations. J. Silk **52**(9), 65–71 (2015). (in Chinese)
12. Optical Motion Capture System. https://www.realis-e.com/. Accessed 25 Dec 2023
13. Overview of the PERCEPTION NEURON Series. https://www.noitom.com.cn/. Accessed 25 Dec 2023

The Digital Integration Path of Aesthetic Education and Ideological Education: Based on the Design Application of China's Yao Ethnic Group's Ecological Textile Process

Xing Yuan[1,2,3]([✉]), Nataliia Chuprina[1]([✉]), and Tiantian Wang[2]

[1] Kyiv National University of Technologies and Design, Kyiv 01011, Ukraine
202006007@hzxy.edu.cn, chouprina@ukr.net
[2] School of Culture and Media, Hezhou University, Hezhou 542899, China
[3] Shaanxi University of Science and Technology, Xi'an 710021, China

Abstract. This study explores the basic functions of China's Yao ethnic group's ecological textile technology in terms of protection, healthcare, identity recognition, historical records, and decorative beautification. It analyzes the historical value, aesthetic education value, and ideological and political value embedded in it. Based on this, the article proposes a feasible digital integration path combining aesthetic education and ideological and political education, creating new possibilities and opportunities for aesthetic education and ideological and political education. The article emphasizes how to utilize digital technology and tools to promote the integration of aesthetic education and ideological education, particularly in conjunction with innovative development strategies of Yao ethnic group's ecological textile process. This line of thinking can provide a continuous creative basis and cultural material source for current and future design, art, and cultural activities, while showcasing the rich cultural connotations and visual imagery of the Chinese nation.

Keywords: Yao Ethnic Group · Ecological Textile Process · Basic Functions · Value Analysis · Innovative Strategies

1 Introduction

This paper investigates the ecological textile process of the Yao ethnic group in Guangxi, China, from an artistic design perspective. The study aims to achieve the following objectives: firstly, to analyze and summarize the basic functions and values of Yao ethnic group's ecological textile process; secondly, to propose a digital integration strategy combining aesthetic education and ideological and political aspects. This strategy involves the creation of gifts, brand shaping, and the integration of digital media for storytelling and promotion, with the goal of driving contemporary innovation in Yao ethnic group's ecological textile process.

The research primarily focuses on the Yao ethnic group in Guangxi as a representative case, as Guangxi is their main settlement area and holds significant cultural value. The

Yao population in Guangxi accounts for approximately 50.9% of the total Yao population in China, reaching 1.683 million people [1]. Guangxi is home to six renowned Yao autonomous counties, namely Jinxiu, Fuchuan, Gongcheng, Du'an, Dahua, and Bama. With the collective development of various ethnic groups, the cultural heritage of Yao ethnic group's ecological textile process has been preserved and promoted. This process not only serves as a traditional craft and material carrier of the Yao ethnic group's social and historical culture but also represents a vibrant and diverse cultural symbol.

Therefore, the study of Yao ecological textile process contributes not only to the preservation and inheritance of Yao cultural heritage but also provides an important window for understanding and appreciating Yao culture. It enriches our understanding of ethnic diversity and human cultural development while providing valuable resources and insights for contemporary art design and cultural exchange.

2   Basic Functions of Ecological Textile Process of the Yao Ethnic Group in Guangxi

2.1 Protective and Health Preservation Function

The clothing selection, production, usage, and development of the Yao ethnic people in Guangxi are influenced by their long-term experience and practical knowledge of mountainous survival and living practices, with practicality, protection, and healthcare being the primary considerations. Historically, the Yao ethnic group was a migratory mountainous ethnic group, and by the Ming and Qing dynasties, they had already spread across the mountainous regions of Guangxi and Guangdong. There is even a folk saying that goes, "Where there are mountains, there are Yao people," highlighting the profound impact of the living environment on the Yao people and the formation of practical ethnic clothing.

For example, in the Yao communities of Pan Yao, Lingzu Chashan Yao, Shanzi Yao in Jinxiu, Guangxi, and Guoshan Yao in Hezhou, women's attire includes a large embroidered apron. This apron is made of thick and durable material, capable of reducing the wear and tear on the body and clothing during mountainous labor [2]. Additionally, the practice of "tying the legs" is prevalent in various branches of the Yao ethnic group. This helps alleviate the impact of mountainous labor on the legs, effectively preventing scratches and entanglements from thorns and branches, while also serving as a rope for climbing and traction. Among them, the leg-tying tradition of Nandan Bai Ku Yao is the most famous, where men uniformly wear white trousers and tie their legs. They use the "cloth folding" method for garment production (see Fig. 1), which eliminates the need for cutting and allows the fabric to be folded into pants. Even if there is wear and tear, the fabric can be refolded and reused, making it highly suitable for the resource-scarce mountainous lifestyle.

In the Guoshan Yao region of Hezhou, Guangxi, the local Yao ethnic people incorporate the use of fragrant sachets filled with a variety of herbal ingredients, known to have invigorating and insect-repellent properties (see Fig. 2). Furthermore, in the production of textiles, they employ traditional indigo dyeing techniques using leaves and rhizomes of plants like Polygonum tinctorium, Persicaria tinctoria, and Indigofera tinctoria, which grow abundantly in the surrounding Yao mountains. Through a fermentation reaction involving lime, rice bran water, and rice wine residue, a practical indigo dye precipitate is obtained (see Fig. 3). The resulting fabric exhibits a natural blue color and emits a long-lasting herbal fragrance. The Yao people believe that this fragrance aids in preventing colds and repelling mosquitoes. These practices are derived from the Yao ethnic people's extensive experience in mountainous labor, with a focus on promoting health and safety.

Fig. 1. Nandan Bai Ku Yao Women's Skirt.

Fig. 2. Guoshan Yao Fragrant Sachet.

Fig. 3. Ecological Textile Process of the Yao Ethnic Group: Fermentation Process of Blue Dye Production.

2.2 Identity Recognition Function

Visual identifiability is a significant visual characteristic in the ecological textile process of the Yao ethnic group in Guangxi. Specific clothing attributes such as style, color, decorations, and patterns are used for differentiation, enabling the identification of age, social status, behavior, and preferences. This serves as an important basis for Yao people to understand the Yao ethnic identity across different regions and subgroups. Additionally, the Yao ethnic group incorporates the strengths of neighboring ethnic groups and integrates them into their attire and behavior to foster interethnic relationships. For instance, the flatland Yao subgroup in Fuchuan, which has been heavily influenced by Han culture, fully incorporates the structural advantages of Tang dynasty clothing into their male attire, resulting in a clean and elegant style(see Fig. 4). This is also one of the significant pieces of evidence highlighting the mutual influence between Yao culture and the cultures of surrounding ethnic groups, demonstrating the inclusive nature of Yao culture.

In general, the attire of the Yao ethnic group conveys two types of information. The first type of information is directed towards external communities and subgroups. Through identifiable clothing, individuals display their affiliation with a specific subgroup, region, or belief system, allowing for immediate recognition of their identity through visual differences. For instance, the Bai Ku Yao subgroup in Nandan, Guangxi, distinguishes themselves from other subgroups by wearing distinctive wide white trousers with large circular patterns at the back, representing the emblem of the Great Plateau King (see Fig. 5). Similarly, the Pointed Hat Yao subgroup in the Babu region of Hezhou differentiates themselves from other subgroups by wearing layered headgear weighing several tens of kilograms, while internally, the Pointed Hat Yao subgroup distinguishes between the Eastern Mountain Yao and Western Mountain Yao through variations in sleeve embroidery colors and headgear details (see Fig. 6).

The second type of information is directed towards internal communities and subgroups. Attire serves as a means for individuals to display personal identity information to their fellow community members, such as wealth status, social standing, adulthood, marital status, and occupation. For example, in Pang Xinmin's "Investigation of the Yao Mountains in Guangdong and Guangxi" during the Republican era, it is documented in the clothing section how Yao men used the number of earrings to showcase their wealth [3]. The attire of women is directly proportional to the affluence of their families, with wealthier families exhibiting more elaborate clothing. Furthermore, elderly members of the Yao community and Yao spiritual leaders possess distinct headgear and other forms of attire. Throughout centuries, the Yao ethnic group has endowed clothing with profound cultural functions and values through these simple yet specific markers of identity and experiences.

Fig. 4. Fuchuan Flatland Yao Men's Attire.

2.3 Historical Documentation Function

The patterns and designs found in the ecological textile processes of Guangxi, such as those seen in Yao ethnic clothing, serve as records of Yao ethnic history. Their creation and origin have specific purposes. These patterns combine Yao ethnic legends and unveil historical stories that reveal the origins, formation, development, and evolution of the Yao ethnic group. Throughout history, due to the narrow-minded ethnic prejudices of feudal regimes, there has been a scarcity of official records documenting Yao ethnic history. According to existing resources, the Yao ethnic group uses a specific script called "Ancient Yao Script" during folk rituals such as sacrificial ceremonies, vows, and divination, to record and convey specific content [4]. These records include the Yao ethnic group's "Guoshan Bang" (Mountain Crossing List), religious scriptures, and handwritten folk songs. However, the knowledge of this "Ancient Yao Script" is predominantly held by a select minority group, including Yao spiritual leaders, Daoist priests, and song masters, and its usage is limited in scope. Additionally, the "Shi Pai Gong Yue" (Stone Tablet Covenant) of the Yao ethnic group in Guangxi is written in Chinese characters, as the Yao ethnic group did not develop and widely use its own script in everyday life. Consequently, written historical records specific to the Yao ethnic group are much rarer.

Fig. 5. Nandan Bai Ku Yao Women's Attire - Festive Dress.

Fig. 6. Hezhou Guoshan Yao Ethnic Group - Festive Dress.

2.4 Decorative and Beautification Function

The ecological textile processes of the Yao ethnic group in Guangxi are a unique expression of their cultural heritage. From an aesthetic perspective, Yao ethnic clothing is a product of their perception, pursuit, creation, and worship of beauty. As a mountainous ethnic group historically residing in mountain areas, their aesthetics exhibit distinct characteristics of mountainous ethnic groups, characterized by the use of natural materials and simple designs.

Yao ethnic clothing typically incorporates five colors: green (blue-green), white, red, black, and yellow. Fabrics are often dyed using methods such as indigo dyeing and wax resist dyeing. Embroidery decorations are applied to the chest, back, cuffs, pant legs, and waist of the garments to enhance their overall appearance. Additionally, different subgroups within the Yao ethnic group exhibit variations in materials and color usage. For example, in Fuchuan, Guangxi, the Yao ethnic group excels in weaving Yao brocade, which features a textured surface and is predominantly red, white, and yellow. In Nandan, Guangxi, the Bai Ku Yao subgroup specializes in embroidery. They raise a local silkworm species known as "golden silk worms" and use a unique method to extract silk. The silkworms are placed on flat wooden boards, allowing them to spin freely. Once the silk layers accumulate into a fabric-like structure, a piece of silk cloth is obtained.

Based on data obtained from field research, the method of silk extraction used by the Bai Ku Yao subgroup in Nandan is identical to the method employed by the Miao ethnic group in Danzhai, Guizhou, for producing the Miao ethnic group's "Hundred Birds Coat." This raises questions: Was there historical cultural exchange between them? Or did ethnic integration occur in the past? To explore these potential connections, further research can be conducted from linguistic perspectives to study the origins and evolution of their languages, from archaeological perspectives to investigate the historical relationship between their cultural artifacts and sites, and from anthropological perspectives to provide genetic evidence. These studies can provide robust scientific support for ethnic unity and stable relationships.

The aesthetic spirit of the Yao ethnic group's ecological textile processes stems from generations of cultural heritage and ongoing aesthetic practices. From the perspective of aesthetic experience, Yao women imbue meaning into imagery through techniques such as simplification, deformation, exaggeration, and transformation, drawing from their understanding and perception of ethnic history and the natural environment [5]. This results in clothing styles with distinctive Yao ethnic aesthetic characteristics. For example, the headscarves worn by Yao women in Hezhou, Guangxi, feature numerous sun patterns symbolizing auspiciousness, as the sun is always present by their side [6]. Additionally, the five-finger imprints on the pant legs of Bai Ku Yao trousers in Nandan have origins in ethnic historical legends and reflect the spirit of ethnic unity through the women's aesthetic conceptualization. It is through this process of evoking aesthetic emotions and experiences through clothing that the aesthetic significance of Yao ethnic clothing is elevated.

3   Value Analysis of Yao Ethnic Group's Ecological Textile Processes

The ecological textile processes of the Yao ethnic group are the result of the accumulated wisdom of the Hua Yao people through long-term production practices. It not only meets the daily needs of the Hua Yao people but also serves as artistic creations to satisfy the aesthetic demands of the surrounding society. This reflects the positive social functions and values of the Yao ethnic group's ecological textile processes, which are primarily manifested in three aspects: historical value, aesthetic education value, and ideological and political value.

3.1   Analysis of Historical Value

The ecological textile processes of the Yao ethnic group are an important part of the historical and cultural heritage of the Chinese Yao ethnic group and a significant legacy of Chinese culture. Their formation and development have witnessed the entire historical process of the Yao ethnic group. Research has shown that in traditional Yao society, there was no widely used written language, except for some symbols resembling writing that might appear in important rituals and divination. Therefore, oral transmission and techniques like pick-up weaving and embroidery became important means of recording, transmitting, and disseminating ethnic historical memory [7].

For example, the pick-up weaving artwork of the Yao ethnic group, such as "The Coronation of the Ancestors," depicts the scene of Yao ancestors' leaders ascending the golden palace (see Fig. 7). Similar artworks contain rich content, earning the Yao ethnic group's pick-up weaving art the reputation of being "living historical books worn on the body." Furthermore, by studying the spatial usage, scenes, customs, and rules related to Yao pick-up weaving, we can gain insights into the historical aspects of Hua Yao society, providing valuable historical evidence for contemporary folklore studies.

Fig. 7.   Hunan Hua Yao Embroidery (Pick-Up Weaving).

3.2   Analysis of Aesthetic Education Value

The ecological textile processes of the Yao ethnic group are an aesthetic product created, appreciated, preserved, and passed down by the collective creativity of the ethnic community through a long history of choices. It embodies the Yao people's emotional pursuit of beauty and their aesthetic attitudes. The aesthetic value of this craft lies in shaping the ethnic sense of beauty and cultivating generations of Yao women's love and pursuit of beauty. Additionally, it inclusively incorporates excellent cultural elements from neighboring ethnic groups such as the Han and other Yao ethnic groups, achieving mutual integration. For example, patterns like the "Wanzi" pattern (resembling the Chinese character "万") and "Fuzi" pattern (resembling the Chinese character "福") are new forms formed by integrating traditional Han patterns. This also reflects the spirit of mutual trust, tolerance, and common development among members of the Chinese ethnic family.

The ecological textile processes of the Yao ethnic group, especially the process of making Yao ethnic costumes, is an important way to cultivate individual aesthetic sense and inherit ethnic culture. In traditional Yao society, the inheritance of costume techniques mainly occurs through oral transmission and immersive exposure among families and ethnic groups. Young Yao women learn to observe and perceive beauty from a young age under the guidance of their families and elders. They become familiar with the beautiful stories, historical legends, and totem beliefs embedded in the patterns of the costumes, which are all cultural accumulations of the Yao ethnic group.

Yao elders repeatedly teach young female family members the skills of weaving brocade and embroidery, enabling them to gain aesthetic experiences related to beauty, colors, shapes, and techniques (see Fig. 8). At the same time, this process also cultivates virtues such as patience, meticulousness, and perseverance among the Yao people, constantly improving the ethnic sense of beauty. This cultivation of aesthetic sense accompanies Yao women throughout their lives and is characterized by attention to detail and uniqueness.

Therefore, the process of making Yao ethnic costumes is not only an important part of Yao culture but also an important avenue for the Yao people to enhance their aesthetic cultivation. Through this process, the Yao people can inherit and promote their own ethnic culture while embodying their pursuit of beauty and unique aesthetic concepts.

3.3 Analysis of Intellectual Value

The ecological textile processes of the Yao ethnic group is the comprehensive result of their knowledge of materials, stitching techniques, color combinations, forms, dyeing, weaving, and embroidery. It reflects the Yao people's exceptional craftsmanship and practical philosophy, which has been passed down through generations as folk wisdom. Integrating these elements into higher education can serve as an important medium for cultivating students' innovative spirit and practical abilities.

The ecological textile processes of the Yao ethnic group are an artistic achievement created by the Yao people to satisfy their spiritual needs. It embodies their pursuit of a better life, showcasing their positive, optimistic, and down-to-earth spirit with a strong local flavor, and reflecting the unique aesthetic style of the working people. Techniques such as cotton cultivation, thread making, dyeing, embroidery, batik, and brocade weaving are integrated into the daily lives of the Yao ethnic group, embodying their wisdom and talent while showcasing the practical creativity of the working people.

Fig. 8. Yao Ethnic Family Textile Scene.

In the context of university education, if these ecological textile processes elements can be organically integrated into relevant disciplines, they can enrich the content of practical courses, allowing students to personally experience the process and aesthetic charm of crafting, understand the essence of Chinese culture, expand their appreciation of art, deepen their understanding of traditional fine arts, and cultivate a correct aesthetic perspective, thereby enhancing their aesthetic sensibility. Furthermore, if the aesthetic consciousness, practical philosophy, compositional relationships, and cultural symbolism inherent in the ecological textile craftsmanship of the Yao ethnic group can be extracted and applied to modern cultural and creative product design, it will enrich the expressive language of design and enhance the cultural depth of modern product design. From the perspective of cultural heritage, this provides a valuable practical approach for understanding the labor wisdom of the Yao ethnic group and continuing their artistic traditions.

4   Digital Integration Path: Innovative Strategies Based on Yao Ethnic Group's Ecological Textile Craftsmanship

Innovation and development are the themes of the present era [8]. When engaging in innovative practices, one should be guided by problems, needs, and digitization. By following these three fundamental principles and employing "Internet+" thinking, social thinking, collaborative thinking, and coordinated development thinking, the ecological textile craftsmanship of the Yao ethnic group in Guangxi can unleash a more profound and enduring source of inexhaustible motivation.

4.1   Branding or Brand Building

The key to the innovative development of Guangxi's Yao Ethnic Group's ecological textile processes lies in shaping the brand. In the context of economic globalization, Chinese products are gradually entering the international competitive stage. At the same time, foreign design brands have boldly incorporated Chinese ethnic elements into their design works, resulting in many outstanding cases. For example, Italian brand Gucci imitated the style of traditional Chinese enamel porcelain in their 2018 spring/summer collection, directly applying the patterns, colors, and shapes from enamel porcelain to clothing, making the garments look novel and eye-catching, and gaining popularity among foreign consumers. Belgian fashion designer Dries Van Noten incorporated patterns, color schemes, and embroidery elements from Chinese Manchu costumes into his 2019 autumn/winter runway show, combining them with modern plaid and prints to create impressive visual effects. In these cases, brands and designs played a decisive role, and these products were well-received by domestic consumers. The success lies in the ability of these brands and products to convey luxurious culture and the noble identity and significance represented by these symbols. However, a careful analysis reveals that foreign designers often directly replicate Chinese elements without fully embodying the cultural significance behind them [9].

In fact, for the innovative development of Guangxi's Yao Ethnic Group's ecological textile processes, one crucial aspect is to shape the brand. It not only requires the full utilization of Yao ethnic cultural elements but also emphasizes the communication of the profound connotations of Chinese culture. Brand building should be based on a deep understanding and respect for Yao ethnic culture, integrating the unique textile craftsmanship, patterns, and color schemes of the Yao ethnic group with modern designs to create products that possess both Yao cultural characteristics and a sense of modern fashion. Additionally, the brand should convey the values, lifestyles, and aesthetic concepts of Yao culture to domestic and international consumers through promotion and storytelling, enabling them to better understand and appreciate the beauty of Yao textile art. Through such brand shaping and product design, the products of Guangxi's Yao Ethnic Group's ecological textile craftsmanship can gain greater recognition and competitiveness in the international market, showcasing the charm and uniqueness of Chinese culture.

Therefore, the innovative breakthroughs for Guangxi's distinctive Yao Ethnic Group's ecological textile processes can be approached from the following aspects:

Emphasize the Shaping of a Distinctive Brand for Guangxi's Ecological Textile Processes. Establish brand images focused on eco-fashion, eco-fabrics, eco-plant dyes, and other ecological textile-related areas. branding can effectively ensure the reputation and value of businesses, attracting more consumer attention and recognition.

Strengthen Original Design with Guangxi's Yao Ethnic Elements. Pay attention to incorporating the regional characteristics of Guangxi's Yao ethnic group into original designs, such as using Yao ethnic patterns, motifs, a nd color schemes in harmony with elements from neighboring ethnic groups. Doing so can expand the consumer base for products and attract more attention and recognition for Yao culture.

Cultivate Innovative Talents with an Understanding of Yao Ethnic Cultural Aesthetics. Emphasize the cultivation of designers, teachers, and other innovative talents who understand Yao ethnic cultural aesthetics. They can provide a sustainable source of creativity and talent for Yao ethnic ecological textile processes. With the support of these professionals, continuous innovation and competitiveness can be maintained.

Through the implementation of these measures, Guangxi's Yao Ethnic Group's ecological textile processes can establish a distinctive brand image, introduce more products with original designs and Yao ethnic cultural characteristics, and attract more consumer attention and appreciation, thereby achieving greater success in the market.

4.2 Building a Digital Marketing Model

Building a digital marketing model is the "key" to the innovative development of Guangxi's Yao Ethnic Group's ecological textile processes. At present, China is undergoing a transition from a traditional agricultural society to a modern and information-based society, which has given rise to production and consumption models with distinct characteristics of the times, such as the Internet, Internet of Things (IoT), and metaverse. This transformation also presents development opportunities for the innovation of Guangxi's Yao Ethnic Group's ecological textile processes. It is crucial to closely follow the actual social needs and integrate the current new consumption and production sales models into the inheritance of tradition. The business logic of the Internet era is a platform model centered around communities [10].

The key points for implementing a digital marketing model for Guangxi's Yao Ethnic Group's ecological textile processes are as follows:

Online Platform Sales. Establish online sales channels by leveraging internet platforms to cater to the shopping habits of younger generations. Create dedicated e-commerce websites, social media platforms, or online marketplaces to reach a wider consumer base for Yao ethnic ecological textile products.

Digital Recording and Showcasing. Utilize digital technology to record and showcase Yao ethnic weaving and embroidery techniques, such as embroidery and brocade weaving. Present the uniqueness of Yao ethnic ecological textile processes through photography, videos, virtual reality, and other means to increase consumer understanding and interest in the products.

Community Building and Interaction. Build a community platform for enthusiasts of Yao ethnic culture. Through online social media, forums, blogs, etc., allow people to share their experiences, stories, and perspectives. Such platforms can facilitate communication, interaction, and collaboration among users while providing more opportunities for the promotion and dissemination of ecological textile processes.

Cross-industry Collaboration and Promotion. Collaborate with brands, designers, artists, and other related fields to promote Yao ethnic ecological textile processes. Through collaborative projects, co-designed products, or exhibitions, blend Yao ethnic culture with other elements to attract more attention and interest.

Currently, the younger generation has grown up in an internet-centric environment. Traditional marketing methods no longer meet their consumption habits and mindset. Therefore, the sales of traditional Yao ethnic ecological textile processes products should adapt to the changing consumer habits by combining offline marketing methods with online platforms, primarily internet-based. This approach has two advantages: first, it allows for the digital recording of Yao ethnic weaving and embroidery techniques through the digital characteristics of internet platforms; second, it enhances the promotion of Yao ethnic weaving and embroidery techniques in the interconnected online space, providing a platform for communication and exchange among ethnic culture enthusiasts.

According to data released by the National Bureau of Statistics of China for online retail sales from January to June 2021, the national online retail sales reached 6,113.3 billion yuan, a year-on-year growth of 23.2%. The sales of clothing and related products increased by 24.1%. These figures reflect the continuous rise in the online consumption level of the Chinese people and the increasing demand for online shopping. Therefore, building an integrated "Internet+" marketing model that combines online and offline channels is necessary for the development of Guangxi's Yao Ethnic Group's ecological textile processes to adapt to the current trends.

4.3 Design-Oriented Souvenirs

Designing branded and serialized fun souvenirs is an accelerator for the innovative development of Guangxi's Yao Ethnic Group's ecological textile processes. Souvenirs are currently a popular category of tourist products, loved by consumers for their portable and practical characteristics. Designing serialized and lifestyle-oriented fun souvenirs aims to continuously introduce products that cater to consumer needs, combining cultural, practical, aesthetic, and packaging features. This approach not only assists brand development but also promotes Yao ethnic cultural characteristics, showcasing the unique features of the Yao ethnic region in Guangxi. It helps enhance consumers' understanding and identification with Yao ethnic cultural products.

Therefore, in the later stages of design, it is essential to fully utilize modern art design concepts and innovative design methods. Consider the characteristics, cultural tone, and brand category of Yao ethnic cultural products from the perspectives of visual identity, brand meaning, and cultural communication in order to design and develop souvenir products. Firstly, ensure that the souvenir products accurately convey Yao ethnic cultural characteristics and showcase the appearance and folk customs of the Yao ethnic region in Guangxi. Inspiration can be drawn from traditional patterns, motifs, colors, and other elements involved in Yao ethnic ecological textile processes, integrating them into product design to establish a close connection with Yao ethnic culture. Design visually appealing appearances and packaging using these elements to make the souvenir products stand out in the market and align with the brand image. Emphasize the story and background of Yao ethnic ecological textile processes culture in product promotion and packaging. Through various channels such as product labels, brochures, promotional materials, etc., communicate the history, culture, and craftsmanship of the Yao ethnic group to consumers, strengthening their sense of identification and emotional connection with the products. Through such design, the brand can be further reinforced, enhancing brand recognition and acceptance, as shown in Fig. 9.

Fig. 9. VR model for design of Yao ethnic textile elements.

4.4 Conducting Promotion Through Digital Cartoon Characters

Digital marketing serves as a showcase for the innovative development of ecological textile processes within the Yao ethnic group in Guangxi. Traditional forms of news and advertising promotion are relatively limited, whereas digital media brings forth the characteristics of agility, efficiency, and real-time interaction in disseminating traditional culture. However, digital marketing also faces challenges such as holography, fragmentation, and the digital divide [11].

Short videos and mobile-based social networking platforms such as self-media present the greatest opportunities for promoting and disseminating Yao ethnic ecological textile processes in the modern era. We should fully recognize the spillover effects brought about by these platforms, as they can significantly enhance the economic income and social visibility of the Yao ethnic ecological textile processes brand. For instance, in the 2019 Bilibili New Year's Eve live broadcast, pipa player Fang Jinlong captivated netizens with a series of musical performances. Within four days after the live stream, the video garnered over 46 million views, generating more than 100,000 discussions under the Weibo trending topic "Bilibili New Year's Eve" and accumulating 220 million clicks and reads. This directly sparked the "Chinese music trend" and boosted the sales of musical instruments. Influencer Li Ziqi, known for creating high-quality short videos with Chinese aesthetic elements, has gained over 14 million fans overseas and her videos on YouTube have been viewed over 1.33 billion times, leading to a significant increase in brand sales. There have also been successful promotional effects achieved through the fusion of Yao ethnic character imagery and elements of Yao textile processes in the design of animated characters on the internet (see Fig. 10). These cases demonstrate the powerful advantages of new media communication in cultural promotion.

The core of popular online videos lies in the creation of high-quality content and the packaging of brand stories. Therefore, Yao ethnic ecological textile processes brands should fully leverage their own strengths and audience preferences, combining the two to create compelling and interesting brand stories, and consistently deliver high-quality content to better promote the popularization of Yao ethnic cultural knowledge and brand communication.

Fig. 10. Cartoon characters that incorporate elements of Yao textile craftsmanship.

5 Conclusion

In conclusion, Yao ethnic ecological textile processes, as an outstanding representative of traditional Chinese crafts, encompasses multiple characteristics such as protection, health preservation, identification, record-keeping, decoration, and beautification. It provides an important avenue and perspective for us to understand the social and cultural diversity of China. We should fully recognize and explore the positive role and aesthetic value of Yao ethnic ecological textile processes in cultivating aesthetics, nurturing emotions, and shaping character, as it integrates various means of understanding, exploring, experiencing, and creating beauty. It can expand and enrich the current teaching content of aesthetic education in schools. Teachers can guide students to experience, appreciate, and create Yao ethnic ecological textile processes by teaching them the design, production, and decoration techniques of the Yao ethnic group. This deepens their understanding of traditional culture and cultivates their sensitivity and aesthetic abilities towards beauty. Additionally, it further enriches the ways in which we cultivate students' moral character and promote the spirit of Chinese national aesthetic education.

Acknowledgements. The authors would like to thank the contributions and support of the supervising professors during the writing process.

Foundations. 2023 Guangxi Philosophy and Social Science Research Youth Project (China): "Exploration, Organization, and Application of Elements of Ethnic Interaction and Exchange in the Cultural Dress of the Yao People in the Southern Ling Corridor (Guangxi Section)" (Program Code: 23CMZ014); Guangxi Educational Science Planning Project(China): "Research on the Integra-tion Path of 'Art Education + Political Education' Design Education Based on GUangxi's Intan-gible Cul-tural Heritage Resources" (Program Code: 2021C360).

References

1. Office of the Leading Group of the Seventh National Population Census of the State Council. China Population Census Yearbook 2020, vol. 1. China Statistics Press, Beijing (2022)
2. Xiong, H.Y., Zhan, B.H., Ou, Y.J.: Picture Album of Jinxiu Yao Ethnic Clothing. China Textile Press. China Textile Publishing House Co. Ltd., Beijing (2019)
3. Pang, X.M.: Investigation of the Yao Mountains in Guangxi and Guangdong. Chung Hwa Book Co. Ltd., Shanghai (1935)
4. Xu, Z.X.: Chinese and ancient Yaowen. Chin. Cult. (03), 38–39 (2003). (in Chinese)
5. Peng, H.Z.: Folk Aesthetics of Ethnic Groups. Guangxi Normal University Press, Guilin (2000)
6. Hu, Q.S., Tao, H.Y.: Hezhou Yao Ethnic Group. Guangdong World Publishing Corporation, Canton (2015)
7. Liang, Y., Yuan, X.: Eucational function of traditional brocade weaving techniques of Zhuang and Dong nationalities. J. Guilin Normal College **34**(02), 50–54 (2020). (in Chinese)
8. Conway, G., Jeff, W., Sara, D.: Science and Innovation for Development. UK Collaborative on Development Sciences, London (2010)
9. Lu, T.Y.: Strategies of symbolization and innovation of brands in a context of "Cultural Consumption". South. Cult. Forum (1), 184–187 (2021). (in Chinese)
10. Luo, M., Li, L.Y.: The innovation of businness model in internet era: from value creation perspective. China Ind. Econ. (1), 95–107 (2015). (in Chinese)
11. Fu, S.J.: Research on innovative strategies for traditional cultural communication: based on the perspective of digital media. View Publ. (23), 67–69 (2020). (in Chinese)

Research on Digital Identification for Cultural Protection of Yao People Clothing Patterns in Northern Guangdong

Yao Zhang[1,2] and Zhi Yang[3(✉)]

[1] Beijing Institute of Technology, Zhuhai, China
[2] Institute of Creative Industries Design, National Cheng Kung University, Tainan, Taiwan
[3] Wuhan Institute of Design and Sciences, Wuhan, China
373129643@qq.com

Abstract. Patterns serve as significant cultural and artistic symbols among the Yao people in northern Guangdong, China. They play a crucial role in clothing art, embodying national culture and historical heritage. This research adopts various research methods, including literature research, case studies, and field investigations, to systematically identify patterns found in the traditional costumes of the Yao people in northern Guangdong, China. Additionally, it utilizes semi-structured interviews to analyze, organize, and categorize these patterns within the cultural context of the Yao people in this region. To enhance the understanding of these patterns, digital technology is used to draw and extract vector graphics of the patterns, followed by a comprehensive analysis of their units, color combinations, and compositional features. Furthermore, this study delves into the characteristics, origins, and cultural symbolism behind these patterns. This research aims to improve the digital identification of Yao costume patterns in northern Guangdong, China. The software was also used to extract typical pattern units, and through the combination of basic unit patterns, transform and design a modern pattern series with the style of the Yao people in northern Guangdong. The results of this study are propitious to the protection, digital identification and inheritance of the outstanding traditional pattern culture of the Yao nationality in northern Guangdong, and have high practical value to the future research on the modern digital application of the traditional pattern of the Yao nationality in northern Guangdong.

Keywords: Yao people in northern Guangdong · Clothing patterns · Culture · Digital identification · Protection · Application

1 Introduction

1.1 Research Motivation

The Yao people are one of the most populous ethnic minorities in Guangdong Province. Their costumes were selected into the first batch of national intangible cultural heritage in 2006 [1]. The Yao people residing in northern Guangdong have historically inhabited the hills of the Liannan region of China, predominantly engaging in farming and boasting a lengthy cultural history. The primary branches, Paiyao and Guoshan Yao, both belong to the Panyao branch among the three principal branches of the Yao people, with historical records dating back to the Sui and Tang Dynasties. Lacking a written language, they rely solely on oral communication for the transmission of their national culture.

Patterns serve as pivotal cultural and artistic symbols for the Yao people in northern Guangdong, China. They play an important part in clothing art by maintaining national culture as well as historical and cultural heritage. The current research on Yao patterns in northern Guangdong mainly focuses on the cultural connotation and semantic expression of national emotions [2]. The research areas are concentrated in Ruyuan County, Shaoguan and Liannan County, Qingyuan. Despite the establishment of Yao cultural research bases and research centers, the investment in human and material resources is relatively modest, yielding a restricted scope and impact, and as a consequence inadequate protection of local traditional costumes [3]. Simultaneously, due to the impact of economic development, regional culture, and the lack of inheritors of traditional handicrafts, a large number of precious and excellent clothing cultures are disappearing rapidly. Therefore, it is imperative to conduct research on Yao clothing culture and protect the Yao clothing patterns in northern Guangdong. Protective, excavational and archival initiatives such as this research are essential to promote the sustainable development of national costume art.

In recent years, China has progressively placed greater emphasis on the protection and development of our country's traditional culture. In 2022, the Chinese government promulgated the regulations of the "14th Five-Year Plan for Cultural Development" to explicitly strengthen the protection and inheritance of intangible cultural heritage and enhance the practical capacity of intangible cultural heritage [4, 5]. The regulations focus on the development of digital preservation solutions for the cultural industry.

Currently, scholars' research on the clothing patterns of the Yao people in northern Guangdong focuses primarily on culture and history, with a noticeable absence of digital innovative inheritance and application of the Yao people's patterns in northern Guangdong. With the development of technology, computer-aided design technology is conducive to the digital protection and inheritance of traditional national patterns, and its flexible application in modern design present conspicuous advantages, attracting the attention of an increasing number of scholars.

For traditional ethnic patterns, ethnic characteristics constitute their fundamental vitality, and the key lies in how to preserve and regenerate them in the digital process. In this context, studying how to digitally identify, protect, and inherit the clothing pattern culture of the Yao people in northern Guangdong has significant theoretical support for safeguarding the intangible cultural heritage, specifically Yao embroidery. It holds substantial social value and importance. Therefore, this topic merits further research.

1.2 Research Purposes

The Yao people of northern Guangdong use patterns as cultural memory markers. They are brightly colored and diverse in form, constituting an important part of costume art. Digital identification is a significant instrument for capturing and conserving the unwritten aspects of Yao culture and tradition. Through the identification of the Yao costume pattern culture in northern Guangdong and the establishment of a pattern database, these digital records provide rich sources of inspiration for modern pattern design, in addition to protecting and sharing an important aspect of the national culture in northern Guangdong.

The purpose of this study is threefold:

1. Explore the intertwined patterns of Yao Culture and identities woven into costume patterns.

   To achieve this purpose, we undertook an on-site investigation in Liannan Yao Autonomous County, a gathering place for the Yao people in northern Guangdong. This allowed us to gather information first-hand, amass a substantial collection of physical clothing patterns, and obtain second-hand information based on literature. By conducting interviews with intangible inheritors of Yao embroidery and local embroiderers possessing expertise in embroidery techniques, we analyze the distinctive features and cultural connotations inherent in the embroidery patterns adorning Pai Yao costumes.

2. Develop a digital system for recognizing and cataloging the rich heritage of Yao costume patterns.

   Taking into account the cultural context of the Yao people in northern Guangdong, we studied the two main branches of the Yao people in northern Guangdong. Specifically, we delved into the principal artistic features of the embroidery patterns adorning the costumes of Paiyao and Guoshan Yao. Following that, we meticulously analyzed, organized, and categorized the acquired data, utilizing computer-based methodologies to extract pattern units with distinctive characteristics typical of the Yao people in northern Guangdong with the goal of establishing a typical pattern unit library. This subsequent step involved conducting an in-depth analysis of these units, exploring their composition and color matching characteristics using a comprehensive approach aimed at improving the digital identification of cultural protection of Yao ethnic costume patterns in northern Guangdong.

3. Design a series of contemporary patterns based on the unit patterns of the Yao people in northern Guangdong.

   This final purpose aimed to provide innovative ideas and methodologies for the research and development of digital inheritance and protection of Yao ethnic patterns in the northern Guangdong region.

2   Literature Review

2.1   Research on Yao Costume Patterns

With regard to ancient domestic works and local chronicles, available work has focused on the history, branches, costume characteristics and cultural connotations of Yao costumes.

Xuemei Long and Zhihui Pan provided a detailed introduction to the common embroidery patterns and techniques of the Yao people in northern Guangdong, as well as the costumes and patterns of Bapai Yao and Guoshan Yao. This work holds significant reference value for the study of Yao clothing in northern Guangdong [6]. Juhua Deng described embroidery stitches, sources of clothing patterns, stories, and legends related to the patterns, along with the artistic characteristics of embroidery patterns and their application in Yao costumes [7]. Xiaowen Li conducted a relatively systematic discussion on clothing classification and characteristics, cultural connotation, artistic style, and cultural exchanges between ethnic groups of minorities in Guangdong [8]. Through analysis of pictures and text, Xiaowen Li provided a multifaceted analysis and discussion of Yao costumes in northern Guangdong with valuable insights related to historical evolution, craft characteristics, form, cultural connotation, and artistic value [9]. This is a significant work that provides detailed examination of the costumes worn by the Yao people in northern Guangdong. Zanmin Chen analyzed the connotation and artistic characteristics of Ruyuan's embroidery patterns and documented relevant information about the costumes and embroidery of the Yao people in northern Guangdong [10–12]. Shijie Yu deconstructed the composition of Yao costume patterns to provide valuable analysis of the connection between Yao costume patterns and their nationality which lead to insightful interpretations concerning the original beliefs and cultural connotations behind Yao costumes [13].

In published papers addressing related topics, the ethnology expert, Qixin Chen, conducted an in-depth field trip to Ruyuan Bibei Yao Village. He categorized the basic patterns of their embroidery into five distinct categories, a classification widely acknowledged by numerous scholars [14].

Other scholars have provided interpretations of the artistic characteristics, historical origins, symbolic meanings, and customs and beliefs associated with the patterns of the Yao people in northern Guangdong. These perspectives stem from disciplines such as anthropology, ethnology, and iconography, offer new insights into the subject [15–20].

With regard to research on the application of Yao ethnic pattern design, some scholars have developed fashion and home products by interpreting design language derived from typical patterns of Yao ethnic embroidery. This approach has introduced novel concepts for the preservation and innovative design of traditional Yao ethnic patterns [21–24].

2.2 Research on Pattern Digitization

The current research on Yao patterns in northern Guangdong predominantly centers around the socio-cultural perspective, investigating the characteristics of Yao patterns and their generation and evolution from the viewpoints of anthropology, history, and ethnology, to produce insights into social factors, aesthetic features, and production techniques. However, there is a noticeable dearth of studies on the digital conservation of Yao patterns in this region. With the advancement of digital technology, the inheritance, protection, and innovative development of traditional clothing patterns and their production techniques have become much more accessible, intelligent, and shareable [25].

Numerous research papers emphasize digital protection, with scholars primarily concentrating on interactive design at the terminal interface for traditional clothing patterns. Additionally, some use parting technology to generate computer simulations of clothing patterns and use shape and other analysis methods to derive designs from traditional clothing patterns. For instance, Han Xu analyzed the morphological structure of Buyi batik patterns, extracted typical patterns for digitization, employed corresponding design methods to generate new patterns, and integrated them into the design of women's leather shoes through use of 3D digital software modeling [26]. Furthermore, Man Zhou et al., based on the analysis of elements and composition rules of Kirgiz tapestry patterns, used computer programming language to develop the Kirgiz tapestry pattern design system [27]. Additionally, Haiying Zhao et al., employed computer-aided design technology to decompose typical patterns of ethnic minorities, extract pattern primitives, and construct a multi-level pattern primitive library to preserve ethnic characteristics, thereby facilitating achievement related to the goals of inheritance, innovation, and vectorized design [28].

In conclusion, work to protect and digitally document traditional patterns can play an important role in preserving and integrating the evolution of traditional clothing designs with contemporary trends. This study aims to add to this work by leveraging modern digital technology to refine and digitally identify traditional Yao patterns, offering practical value for innovative design, pattern inheritance, and development.

3   Research Methods

Pattern basic unit exemplar in clothing resembles a pattern lexicon derived from the cultural attributes specific to an ethnic group. It serves as a fundamental graphical unit recurrently employed throughout the entire composition. The subsequent diverse and innovative patterns, to be transformed, must be crafted and designed in accordance with this foundational element, which serves as the emblem and symbol of a particular group (nation) [29]. Pattern primitives not only preserve the national symbolism inherent in the original pattern but also streamline the pattern redesign process, offering insights for more effective continuity and innovation within the national pattern culture [30]. To attain the research objective of digitally recognizing Yao ethnic costume patterns in northern Guangdong, the study employed the ensuing research methodologies.

Initially, an investigation was conducted in Damaishan Town, Zhaigang Town, Sanpai Town, Sanjiang Town, and Nangang Town in Liannan Yao Autonomous County, located in northern Guangdong. A total of 21 Yao villagers were interviewed, including three government officials—specifically, the Director of Damaishan Cultural Station, the Director of Sanpai Town Cultural Station, and the Deputy Secretary of Sanpai Town Nangang Village. Also among the interviewees were five inheritors, including Shen Peiying, Fang Weiyan, Deng Shengyimei, Fang Chunhua—inheritors of Liannan Heritage Embroidery—and Fang Erguisha, the inheritor of intangible cultural heritage indigo. Interviews were also conducted with two craftsmen in Li Gaochong from Liannan Millennium Yao Village, as well as eleven village craftsmen including Youling embroiderers and local Yao villagers. In addition, investigative visits were made to Yirong Yao Embroidery Workshop, Weiyan Yao Embroidery Craft Workshop, and Zuimei Yao Embroidery Workshop (all located in Liannan Yao Autonomous County) for the purpose of examining and documenting characteristics of their current product lines.

Interview duration for the 21 subjects mentioned above ranged from 20 to 30 min. The content of each interview was coded independently to generate textual data. Subsequently, open coding was employed on the interview data, primarily involving the initial conceptualization of the textual data post-interviews. The resulting concepts were further refined and summarized to establish categories. In accordance with the categorization of Yao costume patterns by prior scholars, the patterns of the actual costumes captured during the survey were systematically classified.

Secondly, digitally restore the actual clothing items. Based on the actual measurement data, styles are drawn according to the organized clothing categories. The computer graphics software Adobe Illustrator was used to digitize typical patterns, analyze the pattern characteristics, disassemble the patterns into primitives, then classify and sort them according to different themes, to establish a pattern primitive library, and complete the digital catalog of patterns.

Finally, a total of 327 questionnaires on Yao ethnic patterns were completed. Building upon the previously established digital identification system for restoring the patterns of the Yao people in northern Guangdong, and in conjunction with the analysis of quantitative survey results, the basic patterns underwent redesign through structural reorganization and morphological displacement design methods. Subsequently, multiple sets of derivative patterns were created based on specific arrangement rules.

4   Data Analysis

4.1   Analysis of Embroidery Patterns of the Yao People in Northern Guangdong

The embroidery patterns of the Yao people draw inspiration from nature and are shaped by the inherent ecology of inhabiting mountainous and jungle regions. These patterns encapsulate landscapes, forests, mountain flora, plants, people, and animals, with the most distinctive elements of these subjects selected to form geometric designs. The patterns convey abstract characteristics, rich in content and vivid in imagery, each holding unique meanings. The wisdom of the Yao people underlies these patterns, which are not merely products of their imagination. During production and labor, abstract patterns are transformed with needle and thread meticulously sewn into clothing fabrics, drawing inspiration from their daily familiar life scenes. Unfortunately, they lack written records. The patterns adorning their clothing not only serve an aesthetic function, but also communicate a form of inheritance and memory. These patterns document aspects of religion, belief, history, and life.

In Professor Chen Qixin's research on Ruyuan Yao embroidery at Sun Yat-sen University, the embroidery is categorized into five groups: plant patterns, animal patterns, humanoid patterns, graphic patterns, and symbolic patterns. This classification provided a profound theoretical foundation for subsequent scholars studying Yao patterns in northern Guangdong.

This study also adopts the same five major categories of patterns. It involves digitally drawing the actual objects photographed during the survey and, subsequently, extracting several individual patterns based on the pattern's shape. In turn, each individual pattern undergoes coding, and in conjunction with the interview content, the artistic characteristics and cultural connotations of these individual patterns are analyzed (see Table 1).

Table 1. Extracting multiple patterns from physical objects for digital illustration.

	Real pattern	Digital Drawing	Unit Pattern	Unit Pattern Name (from left to right)	The Source of the Real Pattern
1				1. Bird pattern, 2. Sister pattern, 3. Eye pattern 4.Dragon pattern	Clothes made by Peiying Shen, the intangible inheritor of Yao embroidery
2				1. Youling horse head pattern, 2. Fan pattern, 3. Snake pattern	Yao embroidered clothing made by Ermei Tangsha in Youling
3				1. Bird pattern, 2. Human head pattern, 3. Field pattern	Bag made by Peiying Shen, the intangible inheritor of Yao embroidery
4				1. Phoenix tail, 2. Octagon pattern, 3. Eyeball pattern, 4. Dragon pattern	Bag made by Peiying Shen, the intangible inheritor of Yao embroidery
5				1.Wavy pattern, 2.Bird pattern, 3.Humanoid pattern, 4. Field pat-	Bag made by Peiying Shen, the intangible inheritor of Yao embroidery

(continued)

Table 1. (*continued*)

6			1. Horse head pattern, 2. Small grass pattern, 3. Bridge pattern, 4. tree pattern, 5. Humanoid pattern	Yao embroidered clothing made by Ermei Tangsha in Youling
7			1. Bird pattern, 2. Snake pattern	Clothes made by Peiying Shen, the intangible inheritor of Yao embroidery
8			1.Pine pattern, 2. Eye pattern, 3. Panwang Seal, 4. Dragon pattern	Clothes made by Peiying Shen, the intangible inheritor of Yao embroidery

4.2 Digital Identification of Pattern Units

For this study, pattern units are created by extending the concept of metadata in computer systems. This involves dividing the pattern in a specific manner and extracting fundamental pattern units that possess regional and independent characteristics associated with certain national cultural traits. These pattern units exhibit stability, inheritance, and typicality. The pattern unit is constituted by the combination of graphic elements, color matching, and composition. During the field research, it was observed that traditional Yao costumes in some towns within the northern Guangdong Yao Autonomous County have been influenced by modern industrial production, showing a tendency towards mechanization. Many women who were previously able to hand-embroider traditional patterns no longer comprehend the connotations and meanings of these patterns. Even the names of traditional patterns are not clearly explained, posing a risk of losing these traditional patterns. Therefore, digitizing the typical patterns of the Yao people in northern Guangdong and establishing a pattern database represents one of the strategies for preserving and revitalizing the clothing pattern culture of the Yao people in northern Guangdong.

Pattern units serve as the fundamental structural elements comprising the traditional clothing patterns of the Yao people in northern Guangdong. Illustrating these pattern units and scrutinizing their characteristics contribute to an understanding of the principles underlying the Yao people's pattern composition. This exploration enables a deeper appreciation for the decorative art and pattern culture of the Yao people, establishing a theoretical foundation for pattern identification among the Yao people in northern Guangdong. Consequently, this study categorizes collected Yao patterns in northern Guangdong through field surveys and literature collection, analyzes the characteristics of pattern units, and performs digital identification of patterns.

The organized and refined unit patterns are as follows (see Table 2):

Plant Pattern. Plant patterns play a significant role in Yao costumes. Among the pattern elements derived from plant patterns are octagonal flowers, pine tree patterns, tree patterns, grass patterns, sycamore flowers, lotus flowers, osmanthus flowers, and ginger flowers. In crafting a pattern, Yao women in northern Guangdong selectively choose the most distinctive parts of plants, including stems and leaves, petals, stamens, and fruits, and abstract, refine, and transform them. It is not merely a replication of natural plants but an expression of the form of geometric figures. For instance, in Pai Yao embroidery, the octagonal pattern (Pai Yao) frequently serves as the core part of the Panwang Seal on the Pai Yao plate. In Guoshan Yao, the sycamore flower pattern only depicts the shape of leaves and stalks, with palmately divided leaves and longer stalks. Similarly, in the case of the octagonal pattern (Pai Yao), the petals are abstracted into irregular pentagons, devoid of stems and leaves, presenting an aerial perspective of flowers [6].

Animal Pattern. Throughout the life of the Yao people's embroidery patterns, animals are commonly featured, including horse head patterns, deer patterns, dragon patterns, birds, spiders, fishbone patterns, and snake patterns. These animal patterns are utilized with varying frequencies across different branches and are combined in different ways on distinct embroideries. For instance, Ruyuan Guoshan Yao embroidery prominently features deer patterns embroidered with white, black, or green silk threads, while Liannan Youling primarily incorporates horse head patterns. Animal patterns and plant patterns are typically blended together to produce compositions. For instance, the combination of bird patterns and forest patterns evokes the sensation of hearing birds chirping in the forest. These combinations result in the creation of a harmonious and natural ecological landscape.

Humanoid Pattern. There are only two types of humanoid patterns: male and female. Human-shaped patterns are commonly found in Ruyuan Yao embroidery, but they are less prevalent in Liannan designs. Simple straight lines are used to create figures with the arms akimbo and feet spread apart. Both men and women are dressed in a similar style, differing only in the headdress.

The body shapes of men's and women's patterns are similar, with a distinction lying in the patterned headwear. Men wear a headscarf, while women wear a horned hat. Both genders have hands on their hips and feet apart. The patterns are highly simplified,

Table 2. Yao ethnic patterns in northern Guangdong and digital drawing of pattern units.

Pattern Category	Pattern Naming	Representative Pattern Unit
Plant pattern	Pine pattern	
	Octagon flower pattern	
	Dalian flower stamen pattern	
	Sycamore pattern	
	Field pattern	
	Others (Pine cone pattern, Stamen pattern, Forest pattern)	
Animal Pattern	Horse head pattern	
	Dragon pattern	
	Deer pattern	
	Cockscomb pattern	
	Bird pattern	
	Fish pattern	
	Snake pattern	
Symbolic pattern	Panwang Seal□Chinese character Wan pattern pattern	

(continued)

Table 2. (*continued*)

Human-oid pattern	Men's pattern, Brothers' pattern	
	Woman's pattern, Sister's pattern	
Graphic pattern	Others (half-bean pattern, river pattern, river pattern, Japanese character pattern, Bridge pattern, Mountain pattern, Star pattern, Snowflake pattern, Eye pattern, Fan pattern)	

frequently featuring a single human-shaped motif arranged in repeated sequences to form two-sided continuous patterns.

During the investigation, it was observed that in the Damai Mountains of Liannan, there are sister patterns and brother patterns in the embroidery. These patterns depict single male and female figures in a two-sided continuous composition, symbolizing the deep bond between brothers and sisters.

Graphic Pattern. Graphic patterns draw inspiration from common buildings or daily necessities in daily life. Many patterns are no longer direct imitations of the original objects but take the form of abstract geometric figures. These patterns are typically utilized for interval decoration between patterns and as embellishments on the edges of clothing. They primarily employ repeated geometric motifs to play a coordinating role. The names assigned to these patterns are closely linked to the lives of the Yao people. For instance, the zigzag pattern (Ruyuan) and tofu plaid pattern (Ruyuan) have names established by folk conventions. The zigzag pattern (Ruyuan) is attributed to the dense forests in the Yao Mountains where logging serves as a primary livelihood for the Yao people. On the other hand, the tofu plaid pattern (Ruyuan) is derived from the Yao people adopting aspects of the Han people's lifestyle, involving the exchange of high mountain tea for beans, thus forming an eating pattern. Due to the exquisite beauty of the tofu plaid pattern, the Yao people in northern Guangdong documented it through embroidery.

Symbolic Pattern. Symbolic patterns primarily convey reverence for ancestors, religious convictions, and the commemoration of heroes, such as the Panwang seal, spider pattern, and Chinese character Wan pattern pattern. For instance, the Panwang Seal holds significant importance in Yao costumes. The origin of the Panwang seal pattern is closely tied to the narrative of Panhu God, the Yao people's ancestor. The myth and legend that Panhu dragon dog made a contribution in helping the dynasty to eliminate the bandits during the war, was given a princess as his wife, and then retreated into the mountains and forests to propagate. This story has been passed down through generations in each branch of the Yao people, who consider the Panhu dragon dog as their clan protector.

They embellish their clothing with the embroidered Panhu seal pattern, venerating it as a clan totem.

The Chinese character Wan pattern is also prominently featured in Yao patterns, originating from Buddhism and introduced by the Han people. It is employed to pray for the prevention of disasters, ancestral blessings, and to symbolize good fortune and luck. Additionally, it signifies concepts such as eternal life and reincarnation.

4.3   Composition and Color Matching

Composition of Patterns of Yao People in Northern Guangdong. Pai Yao's embroidery patterns can be classified into three categories: single flower patterns, double flower patterns, and combined patterns, based on the arrangement of patterns. Pai Yao features nearly thirty types of single flower patterns, serving as the fundamental embroidery units that compose the vibrant patterns on Yao costumes (see Fig. 1). For instance, individual patterns like the pine tree pattern, horse head pattern, and fish pattern, can be utilized independently or repeated to create two-sided continuous patterns.

The double flower pattern represents a novel combination formed by two-unit patterns. Some of these innovative patterns involve combining existing unit patterns by altering their color often to convey entirely new meanings. Illustrated in Fig. 1, the combination of the dragon horn pattern, snake pattern, and fan pattern results in the creation of a more animated scene depicting flying dragons and dancing snakes. This scene corresponds to the classic story of the Yao people's ancestors that portray divine dogs, crossing the sea in Yao myths and legends. Double flower patterns are commonly found on belts, cuffs, collars, pants, and other attire items.

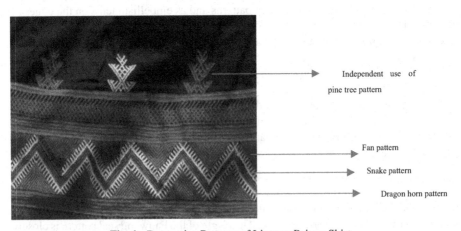

Independent use of pine tree pattern

Fan pattern

Snake pattern

Dragon horn pattern

Fig. 1. Decorative Patterns of Liannan Paiyao Skirt

Combination patterns involve a fusion of various single flower patterns and multi-flower patterns with predetermined combinations, creating a continuous pattern through specific arrangements that depict more intricate scenes. In the patterns of the Yao people in northern Guangdong, symmetry and continuity stand out as the most common composition methods. Continuous patterns are typically composed in various forms such as symmetrical, upright, scattered, and diagonal. The unit patterns exhibit diverse transformations, with each composition method displaying freedom and flexibility. These extensive embroidery patterns are commonly adorned on skirts, shawls, headscarves, and hats. By examining representative examples of multi-flower patterns, we can discern the general rules governing combined pattern composition. Illustrated in the subsequent field survey is an instance of multi-flower combination patterns in Liannan Youling (see Fig. 2).

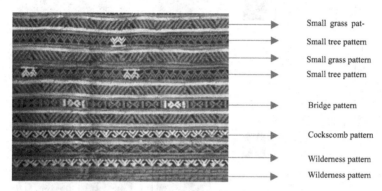

Small grass pat-

Small tree pattern

Small grass pattern

Small tree pattern

Bridge pattern

Cockscomb pattern

Wilderness pattern

Wilderness pattern

Fig. 2. Decorative Patterns of Skirt in Liannan Paiyao Youling

From top to bottom, there are patterns such as the small grass pattern, field pattern, small tree pattern, bridge pattern, and cockscomb pattern. These patterns recur, and when amalgamated, depict a pastoral scene with vegetation and bridges. Single or multiple patterns are linked end-to-end and systematically arranged with other patterns to create a cohesive continuous pattern, providing a unified yet diverse and intricately layered overall design.

Color Patterns of Yao People in Northern Guangdong. Historically, the Yao people have been renowned for their habit of wearing "five-color clothes." Dating back to the Han Dynasty, the Yao ancestors adorned their garments with five colors: red, yellow, blue, white, and black, establishing a distinctive symbol in Yao clothing. According to research findings, Paiyao costumes predominantly utilize black fabric as the base, enriched with embroidery in red, white, yellow, blue, and other colors. The color saturation is notably high, creating a strong color contrast. Concerning color and pattern coordination, variations can occur within the same pattern or different colors can be incorporated at various intervals to produce a splendid and beautiful color-matching feature.

The choice of clothing colors among the Yao people in northern Guangdong is intricately linked to their daily life and beliefs. The prevalence of black as the primary color holds historical significance for the Yao people who, as a migratory nation, associate black with the concept of land. Throughout history, the Yao people often experienced land scarcity, and black symbolizes both their yearning for the land and their sorrow at

Table 3. Application Examples of Digital Creative Design of Yao Ethnic Costume Patterns

Creative pattern naming	Use representative pattern unit names	Unit Pattern	Basic unit of creative design	Design of combined creative patterns
Creative pattern 1	Stamen pattern			
Creative pattern 2	Octagon flower pattern, Dragon pattern			
Creative pattern 3	Pine cone pattern, pine tree pattern, Dragon pattern, Panwang seal, Chinese character Wan pattern, Eye pattern, Star pattern, etc.			

(continued)

Table 3. (*continued*)

Creative pattern 4	Deer Pattern, Humanoid pattern, Octagonal pattern			
Creative pattern 5	Sycamore pattern, Bird pattern Wilderness pattern			
Creative pattern 6	Pinecone pattern, Stamen pattern			
Creative pattern 7	Star pattern, Half-bean pattern, Japanese character pattern, Girl pattern			

losing it. Black also represents the wisdom and composure of the nation. When combined with other vibrant colors, it reflects the positive and enthusiastic attitude toward life by the Yao people, embodying their yearning and reverence for their ancestors, land, and nature.

4.4 Examples of Digital Recognition and Application of Yao Costume Patterns

Based on the summary, it can be deduced that the patterns of the Yao people in northern Guangdong are shaped by historical, cultural, religious beliefs, traditional etiquette, and living customs. These factors contribute to the composition and stylistic characteristics of the patterns. Utilizing computer software to digitally extract unit patterns and conduct feature analysis proves beneficial for discerning the art and culture of Yao patterns in northern Guangdong. More significantly, through the reorganization of unit patterns, new pattern types infused with Yao style can be rapidly designed, ensuring its seamless integration into modern mainstream culture. By blending with contemporary aesthetic characteristics, the Yao traditions can be passed down and developed over time.

There are two approaches to design based on unit patterns. One involves the direct application of formal beauty methods to combine and arrange the refined basic units. The other approach is to select a basic unit pattern and make appropriate adjustments in color and shape, transforming it into a design suitable for patterns such as two-sided continuous or four-sided continuous patterns (see Table 3).

Select representative Yao ethnic pattern units in northern Guangdong and reorganize them to create a series of new patterns. As illustrated in Table 3-Creative pattern 1, the stamen-shaped pattern unit is employed, coupled with traditional color matching, to generate a new pattern characterized by strong color contrast and simple geometry. In Table 3-Creative pattern 2, the pattern unit of a Panwang Seal and Snowflake pattern is utilized, combined with modern color matching, resulting in a new pattern with a delicate style and rich layers. Table 3-Creative pattern 3 incorporates numerous pattern units, including the pinecone pattern, octagonal pattern, Chinese character Wan pattern, and dragon pattern. These pattern units undergo reorganization and redesign through symmetry, combination, repetition, change, etc.

5 Conclusion

This study conducted field research in the Liannan Yao Autonomous County, collecting a significant number of typical Yao clothing patterns. It digitally analyzed these patterns, utilizing Adobe Illustrator software to extract representative pattern units. Through a comprehensive review of physical objects and literature, the characteristic features, composition, and color matching principles of the five major classification patterns were identified and summarized. The software was then employed to produce innovative design applications, resulting in modern patterns in two dimensions. This approach not only preserves the intangible cultural heritage characteristic of typical Yao patterns in northern Guangdong, but it also streamlines the pattern design process.

The establishment of digital identification for Yao ethnic costume patterns in northern Guangdong serves as the cornerstone for preserving, passing down, and creatively utilizing these patterns while ensuring efforts to culturally protect Yao culture and traditions. This study explores the practical significance of traditional patterns and introduces fresh viewpoints for digitally safeguarding and advancing Yao patterns in northern Guangdong.

References

1. https://www.ihchina.cn
2. Ye, Y., Xiao, J.: Characterization and development of Yao embroidery in northern Guangdong. Silk **51**(9), 62–66 (2014)
3. Ye, Y.: The current situation and decorative characteristics of the Yao people's clothing in northern Guangdong. Silk **48**(11), 54–57 (2011)
4. https://www.gov.cn/zhengce/2022-08/16/content_5705612.htm?eqid=f59ffd82000055e700 0000066480271c
5. https://www.gov.cn
6. Long, X., Pan, Z.: Yao Embroidery: Liannan Yao Clothing Embroidery Technology (2009)
7. Deng, J., Pan, W., Mo, R.: Yao Embroidery. Guangdong People's Publishing House, Guangzhou (2008)
8. Li, X.: Costume culture of ethnic minorities in Guangdong (2004)
9. Li, X.: Colorful——Guangdong Yao Embroidery. Guangdong Education Press, Guangzhou (2012)
10. Li, X.: Colorful: The Embroidery of the Yao Nationality in Guangdong. Guangdong Education Publishing House, Guangzhou (2012)
11. Li, X.: Pictures of the Yao people in Guangdong. Guangdong People's Publishing House, Guangzhou (2012)
12. Chen, Z.: History Books Worn on the Body: Interpretation and Application of Ruyuan Yao Embroidery. Guangdong People's Publishing Hous, Guangzhou (2013)
13. Yu, S.: The cultural connotation of Yao ethnic costume patterns. J. Guangxi Univ. Nationalities (Philosophy and Social Sciences Edition) (1994)
14. Chen, Q.: Also talking about the embroidery patterns on the costumes of the Yao people in Ruyuan. Guangxi Ethnic Stud. (3), 116–124 (1987)
15. Hu, X., Luo, L.: Iconological analysis of embroidery patterns of the Yao people in Ruyuan, northern Guangdong—taking "Panwang Seal" as an example. Silk (2020)
16. Hu, X.: The application of iconography in the analysis of clothing patterns of the Yao people in northern Guangdong. Silk (2020)
17. Xie, L.: Research on the decorative graphics of the "Panwang Seal" of the Ruyuan Yao people in northern Guangdong. Ethnic Art (2), 164–166 (2014)
18. Xie, L.: The symbolic cultural connotation of the "deer pattern" embroidery pattern of the Ruyuan Yao people. J. Guangxi Normal Univ. (Phil. Soc. Sci. Ed.) **51**(4), 81–87 (2018)
19. Li, J.: A study of the totem worship patterns of the Ruyuan Yao people. Decoration (2), 114–115 (2011)
20. Li, J.: Research on the embroidery patterns of horn hats and flower handkerchiefs of the Yao people in Dongping, Ruyuan. Decoration (6), 84–86 (2016)
21. Ye, Y.: Innovative design of patterns of Yao people in northern Guangdong. Silk **52**(1), 60–65 (2015)
22. Yin, N.: The application of Guangdong Liannan Yao embroidery in the design of modern home textile products. Text. Herald (2), 71–73 (2018)
23. Jia, Y., Feng, S.: Feasibility exploration of fashionable design of Yao embroidery in northern Guangdong. Creat. Des. (5), 37–39 (2011)

24. Jiang, R., Dong, J.: Extraction and application of clothing cultural factors of the Yao people in northern Guangdong. Packa. Eng. **41**(4), 341–346 (2020)
25. Cui, R.: Review and value explanation of research on Chinese traditional textile clothing patterns. Packa. Eng. Art Ed. **43**(6), 11–23 (2022)
26. Xu, H., Chen, H.: Innovative design application of Buyi batik patterns in women's leather shoes. Leather Sci. Eng. (2023)
27. Zhou, M., Xin, X., Zhang, H., Qian, J.: Development of online design system for Kirgiz tapestry patterns. Wool Text. J. **50**(9) (2022)
28. Zhao, H., Zhang, J.: Xinjiang folk art patterns digital technology. Comput. Syst. Appl. **20**(12), 167–172 (2011)
29. Li, J., Tang, J.: Research on the shape of flowers in Rongshui Miao costume patterns. Spec. Topic Disc. (2022)
30. Qian, J.: Analysis and application of Kirgiz traditional textile pattern primitives. Silk (2021)

Cross-Cultural Digital Transformation

Strategic Pathways to Net Zero by 2050: Vietnam's Adoption of South Korea's Policies

Minh Bui Duc[1] and Lin Wang[2(✉)]

[1] Hanyang University, Seoul 04763, Republic of Korea
[2] Incheon National University, Incheon 22012, Republic of Korea
linwang0@gmail.com

Abstract. This research conducts an in-depth analysis of Vietnam's strategies to reach the Net Zero target by 2050, contrasting them with South Korea's more established methods. It employs a comprehensive approach that includes a literature review, interviews with experts, and data analysis, all tailored to enhance Vietnam's climate policy framework. These findings highlight South Korea's success in emission reduction and clean technology adoption, serving as a model for Vietnam. The urgency for Vietnam to reform its climate strategy is apparent, as the research advocates for a robust legal framework, comprehensive sectoral integration, and a focus on transparent, equitable policy development. Vietnam's revised strategy should be underpinned by a sturdy legal system and encompassing planning that considers its economic growth, social fairness, and energy transitions, with bespoke strategies for emission cuts and carbon sequestration. The research suggests that Vietnam engages more in international cooperation, especially in carbon markets, to access global financial and technology resources. It also calls for regular policy reviews to adapt to technological and scientific developments. The study stresses the importance of setting transparent and equitable climate goals to ensure stakeholder support and the durability of climate policies. These strategic recommendations are geared towards guiding Vietnam on a path to a sustainable, low-carbon future by 2050, in line with international climate objectives.

Keywords: Net Zero · International Climate Cooperation · Vietnam & South Korea

1 Introduction

As the challenge of climate change becomes increasingly urgent, this study undertakes a comparative analysis of Vietnam's and South Korea's strategies for achieving the Net Zero 2050 goal. Despite Vietnam's significant progress in economic growth and poverty reduction, the country is now facing the challenge of mitigating its rising greenhouse gas emissions. [1–4]. South Korea's experience in implementing effective environmental policies and adopting clean technology provides valuable lessons for Vietnam [5–8]. The literature review scrutinizes both countries' latest environmental laws and policy developments, focusing on South Korea's recent advances in Net Zero initiatives. This

© The Author(s), under exclusive license to Springer Nature Switzerland AG 2024
P.-L. P. Rau (Ed.): HCII 2024, LNCS 14701, pp. 197–209, 2024.
https://doi.org/10.1007/978-3-031-60904-6_14

research aims to analyze and assess Vietnam's current strategies as well as the practices of South Korea, identifying opportunities for Vietnam to enhance its policies and strategies. Through the synthesis of legal texts, reports, and studies, as well as exploring the perspectives of policymakers in Vietnam, this work seeks to propose additional policies compatible with Vietnam's unique developmental challenges. Guided by the hypothesis that Vietnam can adapt and learn from South Korea's approach, the study focuses on understanding the specific policy and strategic improvements needed to progress efficiently toward Net Zero. The expected outcomes include an enhanced understanding of Vietnam's policy landscape, strategic recommendations based on South Korea's experience, and deeper insights into the challenges and opportunities of achieving Net Zero goals. This foundational research aims to inform policymaking and facilitate Vietnam's strategic progress toward a sustainable, low-carbon future by 2050.

Methodologically, the study uses SPSS for a descriptive statistical overview and ANOVA tests to pinpoint significant policy differences between the policies and strategies by sectors and elements. Content analysis further explores the qualitative facets of these strategies, offering insight into the nuances of each country's policy environment. The study's analytical rigor, combining legal and policy analysis with statistical validation, offers a solid base for evaluating Vietnam's strategies and learning from South Korea's experiences.

2   Literature Review

2.1   Net Zero 2050 Explained - Understanding Its Global Significance and Role

Net Zero, defined in the Paris Agreement, strives for a balance between GHG emitted and removed from the atmosphere. It's not just about reducing emissions but also using carbon removal technologies. The terms 'Net Zero' and 'Carbon Neutrality' are used differently across countries and require policies, technology, and financing to reduce primarily CO_2 emissions. Achieving Net Zero by 2050 is crucial to limiting global temperature rise and mitigating climate change impacts, as the IPCC's 2019 report highlights. Delays in emission reductions could have long-term detrimental effects.

The world has been actively addressing climate change with critical milestones since the UNFCCC's Paris Agreement 2015, which introduced the Net Zero target. Countries have made commitments to finance, technology, and capacity building. Key developments include the 2015 adoption of the Paris Agreement, 2018 COP24's implementation rules, and 2021 COP26's notable agreements by 195 countries to achieve net-zero emissions by 2050. South Korea and Vietnam have pledged to meet Net Zero targets, with South Korea focusing on clean energy and Vietnam setting sector-specific emission reduction goals for 2050.

2.2   Comparative Commitments: Climate Strategies of Vietnam and South Korea

In the global fight against climate change, both Vietnam and South Korea have made steadfast commitments to achieve the Net Zero target by 2050. South Korea has enacted numerous strategies and laws, such as the "2050 Carbon Neutral Strategy" and the

"Korean New Deal" [9–12], which include substantial investments in renewable energy. These advancements are evidenced by large-scale wind and solar energy projects [6] and a robust development in the new energy sector [13]. On the other hand, Vietnam, following the COP26 summit, has implemented essential strategies and plans aimed at reducing emissions but lacks an official legal document on Net Zero [4, 14–16] (Fig. 1).

Both countries, with similar geographical and cultural backgrounds, possess significant potential for renewable energy development and share stable political commitments to sustainable development goals [17–19].

Vietnam GHG emissions target by 2050 (Vietnam NDC update,2022)

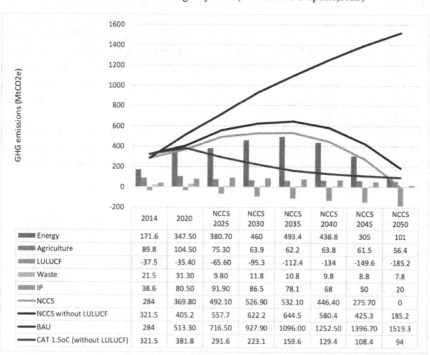

	2014	2020	NCCS 2025	NCCS 2030	NCCS 2035	NCCS 2040	NCCS 2045	NCCS 2050
Energy	171.6	347.50	380.70	460	493.4	438.8	305	101
Agriculture	89.8	104.50	75.30	63.9	62.2	63.8	61.5	56.4
LULUCF	-37.5	-35.40	-65.60	-95.3	-112.4	-134	-149.6	-185.2
Waste	21.5	31.30	9.80	11.8	10.8	9.8	8.8	7.8
IP	38.6	80.50	91.90	86.5	78.1	68	50	20
NCCS	284	369.80	492.10	526.90	532.10	446.40	275.70	0
NCCS without LULUCF	321.5	405.2	557.7	622.2	644.5	580.4	425.3	185.2
BAU	284	513.30	716.50	927.90	1096.00	1252.50	1396.70	1519.3
CAT 1.5oC (without LULUCF)	321.5	381.8	291.6	223.1	159.6	129.4	108.4	94

Data sources: Draft NCCS, NDC 2020, and Climate Action Tracker.

Fig. 1. The Proposed National Climate Change Strategy (NCCS) Targets

This study asserts that learning from international experiences, mainly from South Korea, can enhance and effectively optimize Vietnam's Net Zero strategy, leveraging existing conditions to achieve emission reduction targets more efficiently.

2.3 Strategic Frameworks: Evaluating and Propelling National Net Zero Initiatives

In the evaluation and development of national strategies to achieve Net Zero targets, the use of a structured framework based on various indicators [20–22] is essential. These indicators help shape policies to reduce greenhouse gas emissions and promote sustainable development. A prominent example is the set of indicators from the Climate Action Tracker (CAT) [23], which allows for a comprehensive assessment and comparison of national commitments against the objectives of the Paris Agreement.

The CAT framework includes ten elements such as the target year, the scope of emissions, the inclusion of international aviation and maritime emissions, and approaches to global emissions reduction with three main elements group, particularly: Scope of Emissions, Architecture, and Transparency. This framework also determines the legal status of Net Zero targets, differentiates between emission reduction and carbon removal targets, and establishes review processes to ensure continuous progress.

Frameworks like this provide a systematic approach to policy-making that is effective and fair and comprehensive, meeting the needs of all stakeholders. This approach is demonstrated by the United Nations Sustainable Development Goals (SDGs) [24, 25].

The Net Zero National Target Design framework shows that South Korea has implemented a comprehensive set of legal documents, including the "2050 Carbon Neutral Strategy" and the "Green Growth Act," showing a well-structured approach to achieving Carbon Neutrality. Conversely, Vietnam is still developing its strategy to include a more rigorous legal framework.

This approach emphasizes the importance of countries adopting a clear and organized method to achieve their Net Zero goals effectively. Such frameworks and indicators are essential for countries to accurately assess their progress and make the necessary adjustments to reach their climate objectives (Fig. 2).

Fig. 2. Climate Action Tracker National Net-zero Target Design

3 Method

3.1 Conceptual Model and Research Questions

The study asks questions based on a literature review to inform research hypotheses and understand Vietnamese experts' perspectives on achieving the Net Zero goal. This phase is designed to answer two primary research questions: which policies and strategies should Vietnam enhance, and what can it learn from South Korea's experience? The goal is to determine whether Vietnam can apply Korea's experience in implementing policies towards Net Zero 2050, adapting them to fit Vietnam's unique contexts and challenges. Research process - Fig. 3 below follows Siming Zhai's theoretical framework research [26]. Research questions:

1. What enhancements to policy and strategy are critical for Vietnam in achieving the Net Zero target?
2. How can Vietnam utilize lessons from South Korea to develop effective Net Zero strategies?

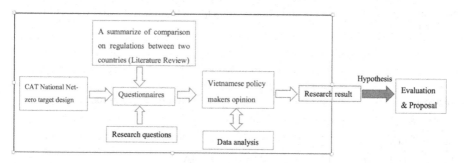

Fig. 3. Research process

3.2 Questionnaire Construction and Survey Procedure

The construction of the questionnaire and the survey procedure are pivotal to understanding the effectiveness of Vietnam's Net Zero strategy and policies. Insights from experts (15 people) in Vietnamese government agencies, gathered through the questionnaires, provide invaluable information. Experts contribute their specialized knowledge and offer an insider's perspective, combining theoretical knowledge with practical experience to ensure high reliability and the ability to propose practical solutions suitable for Vietnam. The diversity of 15 expert opinions based on unique experiences and qualifications enriches the research, paving the way for practical solutions.

This research employs a questionnaire method to capture Vietnamese experts' assessments of Vietnam's current Net Zero policies and strategies and potential lessons from South Korea's approach. Questions are crafted to evaluate the status quo of Vietnam's efforts and then identify actionable strategies that could be adopted, drawing on South

Korea's experiences. Responses will be quantified using a 5-point Likert scale, ranging from 1 for "Strongly Disagree" to 5 for "Strongly Agree," ensuring nuanced data collection as procedure research of Siming Zhai [27]. Experts' opinions will provide additional depth, helping to validate the research outcomes and directly inform on the study's hypotheses and questions.

3.3 Data Analysis

The methodology section will detail the data coding approach and the analytical methods used. It will describe how questionnaires will be coded and analyzed using tools such as SPSS, emphasizing the importance of reliability analysis to ensure the consistency and credibility of expert responses. Following previous research methods [28], descriptive data analysis and other statistical techniques, such as ANOVA, will be applied to interpret findings and draw conclusions about the current state of Vietnam's strategies, providing insights to answer the research questions (25 items) and support the hypotheses.

This approach is intended to offer a comprehensive view of Vietnam's efforts towards Net Zero, identifying strengths, areas needing improvement, and potential for adopting successful strategies from South Korea. The resulting data will be the foundation for proposing necessary strategies and policies to help Vietnam achieve its Net Zero targets (Table 1).

Table 1. Coding Rules

Elements	Question 1	Question 2	Question 3	Question 4
Target Year	TY1	TY2		
Scope of Emissions	SE1	SE2		
International Invitation and Shipping	IAS1	IAS2		
Removal outside Borders	RB1	RB2	RB3	
Legal System	LS1	LS2		
Separate reduction and removals targets	SRT1	SRT2	SRT3	SRT4
Review Process	RP1	RP2	RP3	
CO2 Removal	CDR1	CDR2	CDR3	
Comprehensive Plan	CP1	CP2		
Clarity on fairness of target	CFT1	CFT2		

4 Result

4.1 Insights on Vietnam's Net Zero Policy Framework and Korean's Lessons

In Chapter 4, the focus is on analyzing the collected data to discuss the results of the study on Vietnam's Net Zero strategy.

The reliability of the questionnaire is confirmed with a high Cronbach's Alpha, indicating consistent expert responses.

Reliability Statistics results:

- Cronbach's Alpha: **0.81.**
- Cronbach's Alpha Based on Standardized Items: **0.82.**
- N of Items: **25.**

The ANOVA one-way test results (p = 0,050) indicate significant differences among the groups of elements considered in the study. These differences suggest that each group of elements has varying impacts on policy implementation.

Group of Elements Comparison Analysis (Table 2)

Scope vs. Architecture. The mean difference between Scope and Architecture is 0.08, with a p-value of 0.802. This indicates that there is no statistically significant difference between the impact of Scope and Architecture on policy implementation. With Scope having a higher mean than Architecture (3.97 compared to 3.89), it suggests only a marginal difference that is not statistically significant.

Scope vs. Transparency. The mean difference is more substantial at 0.28, with a p-value of 0.064, which is just above the conventional threshold for significance (0.050). This result suggests there is a trend towards Scope having a more significant impact on achieving Net Zero targets compared to Transparency, although it does not reach the standard level of statistical significance. This close-to-significance result may warrant a **closer** examination or a follow-up study with a larger sample size to conclusively determine the relative impact of Scope on policy effectiveness.

Architecture vs. Transparency. The mean difference here is 0.20, with a p-value of 0.226. This lack of statistical significance suggests that Architecture and Transparency likely have a similar level of impact on policy implementation. The slightly higher mean for Architecture compared to Transparency (3.89 vs. 3.69) indicates a slight tendency for Architecture to be more influential but not significantly so.

In summary, the data suggests that among the elements considered, Scope may have a more prominent role in influencing policy implementation towards Net Zero goals, particularly when compared to Transparency. However, none of the pairwise comparisons among the three elements demonstrated a statistically significant difference at the 0.050 level, which implies that while there may be trends and tendencies, there is no conclusive statistical evidence to differentiate the impacts of these elements on policy implementation. Further investigation with more data could provide additional insights.

Scope Elements Comparison Analysis (Table 3). The provided data indicates the results of a one-way ANOVA comparison within the "Scope" elements. The analysis shows how these elements differ from each other in terms of their mean scores and how significantly they impact policy implementation.

The comparison between TY and IAS shows a statistically significant difference with a p-value of 0.023, suggesting that the impact of IAS on policy implementation is notably different from that of TY. In particular, IAS appears to have a less substantial

Table 2. Group of Elements Comparison Analysis

G. Elements	Mean	SD	G. Elements	Mean	SD	F-value	p-value
Scope	3.97	0.34	Architecture	3.89	0.31	3.310	0.802
Scope	3.97	0.34	Transparency	3.69	0.29		0.064
Architecture	3.89	0.31	Transparency	3.69	0.29		0.226

effect when compared to TY, as indicated by the lower mean score of 3.80 for IAS versus 4.37 for TY.

The comparison between TY and RB also shows a statistically significant difference with a p-value of 0.006. This is also a notable finding, implying that RB differs from TY in terms of impact on policy implementation, with RB having an even lower mean score of 3.71.

The comparisons of SE with both IAS ($p = 0.730$) and RB ($p = 0.450$) and the comparison of IAS with RB ($p = 0.970$) did not yield statistically significant differences. This suggests that, while there are observable differences in the mean scores, they do not statistically significantly differ from each other in terms of their impact on policy implementation.

Interpretation. The significant p-values in TY comparisons indicate that TY is a critical element within the scope category, showing distinct differences when compared with IAS and RB. The lack of significance in the differences between SE and the other two elements (IAS and RB) suggests that SE's impact on policy implementation is not statistically distinguishable from that of IAS and RB. The high p-value (0.970) in the IAS vs. RB comparison suggests that there is no evidence to support a significant difference in their impact on policy implementation.

Table 3. Scope Elements Comparison Analysis

Element	Mean	SD	Element	Mean	SD	F-value	p-value
TY	4.37	0.48	SE	4.00	0.65	5.461	0.240
TY	4.37	0.48	IAS	3.80	0.32		0.023*
TY	4.37	0.48	RB	3.71	0.42		0.006*
SE	4.00	0.65	IAS	3.80	0.32		0.730
SE	4.00	0.65	RB	3.71	0.42		0.450
IAS	3.80	0.32	RB	3.71	0.42		0.970

* $p < 0.050$

Architecture Elements Comparison Analysis (Table 4). LS has a mean of 4.33, which is significantly higher than both SRT's mean of 3.68 and RP's mean of 3.67. The p-values for both comparisons are less than 0.001, indicating a highly significant statistical difference. This significant difference suggests that LS is a critical element within the architectural category, having a more substantial impact on policy implementation related to architectural considerations than both SRT and RP.

The comparison between SRT and RP shows an insignificant mean difference, with a p-value of 0.990. This lack of significance suggests that there is no statistical evidence to differentiate the impact of SRT and RP on policy implementation within the context of architectural considerations. The means of SRT and RP are very close (3.68 vs. 3.67), further supporting the conclusion that their impacts are statistically indistinguishable.

Table 4. Architecture Elements Comparison Analysis

Element	Mean	SD	Element	Mean	SD	F-value	p-value
LS	4.33	0.36	SRT	3.68	0.47	13.214	< 0.001*
LS	4.33	0.36	RP	3.67	0.38		< 0.001*
SRT	3.68	0.47	RP	3.67	0.38		0.990

* $p < 0.050$

Interpretation. The findings highlight the importance of LS as a factor in architectural policy considerations. Its statistically significant difference in means from SRT and RP underscores its potential as a key influencer in policy effectiveness.

Given the strong statistical significance ($p < 0.001$), LS should be a priority in the discussion of architectural elements when considering policies aimed at achieving Net Zero targets.

The similarity in the impact of SRT and RP implies that these elements may be of secondary importance compared to LS or that they contribute similarly to the architectural aspects of policy implementation.

These results are valuable for policymakers, suggesting that LS warrants focused attention in the strategic planning and execution of policies within the realm of architecture to drive toward Net Zero goals. Further studies could explore the specific characteristics of LS that contribute to its significant impact.

Transparency Elements Comparison Analysis (Table 5). A significant mean difference of 0.44 ($p = 0.030$) suggests that CDR has a more pronounced influence on transparency-related policy outcomes compared to CP. The mean score of CDR is 3.91, which is notably higher than CP's mean score of 3.47, reinforcing the statistical finding.

The comparison between CDR and CFT shows a non-significant mean difference ($p = 0.430$), indicating that there is no strong evidence to suggest a difference in their impact on transparency in policy implementation. While the mean score of CDR is higher than that of CFT (3.91 vs. 3.70), the difference is not statistically significant.

Similarly, the mean difference between CP and CFT is not statistically significant ($p = 0.359$), suggesting that these elements have similar influences on policy transparency. The mean scores are relatively close (3.47 for CP and 3.70 for CFT), further supporting this conclusion.

Interpretation. The significant difference between CDR and CP points to CDR as a potentially critical element in enhancing transparency within policy frameworks. This could imply that strategies or actions that are part of the CDR element are more effective in promoting transparency. The lack of significant differences between CDR and CFT, and CP and CFT, suggests that these elements may contribute similarly to transparency-related outcomes or that the sample size or variability within the data does not allow for a clear distinction between their impacts.

Policymakers may consider focusing on the aspects of CDR that contribute to its greater influence on transparency, possibly integrating these aspects into the development and refinement of transparency measures within policy initiatives. These findings can inform strategic decisions in policy development, especially in contexts where transparency is crucial to achieving policy objectives and public trust.

Table 5. Transparency comparison Analysis

Element	Mean	SD	Element	Mean	SD	F-value	p-value
CDR	3.91	0.43	CP	3.47	0.52	3.812	0.030*
CDR	3.91	0.43	CFT	3.70	0.37		0.430
CP	3.47	0.52	CFT	3.70	0.37		0.359

* $p < 0.050$

The results underscore the necessity for Vietnam to tailor its strategies based on these findings, particularly when adopting policies informed by the South Korean experience. It is clear that some elements within each group are more influential than others, and recognizing these differences is crucial for prioritizing areas of focus as Vietnam advances toward its Net Zero 2050 goal.

The next step in the research would involve a closer look at the specific conditions in Vietnam that might affect the implementation of these elements, ensuring that the final policy recommendations are well-suited to the unique challenges and opportunities present in the Vietnamese context.

The consensus among experts is that Vietnam should model its Net Zero strategies on South Korea's experience, emphasizing the critical role of a robust legal system and a comprehensive, multi-sectoral plan. Strategies must be specific, distinguishing between emission reductions and carbon removal, and should consider international collaboration, particularly in the carbon market. Regular review processes and transparent, fair targets are essential for adaptability and stakeholder engagement. Less focus on emissions scope and international transport suggests these areas need more attention. Overall, Vietnam's climate change policy must be legally solid, technically specific, strategically collaborative, and socially equitable to be effective.

4.2 Insights into Study Findings and Recommended Action Plans

Based on the findings and data presented in the previous sections, it is evident that Vietnam's path to achieving Net Zero by 2050 will benefit from a nuanced understanding of different policy elements and their impacts. The research outcomes suggest that certain policy components have a more pronounced influence on the effectiveness of Vietnam's climate strategy. To capitalize on these insights, Vietnam should prioritize the development and enforcement of a strong legal framework, which has been identified as a key driver in policy implementation.

The empirical evidence from the questionnaire indicates that Vietnam must focus on enhancing legal structures (LS), as they are crucial for the architectural integrity of policy frameworks. These structures should be comprehensive and enforceable, providing a stable foundation for various sector-specific strategies. Furthermore, the study's findings recommend that Vietnam take a holistic approach to policy development, integrating aspects that cover the breadth of emissions (Scope) and transparently outlining policy intentions and outcomes (Transparency).

In learning from South Korea's experience, Vietnam can harness strategic advantages by adopting a multi-faceted approach to policy enhancement. This includes emphasizing emission reduction and carbon removal strategies that are tailored to the country's unique environmental and socioeconomic contexts. While the study highlights the importance of elements such as Target Year (TY) and International Aviation and Shipping (IAS), it also points to the need for Vietnam to give more attention to emissions scope and international transport, as these areas have received less focus.

The research underlines the significance of international cooperation, especially in carbon markets (RB), which can provide Vietnam access to global carbon funds and state-of-the-art technologies. Engaging in such collaborative efforts can also bolster the country's position in international climate negotiations and carbon trading platforms.

Regular assessment and review processes are advised to ensure policies remain relevant and effective in the face of rapid technological and scientific advances. This adaptability is crucial for maintaining the momentum towards Net Zero goals and adjusting strategies as necessary based on ongoing evaluations.

The proposed solutions also call for setting clear and fair climate targets, fostering stakeholder engagement, and ensuring long-term sustainability of the climate agenda. Establishing transparent targets will not only facilitate monitoring and accountability but also enhance public and stakeholder trust in Vietnam's commitment to climate action.

In essence, the study provides a strategic roadmap for Vietnam, outlining that the successful implementation of climate policies requires a balance between legal robustness, technical specificity, strategic collaboration, and social equity. These elements, when integrated effectively, will form the cornerstone of Vietnam's sustainable and low-carbon future. As the country moves forward, it will be imperative to tailor these strategies to the national context, drawing from international examples yet remaining distinctly Vietnamese in application and execution.

5 Conclusion

The study's conclusion underscores the urgent need for Vietnam to enhance its climate change strategies and policies, drawing key insights from South Korea's successful approach towards achieving Net Zero by 2050. The study reveals a consensus among experts that Vietnam must prioritize the establishment of a robust legal framework and a comprehensive, integrated plan that spans various sectors and aligns with international standards and practices.

Key findings indicate that experts advocate for a strong legal system (LS) as the cornerstone of effective policy implementation. The focus on a comprehensive plan (CP) reflects the necessity for a multi-pronged approach that accounts for the nuances of economic development, urban planning, and energy policies. Emphasis on separate strategies for emission reduction (SRT) and carbon removal (CDR) highlights the need for tailored solutions that leverage Vietnam's unique geographic, economic, and social landscape.

Furthermore, the study suggests that Vietnam should be open to international cooperation, particularly in the carbon market (RB), to benefit from global carbon finance and technology. The significance of regular review processes (RP) underscores the importance of adaptive policies that evolve with new findings and technological advancements. Lastly, the mention of clarity and fairness in target setting (CFT), though less frequent, points to the need for transparency and equity to ensure stakeholder buy-in and long-term policy sustainability.

In conclusion, the study provides strategic recommendations for Vietnam to learn from South Korea's experience and adapt it within its unique developmental context. The research emphasizes the need for Vietnam to craft policies that are not only legally sound and technically specific but also strategically collaborative and socially equitable. This holistic approach is vital for Vietnam to effectively progress towards a sustainable, low-carbon future by 2050.

References

1. Nguyen, L.T.H.: Impacts of foreign direct investment on economic growth in Vietnam. J. Econ. Bank. Stud. **4**, 01–15 (2022)
2. Dang, P.T., Baruah, B.: An evaluation of Vietnam's pathway to net-zero by 2050: reconciling the developmental state and civil society. In: 11th Congress of the Asian Association of Environmental and Resource Economics (2022)–A Pathway Towards Carbon Neutrality in Asia (2022)
3. Vietnam Ministry of Natural Resources and Environment. Technical report: National greenhouse gas inventory for 2016 (2022)
4. Agarwal, V., et al.: Charting a path for Vietnam to achieve its net-zero goals. McKinsey & Company, Sustainability Practice (2022)
5. Kim, J., Moon, J., Kim, Y.G.: Thematic Section: Green Transition and National Efforts towards Net-Zero Target, vol. 43 (2030)
6. Invest Korea. Facilitation of Energy Supply through Development of Catching-up Technologies (2022). https://www.investkorea.org/ik-en/cntnts/i-321/web.do#n
7. Lee, D., Kim, K.: Research and development investment and collaboration framework for the hydrogen economy in South Korea. Sustainability **13**(19), 10686 (2021)
8. Offshore Wind Staff. Korea's Largest Offshore Wind Turbine Stands Complete. Offshore Wind (2022). https://www.offshorewind.biz/2022/01/27/koreas-largest-offshore-wind-turbine-stands-complete/
9. Republic of Korea. 2050 Carbon Neutral Strategy of the Republic of Korea: Towards a Sustainable and Green Society. United Nations Framework Convention on Climate Change (2020)

10. Republic of Korea. Korean New Deal (Version 1,2) (2021)
11. Republic of Korea. First National Basic Plan for Carbon Neutrality and Green Growth (2023)
12. Republic of Korea (2022). Framework Act on Carbon Neutrality and Green Growth for the Climate Change
13. Stangarone, T.: South Korean efforts to transition to a hydrogen economy. Clean Technol. Environ. Policy **23**, 509–516 (2021)
14. Urakami, A.: Are the barriers to private solar/wind investment in Vietnam mainly those that limit network capacity expansion? Sustainability **15**(13), 10734 (2023)
15. Do, T.N., Burke, P.J.: Phasing out coal power in a developing country context: insights from Vietnam. Energy Policy **176**, 113512 (2023)
16. Nguyen, T.C., Chuc, A.T.: Green finance in Viet Nam: barriers and solutions. No. 886. ADBI Working paper (2018)
17. Bach, T.N.T.: Similarities of Vietnam and South Korea-linking to the strategy cooperation partnership and its future direction. Int. J. Soc. Sci. Manag. 1(3), 88–92 (2014)
18. Shwalb, D.W., et al.: East and Southeast Asia: Japan, South Korea, Vietnam, and Indonesia. In: Handbook of Cultural Developmental Science, pp. 445–464. Psychology Press (2014)
19. Vu, T.: Paths to Development in Asia: South Korea, Vietnam, China, and Indonesia. Cambridge University Press, Cambridge (2010)
20. Levin, K., et al.: Designing and communicating net-zero targets (2020)
21. Fankhauser, S., et al.: The meaning of net zero and how to get it right. Nat. Clim. Change **12**(1), 15–21 (2022)
22. Jeudy-Hugo, S., Re, L.L., Falduto, C.: Understanding countries' net-zero emissions targets (2021)
23. Tracker, Climate Action. Climate target updates slow as science ramps up need for action. Update (2020)
24. Carlsen, L., Bruggemann, R.: The 17 United Nations' sustainable development goals: a status by 2020. Int. J. Sust. Dev. World **29**(3), 219–229 (2022)
25. Whittingham, K.L., et al.: The impact of the United Nations sustainable development goals on corporate sustainability reporting. BRQ Bus. Res. Q. **26**(1), 45–61 (2023)
26. Zhai, S., Wang, L., Liu, P.: Not in control, but liable? attributing human responsibility for fully automated vehicle accidents. Engineering (2023)
27. Zhai, S., Wang, L., Liu, P.: Human and machine drivers: sharing control, sharing responsibility. Accid. Anal. Prev. **188**, 107096 (2023)
28. Wang, L., et al.: Individual entrepreneurial orientation, value congruence, and individual outcomes: does the institutional entrepreneurial environment matter? Bus. Strat. Environ. **30**(5), 2293–2312 (2021)

Educational Methods and Practices for Futures-Thinking-Based Interaction Design Curricula

Zhiyong Fu and Ping Gong[✉]

Academy of Art and Design, Tsinghua University, Beijing 100084, China
2201710163@cug.edu.cn

Abstract. The core of interaction design lies in shaping and optimizing the interactive experience between users and products, enabling design solutions to help users achieve their intentions and goals. However, with social development, the term "design" has surpassed the traditional fields of products and information. People expect design to play a greater role in social and technological intervention and extend it to interdisciplinary fields such as culture, policy, and society. However, traditional interaction design courses based on "design thinking" may overlook the cultivation of students' abilities to grasp forward-looking trends and explore diverse uncertainties. Therefore, this paper proposes an educational approach for interaction design courses based on "futures thinking (FT)". By systematically training students in futures thinking, speculative thinking, systems thinking, aggregation capability, prototyping ability, and reflective ability, this approach breaks through the limitations of traditional "design thinking." It guides students to understand the influence of futures thinking and future-oriented methodologies on future interaction patterns, explore the interactive connections between activities, media, space, and environments, and realize future-oriented exploration and practice in interaction design.

Keywords: Futures Thinking · Interaction Design · thinking toolkit · Educational Practices

1 Introduction

The 21st century is an era of uncertainty, situated within a world characterized by exponential rates of change [1]. The pace of design and development of products and services has accelerated, with their shelf life constantly being disrupted by new products. As the field of design engages with larger and more complex issues, new methods and skills become necessary. Design education must keep pace with and anticipate these changes. However, with the development of society, the demand for design is no longer confined to traditional products and information domains. Modern society expects design to engage more deeply in socio-technical interventions and to expand into interdisciplinary fields such as culture, policy, and society. This trend presents new challenges and opportunities for the field of interaction design, requiring designers to continuously

P.-L. P. Rau (Ed.): HCII 2024, LNCS 14701, pp. 210–223, 2024.
https://doi.org/10.1007/978-3-031-60904-6_15

expand their perspectives and skills to adapt to the evolving needs and environments. Many thought leaders have also clearly pointed out the changes in the field of design. For example, John Chris Jones [2] proposed four levels of design: components, products, systems, and communities, advocating for new design methods that go beyond craftsmanship to address new challenges such as traffic safety and air quality. Meredith Davis [3] introduced the concept of complexity levels in communication design, where complexity increases with the scope of the system and human experience, with communication design ranging from logo design to corporate identity design, brand design, and service design. Richard Buchanan [4] introduced four design sequences, including communication design (symbols), industrial design (products), traditional disciplines of action design (actions), and systems design (thoughts), along with the blurred boundaries of new understandings of design. Arnold Wasserman [5] proposed exponential design and explained its four versions: Design 1.0 centered on artifacts (e.g., manufacturing and sales); Design 2.0 centered on humans (e.g., strategic and embedded architecture); Design 3.0 centered on society (e.g., changing the world); and Design 4.0 for the post-human era (e.g., sustainable prosperity of a planet). Norman [6] introduced the DesignX concept in 2014, going beyond the quantity of design to shift focus from products and services to broader societal issues.

As a field within the discipline of design, the field of interaction design has experienced rapid development and transformation in recent years. Traditionally, design has primarily focused on the domains of products and information. However, with the continuous evolution of society and advancements in technology, expectations regarding design have also been evolving. Interaction design, as a significant branch of design, is concerned with shaping and optimizing the interactive experiences between users and products, enabling design solutions to assist users in achieving their intentions and goals. In traditional interaction design courses, Design Thinking (DT) is a human-centered design approach that is based on understanding user needs, defining design directions, generating creative ideas, rapidly iterating prototypes, and collecting feedback for innovation in products, services, processes, and organizations. Through DT, designers primarily develop feasible solutions based on human expectations. However, in the present context, interaction design requires continual consideration and exploration of how to leverage design's role in various domains and environments to address complex societal issues and challenges. This includes understanding future trends, exploring diverse unknowns, and applying design thinking and methods in practical social practices. Through interdisciplinary collaboration and innovation, designers can make positive contributions to building a more human-centered and intelligent future society.

Contemporary curriculum design requires a more comprehensive approach that considers the intersections and interrelationships between curriculum elements and larger practical-level subsystems, while also taking into account learners' developmental progress in core competencies. A coherent and overarching theoretical approach supporting complex curriculum blueprints will ensure the integrity of the entire curriculum approach [7]. Systems thinking can provide curriculum designers with this conceptual shift. Therefore, this paper proposes a futures-thinking-based systems thinking, namely a collaborative thinking toolkit aimed at understanding the dynamic relationships, dependencies, and interactions among various elements within and across systems and subsystems [8, 9]. It is considered a highly relevant perspective for understanding, predicting, and enhancing the adaptive capacity of complex systems, such as curricula [10]. In this paper, employing systems thinking as a theoretical reference, our goal is to provide curriculum designers with a toolkit based on futures thinking, enabling learners to better design and capture their learning journeys by understanding the various components of the curriculum, while remaining prepared to practice at all times to adapt to rapidly evolving complex design environments. The term "thinking toolkit" refers to a set of ideas, viewpoints, and methods based on soft systems thinking, which will enable educators to visualize, create, improve, implement, and evaluate new or existing curriculum designs.

2 Methodology

By structuring the curriculum as a complex adaptive system, we utilize soft systems thinking to develop an initial prototype of a conceptual curriculum toolkit, grounded in an assessment of relevant literature, for practical application in interaction design education and broader educational contexts. Following reflective case studies, the prototype is further refined.

3 Conceptual Framework

The framework is guided by various perspectives of systems thinking, where the interactions between different systems and subsystems can be analyzed based on views of boundaries, relationships, and internal and external perspectives of various system elements [11–13]. When constructing the curriculum as an adaptive system, each learning subsystem will be appropriately interconnected with other subsystems and engage in communication to achieve self-regulation and adapt to environmental influences. Although this system is simplified, its systems thinking perspective aligns with the "soft systems" approach, serving as a way to generate insights and understanding of real-world engagement, and allowing different stakeholders to construct similar curriculum questions or issues in different ways [14]. Soft systems thinking is considered an appropriate approach to the complex structure of "messy" real-world problems. Whereas the hard systems approach informs how systems and their subsystems operate, the soft systems approach describes why systems operate in the way they do [15, 16]. It is a holistic approach to understanding how components of subsystems intersect, relate, and interact within the context of larger systems [17, 18].

Based on the theoretical foundation mentioned above, we conceptualized a future-thinking toolkit called "3P-6Fs" (Fig. 1), which illustrates the Personal (P1), Program (P2 and 6Fs), and Practice (P3) dimensions of course elements that intersect and interact through course interactions. The Personal dimension delineates the core considerations learned at the learner's level; the Program dimension describes the characteristics or elements of the curriculum, both explicit and implicit; and the Practice dimension delineates the broader learning capacity of learners within the design industry.

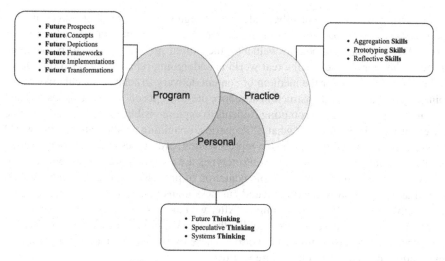

- **Future** Prospects
- **Future** Concepts
- **Future** Depictions
- **Future** Frameworks
- **Future** Implementations
- **Future** Transformations

Program   Practice

- Aggregation **Skills**
- Prototyping **Skills**
- Reflective **Skills**

Personal

- Future **Thinking**
- Speculative **Thinking**
- Systems **Thinking**

Fig. 1. 3P-6Fs system thinking toolkit

3.1 Personal Level

At the individual level, students embark on their journey in the interaction design course by initiating contemplation and reflection on designing the future. There exists a logical coherence and progression among these three modes of thinking. Futures thinking provides students with a method to contemplate future trends and possibilities, aiding them in understanding and anticipating future directions. Following initial considerations and explorations of the future, students then engage in "speculative thinking," which focuses on fostering their critical thinking and analytical abilities, enabling them to scrutinize and evaluate future possibilities from multiple perspectives. Finally, "systems thinking" emphasizes teaching students how to integrate various factors and causal relationships to comprehensively and systematically understand patterns and trends in future development. Thus, these three modes of thinking form a logically coherent process, progressing from initial awareness of the future to deep contemplation and analysis, ultimately leading to the establishment of a systematic understanding of the future.

Future Thinking. FT is a creative exploratory process that employs divergent thinking to envision diverse scenarios, acknowledges uncertainty, and seeks multiple potential answers. As a mode of thinking, FT is grounded in disciplines such as futurology, forecasting, sociology, and science fiction. Concurrently, within the design domain, there are numerous theories and practices centered around the future, time, and trends. They share a common objective, which is to expand the range of future alternatives. In the context of interaction design, "Futures Thinking" refers to designers considering potential future environments, user behaviors, needs, and responses, and then being able to accurately anticipate and respond to these environmental behaviors. It is a crucial component of curriculum training. During the Futures Thinking training phase, students primarily explore existing weak signals, engage in multidimensional data collection, thereby triggering imaginations of future societies and clarifying project positioning.

Speculative Thinking. Typically, students in design rely more on static environments and investigations of past or existing conditions rather than anticipation of future scenarios. While these methods are valuable, they often present a static or perpetuated image of the world, whereas the real world is undergoing rapid changes. At this stage, students need to consider the medium of content delivery to achieve speculative touchpoints. During this period, instructors introduce the concepts of "speculative design" and "speculative prototyping," prompting students to explore visible, plausible, and possible spaces through the inquiry of "what if" scenarios, imagining an alternate parallel world to infer design possibilities. In design representation, prototypes are commonly used to rapidly materialize and express ideas. Prototypes are rough physical representations of products or environments, or the implementation of processes and service experiences, as well as the internal infrastructure and business plans required to deliver these products or environments [19]. For example, 'After we have established the environment of a world and written the stories to unfold within it, what props will the protagonists use to advance the narrative within that world?' These props also serve as prototypes, thus constituting 'evidence from the future world'.

Systems Thinking. Before engaging in systems thinking, students need to undergo a process of goal transformation. The 'transformation' step involves converting subjective descriptions from the preceding stages into primary research questions within a design context. During this conversion process, students utilize design tools such as the Future Triangle and Future Signals to transition from data to questions. The Future Triangle primarily presents the driving forces behind developmental trends, such as the gravity of history, the thrust of the present, and the pull of the future. Future Signals primarily conduct research across three dimensions: signals, issues, and interpretations, driven by visible clues to prompt anticipated actions. As a generic model, Future Signals are employed to comprehend weak signals and assess their characteristics. At this stage, students are required to: list key findings, i.e., all key findings need to be listed in the thematic description and all relevant content marked; merge similar findings, i.e., preliminary organization of key findings, ensuring the most vivid statements are preserved during consolidation; and select processed findings, choosing key findings that generate further discussion and debate. Throughout this process, the future transitions from 'decomposition' to 'transformation,' with future trends being extended through the analysis of 'future signals' and background depth being excavated through the analysis of 'future traces,' thereby transforming the project into specific design requirements.

3.2 The Program Level 6Fs

The six task stages of the curriculum constitute the curriculum elements known as the '6Fs,' defining and interconnecting various curriculum tasks within a curriculum framework. They are: Future Prospects, Future Concepts, Future Depictions, Future Frameworks, Future Implementations, and Future Transformations (Table 1), collectively referred to as the transformation and construction of visions (Fig. 2). In Interaction Design - Systems Design theory, Interaction Design has systematic objectives, characterized by structured features, and observed from a panoramic view to study the whole, emphasizing the reinforcement of scenarios and environments rather than the users themselves. This provides a comprehensive analytical framework for design and is also highly effective in addressing complex issues. In the development of future interactions, attention should not only be paid to specific technological innovations but also to the conceptualization of future societies, capturing the changes in social life brought about by the future wave of human-computer interactions at a higher level.

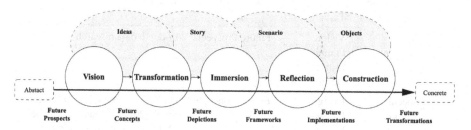

Fig. 2. The Design Future Transformation Diagram of the Program Level 6Fs

Future Prospects and Future Concepts also referred as "vision". This is the first step in a futures thinking-based design process that inspires users to articulate their deep desires and fears, and enables designers to establish the starting point and end goal of the creative process (Fig. 3). The process from envisioning the future to describing it is referred to as "transformation". The vision of the research object is typically a self-description, and the transformation step involves translating this subjective description into a research question within the design context (Fig. 4). The process mentioned above until Future Depictions, we refer to it as "immersion" (Fig. 5). Design artifacts, products, services, systems, or rules, etc. that fulfill the "vision" of the object of study; And set up a detailed scenario to draw a picture of how the object would accomplish the wish through the creation. In this step, the solution will be regarded as a Diegetic Prototyping system based on the intelligent Internet of Things technology, which in addition to the function of each touch point, will focus more on the data link and information flow relationship between system elements. This is a way to not only present design creations to people, to allow them to see the story of the future, but also to become participants in the story, so that they can actually experience the realization of that vision. The transition from Future Frameworks to Future Implementations requires a process of "reflection". This step is the pause button step for the design process. During this brief pause, creators are encouraged to think about the long-term impact of their designs. The influences at different levels and the trends under different development directions are decomposed. When calculating the impact, we can use the future board tool to mark the development of the product and its positive and negative effects on society, economy and technology on the given timeline, so as to reflect on the value and necessity of the design. To see if the direction is consistent with the original vision. The final step, known as the Future Transformations, is also referred to as "construction". This step is the creative process of design. After determining the direction of the design without yaw, further deepen the design to achieve the design goal. Depending on the design goal, the content of the build will vary. In the pursuit of practical design projects, can be transformed into a realistic program; In the pursuit of possibilities, the project shows the story or scene, makes the dialogue more convenient and easier, and realizes the imagination of the future to the concrete reality.

Table 1. The program level 6Fs Elements

Stage	Curriculum Organization	Teaching Tasks	Task Phase	Task Design
1	Future Thinking	Vision Planning, Project Description	Future Prospects	In-depth data research
2	Speculative Thinking	Design Fiction, Speculative Prototypes	Future Concepts	Utilizing tools such as "Future Sign" [20] and "Future Triangle" [21] to translate signals into problems
3	Systems Thinking	Trend Analysis, Scenario Construction	Future Depictions	Utilizing tools like STEEP [22] and CLA [23] to model vision-objective-problem-system
4	Aggregation Skills	Content Experience, Interaction Behavior	Future Frameworks	Linking content experience and interaction behavior through design tools
5	Prototyping Skills	Prototype Assembly, Media Propagation	Future Implementations	Transforming future scenarios into interactive prototypes and disseminating design propositions
6	Reflective Skills	Presentation, Reflection Evaluation	Future Transformations	Learning and reflecting from projects to achieve knowledge expansion and skill enhancement

Fig. 3. Vision Design Tools

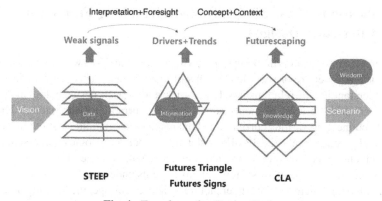

Fig. 4. Transformation Design Tools

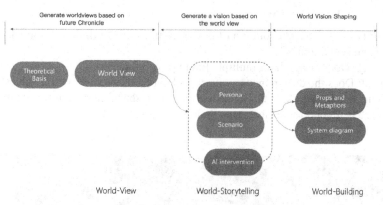

Fig. 5. Immersion Design Tools

3.3 The Practice Level

The practical-level elements of the toolkit focus on the broader picture for graduates entering practice as interaction design professionals. As learners transition into their next stage of comprehensive learning, our toolkit presents three key competency processes: 1) Cultivating learners' aggregative capabilities, a process that not only trains thinking methods but also strengthens skill development to 'calibrate' their skills, knowledge, and behaviors; 2) Cultivating learners' design prototyping capabilities, completing creative outputs and retrospection; 3) Cultivating learners' reflective capabilities, ensuring learners' 'continuous development' training. This process requires students to integrate and output previous knowledge, signals, concepts, and scenarios, training their ability to transform thinking while assessing their design output capabilities.

4   Implications of the 3P-6Fs Systems Thinking Framework for Curricular Designs

We anticipate that a systems thinking toolkit will provide educators with valuable insights when redesigning entire or specific elements of a curriculum. This can be achieved by better understanding the relationships, boundaries, and impacts nested within individual, project, and practice-level elements across various curriculum subsystems. Through explicitly connecting various curriculum elements and considerations at the individual, project, and practice levels, the 3P-6Fs model offers a better ecological understanding of curriculum elements. The toolkit provides designers with a range of heuristic methods to address key questions, such as: How to help students understand potential curriculum blueprints and help them see the bigger picture by addressing specific learning outcomes.

To illustrate the utility of our toolkit for interaction design learners, we describe practical cases of the 3P-6Fs systems thinking toolkit in curriculum design and its application assessments in four key areas.

1. Trend: Does the future evolution of design conform to the design vision and can it anticipate social trends?
2. Diversity: Does design have multiple future possibilities?
3. Concept: Does the design incorporate consideration of world view and values?
4. Sociality: Did the thinking that came with designing the event make it worth reflecting on later? Is it good for society as a whole?

Fig. 6. Case 1 of Curriculum Practice

The curriculum practice, guided by the five core tasks mentioned earlier, led students through a progression from futures thinking, speculative thinking, and systems thinking to aggregation capability and prototyping capability, with their progress reflected in staged assignment reports. In practical application, design teams engaged in constructing interactive scenarios for a future 'carbon-based civilization,' using various preset scenarios and the 3P-6Fs framework. Here, students assumed the role of 'reflective practitioners' in the design process. At this stage, students were tasked with synthesizing

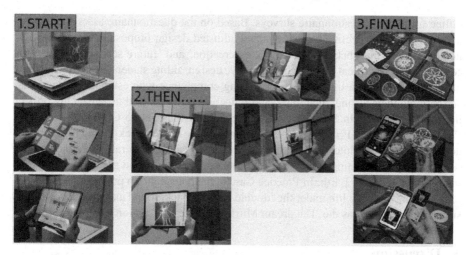

Fig. 7. Case 2 of Curriculum Practice

Fig. 8. Case 3 of Curriculum Practice

their prior knowledge, signals, ideas, and visions into comprehensive outputs, aiming to cultivate their ability to transform thinking and assess their design output capabilities, primarily showcased in the final assignment presentations. During the retrospective evaluation phase, instructors explained fundamental evaluation methods and criteria, allowing students to employ diverse evaluation methods based on the presentation format of each group's work. For instance, in Practice Case 1, the 'Plant Change Initiative' project group collected feedback and co-creation ideas from visitors through both online and offline channels, employing QR code sharing online and distributing design posters offline for related questionnaire surveys. Based on the questionnaire assessments, students conducted reflective evaluations and adjusted design proposals, optimizing and iteratively designing between 'feedback co-creation' and 'future scenarios.' This process constitutes a critical juncture in interactive design, aiding students in reviewing their decision-making in design projects, assessing compliance with established standards, and refining their testing, analytical, and reflection skills, as well as enhancing project improvement plans. In Practice Case 2, the case of the 'Future Cosmic Community Waste Recycling and Printing System' under a double carbon background is described, detailing how the 'printer' achieved an almost 100% conversion rate of garbage in the 'First Oasis,' maintaining cleanliness in the space community and gradually popularizing resource reuse on Earth. In Practice Case 3, the course group proposed the concept of protecting the slow life under the 'double carbon' background and introduced future sign prototypes such as the 'Daydream Mirror' and the 'Perception Lamp'.

5 Discussion

In the respective course practice cases (Figs. 6, 7 and 8), Each group will combine the virtual space they build and simulate relevant experiences to demonstrate their alternative future solutions. Experts in the field of future research and design will evaluate the trend, concept, diversity and sociality of each scheme, and pay attention to whether the derivation process of its results is based on evidence and reasonable (Fig. 9).

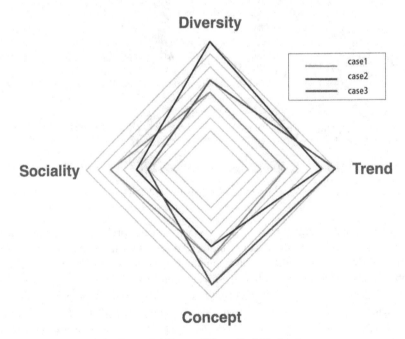

Fig. 9. Radar Chart of Three Case Evaluations

1. Trends: These cases aim to predict future development trends and align with design visions. Case 1 demonstrates reflections on future societal trends, Case 2 emphasizes trends in resource utilization and environmental protection, while Case 3 reflects attention to the trend of slow living and emotional needs.
2. Diversity: These designs showcase various possibilities for the future. Case 1 showcases design diversity by constructing diverse interactive scenarios, Case 2 presents different resource utilization scenarios, and Case 3 demonstrates diversity in future product design.
3. Conceptualization: The designs fully consider worldviews and values. Case 1 reflects deep reflections on the future direction of society, Case 2 focuses on values such as resource recycling and environmental protection, while Case 3 emphasizes the importance of slow living and emotional needs.
4. *Societal Impact: These designs have a positive impact on society.* Case 1 helps provoke thoughts on future societal development, Case 2 provides environmental solutions for space communities, and Case 3 encourages reflection and improvement of lifestyles.

Based on the P3-6Fs theoretical framework, we can see that the future evolution of design must be built upon a framework based on capabilities or outcomes to ensure the continuous development of students in various abilities and sub-abilities. Such design requires comprehensiveness and flexibility, capable of effectively assessing the complex knowledge, skills, and behaviors students acquire in different design contexts, activities, and assessment tasks. By using a learning-teaching-assessment plan to track students' progress in the curriculum, we can better understand whether the future evolution of design aligns with the design vision and whether it can anticipate societal trends. At the same time, aligning capabilities and outcomes with the learning-teaching environment and activities ensures that the future evolution of design can adapt to societal trends and meet evolving needs. Ultimately, by fostering connections among students, teachers, and project designers, we can collectively reflect on whether the future evolution of design is consistent with the design vision and accurately anticipate future societal development trends.

6 Conclusion

Utilizing the 3P-6Cs curriculum toolkit in interactive design courses offers a holistic perspective, enhancing learners' understanding of how the integration of future-oriented design elements shapes their readiness for lifelong practice. Its primary aim is to elucidate the logical interconnections across various facets of the curriculum landscape as students' progress from individual to project-based to practical levels. Grounded in systems thinking, it empowers learners to explore future scenarios more effectively, transitioning from recognizing weak signals to conducting in-depth analyses of developmental trends. Concurrently, by leveraging tools associated with futures thinking, it fosters more productive design dialogues, uncovering novel design metaphors and narrative arcs. This not only nurtures the generation of novel insights but also bolsters students' capacity for imagination and innovation.

The principal objective of the 3P-6Cs curriculum toolkit is to cultivate students' proficiency in futures thinking-based methods for interactive design, addressing deficiencies in strategic planning, innovation, and foresight. Through interdisciplinary collaboration, it tackles issues of problem-solving, grappling with complexity and uncertainty, and envisioning the medium to long-term future. The curriculum toolkit facilitates teaching across various levels, progressing logically from data to information to knowledge to wisdom to feedback.

Moreover, we introduce pertinent theories from futures studies and position futures thinking as the cornerstone of teaching pedagogy. Echoing Steve Jobs' sentiments expressed in his Stanford University commencement address, "You can't connect the dots looking forward; you can only connect them looking backward. So you have to trust that the dots will somehow connect in your future." In confronting the challenges of the Anthropocene era, it becomes imperative to contemplate how to reflect, innovate, and act based on the ethos of symbiosis between humans and technology, as well as nature and the Earth, in order to design a future that is more sustainable, resilient, and conducive to happiness.

Disclosure Statement. The authors declare no potential conflicts of interest with respect to the research, authorship, and/or publication of this article.

References

1. Scupelli, P., Wasserman, A., Wells-Papanek, D., et al.: The futures of design pedagogy, learning, and education. In: 21st DMI: Academic Design Management Conference, Next Wave, pp. 1–2 (2018)
2. Jones, J.C.: Design Methods. John Wiley & Sons, Hoboken (1992)
3. Davis, K.: Intersectionality as buzzword: a sociology of science perspective on what makes a feminist theory successful. Fem. Theory **9**(1), 67–85 (2008)
4. Buchanan, R.: Wicked problems in design thinking. Des. Issues **8**(2), 5–21 (1992)
5. Scupelli, P., Wasserman, A., Brooks, J.: Dexign futures: a pedagogy for long-horizon design scenarios (2016)
6. Norman, D.A., Stappers, P.J.: DesignX: complex sociotechnical systems. She Ji: J. Des. Econ. Innov. **1**(2), 83–106 (2015)
7. McKimm, J., Jones, P.K.: Twelve tips for applying change models to curriculum design, development and delivery. Med. Teach. **40**(5), 520–526 (2018)
8. Arnold, R.D., Wade, J.P.: A definition of systems thinking: a systems approach. Proc. Comput. Sci. **2015**(44), 669–678 (2015)
9. Plack, P., Margaret, M., Scott, R.: Systems thinking in the healthcare professions: a guide for educators and clinicians (2019)
10. Quirk, M., Chumley, H.: The adaptive medical curriculum: a model for continuous improvement. Med. Teach. **40**(8), 786–790 (2018)
11. Cabrera, D., Colosi, L., Lobdell, C.: Systems thinking. Eval. Program. Plann. **31**(3), 299–310 (2008)
12. Ackoff, R.L.: Systems thinking and thinking systems. Syst. Dyn. Rev. **10**(2–3), 175–188 (1994)
13. Checkland, P.: Four conditions for serious systems thinking and action. Syst. Res. Behav. Sci. **29**(5), 465–469 (2012)
14. Khanna, P., Roberts, C., Lane, A.S.: Designing health professional education curricula using systems thinking perspectives. BMC Med. Educ. **21**, 1–8 (2021)

15. Pourdehnad, J., Wexler, E.R., Wilson, D.V.: Integrating systems thinking and design thinking. Syst Thinker. **22**(9), 2–6 (2011)
16. Reynolds, M., Holwell, S.: Introducing systems approaches. In: Reynolds, M., Holwell, S. (eds.) Systems Approaches to Making Change: A Practical Guide, pp. 1–24. Springer, London (2020). https://doi.org/10.1007/978-1-4471-7472-1_1
17. Železnik, D., Kokol, P., Vošner, H.B.: Adapting nurse competence to future patient needs using Checkland's soft systems methodology. Nurse Educ. Today **48**, 106–110 (2017)
18. Waldman, J.: Thinking systems need systems thinking. Syst. Res. Behav. Sci. **24**(3), 271–284 (2007)
19. Brown, T., Katz, B.: Change by Design: How Design Thinking Transforms Organizations and Inspires Innovation. Harper Busines, New York (2009)
20. Hiltunen, E.: The future sign and its three dimensions. Futures **40**(3), 247–260 (2008)
21. Inayatullah, S.: Six pillars: futures thinking for transforming. Foresight **10**(1), 4–21 (2008)
22. Agan, B., Balcilar, M.: On the determinants of green technology diffusion: an empirical analysis of economic, social, political, and environmental factors. Sustainability **14**(4), 2008 (2022)
23. Inayatullah, S.: Causal layered analysis: poststructuralism as method. Futures **30**(8), 815–829 (1998)

What is Priming You in APP? The Study of Cultural Difference in Consumers' Self-construction and Perception by Exploring the Splash Screen Design for Mobile Banking Apps

Guo-Ruei Huang and Tseng-Ping Chiu[✉]

Department of Industrial Design, National Cheng Kung University, Tainan, Taiwan
{p36124160,mattchiu}@gs.ncku.edu.tw

Abstract. As modern mobile technology advances, the significance of online banking continues to grow. Consumers can now conveniently conduct banking transactions anytime, anywhere through mobile devices, no longer restricted by the operating hours and locations of financial institutions. However, attracting customers from the very first interaction and encouraging continued usage is crucial for mobile banking apps. The initial screen that appears when the app is opened, known as the "Splash Screen," plays a key role in shaping users' first impressions. These impressions influence users' thoughts and evaluations of the mobile banking app, indirectly affecting user revisit rates and trust levels. This study utilizes cultural psychology to explore consumers' perceptions of the mobile banking app, understanding the emotional and perceptual differences influenced by culture. In Study 1, secondary data from the Splash Screens of numerous Taiwanese mobile banking apps were gathered, analyzing the frequency and screen coverage of visual elements to comprehend the design trends of Splash Screens in East Asian (Taiwanese) culture. In Study 2, a virtual bank's Corporate Identity System (CIS) was employed as material for a questionnaire survey using dual-factor analysis. The study investigated differences in consumer perceptions, emotions, and usage intentions regarding the thematic visual presentation of the mobile banking splash screen. Finally, culturally informed design recommendations for the Splash Screens of mobile banking apps are proposed, aiming to align with cross-cultural user needs. The goal is to establish a positive emotional experience and enhance user loyalty from the very first interaction with the mobile banking app.

Keywords: Cross-cultural communication · Cultural differences · Culture and psychology · splash screen · user interface · user experience · emotion response · mobile banking · self-construction

1 Introduction

With the continuous development of internet technology, the global usage of online banking has been steadily growing year after year. Statista predicts that by the year 2028, the global penetration rate of online banking will grow to 48.28% [1], highlighting the

P.-L. P. Rau (Ed.): HCII 2024, LNCS 14701, pp. 224–244, 2024.
https://doi.org/10.1007/978-3-031-60904-6_16

significant demand for online banking services among consumers. In four years, it is estimated that there will be an additional 756 million online banking users globally.

"Mobile banking" is a crucial development in the financial sector, where financial companies and banks provide internet-based financial services through portable technologies [2]. Users can conveniently check account balances, transfer funds, pay bills, and plan financial investments anytime, anywhere using their smartphones or other mobile devices, without the need for a computer to access online banking. On the other hand, mobile banking brings numerous advantages to banking institutions, enhancing operational efficiency, reducing labor costs, and a well-designed mobile banking app coupled with effective marketing strategies can attract new customers and retain existing ones, effectively increasing customer loyalty to the bank [3]. However, retaining and attracting mobile banking users may not be easy, as mobile banking brands must captivate customers at the very first interaction to ensure that customers choose to continue using their mobile banking apps in the future.

In previous studies on the interface design of online banking, it has been suggested that whether a visitor becomes a loyal customer of online banking may depend on the first impression of the interface [4]. The Splash Screen serves as the first point of contact for building the initial experience of the app, creating the user's first impression of the app [5]. However, past psychological research has found that the first impression can influence users' thoughts and evaluations of subsequent information [6]. In other words, the Splash Screen, as the first point of contact for the user interface, may lead individuals to form preliminary subjective judgments and perceptions of the interface and brand, indirectly affecting user revisit rates and trust levels.

In the field of social psychology, significant cultural differences in self-construction patterns and perception can be observed between East Asians and Westerners. For instance, East Asians tend to think holistically, emphasizing the contextual relationships within a group, and attributes among objects that resonate with each other can help them better understand their meanings. On the other hand, Westerners tend to think analytically, directly perceiving the meaning of individual objects themselves [7, 8]. These cultural differences may impact how people interpret and evaluate colors, shapes, images, and text [9, 10]. Therefore, applying cultural cognitive psychology to explore the Splash Screen of mobile banking, understanding the cultural aspects in interface design, can help design creators create more culturally relevant and effective products and messages.

In the preliminary exploration, significant differences were observed in the Splash Screens of Eastern and Western banks. Western bank apps often prioritize the display of the corporate logo. Interestingly, in Eastern bank apps, visual backgrounds, mascots, or thematic visual presentations are frequently featured (see Fig. 1). In the Eastern world, mascots are commonly present in various local contexts, including branding, regional cultural developments, academic institutions, and sports events. Mascots are widely utilized in Eastern cultures for commercial communication and marketing, as their presence tends to elicit more positive emotions in consumers, leading to a higher willingness to make purchases. Therefore, delving into how the combination of mascot imagery and background elements in the Splash Screen of a banking app influences consumers' willingness to use the interface is of particular interest.

The primary focus of this study is to investigate the visual presentation of the splash screen, aiming to understand its perceptual impact on consumer self-construction and the intention to use mobile banking. The visual presentation of the splash screen is categorized into two components: (1) the presence or absence of a mascot and (2) the presence or absence of background information. Through secondary data analysis and a questionnaire survey employing 2-way ANOVA, differences in consumers' visual perception, emotions, and usage intentions regarding the visual presentation of the splash screen in mobile banking will be explored. The study aims to comprehend how consumers from diverse cultures respond to various splash screens, catering to the needs of cross-cultural consumers.

Fig. 1. Visual Presentation Differences in Mobile Banking App Splash Screens

2   Literature Review

2.1   The User Experience of the Splash Screen

When users first use an app, the Splash Screen becomes the initial screen displayed to them. While current website development primarily focuses on reducing Page Loading Time (PLT), past research in computer science has found that a shorter PLT does not necessarily result in a better user experience. A visually engaging loading screen can temporarily capture the user's attention, and although it doesn't reduce the user's wait time, it can alleviate the user's tension, providing a higher level of pleasure and awakening. This pleasant waiting process can leave users with a positive impression of the app [11, 12]. As demonstrated in Asch's past psychological research, the first impression created in the same event may influence people's thoughts and evaluations of subsequent information [6]. Therefore, the first impression established by the Splash Screen may lead to initial subjective judgments and perceptions of the brand and interface, indirectly impacting the user's subsequent interface usage experience and emotional perception.

Typically, a Splash Screen will display the app's logo, app name, call-to-action slogans, etc., focusing on representing the brand's corporate identity system. Sometimes, it may include background or pattern decorations [13]. Interestingly, the Splash Screen's function also extends to creating the app's brand tone and providing hints about the app's functionalities at the user's first interaction. This can potentially increase user understanding of the app's features at the outset, reduce uncertainty in usage, and make users more willing to use the app, ultimately enhancing user loyalty.

H1. When the visual presentation of the splash screen includes visual cues hinting at the app's functionality, users will have a positive perception.

2.2 Intentions and Attitudes

In this study, the Decomposed Theory of Planned Behavior (DTPB) serves as the theoretical framework for understanding user behavioral intentions in mobile banking [14, 15]. Simultaneously, it explores the elements of character image that influence consumers' positive attitudes [16], with the aim of discussing how the Splash Screen creates positive emotional and perceptual differences.

Comparing the elements of DTPB with positive character imagery, it is evident that the positive character portrayal aligns with certain aspects of all three frameworks within DTPB. (see Fig. 2), this study hypothesizes that when the mascot's character image is combined with surrounding environmental conditions to form a thematic visual presentation, it will generate a greater intention among users to use mobile banking. This is anticipated to have a positive impact on consumers' attitudes towards mobile banking, their assessments of the app's functional capabilities, and their inclination to trust the mobile banking brand.

H2. The thematic visual presentation on the splash screen will increase user attention to mobile banking, enhance user understanding of the app's functionalities, and boost user trust in the banking app.

	Attitude-related behavior			Perceived behavioral control			Trust related behaviors		
	Related advantage	Compatibility	Complexity	Self-efficacy	Resource facilitation	Technology facilitation	Disposition to Trust	Structural assurance	Trust belief
	Image enhancement	Consistent with Need	Ease of use	Information judgment ability	Resource	Technical compatibility of hardware	Trust or not	Technical Structures	Service provider
Symbolic representation	v	v	v	v			v		
Emotional Value	v	v	v	v			v		
Self-image Congruence	v	v	v	v			v		

Fig. 2. DTPB and consumer preference factors for character roles

2.3 Cross-cultural Perspective and User Interface Experience

Research in cross-cultural psychology consistently demonstrates significant differences in self-construal patterns between Eastern and Western cultures, influencing their distinct thinking styles. Western cultures typically nurture independent self-construal patterns, leading Western individuals to exhibit analytical thinking and engage in low-context communication. Conversely, Eastern cultures tend to foster interdependent self-construal patterns, resulting in individuals from the East demonstrating holistic thinking and participating in high-context communication [8, 17, 18]. These cultural differences also manifest in composition variances in paintings, photographs, and designs. Westerners tend to focus on the subject itself, while East Asians contemplate the relationship between the subject and the background, creating a thematic visual presentation [10]. This illustrates the divergence in attention and perceptual habits between Eastern and Western cultures, reflecting distinct aesthetic preferences. Therefore, this study posits the hypothesis that, due to the preference of Eastern consumers for perceiving context-laden thematic visuals, there may be a trend for businesses to create more context-rich splash screens for mobile banking applications.

H3. The Splash screen of East App may have more Thematic visual presentation.

Before using mobile banking, there may be various emotional experiences, such as the stress of forgetting to pay a credit card bill, which can put consumers in a tense state. Therefore, understanding whether the splash screen can provide emotion-regulating functionality is crucial. The Emotional Circumplex Model is a cognitive structure conceptualizing emotion (see Fig. 3). In Jennie Tsai's cross-cultural research, significant differences were found in the ideal emotional expressions across cultures. Westerners tend to prefer High Arousal Positive (HAP), emphasizing highly arousing positive states, while Easterners value Low Arousal Positive (LAP) in expressing pleasurable feelings [19, 20]. Easterners lean towards holistic thinking in perceiving things. Therefore, this study posits the hypothesis that through the positive emotional experiences provided by mascots and the thematic visual presentation created by the context, aligning with the perceptual needs and habits of East Asian consumers, they will exhibit Low Arousal Positive (LAP) emotions.

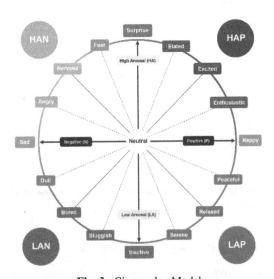

Fig. 3. Circumplex Model

H4–1. When the splash screen is a thematic visual presentation, the emotional dimension of East Asian users will be more inclined to LAP.

H4–2. In the visual presentation of the splash screen, the values of high arousal emotions will be less obvious for East Asian users.

3 Study 1

Study 1 aims to analyze the visual presentations of existing mobile banking app splash screens in the market through quantitative methods. The goal is to investigate the design trends of splash screens on the financial company and bank side for mobile banking apps.

3.1 Method

Secondary Data Collection. Through inquiries with the Banking Bureau of the Financial Supervisory Commission, R.O.C [21], an inventory of existing commercial banks in Taiwan was conducted. There are a total of 34 commercial banks, with some banks having sub-brands offering mobile banking apps. In total, there are 37 mobile banking apps available in the market. After initial screening, four mobile banking apps were excluded as they directly lead to the login screen without a splash screen. It was confirmed that there are 33 mobile banking apps in Taiwan's consumer market with a designed splash screen (Table 1).

Table 1. Current Status of Taiwan Mobile Banking App Splash Screens

type	Quantity	Quantity ratio
Mobile Banking APP with Splash Screen	33	89.2%
Mobile Banking APP without Splash Screen	4	10.8%
Total number of mobile banking apps	37	100%

Data Analysis. Capture screenshots of the Splash screens of these 33 mobile banking apps, calculate the percentage of each visual element on the screen, and analyze the trends in their Splash screen visual presentations. Visual elements are categorized into the following two types: (1) Foreground (Logo, Logotype, Mascot, Slogan) (2) Background (Meaningful Pattern, Meaningless Pattern, Photo).

3.2 Result

The results show that among the mobile banking apps in the current Taiwanese market, there is a relatively high usage rate of background visual presentations in Splash Screens (Meaningful Pattern average screen ratio = 14.07%, Meaningless Pattern average screen ratio $= 21.31\%$). In contrast, the logo graphic on the screen has a much lower average screen ratio, accounting for only 1.42%, indicating a trend among East Asian mobile banking apps to use background patterns. (see Table 2).

In the foreground section, the results highlight a prominent presence of mascots in the screen composition (Mascot average screen ratio $= 5.3\%$). Interestingly, when mascots are used in Splash Screens, they are often accompanied by meaningful background images to create a thematic visual presentation.

Table 2. The screen ratio of visual elements on the Splash Screen

Visual Element	Quantity	Quantity ratio	Average screen ratio
Logo	33	100%	1.42%
Logotype	25	75.8%	1.12%
Mascot	5	15.15%	5.3%
Slogan	13	39.3%	2.31%
Meaningful Pattern	11	33.3%	14.07%
Meaningless Pattern	12	36.3%	21.31%
Photo	2	6.06%	57.96%

4   Study 2

Through the results of Study 1, insights were gained into the presentation styles of Splash screens in mobile banking apps on the market, identifying the trend of East Asian (Taiwanese) banking apps using mascots and backgrounds on the Splash screen. Therefore, Study 2 aims to explore the effects of these two factors on the Splash screen. The research adopts a 2 (presence/absence of contextual background) $\times$ 2 (presence/absence of mascot) factorial experimental design and designs four types of Splash screens. The dependent variables include user experiential perceptions, emotional responses, and intention-to-use scores, aiming to deeply understand the subjective perceptions and usage intentions of East Asian consumers regarding the Splash screen in mobile banking concerning mascots and contextual backgrounds.

4.1   Method

Creation of Visual Stimuli. Materials Creation of Visual Stimuli Microsoft Designer's Image Creator was used to generate sketches of visual components (mascots, contextual backgrounds, logos), and through AI-based algorithms, random sketches were generated as references and further redesigned. Six vector-style humanoid mascots, six banking contextual backgrounds, and six minimalist-style bank logos were created for the generation of four types of Splash screens: (A) Thematic visual presentation Splash Screen, mainly featuring the combination of contextual background and mascot; (B) Mascot-only Splash Screen, primarily showcasing the mascot; (C) Contextual background-only Splash Screen, primarily displaying the contextual background; (D) Logo-only Splash Screen, showing only the logo. (see Fig. 4) Each type provided six samples for participants to view and evaluate. To avoid color preferences, all visual stimuli and Splash Screen background colors were set in grayscale.

Fig. 4. Splash Screen Sample Design

Participants. In this study, a total of 156 East Asians (37.17% male, 62.82% female) participated in the questionnaire test. The age range of the participants was concentrated in the young adult to middle-aged group, between 21 and 40 years old.

Procedure. At the beginning of the experiment, participants were assigned to one of four different types of Splash screens. They were informed that they were in a situation: "You swiped your card at the store checkout, so you want to check your bank balance and transaction details. You open the mobile banking app you usually use, and upon opening the app, you see the Splash Screen of this mobile banking app…". Subsequently, a Splash screen image was presented, and participants were asked to answer the first series of questions: "This Splash screen makes me feel quite positive," "This Splash screen makes me feel quite rational," "This Splash screen makes me feel quite professional." These questions aimed to explore users' subjective feelings about the presented Splash screen. The second series of questions were designed to understand participants' emotional responses: "This Splash screen makes me feel very excited (HAP)," "This Splash screen makes me feel very relaxed (LAP)," "This Splash screen makes me feel very tense (HAN)," "This Splash screen makes me feel very bored (LAN)." They were then asked three questions related to the Decomposed Theory of Planned Behavior (DTPB): "If the Splash screen is presented in this way, I would pay more attention to this mobile banking app," "If the Splash screen is presented in this way, I would better judge the purpose of this mobile banking app," "If the Splash screen is presented in this way, I would trust this mobile banking app more" (participants responded on a 7-point scale). At the end of the study, participants completed a survey on basic personal information, reporting age, gender, education level, employment status, nationality, monthly income.

4.2 Result

Emotional Responses. Regarding positive emotions, the data indicates that East Asian participants, after viewing Splash screens with thematic visual presentations, showed higher levels of relaxation (LAP) (M = 4.634, SD = 0.181). There were significant main effects observed in the situational background condition, F (1,152) = 11.313, p < .001, and the mascot presence condition, F(1,152) = 12.219, p < .001. Additionally, there was a significant interaction effect in the thematic visual presentation (situational background * mascot) condition, F(1,152) = 4.045, p = .046 (Fig. 5).

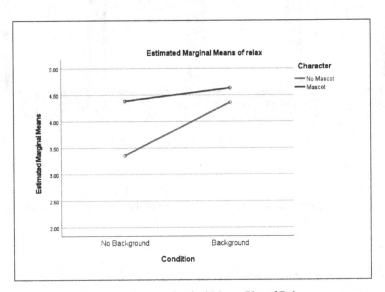

Fig. 5. Estimated Marginal Means Plot of Relax

Interestingly, East Asian participants in the mascot-present condition significantly reported more excitement (HAP) emotions, F (1,152) = 4.059, p = .046. Moreover, they significantly reduced feelings of tension (HAN), F (1,152) = 13.154, p < .001, and decreased feelings of boredom (LAN), F (1,152) = 13.154, p < .001.

Thus, the data suggests that thematic visual presentations and the presence of a mascot enhance the positive emotional experiences of East Asian users in Splash Screens while reducing negative emotional experiences (Fig. 6).

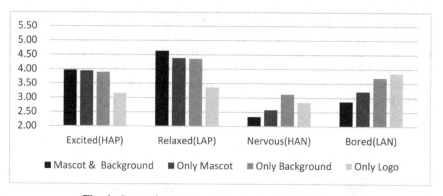

Fig. 6. Scores for Emotional Responses to Splash Screens

User Experience Imparted by the Splash Screen. Regarding positive emotional experiences, there was a significant difference between the condition with the presence of a situational background (M = 4.908, SD = 0.166) and the condition without a situational background (M = 4.237, SD = 0.170). F(1,152) = 5.663, p = .019, indicating that East Asian (Taiwanese) participants had higher positive emotions towards the Splash Screen with a situational background. Thematic visual presentation (the combination of a mascot and situational background) also contributed to enhancing positive emotions (M = 4.923, SD = 0.164), although the difference was not substantial compared to the Splash Screen with only a situational background (M = 4.908, SD = 0.166). When the mascot appeared independently on the Splash Screen, it also led to a preliminary improvement in consumers' positive emotional experiences (M = 4.793, SD = 0.173). These values indicate that presenting the Splash Screen through a situational background (bank-related visual features) or the inclusion of a mascot can initially boost East Asian consumers' positive emotions towards the displayed splash screen (Fig. 7).

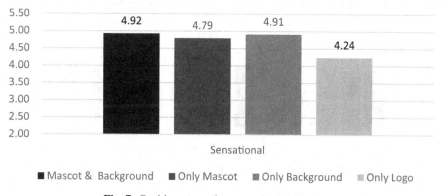

Fig. 7. Positive perception score for splash screen

In terms of rational perception and professionalism perception, Taiwanese participants experienced higher levels of rational perception (M = 5.042, SD = 0.167) and
higher professionalism perception (M = 4.871, SD = 0.172) in the Splash Screen with
only a situational background. Through correlation analysis, a particularly significant
association between rational perception and professionalism was found, r(154) = .831,
p < .001 (Fig. 8).

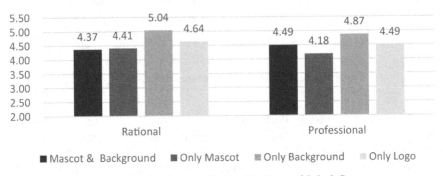

Fig. 8. Professionalism and Rationality Score of Splash Screen

Intention to Use Mobile Banking. The results indicate that the presentation of visual
elements on the splash screen significantly increases the intention of East Asian consumers to use mobile banking, especially under the condition of having a situational
background. Consumers, in this context, show heightened attention to the specific mobile
banking app (M = 4.379, SD = 0.183), a more perceptible understanding of the app's
functionalities (M = 4.737, SD = 0.182), and a greater inclination to trust the mobile
banking service (M = 4.646, SD = 0.189). The findings suggest that, for East Asian
consumers, going through a thematic visual presentation with a situational background
on the splash screen may enhance their intention to use mobile banking (Fig. 9).

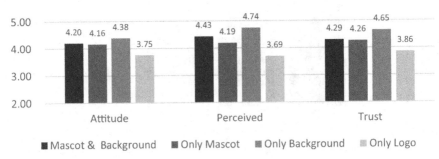

Fig. 9. Mobile banking usage intent score for splash screen

5 Conclusion and Discussion

Both studies revealed visual display patterns on Splash Screens of mobile banking apps. Study 1 investigated the Splash screens of existing commercial banks in Taiwan, categorizing visual information into (1) foreground and (2) background. Specifically, Study 1 found that in the Splash Screens of East Asian mobile banking apps, there is a significant utilization of visual elements in the background to enhance the visual richness of the Splash Screen. This choice aligns with the interdependent self-construal prevalent in East Asian individuals, who tend to use holistic analysis to perceive the relationship between characters (objects) and the background. When mascots are used on the Splash Screen, they are often paired with background imagery, standing out prominently in the Splash Screen. This indicates a tendency for more thematic visual presentations in East Asian mobile banking app Splash Screens (H3).

Study 2 aimed to investigate the differences in subjective experiences, perceived emotions, and usage intentions among East Asian consumers in response to the thematic visual presentation of Splash screens. The study employed a two-factor experimental design, including (1) mascots and (2) contextual background. Utilizing the emotional descriptors derived from the quadrants of the Arousal-Valence circumplex model (HAP, LAP, HAN, LAN), the research explored consumers' emotional responses to visual stimuli (Splash screens). The results revealed that, in the thematic visual presentation, East Asian individuals significantly exhibited a higher state of relaxation. Among East Asian individuals who tend to use holistic analysis, receiving visual stimuli in the form of thematic visual presentations triggered a "low arousal positive" emotional state. The findings align with cultural emotion research by Jennie Tsai and others, suggesting that individuals in interdependent self-construal cultures, when experiencing positive emotions, demonstrate a relaxed state of positive emotion characterized by low arousal.

In terms of the impact of the splash screen on the intention to use the mobile banking app, the study revealed that thematic visual presentation significantly influenced the usage intention of East Asian consumers. Particularly, under the condition of exclusively utilizing a situational background in the Splash screen, consumers were more likely to perceive the functionalities of the mobile banking app ($M = 4.737$) and trust the mobile banking app ($M = 4.646$). This indicates that for East Asian consumers, the visual presentation of the splash screen, especially when featuring thematic visual elements and a situational background, can significantly enhance their intention to use the app. In conclusion, the experimental results of this study found that East Asian consumers, upon receiving a thematic visual presentation in the mobile banking app's splash screen, tend to exhibit higher positive emotional experiences (low arousal positivity) and demonstrate increased perception and trust tendencies towards the mobile banking app itself.5.1 Splash screen design suggestions for cross-cultural thinking.

Based on the findings, the study proposes three practical recommendations for designing Splash screens for East Asian mobile banking apps: (1) Thematic visual presentation with the combination of mascots and contextual background effectively provides a positive emotional experience for East Asian consumers, creating a relaxed atmosphere and alleviating the seriousness or tension associated with banking or financial transactions. (2) The waiting time for app loading can be tedious and boring. Having mascots on the Splash screen reduces boredom for East Asian consumers. Interestingly, mascots also increase their excitement, making the waiting time more engaging and enhancing user loyalty. (3) Design the Splash screen based on the nature and appeal of the bank's brand. For creating a professional and rational brand image, the design can incorporate functional contextual backgrounds (such as bank buildings and visual elements of banknotes and coins) to allow East Asian consumers to perceive professionalism and enhance trust by understanding the app's functionalities through the contextual background.

5.1 Contribution

In conclusion, this study on mobile banking app splash screens reveals that a thematic visual presentation, incorporating mascots and contextual backgrounds, effectively heightens positive emotional experiences and boosts the usage intention of East Asian consumers. Prior cultural studies have seldom delved into the visual perception disparities in splash screen design. The splash screen plays a pivotal role in shaping the initial impression of an app, and this initial impression significantly influences users' subsequent perceptions of the app and brand image, potentially positively impacting user experience and perception. This study identifies the influence of thematic visual presentations on the self-construction model and perception of East Asian cultural consumers. Finally, three practical recommendations are proposed to align mobile banking app splash screens with user expectations from different cultures, aiming to create a positive emotional experience and enhance user loyalty and trust when using the mobile banking app.

5.2 Limitations and Future Research

In the usage of mobile banking, various purposive behaviors such as checking accounts, credit card payments, and investment planning may induce specific emotions in users. For instance, being late in credit card payments within a five-minute timeframe could create anxiety in users entering the app. It is uncertain whether a thematic visual presentation in such scenarios can still significantly relax users. In the future, eye-tracking devices will be employed to understand users' eye movement patterns and physiological responses during Splash screen interactions. This aims to systematically establish cross-cultural design guidelines for app Splash screens.

Appendices

Appendix 1. Visual Stimulus Samples

(See Figs. 10, 11, 12 and 13).

Fig. 10. Sample of Thematic visual presentation Splash Screen

Fig. 11. Sample of Mascot-only Splash Screen

Fig. 12. Sample of Contextual background-only Splash Screen

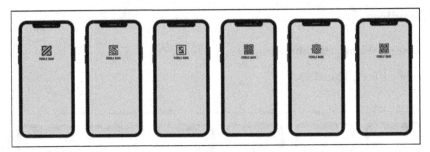

Fig. 13. Sample of Logo-only Splash Screen

Appendix 2. Questionnaire

(See Table 3 and Figs. 14, 15, 16, 17, 18, 19, 20, 21, 22 and 23).

Table 3. Questionnaire questions

	Code	Questions
Feeling	Sensational	1. This splash screen makes me feel pretty good
	rational	2. This splash screen makes me feel quite rational
	professional	3. This splash screen makes me feel quite professional
Emotion	excited	4. This splash screen makes me feel very excited
	relax	5. This splash screen makes me feel very relaxed
	nervous	6. This splash screen makes me feel very nervous
	bored	7. This splash screen makes me feel very bored
Intention	attention	8. I will pay more attention to this mobile banking APP
	Perceived	9. I can better Know the purpose of this mobile banking APP
	Trust	10. I will trust this mobile banking APP more

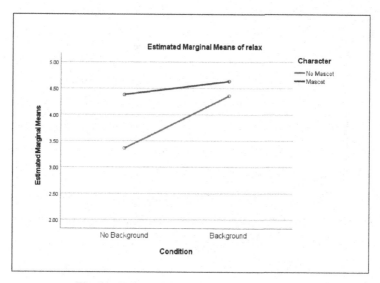

Fig. 14. Estimated Marginal Means Plot of relax

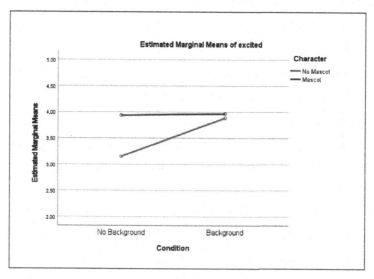

Fig. 15. Estimated Marginal Means Plot of Excited

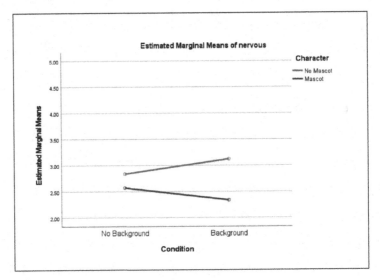

Fig. 16. Estimated Marginal Means Plot of Nervous

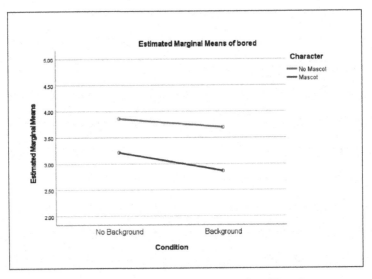

Fig. 17. Estimated Marginal Means Plot of Bored

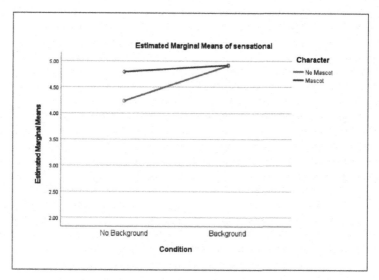

Fig. 18. Estimated Marginal Means Plot of Sensational

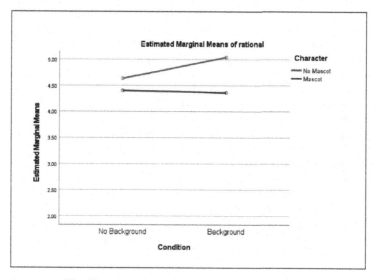

Fig. 19. Estimated Marginal Means Plot of Rational

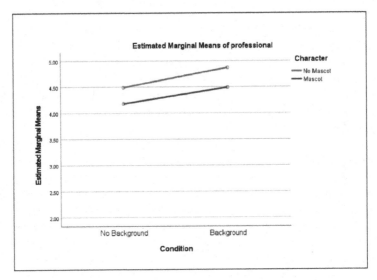

Fig. 20. Estimated Marginal Means Plot of Professional

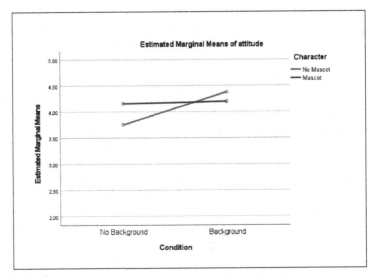

Fig. 21. Estimated Marginal Means Plot of Attitude

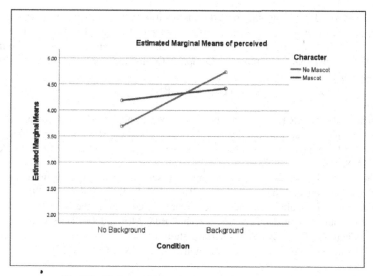

Fig. 22. Estimated Marginal Means Plot of Perceived

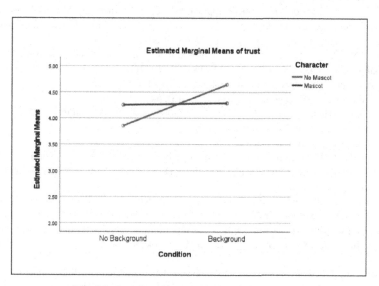

Fig. 23. Estimated Marginal Means Plot of Trust

References

1. Statista Market Insights , W.B., Eurostat. Banking - Worldwide. Accessed 04 Jan 2024. https://www.statista.com/outlook/co/digital-connectivity-indicators/banking/worldwide
2. Tam, C., Oliveira, T.: Literature review of mobile banking and individual performance. Int. J. Bank Mark. **35**(7), 1044–1067 (2017)
3. Wang, Z., Huang, X.: Understanding the role of digital finance in facilitating consumer online purchases: an empirical investigation. Finan. Res. Letters **55**, 103939 (2023)

4. Kim, J., Moon, J.Y.: Designing towards emotional usability in customer interfaces—trustworthiness of cyber-banking system interfaces. Interact. Comput. **10**(1), 1–29 (1998)
5. Goel, G., Tanwar, P., Sharma, S.: UI-UX design using user centred design (UCD) method. In: 2022 International Conference on Computer Communication and Informatics (ICCCI), pp. 1–8 (2022)
6. Asch, S.E.: Forming impressions of personality. Psychol. Sci. Public Interest **41**(3), 258–290 (1946)
7. Masuda, T., Nisbett, R.E.: Attending holistically versus analytically- comparing the context sensitivity of Japanese and Americans. J. Pers. Soc. Psychol. **81**(5), 922–934 (2001)
8. Markus, H.R., Kitayama, S.: Cultures and selves: a cycle of mutual constitution. Perspect. Psychol. Sci. **5**(4), 420–430 (2010)
9. Zhang, Y., Feick, L., Price, L.J.: The impact of self-construal on aesthetic preference for angular versus rounded shapes. Pers. Soc. Psychol. Bull. **32**(6), 794–805 (2006)
10. Masuda, T., et al.: Culture and aesthetic preference: comparing the attention to context of East Asians and Americans. Pers. Soc. Psychol. Bull. **34**(9), 1260–1275 (2008)
11. Lu, J., Chen, Q., Chen, X.: App interface study on how to improve user experience. In: 2012 7th International Conference on Computer Science & Education (ICCSE), pp. 726–729 (2012)
12. Wang, Y., et al.: The effect of mobile applications' initial loading pages on users' mental state and behavior. Displays **68** (2021)
13. Yu, W., Gao, J.: Fine design of music application user experience based on first sense interactive node optimization: example of splashscreen. In :Advances in Usability, User Experience, Wearable and Assistive Technology, pp. 37–43 (2020)
14. Shih, Y.Y., Fang, K.: The use of a decomposed theory of planned behavior to study Internet banking in Taiwan. Internet Res. **14**(3), 213–223 (2004)
15. Lu, M.-T., et al.: Exploring mobile banking services for user behavior in intention adoption: using new hybrid MADM model. Serv. Bus. **9**(3), 541–565 (2014)
16. Chen, C.-Y., Huarng, K.-H., González, V.I.: How creative cute characters affect purchase intention. J. Bus. Res. **142**, 211–220 (2022)
17. Hall, E.T.: Beyond culture (1976)
18. Markus, H.R., Hamedani, M.G.: People are culturally shaped shapers: The psychological science of culture and culture change. In: Cohen, D., Kitayama, S. (eds.) Handbook of Cultural Psychology, pp. 11–52 (2019)
19. Tsai, J.L.: The cultural shaping of emotion (and other feelings). In: Biswas-Diener, R., Diener, E. (eds.). Noba Textbook Series (2013). http://nobaproject.com/modules/culture-and-emotion
20. Tsai, J.L., Clobert, M.: Cultural influences on emotion: established patterns and emerging trends. In: Cohen, D., Kitayama, S. (eds.) Handbook of Cultural Psychology, pp. 292–318 (2019)
21. Bureau, B.: Financial supervisory commission Domestic Banks (2024). https://www.banking.gov.tw/en/home.jsp?id=24&parentpath=0,100&mcustomize=FscSearch_BankType.jsp&type=1

The Application of Digital Media in Macao's Cultural Communication - A Case Study of Macao Light Festival

Cailin Huang, Ke Song$^{(\boxtimes)}$, and Hokkun Wan

Faculty of Humanities and Social Sciences, Macao Polytechnic University, Macao, China
senking1025@foxmail.com

Abstract. The rapid development of digital media has created better conditions for cultural dissemination, innovation, and multicultural integration. Changes in new media technology have facilitated media convergence while dramatically changing the way culture is communicated. As a city with a long history and diverse cultures, Macao has unique historical and cultural symbols, and the Macao Light Festival is an important case to explore the innovative communication of digital media in urban culture. It is found that Macao culture is a typical multicultural culture composed of people from different cultural backgrounds, and this multicultural fusion has become Macao's charm and characteristics. Digital media plays an important role in the integration of Macao's multiculturalism. And it can also enrich the connotation of traditional culture and strengthen cultural ties. The Macao Light Festival uses digital technology to create a unique visual art experience that present Macao's culture, history, and creativity. Through the interaction of digital media, audiences can have a more immersive and personalized participation experience. In addition, the use of digital media enables the Macao Light Festival to reach out to a global audience, attracting participants and artists from different cultural backgrounds and promoting multicultural exchange and dialogue. The development process of the Macao Light Festival reflects the collision and fusion of Macao culture and contemporary digital media. This paper can provide reference and inspiration for other regions in the intersection and proliferation of digital media and cultural activities.

Keywords: Digital Media · Cultural Communication · Multicultural Fusion · Macao Light Festival

1 Introduction

Digital media is a type of media that is encoded in a digital format and is widely available on electronic devices such as computers and smartphones. Widely distributed digital media encompasses a wide range of content, including but not limited to online media, digital games and digital music, virtual and augmented reality, digital art and design, online video, and more recently social media, all enabled by digital technology [1]. The pervasive impact of digital media, characterized by its dynamism, interactivity,

P.-L. P. Rau (Ed.): HCII 2024, LNCS 14701, pp. 245–255, 2024.
https://doi.org/10.1007/978-3-031-60904-6_17

and immediacy, has broken down traditional boundaries, connected people around the world, and influenced communication, culture, and society. The pervasive impact of digital media has redefined the way we communicate, consume information, and engage in cultural exchange [2].

Macao is a city with a long history and diverse cultures. Over the centuries, the fusion of Chinese and Western cultures has resulted in the formation of unique historical and cultural symbols that have demonstrated Macao's unique cultural values to the world. Macao's culture is a typical multi-faceted culture, mainly composed of the Chinese, who have lived in Macao since ancient times, and the Portuguese, who were allowed to settle here for business after the mid-16th century, as well as those who came to Macao from all over the world for missionary work and trade. These cultures come together in Macao to form a multicultural port city. This multiculturalism has made Macao a vibrant and diverse society. This multiculturalism has become not only the unique charm and characteristics of Macao, but also the key to Macao's economic development, and is an important factor in attracting tourists and promoting the development of the tourism industry as well as the cultural and creative industries. The organization of major cultural events is an important means of cultural dissemination and integration. The Macao Light Festival is a characteristic activity of the Macao Government to use digital media technology for urban cultural dissemination and exchange. This paper takes the Macao Light Festival as an example and focuses on qualitative research based on three research methods: case study, interview and observation, and textual analysis, to explore how it can better promote multicultural communication with the help of digital media technology and new media. This will help to provide universal reference suggestions for other regions to better implement the integration of digital media and cultural communication in the future.

This study focuses on the communication of the Macao Light Festival with the following questions: How does the Macao Light Festival use digital technology and new media platforms to promote and showcase Macao's culture, history and creativity in the digital media age? What is the role of digital media in the Macao Light Festival? How has it transformed traditional art forms to provide a unique viewing and engagement experience? How does it use the real-time interactive nature of digital media to engage with audiences? How does the use of digital media in the Macao Light Festival affect multicultural exchange and integration? As a case study of the convergence of digital media and cultural activities, what are the implications of the Macao Light Festival for other regions in promoting the convergence and diffusion of digital media and cultural activities?

2   Literature Review

2.1   Digital Media

Digital media play an important role in cultural communication and have a profound impact on cultural inheritance, communication, and innovation. In the related research on digital media and cultural communication, it can be found that many scholars study from the following perspectives. Huang believes that digital media has a significant impact on the cultural industry, and it is necessary to pay attention to the challenges and opportunities brought by the digital revolution. In particular, with the development of network technology, more and more cultural content is being disseminated, and the infrastructure and operation modes of each sector of the cultural industry have changed dramatically. To adapt to the digital era, cultural heritage institutions need to establish new collection management systems and be equipped with new technologies. At the same time, the positive impacts of the digital revolution are emphasized, including new modes of production, new economic models, and greater accessibility [3]. The important role of digital media in the future development of the cultural industries and the promotion of cultural exchange and innovation is highlighted. Digital media have revolutionized the cultural industries, bringing with them both opportunities and challenges. It undermines traditional practices but also opens new avenues for artistic expression, cultural exchange, and innovation. Digital communication technologies appear in every aspect of the city. Smets, Ballon & Nils Walravens explore the impact of urban experience algorithms on citizens' interactions with the city, both online and offline, and question the extent to which urban spaces can still function as public spaces. The impact of urban experience algorithms on cultural diversity, public engagement, and social interaction. A study of urban spatial planning provides insight into the complex relationships between digital technology, culture, and urban experience [4]. This provides insights into the role of digital technology in shaping urban space, but light shows can also be considered a form of "urban activism art", emphasizing their role as artistic expression in urban space and part of urban activism, which opens new perspectives for this study. Valtysson explores how digital media platforms such as Web 2.0 facilitate cultural participation and influence cultural communication. Drawing on the theories of Habermas, Castells, and Lessig, the study analyzes examples such as Elephant's Dream, YouTube, MySpace, and the BBC's Creative Archive. The study emphasizes the interactive nature of these platforms, blurring the line between content production and consumption. In short, it emphasizes the importance of cultural policy in creating an accessible cultural public sphere by harnessing the participatory nature of digital media [5]. By promoting accessible culture, cultural policy can facilitate inclusive cultural participation in the age of digital convergence. Digital media platforms have revolutionized cultural communication by providing interactive channels for content creation, distribution, and participation. The democratization of cultural communication has been achieved, allowing for increased cultural participation, collaboration, and the creation of an inclusive cultural public sphere. Most of the above studies on digital media have been analyzed from a variety of perspectives, including cultural industries, artistic expression, urban space, and cultural participation. Although the focus of this literature is not on the case study of the Macao Light Festival, it provides insights into the role and impact of digital media in the cultural industry and the importance of digital technologies in shaping urban space and facilitating cultural participation.

2.2 Urban Light Festival

In the digital media era, the light show meets the standards of culture, interaction, and creativity, making it a unique form of artistic communication. Theme light show is a multimedia display design that has gained popularity and widely used in urban light festival in recent years. It breaks the space limitations of single projected images and adds new vitality to modern display and communication design. Urban Light Festival has four main characteristics, which are to make full use of the urban spatial environment, to express the cultural connotation of the city, to highlight the form of light art, and to brainstorm collaborative innovation. Sloan explores how light festivals can go beyond mere spectacle and commodification and contribute to the dissemination of culture. It focuses on the work of artists such as Michel de Broin, Philippe Parreno, Rhonda Weppler, and Trevor Mahovsky, who use light installations to create complex sensory environments. As Sloan describes, these interventions activate human senses, enhance cultural experiences, and contribute to the regeneration of urban spaces. This research highlights the potential of light festivals to promote cultural exchange and engage communities in exploring urban environments [6]. Through these immersive installations and sensory experiences, light festivals facilitate the dissemination of cultural ideas, narratives, and themes. Yin, Fu, & Dai explored the experiences of light festival participants on social media, focusing on the Guangzhou International Light Festival. The study collected data from festival attendees' posts on TikTok and analyzed them using the Jebba Chinese segmentation tool. High-frequency words and phrases were categorized into five dimensions of the Light Festival experience: cognition, novelty, emotion, physical engagement, and social interaction. Modular algorithms and Gephi were used to cluster and visualize the overall festival experience, as well as differences based on gender and age. The results of the study showed that cognitive experiences accounted for the largest percentage of the overall festival experience, followed by physical engagement, and to a lesser extent, social interaction, emotional experiences, and novelty experiences. In addition, the study highlighted the impact of demographic characteristics such as gender and age on the festival experience. Social media platforms, characterized by user-generated content, play an important role in sharing holiday experiences, increasing consumer engagement, and promoting holidays [7].

3 Methodology

This paper presents a qualitative study that utilizes case studies, interviews, observations, and textual analysis. The Macao Light Festival is chosen as a representative and active example to analyze the role of digital media in cultural communication. The study aims to obtain rich, vivid, specific, and detailed data to inspire the overall research. The author conducted five participant observations between December 2023 and January 2024. Additionally, closed-ended interviews were conducted with 10 participants, 6 women and 4 men, who took part in the 2023 Macao Light Festival. Seven of the interviewees were under 30 years old, while three were between 32 and 56 years old. The letter 'W' represents women, and 'M' represents men, with the numbers indicating the order of the interviews. This paper analyzes the #2023 Illuminations of Haojiang and Little Red Book as the selected texts. It combines the videos, pictures, texts, and other contents released by the related media reports to carry out textual analysis. The analysis extracts the characteristics of the Macao Light Festival in terms of cultural contents and the construction process of the activity.

4 The Case Study of Macao Light Festival

4.1 Macao Light Festival

The light show was introduced in Macao as an activity during the 22nd Macao Arts Festival in 2011. The Telenoika Mapping Art Group from Barcelona created the work 'St. Paul's in Light Festival' over three months, after being invited by the Macao Cultural Affairs Bureau. The work uses St. Paul's as a backdrop to depict the history of Macao's founding, the burning of St. Paul's, and the history of Macao's urban transformation. The Macao Light Festival is an annual cultural event that started in 2015. It features light sculpture performances, installations, and interactive games, all centered around a different theme each year in December. The purpose of the festival is to attract tourists to more areas of Macao and promote the city's history and culture. This will extend the length of stay of tourists and increase the revenue of merchants, while also fostering the development of Macao's cultural industry and local cultural and creative talents. The Macao Light Festival has become a highly popular event among both residents and tourists, with its popularity rivalling that of major events such as the Macao Grand Prix and the Macao International Fireworks Display Contest. According to the Macao Tourism Festival, the total number of arrivals during the December 2023 Festival of Lights reached 294,330.

The Macao Light Festival has been held annually for the past nine years. Each edition features a unique theme and form of expression, with the aim of showcasing the story of Macao through the interaction between the Light Festival and its audience. The festival highlights the beauty of the World Heritage buildings and the characteristics of the community, while also bringing new vitality to the old neighborhoods and historic buildings. The creative team is enhancing the program's content by integrating the art of the Light Festival with science, technology, distinctive architecture, history, culture, and cultural and creative industries. This approach allows for cross-disciplinary creativity and injects new vitality into each Macao Light Festival.

4.2 The Application of Digital Media

The Macao Light Festival features light sculpture performances, installations, and interactive games as its primary art forms. Each year, the festival presents unique themes and presents impressive visual effects and artistic images and stories through interactive games with virtual reality (VR) effects. The festival blends art, technology, and interactivity to provide audiences with a new artistic experience. Participants can engage with interactive Light Festival games and immerse themselves in a world of sight and sound. This use of digital media technology enhances the creativity and expressiveness of the Macao Light Festival while increasing the audience's sense of participation and interactivity. The event becomes more attractive and engaging as a result.

Virtual Reality (VR) enables complete immersion in a digital environment, which may not correspond to reality. However, it can provide an interpretive reproduction that combines visual, auditory, tactile, and other sensory stimuli to simulate the experience of a real environment [8]. For instance, the 2018 Light Festival incorporated virtual reality

Fig. 1. VR Game Experience

(VR) technology for the first time. Participants were able to enjoy a 360° immersive flying experience by using VR goggles and an on-site robotic arm (see Fig. 1).

3D mapping is a display technology that can reproduce a three-dimensional scene without the need for glasses. It is characterized by its easy scalability and high display resolution [9]. For instance, during the 2019 Macao Light Festival, a team from Spain, Shenzhen, and Macao presented a 3D display themed on St. Paul's called 'The Adventures of a Little Snowflake.' The display utilized 3D mapping technology. The story follows the journey of a small snowflake, given as a congratulatory gift for the 20th anniversary of Macao's return to China (see Fig. 2).

Augmented Reality (AR) seamlessly integrates digital content into the real-world environment [10]. It integrates components of the digital world into people's perception of the real world, creating an immersive atmosphere by treating the senses as a natural part of the environment. For instance, the Macao Light Festival 2023 showcased an interactive Augmented Reality installation at Nam Van Lake with the theme 'Butterflies in Flight'. The installation aims to encourage visitor participation and engagement through the creation of interactive AR games (see Fig. 3).

Fig. 2. 3D mapping technology

Fig. 3. AR Interactive Game Instructions

4.3 The Realization of Cultural Communication

The Macao Light Festival realizes cultural transmission in three ways: cognitive experience, physical interaction, and social interaction. Participants experience Macao's culture through the understanding of Light Festival art, interactive installations, and event planning. Physical interaction allows participants to directly feel the unique culture and charm of Macao. The social interaction can promote information sharing and emotional exchange among participants, creating a community of shared experiences. The Macao Light Festival successfully spreads the culture of Macao and provides participants with a comprehensive, rich, and deep cultural experience.

Cognitive experience is the process by which individuals construct knowledge and understanding of the external world by perceiving, reasoning, comprehending, and interpreting information. As technologies continue to advance, they can reshape the human experience by augmenting human senses, experiences, and modes of expression [11]. In the Festival of Light Festival, participants perceive, think, understand, reflect, and interpret Light Festival art, interactive installations, and event planning to create a cognitive experience. As an important platform and event for the dissemination of Macao's culture, the Festival of Light Festival effectively promotes participants' perception, experience, and emotional connection to Macao's culture through cognitive experience, commercial infrastructure, aesthetic appeal, and the combination of technology and art. Through the process of perceiving, contemplating, and understanding the art of Light Festival, interactive installations, and event planning, people from all over the world can experience art and culture different from their localities, deepening their identification and understanding of Macao's culture.

My parents and I took a walk around Ban Chan Tong Lane and found Macao in December surrounded by the Light Festival. The colorful lights illuminated you and me as if we were in a large amusement park, making us feel the romance of Light Festival. Taking photos while watching and playing, sharing can be fun. (M1)

The transportation there is very convenient, and there is also a relatively large number of commercial, cultural, and recreational infrastructures. The art museum is also over there, and I like to go there with my friends. Apart from watching the Macao Light Festival, I have also been to the museum to see the exhibitions. (W3)

I get to see these light shows all the time when I work in the neighborhood. I am dazzled by the colorful patterns and images on the building façade, and the change of Light Festival, it creates a unique atmosphere and beauty. I see a lot of tourists coming here to interact with the installations and take photos. (W1)

As a local of Macao, I am proud and excited about the use of technology in the Festival of Light. This event showcases Macao's innovative power and artistic atmosphere as a modern city and allows us to experience first-hand the unique appeal of combining technology and art. (M4)

As far as I know, the use of light interactive games in the Festival of Lights and the use of virtual reality technologies such as naked-eye 3D animation, these technologies are quite important for the field of culture and art, providing us with a more immersive art experience (M2)

I learned about an interesting installation in front of the Coloane Library, depicting a couple of parents and their child immersed in learning about Macao's culture, reading a lot of books and pursuing knowledge about Macao, which gave me the impression that this artwork wanted to express the hope that people would continue to explore Macao's rich cultural heritage, and it is an installation that I like very much. (W4)

The body is at the center of the decision to construct an image, and the impact of digital media and virtual reality on the body provokes questions about embodiment, presence, perception, and consciousness [12]. The physical interaction created by the

Light Festival installation makes the participants more immersive than just spectators, as they interact with the Light Festival installation to change the effect of the installation. The interactive Light Festival installation combines elements of local cuisine, humanities, architecture, and cultural creativity, fully demonstrating the essence of the fusion of Chinese and Western cultures, and playing an important role in promoting Macao's culture. Such an interactive experience offers participants a very different way of cultural engagement from the traditional spectator model. By interacting with the installation, participants co-construct the meaning and effect of the art images. This embodied and participatory experience helps to strengthen participants' sense of identity and emotional connection to Macao culture.

The interactive games at the Festival of Light brought me a completely different feeling. By combining it with virtual reality technology, I was able to participate and interact with the artwork. This kind of interaction gave me a feeling of integration between myself and the artwork. (W2)

I came to this side of the tour after dinner and strolled to the lobby in front of the ground to see the illusion of dazzling Haojiang card point, light, and shadow show this has a lot of surprises, I also went to play in front of the Taipa Ruins of the giant piano plate, this side also has a card point, take pictures to upload or play the official website game also have the opportunity to draw the grand prize, it is a pity that the time is limited, only card two areas. (W5)

We were visiting and were pleasantly surprised to learn from Twitter that there was a Festival of Lights and Shadows in Macao and that there was a punch card activity. We went from the Barrier Gate to the Coloane area to Taipa, and the installations along the way allowed for an interactive experience, where everyone could become a T-Boy Coloane Ambassador, which was presented using light installations and paper sculptures and scanning the QR code with a cell phone would allow you to explore the experience of being a virtual Coloane Ambassador. (M3)

We passed by an interesting installation after dinner on Kanye Street called the Gorgeous Music Box, which had sensors mounted in front of the gears. It was an interesting installation that when we walked up the stairs and reached the front of the gear sensor, it triggered the LED lights to start moving. (W1).

We were particularly impressed with the installation at the Wynn Promenade, where the children had a great time. The "Flower Jump" is very much like the airplane jumping game we used to play when we were kids. The Light Festival interactive flower skipping board, walking on it has a kind of delicate feeling of step by step. (W6)

Digital technology is increasingly integrated into our lives, and social media has become an integral part of our daily lives, providing new ways for people to interact and communicate [13]. Meaningful social interactions are those that have an emotional, informational, or tangible impact that people believe improves their quality of life and facilitates their relationships with others. Meaningful social interactions are also easier to plan and document through pictures or videos [14].

The punch card activities set up by the festival make participants active participants in cultural dissemination, and their sharing behavior creates a network effect on social media, spreading the message and visual presentation of the Macao Light Festival. This participatory behavior not only expands Macao's visibility and image on social media platforms but also encourages a wider audience to become interested in Macao's cultural heritage and artistic expression. This space closely combines urban architecture and cultural communication through scenes combining Light Festival, gradually forming a visual image communication system centered on Macao's unique spirituality and cultural value orientation.

Before we go to the Festival of Lights we look at the official Weibo post, which has a lot of video real-life presentations. Generally, it will post the time and place of the Light Festival and the program, etc., so that it is easy for us to go to the card (W6)

I used to see promotional videos for the Macao Light Festival all over short videos. These videos made me feel that Macao's urban development is gaining momentum, that this space is more vibrant, and that I have more expectations for city life as well. (M2)

I was lucky enough to stumble upon the Festival of Lights on my first visit to Macao, and it was awesome to see the installations and go searching for information about the festival, so I could understand more about the Macao culture spread in the festival. (M4)

Christmas is in the air in Macao, and with this year's Festival of Lights light installations each with a different theme scattered throughout the city's different neighborhoods, following the Festival of Lights route to hit up Macao's attractions seems to be a good choice. (W1)

Macao's Festival of Light Festival allows you to see strong visual impact installations, feel like you've come to an amusement park, so you can't help but be immersed in it, and there are also activities to collect stamps, and I exchanged them for prizes, so it's well worth coming to visit the city. After that, I will share my experience on social media platforms for your reference to hit the route (W5)

5   Discussion and Conclusions

The Macao Light Festival showcases Macao's culture, history, and creativity through innovative applications of digital media, such as digital projection, virtual reality, and interactive installations. By deconstructing and expressing Macao's traditional cultural elements, this festival offers a unique visual art experience that differs from traditional art forms. Interacting with digital media can provide audiences with a more immersive and personalized participation experience. Additionally, the Festival of Light can reach a global audience through platforms such as the Internet and social media, attracting participants and artists from diverse cultural backgrounds and promoting multicultural exchanges and dialogues. The Festival of Light showcases the collision and fusion of Macao culture and contemporary digital media.

References

1. Acerbi, A.: A cultural evolution approach to digital media. Front. Hum. Neurosci. **10**, 636–636 (2016). https://doi.org/10.3389/fnhum.2016.006
2. Stasberger, G.D.: Digital media: shaping communication, culture, and society in the digital age. Glob. Media J. **21**(64), 1–3 (2023). https://doi.org/10.36648/1550-7521.21.64.388
3. Huang, Y.: Public digital libraries: observations and prospects from the Chinese experience. J. Arts Manag. Law Soc. **48**(2), 122–132 (2018). https://doi.org/10.1080/10632921.2017.137 7662

4. Smets, A., Ballon, P., Walravens, N.: Mediated by code: unpacking algorithmic curation of urban experiences. Media Commun. (Lisboa) **9**(4), 250–259 (2021). https://doi.org/10.17645/mac.v9i4.4086
5. Valtysson, B.: Access culture: Web 2.0 and cultural participation. Int. J. Cult. Policy CP **16**(2), 200–214 (2010). https://doi.org/10.1080/10286630902902954
6. Sloan, J.: Experiments in urban luminosity. Senses Soc. **10**(2), 200–216 (2015). https://doi.org/10.1080/17458927.2015.1042244
7. Yin, S., Fu, C., Dai, G.: Exploring the festival attendees' experiences on social media: a study on the guangzhou international light festival. SAGE Open **13**(1), 215824402211451 (2023). https://doi.org/10.1177/21582440221145154
8. Russo, M.: AR in the architecture domain: state of the art. Appl. Sci. **11**(15), 6800 (2021). https://doi.org/10.3390/app11156800
9. Wang, P., et al.: Image quality improvement of multi-projection 3D display through tone mapping based optimization. Opt. Exp. **25**(17), 20894–20910 (2017). https://doi.org/10.1364/OE.25.020894
10. Miller, M.R., Jun, H., Herrera, F., Yu Villa, J., Welch, G., Bailenson, J.N.: Social interaction in augmented reality. PloS One **14**(5), e0216290–e0216290 (2019). https://doi.org/10.1371/journal.pone.0216290
11. Benitez, M., Vogl, M.: Digitally fabricated aesthetic enhancements and enrichments. AI Soc. **36**(4), 1343–1348 (2020). https://doi.org/10.1007/s00146-020-00938-8
12. Byers, K.: Body-movement-interaction: perception and consciousness in interactive digital 3-dimensional audio-visual installations. Body Space Technol. J. **14**, 1–11 (2015). https://doi.org/10.16995/bst.26
13. Khobzi, H., Lau, R.Y.K., Cheung, T.C.H.: The outcome of online social interactions on Facebook pages. Internet Res. **29**(1), 2–23 (2019). https://doi.org/10.1108/IntR-04-2017-0161
14. Litt, E., Zhao, S., Kraut, R., Burke, M.: What are meaningful social interactions in today's media landscape? a cross-cultural survey. Social Media + Soc. **6**(3), 205630512094288 (2020). https://doi.org/10.1177/2056305120942888

Design-Driven Local Rural Transformation: Taking Anji County as an Example

Lyu Ji[✉]

Tongji University, Shanghai 200092, People's Republic of China
jilyu@foxmail.com

Abstract. This paper takes the rural transformation process that occurred in Anji County, Zhejiang Province, China as the research object. Based on the combing of the historical past and overall current situation of the rural areas in Anji County, as well as the elaboration and analysis of multiple rural transformation cases in this area, the research summarizes the dimensions and paths of transformation and development in rural areas in Anji County, and thus proposes a mode of design-driven local rural transformation. This mode may be suitable for guiding and promoting the revitalization and transformation of rural areas in developed areas of eastern China.

Keywords: Design-Driven · Rural Transformation · Anji County · Local Countryside

1 Introduction

This article attempts to sort out and analyze the development and transformation process of some rural areas in Anji County, Zhejiang Province, China, and explore the role and role of design in driving the revitalization of local rural areas in China. Based on this, a design driven model for local rural transformation is constructed. Anji County is a county-level city located in the developed coastal province of Zhejiang Province in eastern China. This land has always been a region with outstanding talents and abundant resources in history. It is rich in local products such as tea, bamboo, and silk. The "Two Mountains" theory, a sustainable development concept, also runs through the rural transformation practice of Anji County in areas such as rural environmental renewal, rural community construction, rural talent gathering, rural industrial development, and rural ecological protection. In the nearly 20 years of transformation practice in rural areas of Anji County, design has played an important role as a guide, intervener, driver, and promoter. By playing an active role in the transformation process at different levels and paths in rural areas, design has improved the infrastructure and internal quality of rural areas, maintained and inherited the original historical style and cultural customs of the countryside, Simultaneously integrating advantageous resources from both urban and rural areas, connecting and empowering different stakeholders in the urban-rural interaction field, exploring the emerging value of rural areas and attracting people to come to, return to, live in, and stay in rural areas for a long time, creating new economic

P.-L. P. Rau (Ed.): HCII 2024, LNCS 14701, pp. 256–263, 2024.
https://doi.org/10.1007/978-3-031-60904-6_18

and industrial models, establishing livable rural communities, and helping rural areas in Anji County achieve rejuvenation, revitalization, and prosperity.

2 The Past and Current Situation of Rural Areas in Anji County

Anji County is located in the northwest of Zhejiang Province, and is a county-level city with a population of about 600000 under the jurisdiction of Huzhou City. It governs a total of 217 administrative villages and communities, and has a history of over 1800 years of urban construction. The name of Anji County comes from the Book of Songs, which symbolizes comfort and beauty. Anji County was first built in the late Eastern Han Dynasty in 185AD, and later developed significantly and gradually flourished in the early Tang Dynasty due to the enlightened policies of the rulers and the construction of water conservancy projects. It became a place to pay tribute to high-quality silk fabrics and tea to the court at that time, and also produced abundant bamboo and bamboo shoots. In history, Anji County has always been the most developed agricultural production area in China due to its unique geographical and natural conditions of being surrounded by mountains and rivers. It is known as the world's granary and the land of fish and rice. The fertile soil, dense river networks, and continuous mountain and river vegetation provide superior and convenient natural conditions for agricultural cultivation and production. Plain farmland is the production area of grain, oil, and silkworms, while mountainous areas are the production areas of bamboo, wood, and tea, Important daily necessities such as rice, silk, and tea are continuously transported from here, as the saying goes, "Su Hu is ripe, and the world is abundant." People in the vast rural areas of Anji are mostly engaged in agricultural production labor, as well as handicrafts, transportation, and commercial trade related to agricultural production such as metallurgy, textiles, bamboo weaving, and water transportation. Apart from the turmoil and famine caused by wars and epidemics throughout history, most of Anji was the most prosperous and economically developed region in the country.

As the time came to the 1970s, the rural areas of Anji County after the reform and opening up began to mine for the needs of economic construction and development. Due to the rich limestone resources, the annual mining output of these mines once reached hundreds of thousands of tons. The high-yield mining industry brought considerable economic income to local villagers, but also caused huge pollution and damage to the local rural ecological environment. At that time, although the mines and cement plants scattered throughout the rural areas of Anji County drove rapid economic growth, the resulting environmental degradation problems also deeply troubled local residents. The harsh environment forced people to not continue living here, and rural residents moved out of this place one after another, turning once beautiful and prosperous villages into desolate "hollow villages". The serious consequences caused by unsustainable development methods have led local governments to pay attention to the ecological environment and population loss issues in local rural areas since the early 21st century. The government has gradually closed mines and attempted to restore the original natural environment in rural areas of Anji County. The natural resources such as mountains, waters, forests, lakes, and grasses owned by the countryside have been restored, protected, and redeveloped, transforming them into cultural and tourism resources, Explore the emerging value of existing resources, bring new economic benefits to local villagers, and achieve a significant balance between economic development and ecological environment protection. Through nearly 20 years of ecological restoration and sustainable development in rural areas, Anji County has become China's first ecological county, the first batch of national comprehensive tourism demonstration zones, and was awarded the United Nations Habitat Award in 2012. In 2021, Yucun Village in Anji County became the "Best Tourist Village" of the United Nations World Tourism Organization. In 2022, the regional GDP of Anji County was 58.24 billion yuan, while the per capita disposable income of farmers in rural areas of Anji County was 42000 yuan, which is five times that of 20 years ago.

3   Yucun: A Case Study of Transformation in Rural Areas of Anji County

Yucun in Anji County has undergone a transformation process from emphasizing economic development to emphasizing ecological development. Yucun is located in Tianhuangping Town, Anji County, with a total land area of approximately 4.8 square kilometers, including more than 6000 acres of mountain forests. The name of the village comes from the Yuling Mountains, a branch of the Tianmu Mountain Range, which is backed by it. It boasts beautiful mountains, rivers, bamboo forests, and abundant natural limestone resources. 20 years ago, the "stone economy" here, which refers to the mining and excavation industry, brought considerable profits to the residents of Yucun. Yucun built three quarries, a cement factory, and a chemical plant for this purpose. Hundreds of tractors ran between the factories, which can generate a net profit of 3 million yuan per year. Although villagers have become wealthy due to the economic income brought by the mining industry, the ecological damage caused by high pollution, high-energy consumption industries, and excessive exploitation of natural resources is also evident. The air and water here are beginning to be polluted, becoming extremely polluted. The residents of the village are unable to breathe clean air and access safe drinking water, and their physical health is also greatly affected. The pollution of land and environment has led to the inability of crops such as mulberry trees, bamboo shoots, and tea, which were once abundant here, to grow in such a harsh environment. The increasingly deteriorating living environment has forced rural residents to leave their hometowns and seek new development opportunities in cities. Due to environmental pollution and the reduction of labor force, rural areas are facing decline and withering.

At the beginning of the 21st century, facing severe natural environment pollution and a large loss of rural population, the local government began to implement engineering projects on rural governance in Anji County. The first step of the project was to shut down the mines and factories in the village, recruit design and planning teams from Tsinghua University and Beijing Forestry University to settle in the countryside, and design and transform the overall appearance of the village and the mines and factories (see Fig. 1). The original mining quarry was designed as a heritage park and camping site, attracting residents and tourists from the city to visit, travel, and camp here. The design team from Shanghai Jiao Tong University has transformed the old chemical factory building with a long history into a rural public library called "Yucun Impression". This zero-carbon building (see Fig. 2), built with sustainable design concepts, includes a book reading area and a bamboo product production area. It has now become a popular leisure venue for local residents and tourists, especially young people. Many entrepreneurial activities and exhibitions are also held here. Local villagers can excavate their own memories here, while foreign tourists can also learn about Yucun through this place. Yucun not only transformed the original mining site into a picturesque forest park, but also provided a community space for migrant workers to start businesses (see Fig. 3). Shared office space and digital nomadic communities were established here, and some social enterprises committed to rural operation and sustainable development also settled in. On weekends and holidays, there will also be rural markets held here, where migrant and local populations from cities and other places interact and live, forming a new local rural community. In such an inclusive and diverse rural community space, it is filled with social and cultural venues for people to interact and exchange. Both old and new residents in the countryside can contribute resources to the countryside through design empowerment, thus creating resonance in the rural community.

Fig. 1. The Landscape of Yucun

Fig. 2. The Public Library

Fig. 3. The Community Space for Migrant Workers to Start Businesses

4   The Dimensions of Design-Driven Local Rural Transformation

Based on the transformation case of rural areas in Anji County, we can extract several dimensions of local rural transformation, including the four main aspects of environment, industry, culture, and society, as well as the paths to promote rural transformation through design, including design driven rural environment updates, design driven rural industry revitalization, design driven rural cultural revitalization, and design driven rural social innovation. These four forms of design driving the emerging development of local rural areas are formed and established on the intervention of design in the three contexts of local space, local products, and local society involved in local rural issues. They respectively represent the main forms of design in intervening in specific rural issues. At the same time, these four forms also influence, complement, and intersect with each other in the design driven emerging development of rural areas. The four forms of design driven local rural problem-solving are also specific manifestations of the three main relationships that design thinking needs to handle when entering the rural context, including the relationship between people and the environment, the relationship between people and things, and the relationship between people and people in local rural areas. These three relationships are based on each other in the rural problem context and are the objects of design thinking intervention in rural problems.

Regarding the intervention of design in the governance of rural space, in the process of driving the protection, renewal, and reconstruction of the environment and texture of rural space, design first reconciles the relationship and contradiction between people and the environment in rural space. Rural space includes both the natural environment and the long-term production and living space of local villagers. It is a product of the mutual influence and integration of the natural and artificial worlds. Therefore, when designing and solving problems arising from rural space environment, the substantive challenge is how to coordinate and balance the relationship between the artificial world and the natural world, that is to say, making good use of natural and artificial objects to construct and shape the overall pattern and texture of rural spatial environment. The natural and artificial objects in rural space provide information and content for solving rural spatial environmental problems, which involves the relationship between objects and people in rural areas, and also affects the relationship between people in rural space. The spatial environment of rural areas serves the production and life of local people, and their utilization, transformation, and production of local things cannot be separated from the spatial environment of rural areas. Similarly, when considering the involvement of design in the governance of rural industries and driving the revitalization of rural industries through design, the relationship between people and things needs to be addressed and faced first, and the relationship between people and the environment is an important foundational factor behind the revitalization of rural industries. Therefore, design not only drives the renewal of rural environment, but also provides an environmental foundation for driving the revitalization of rural industries, as well as cultural revitalization and social innovation. The revitalization of rural industries also indirectly promotes and promotes the reshaping and reconstruction of the rural environment, as well as the revival process of rural culture. A good rural environment creates material conditions for people's long-term production and life, and the gathering and stable production activities of people also make it more possible for the development, inheritance, and continuation of material-based culture. As for the intervention of design in rural social governance, the connection, reshaping, and reconstruction of human relationships in rural society driven by design benefits from the good material environment, prosperous industrial environment, and colorful and active cultural environment in rural areas. Stable and comfortable production and living conditions are the soil for rural social development. When we improve and reconstruct the relationship between people and environment, and between people and things in rural areas through design, The relationship between people in rural areas provides opportunities for innovation, and design driven rural social innovation can also occur.

Overall, the four forms of design that drive emerging rural development and intervene in the context of rural issues constitute the theoretical and practical basis for designing solutions to local rural problems. They are also the forms and methods of design when entering the local rural discourse system. When applying design thinking to address the difficulties and challenges faced by local rural areas through the logic of design driven innovation, we can address specific issues related to the four elements of local rural organic structure in the context of local rural areas, namely rural space, local products, and rural society, including village appearance, landscape, material industry, rural customs, and human society. Through design driven rural environmental renewal and design driven rural industrial revitalization Design driven rural cultural revitalization and design driven rural social innovation are four different ways of design driven innovation, proposing innovative and creative rural problem-solving solutions including rural construction design, rural industry design, rural cultural and creative design, and rural community design.

5 Collaboration and Co-creation: A Mode of Design-Driven Local Rural Transformation

In the process of intervening in local rural issues and driving rural revitalization and development through design, people are the main body that uses design to enter rural areas. In contemporary local rural areas, there are mainly three types of people: original villagers, returning villagers, and new villagers. These three types of people constitute the three main bodies living in local rural areas, and all three types of people can become the main body that uses design driven innovative thinking to enter local rural areas, and these three main entities encompass different types of individuals involved in local rural development. Therefore, the application subject of design in the process of local rural revitalization presents a diversified mode. Rural original residents, new rural residents, temporary rural residents, urban returning residents, urban residents, local governments, local enterprises, social organizations and other stakeholders related to rural issues can all become the subject of using design to intervene and solve local rural problems to achieve rural development, And different entities are not independent of each other, but jointly promote the revitalization of local rural areas in a collaborative and creative way, because every problem context of local rural issues involves people, who are the core of solving rural problems and achieving development. The complex composition of the living subjects in local rural areas inevitably leads to the revitalization and development of local rural areas being the result of collaborative efforts and joint creation by multiple types of subjects.

The process of designing to drive the revitalization of local rural areas is essentially based on the local context, guided by design driven innovative thinking, and involving multiple subjects in a collaborative and creative way to solve rural problems, in order to promote the development and revitalization of local rural areas. Based on the four main specific forms of design driving the emerging development of local rural areas discussed earlier, the collaboration and co-creation among different stakeholders in rural areas are the basic patterns that run through each of these four forms of design driving rural revitalization, and they are also the key path for design driving rural revitalization. Whether it is design driven rural environmental renewal, rural industrial revitalization, or design driven rural cultural revitalization and rural social innovation, they all rely on the joint participation of local rural residents. The emerging participants and implementers of local rural areas must be local rural residents, who are the main participants in the emerging development of rural areas. If design driven innovation is the underlying logic of design-driven rural revitalization, then the collaboration and the co-creation is the indispensable practical mode of design-driven rural revitalization.

E-commerce Platform Mobile Interface Experience Design from a Cross-Cultural Perspective

Jiang Jinchen[1]([✉]), Shi Yini[2], and Peng Kexing[2]

[1] Sichuan Fine Arts Institute, Chongqing 400030, China
jiangjinchen@scfai.edu.cn
[2] Chongqing University, Chongqing 400030, China

Abstract. Objective: Because of the problem of cognitive bias in interface information among cross-cultural users, the research goal is to achieve "cross-cultural adaptation" of e-commerce mobile interface design and improve the experience of cross-cultural users. Method: Combining the literature research method and case analysis method, we analyzed the dimensions of cultural differences between different countries in e-commerce scenarios, sorted out the differences in behavioral habits of cross-cultural users and their involved interfaces in e-commerce contexts, and refined three interface conceptual design processes that are strongly related to cross-cultural. Result: This paper proposes a CID (Cross-Cultural Interface Design) model for e-commerce platform mobile terminals that adapts to cross-cultural differences and further explores a series of cross-cultural interface design strategies between China and the United States with examples. It improved the design strategy by comparing the relevant interfaces of TikTok's American and Chinese versions. On this basis, the design practice of optimizing the interface of the American version of Pinduoduo was completed, and the feasibility of the model was initially verified. Significance: This study is a comprehensive consideration from multiple perspectives of culture, cognition, and experience, which has a certain degree of universality, which provides new perspectives for theoretical research and theoretical references for the development of cross-cultural interface experience design research, and provides new practical paths for the practice of mobile interface design in the cross-cultural e-commerce platform project between China and the United States.

Keywords: Experience Design · Interface Design · Cross-cultural · E-commerce Platform · Mobile Site

1 Introduction

The rapid development of the Internet and mobile technology gives rise to a global marketplace where shopping changes dynamically [1]. The use of electronic platforms by buyers and sellers to transact goods and services is collectively called e-commerce [2]. Nowadays, most corporations can buy, sell, and collaborate worldwide, and even smaller

P.-L. P. Rau (Ed.): HCII 2024, LNCS 14701, pp. 264–279, 2024.
https://doi.org/10.1007/978-3-031-60904-6_19

businesses are forced to place themselves in a global context to survive in this new and challenging business environment [3]. At the same time, more people are accepting and choosing to shop online due to COVID-19, and mobile shopping is gradually overtaking traditional offline and web-based shopping as the preferred shopping method for users [4]. Lee I et al. suggest that as mobile Internet use spreads globally, culture significantly impacts mobile Internet services more than other technological applications [5]. Therefore, to meet the market demand that tends to be globalized, it is necessary to localize exotic mobile software products to cultural differences in different countries. Russo and Boor, and Zahedi et al. demonstrated that users tend to use localized products that conform to their cultural practices and contexts, which has led to a large influx of cultural translation work into interface design [6]. Anthropologists such as Hofstede, Trompenaars, and Hannerz studied cross-cultural in-depth, but the relevant classical theories have not been effectively applied to interface design. The main reason for this phenomenon is that designers tend to use existing cultural models. However, these models are designed for different goals and audiences in other disciplines and are not well adapted to the practice of interface design [7]. Most of the current research on cross-cultural interface design focuses on the influencing factors of the interface and related design strategies in the website. There is a lack of research related to the interface of the mobile terminal, and a mature theoretical system has not been established. Therefore, the research focuses on the design of "localized" interface experiences for cross-cultural consumers.

With the research goal of realizing "cross-cultural adaptation" in interface design, this paper proposes a CID theoretical model of cross-cultural e-commerce mobile interface design based on user experience. It points out the intervention paths of related interface design in different cultural contexts. The research verifies the preliminary feasibility of the model based on case studies. It explores the specific design strategies for e-commerce mobile interface design in China and the United States. This paper aims to assist designers in quickly capturing the part of the interface where cross-cultural differences exist and quickly transforming the interface design based on the existing interface. Cross-cultural interface design for the mobile version of the same app can be completed quickly and effectively.

2 Cross-Cultural Interface Design Model for E-commerce Platform Mobile

2.1 Cultural Dimensions in the Context of Cross-Cultural E-commerce

Based on Hofstede's classical culture theory, Erin Meyer proposed eight dimensions for measuring culture: communication, evaluation, persuasion, leadership, decision-making, trust, opposition, and planning, based on experiments, business practices, and cross-cultural communication. The subdivided attributes of the eight dimensions and the positioning of the attributes in different countries are illustrated in Table 1 [8].

In the communication dimension, communication in low contexts is precise, simple, and straightforward; good communication in high contexts is complex, detailed, and multi-level. In the evaluation dimension, direct negative feedback means that negative feedback given to others is frank and honest; indirect negative feedback means that negative feedback given to others is euphemistic and subtle. In the persuasion dimension, principle priority emphasizes sorting out theories or concepts first; application priority emphasizes starting with a fact, statement, or idea. In the leadership dimension, egalitarianism refers to a flat organizational structure; hierarchy refers to a multi-level and fixed organizational structure. In the decision-making dimension, consensual means that decisions are collectively recognized and made together; top-down means that individuals make decisions. In the trust dimension, task-based means building trust based on business capabilities; relationship-based means building trust through interaction with people. In the opposition dimension, confrontation means that disagreements and debates are favorable for the team or organization; conflict avoidance means that disagreements and arguments harm the team or organization. In the planning dimension, linear time emphasizes completing things in sequence; flexible time emphasizes that tasks can change at any time.

2.2 User Behavioral Habits in Cross-Cultural E-commerce Contexts

When constructing a cross-cultural interface design model for the mobile side of an e-commerce platform, it is necessary to focus on the human factor, which means clarifying the differences in the behavioral habits of cross-cultural users in the e-commerce field. This paper divides user behavior in the e-commerce domain into three phases: pre-shopping, shopping, and post-shopping. Firstly, this paper distinguished East and West countries from the geographical dimension. Taobao, Jingdong, and Pinduoduo are the principal cases in Eastern countries, and Amazon, eBay, and Etsy are the principal cases in Western countries. Through a series of comparative analyses of more typical East-West e-commerce app interfaces, users' behaviors in the three shopping phases and their corresponding touchpoints in East-West countries are condensed (see Fig. 1). The figure shows that in the pre-order stage, consumption philosophy is the main point of difference between Eastern and Western users. Eastern countries' users not only enter e-commerce apps when they have a need but also browse the shopping page when they have no shopping purpose and even make impulse purchases, while users in Western countries generally enter e-commerce apps when they have a clear shopping need. In the shopping stage, shopping psychology, cost perception, logistics efficiency, time concept, etc., are the main differences between Eastern and Western users. Eastern countries users are less trusting of the goods that cannot touch the physical goods, more concerned about cost-effectiveness, delivery time, and shipping costs, and more sensitive to discounts; Western countries users are more critical to the professionalism of the goods and pay more attention to the timeliness of the logistics. In the post-shopping stage, shopping psychology is the main point of difference between Eastern and Western users. Eastern countries' users are prone to impulsive consumption, and the demand for return and exchange services is relatively strong; Western countries' users pay more attention to protecting personal consumption rights and interests.

As mentioned above, consumption philosophy, shopping psychology, cost perception, logistics timeliness, time concept, etc., are the main behavioral differences between Eastern and Western users in e-commerce. The primary interfaces involved are the home

Table 1. Eight dimensions of measuring culture

Cultural Dimension	Attributes	Location Map of Attributes in Different Countries
commu-nication	low contexts/ high contexts	US Netherlands Finland / Australia Germany Denmark / Canada UK (Low-Context) — Poland — Spain Italy Singapore Iran China Japan / Brazil Mexico France India Kenya Korea / Argentina Peru Russia Saudi Indonesia Arabia (High-Context)
evalua-tion	direct nega-tive feedback/ indirect neg-ative feedback	Russia France Italy / Israel Germany Norway Australia / Netherlands Denmark Spain (Direct negative feedbck) — US UK Brazil India Saudi Arabia Japan / Canada Mexico China Korea Thailand / Argentina Kenya Ghana Indonesia (Indirect negative feedback)
persua-sion	principle pri-ority/ application priority	Italy Russia Germany Argentina Sweden Netherlands Australia / France Spain Brazil Mexico Denmark UK Canada US (Principles-first → Applications-first)
leader-ship	egalitarian-ism/ hierarchy	Denmark Israel Canada US / Netherlands Finland UK Germany / Sweden Australia (Egalitarian) — France Poland Saudi Arabia Japan / Italy Russia India Korea / Brazil Spain Mexico Peru China Nigeria (Hierarchical)
decision-making	consensual/ top-down	Sweden Germany / Japan Netherlands UK (Consensual) — US France India Nigeria / Brazil Italy Russia China (Top-down)
trust	task-based/ relationship-based	US Denmark Germany UK Poland / Netherlands Finland / Australia Austria (Task-based) — Saudi Arabia / France Italy Mexico Brazil / Spain Russia Thailand India / Japan Turkey China Nigeria (Relationship-based)
opposi-tion	confronta-tion/ conflict avoidance	Israel Germany Denmark Australia US / France Russia Spain Italy UK / Netherlands (Confrontational) — Sweden India China Indonesia / Brazil Mexico Peru Ghana Japan / Singapore Saudi Arabia Thailand (Aviods confrontation)
planning	Linear time/ Flexible time	Germany Japan Netherlands Poland / Switzerland Sweden US UK Czech Republic / Denmark (Linear-time) — Saudi Arabia / Spain Italy Brazil China / France Russia Mexico India Nigeria / Turkey Kenya (Flexible-time)

page, product list page, product detail page, shopping cart page, checkout page, and product order page. Suppose designers want to convert the interface design between Eastern and Western countries. Based on the above cultural dimensions, factors that differ in the user habits of e-commerce platforms can be derived.

2.3 User Behavioral Habits in Cross-Cultural E-commerce Contexts

The concept of user experience was introduced and popularized by Donald Arthur Norman in the early 1990s. As the Internet market grows, a good user experience is a crucial competition point for various companies. James Garrett defined user experience as how a product relates to and functions in the outside world and formulated five user experience

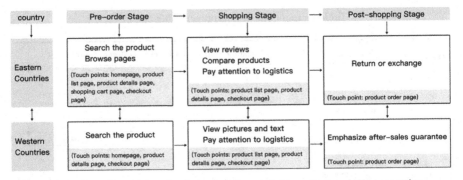

Fig. 1. Flowchart of shopping behavior of users between East and West countries

layers [9]. Israeli researcher Avi Parush proposed a systematic conceptual design system to weaken the gap between user needs and prototypes, offering a practically feasible methodology for interaction designers. The steps of this system are building functional modules, formulating conceptual model elements, creating physical model elements, determining detailed conceptual elements, and designing user interface elements [10] (see Fig. 2).

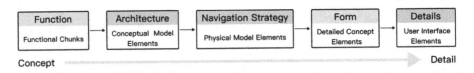

Fig. 2. Interface conceptualization steps

Not all segments in the process involve cross-cultural factors. In the functional part, the user's initial shopping motivation is mainly unaffected by cultural factors. It can be categorized into three types of user shopping motivation based on user behavior: having a clear shopping goal, general shopping goal, and random browsing. In the form part, detailed conceptual elements are mainly designed based on the navigation rules in the previous step and the interface design specifications. However, the interface design specifications of most e-commerce platforms are relatively similar, derived from material design and iOS HIG, so they are less affected by cross-cultural differences. Therefore, cross-cultural interface design needs to focus on architecture, navigation strategy, and details.

2.4   User Behavioral Habits in Cross-Cultural E-commerce Contexts

In the context of cross-cultural e-commerce, this paper constructs a CID (Cross-cultural Interface Design) model for e-commerce platform mobile based on the cultural dimensions and the related interface design process, combining the eight dimensions of culture, the differences in user shopping behaviors, and the interface conceptual design framework (see Fig. 3).

The model transforms cross-cultural interface design into refining cross-cultural factors and interface design. In refining cross-cultural factors, compare the country of the current app with one or more other countries that require cross-cultural interface transformation. From the eight cultural dimensions of communication, evaluation, persuasion, leadership, decision-making, trust, opposition, and planning, we found the dimensions with more significant differences, which means the main cultural difference factors. In the interface design stage, based on the cultural difference factors, the user habit difference factors in the e-commerce context are extracted, namely consumption concept, shopping psychology, cost perception, logistics timeliness, time concept, and the scope layer and structure that are mainly affected by cross-cultural factors are The interface concept design begins with the three user experience elements of layer and presentation layer. The Scope layer corresponds to the architecture layer of the interface conceptualization and consists of conceptual elements, including the connections between the "spaces" in which the user performs functions; the architecture layer corresponds to the navigation and strategy layer of the interface conceptualization and describes the navigation and navigational rules, including paths between the "spaces" and physical constraints in the "spaces"; and the presentation layer corresponds to the detail layer of the interface conceptualization and consists of the user interface elements, which include a detailed look and feel of the interface. Eventually, the above will correspond to the relevant interface design of the e-commerce app, which means its home page, product list page, product detail page, shopping cart page, checkout page, and product order page.

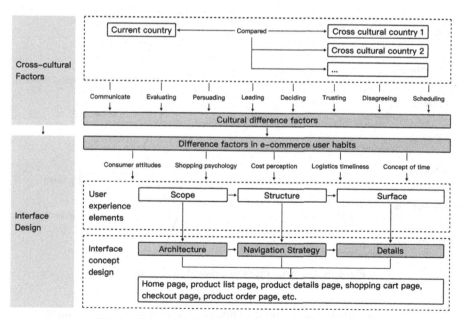

Fig. 3. CID model for e-commerce platform mobile side

3 Case Validation: The United States and China

3.1 Cultural Differences and Design Strategies for E-commerce Mobile in China and the US

This paper chose the US and China as the case validation objects for the CID model. The reason is that the US and China are the top two economies in the world, respectively. Studying the cultural context of these two completely different countries provides interface design strategies that can be transformed into each other and is helpful for in-depth exploration of the theoretical framework in the field of cross-cultural interface design. Theoretical frameworks contribute to a deeper understanding of cultural influences in academia and provide better guidance for companies to be more flexible in understanding and adapting their business practices in different cultural environments.

We can get a comparison chart of Chinese and American cultures from the illustration of the attribute positioning of different countries in Table 1 above, (see Fig. 4). More peculiarly, China does not have a corresponding position in the chart of the Persuasion Culture Dimension. There is no location because the most common worldviews in Asian cultures are so different from European-influenced cultures that an entirely different frame of reference is irrelevant to the persuasion scale. Therefore, Chinese and US cultures do not consider this dimension. The figure shows that the gap between the US and China in communication, trust, and planning is more significant. It is a central cultural dimension in cross-cultural interface design between China and the US.

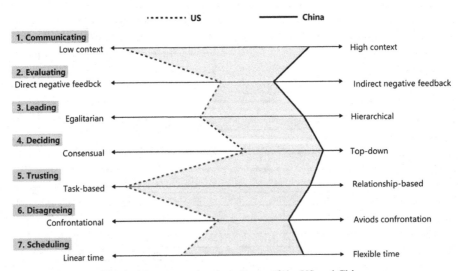

Fig. 4. Map comparing the cultures of the US and China

Therefore, this article focuses on the three cultural dimensions of communication, trust, and planning, combined with the differences in user shopping behavior and habits in Eastern and Western countries mentioned above, and formulates a cross-cultural interface for Chinese and American e-commerce mobile terminals in the architecture layer, navigation layer, and details. The relevant strategies of the three design stages are listed and ranked. See Table 2 for details.

Communication Dimension. The US is a low-context country that seeks precision, simplicity, and clarity in communication. The design strategy for this dimension is to build a clear information structure, which means that products are categorized and organized so that users can easily find the products they are interested in. The design strategy for the navigation layer in this dimension is to set a simple navigation bar and optimize it for search engines. Setting a clean navigation bar means adopting a simple and intuitive navigation bar design to ensure that users can easily navigate through different product categories; optimizing for search engines means ensuring that products are ranked high in search engines through effective Search Engine Optimization (SEO) to increase the chances of users discovering new products. The design strategy at the detail level of this dimension is to optimize the shopping cart design, which means providing a clear list of products and the total price of the shopping cart so that users can easily view and adjust the products in the shopping cart at any time.

China is a high-context country that prefers complex, detailed, and hierarchical communication. The design strategy in this dimension architecture layer is to provide accurate product categorization, which refers to the need for detailed and comprehensive product categorization to adapt to the vast market demand in China and to help users rapidly find the products they need. The design strategy for the navigation layer in this dimension is localized search suggestions, which refers to carefully considering Chinese users' search habits, language habits, and input methods to improve the accuracy and convenience of the search. At the detail level of this dimension, the design strategy is to utilize the urgency marketing strategy and the anxiety psychology. Using an urgency marketing strategy means emphasizing the function of seconds and rush purchase through labels, high saturation colors, and other design expressions to cater to Chinese users' concern and enthusiasm for limited-time freebies and other promotional activities; and exploiting anxiety refers to designing compelling red packets and coupons to create the anxiety that users will lose money if they don't buy them.

Trust Dimension. Trust in the US is more inclined to be built through highly specialized operations. The design strategy in the architecture layer of this dimension is an accurate, personalized recommendation, which means providing users with product recommendations based on their browsing history, purchasing behavior, and interests to increase the personalized shopping experience. The design strategy of this dimensional navigation layer is to display popular digital content with high quality, that is, using interface hot areas to display popular searches and popular lists to help users discover popular products and current trends. The design strategy of the detail layer in this dimension is to provide detailed product descriptions, high-quality product images, and detailed logistics information. Offering detailed product descriptions means providing product information, including specifications, dimensions, materials, etc., to help users understand the characteristics of the product more comprehensively; high-quality product pictures mean providing high-resolution, clear, and bright product pictures so that users can view the details of the product; displaying detailed logistic information means that it is necessary to display precise information on logistics time, price and other information related to the interests, to enhance the user's sense of trust in the platform.

Trust in China is more likely to be built through interpersonal relationships. The design strategy for this dimension is to emphasize the group-buying and promotion atmosphere, which means highlighting related activities on the homepage or in a particular area to meet the shopping culture of Chinese users, who are used to shopping in groups and pursuing discounts. The design strategy in the navigation layer of this dimension is to integrate social media integration, which means that users can share their shopping experience, product evaluation, etc., directly through the e-commerce platform to enhance social interaction. The design strategy at the detail level of this dimension is to provide high-quality evaluations and display rich product graphics. Providing high-quality evaluations means allowing users to check each other's shopping experience and highlighting product evaluations and user ratings; displaying rich product graphics means using vivid pictures and attractive text descriptions to enhance the attractiveness of the products.

Program Dimension. The US prefers to complete matters in order. The design strategy at the structural layer of this dimension is to simplify the shopping process, which means reducing users' shopping resistance and increasing the conversion rate through a straightforward checkout interface and explicit step-by-step guidelines. The design strategy for the navigation layer in this dimension is to provide intuitive filtering and sorting options, which means helping users filter products more accurately according to their preferences and needs. The design strategy at the detail level of this dimension is to provide a clear checkout page, which means that the information on the page for each step of the user's operation should be concise and straightforward to improve the user's shopping convenience.

China preferred a flexible arrangement of events. The design strategy of the structural layer in this dimension is to support multi-path connectivity for the same operation, which means that it considers and accommodates the fact that users complete essential operations such as adding shopping carts and making purchases in different interfaces. The design strategy for the navigation layer in this dimension is to ensure full-link reach for navigation, which means helping the user understand the current location and support a quick return to the previous layer or a direct jump to other related pages. The design strategy for the detail layer of this dimension is to support diversified payment methods and provide an information modification portal. Supporting diversified payment methods means providing payment channels, including Alipay, WeChat Pay, UnionPay, etc., which conform to the payment habits of Chinese users and improve the convenience of payment; and providing a portal for modifying information means that the information can be modified at any stage before the purchase completed.

To summarize, American e-commerce platforms focus on the professionalism of products and services as well as clear shopping directionality to build users' trust through logic and structure; Chinese e-commerce platforms focus on socialized shopping, low-cost logistics, and promotional marketing modes integrating local cultures to attract and satisfy users' needs. After deriving the design strategies, this paper chooses to validate them by utilizing the interface associated with the video shopping process of the Chinese and American versions of TikTok. The prioritization of design strategies is defined to provide specific interface design guidelines for practical projects. Improve designers' design efficiency and users' localized interface experience, and achieve the integration

Table 2. Summary of three-dimensional cross-cultural interface design strategies for mobile in Chinese and American e-commerce companies

cultural dimension	country	architecture	navigation	detail
communication	US	1. Build a clear information structure	2. Simple navigation bar 3. Optimize Search Engine	4. Optimize shopping cart design
	China	5. Comprehensive Product Categorization	6. Localized Search Suggestions	7. Utilizing a Sense of Urgency Marketing Strategy 8. Exploiting Anxiety
trust	US	9. Accurate personalized recommendations	10. High-performance display of digitized popular content	11. Detailed product description 12. High quality product images 13. Display detailed logistics information
	China	14. Emphasis on group purchases and promotions	15. Integrating Social Media	16. Providing high-quality evaluations 17. Display rich product graphics

(continued)

Table 2. (*continued*)

cultural dimension	country	architecture	navigation	detail
program	US	18. Simplify the shopping process	19. Provides intuitive filtering and sorting options	20. Provide clear checkout pages
	China	21. Provide clear checkout pages	22. Guaranteed full-link reach for navigation	23. Support diversified payment methods 24. Provide a portal for information modification

of culture and interface. The reasons for choosing Jitterbug lie in the following two points: (1) Live broadcasting is a new network culture development. Under the influence of the epidemic, the live broadcast e-commerce mode has fully exploded, and the new retail mode of "live broadcast + e-commerce" has accelerated the rise of the new retail mode [11]. As a short-video social networking application with a vast user base, TikTok is one of the representative apps under this marketing model. (2) In September 2023, TikTok Shop was officially launched in the US. TikTok Shop lets users purchase products directly from videos and live streams in the "For You" dynamic by offering video and live streaming shopping services. The Chinese version went live earlier. Therefore, the American and Chinese versions of TikTok are newer case material and provide a more intuitive comparison.

By analyzing the interface of TikTok's Chinese and American versions, we learned valuable experience from the existing market. Further, it deepens the Sino-US cross-cultural interface design strategy generated by the CID model. It provides powerful reference and inspiration for Sino-US digital product interface design on a global scale. The video shopping process-focused interface of TikTok's American version is shown in Fig. 5, and the video shopping process-focused interface of TikTok's Chinese version is shown in Fig. 6. Use blue arrows to express the jump or switching relationship between interfaces and divide the interface into an architecture layer, a navigation layer, and a detail layer. The cross-cultural interface design strategies for e-commerce mobile in Table 2 are further summarized and sorted out. In this paper, the primary design strategy of China and the United States is the P0 strategy, and the remaining secondary strategies are the P1 strategy, (see Fig. 7). As shown in the figure, in the cross-cultural e-commerce interface design transformation between China and the US, if we want to convert Chinese e-commerce products to the American version, the P0 strategies in the architecture, navigation, and detail layers are 1, 18, 10, 19, 11, 12, 20. The P1 strategies are 9, 2, 3, 4, 13, and if we want to convert American e-commerce products to the Chinese version, the P0 strategies in the architecture, navigation, and detail layers are 14, 21, 15, 22, 7, 8, 16, and the P1 strategies are 5, 6, 17, 23, 24.

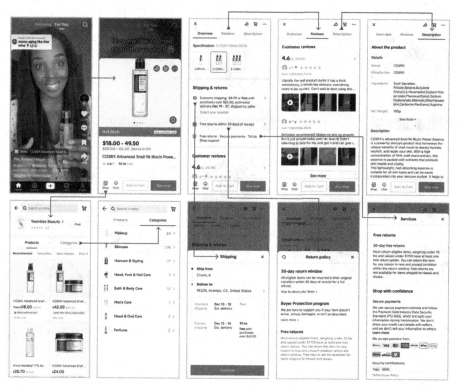

Fig. 5. The interface related to the video shopping process on the American version of TikTok (Image source: TikTok screenshot)

3.2 Design Practices: Optimizing the American Version of Chinese Pinduoduo

From the preceding, we can know the design strategy of Chinese and American e-commerce mobile sites, and this paper is aimed at the Chinese Pinduoduo app to practice the design of the American version. Pinduoduo is a well-known social e-commerce platform in China that adopts the model of group buying and social shopping, focusing on social sharing and team buying. Temu is Pinduoduo's overseas version, launched on September 1, 2022. It is mainly targeted at the mid-range user group and is offered at lower prices to provide users with a value-for-money shopping experience. However, the interface of the current American version of Temu still has a solid local Chinese visual feel, with a low degree of adaptation to local American user habits. In this paper, the interface optimization design is carried out on three main pages of shopping, namely home page, product detail page, and order page, as an example, which is shown in Fig. 8. The home page mainly adopts design strategies 1, 3, 10, 12, which streamline

Fig. 6. Interface related to the video shopping process of TikTok China version (Image source: TikTok screenshot)

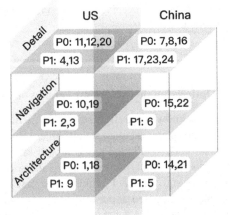

Fig. 7. TikTok China's video shopping process-related interface

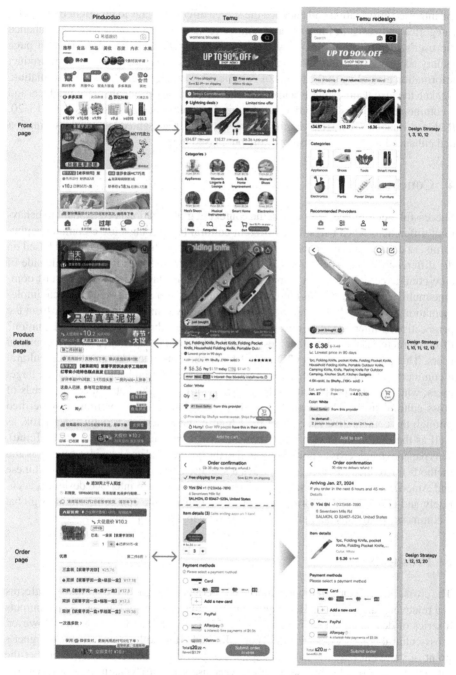

Fig. 8. Temu interface optimization design display

the interface information and enhance the screen effect; use tags to highlight the popular categories and assist in filtering; and remove redundant visual information to enhance the user's identification efficiency and trust in the product. The product detail page mainly adopts design strategy 1, 10, 11, 12, 13. Adjust the content and order of product information according to the habits of American users. Highlight logistics information, weaken the visual atmosphere, and establish a sense of professionalism for products and e-commerce platforms. The order page primarily employs design strategies 1, 12, 13, 20. Reduced visual noise by rearranging the page content, highlighted logistical information and enhanced the user's control over the purchased item.

4 Conclusion

Successful e-commerce platforms in the context of globalization need to adapt to behavioral differences when users from different cultural backgrounds use e-commerce platforms. Localized interface design strategies for each country are implemented based on the differences in user behavior. Cross-cultural interface design for the mobile side of an e-commerce platform is a comprehensive and multi-layered process. It must combine multiple aspects, such as cultural understanding, user insight, and technical implementation, to successfully land in a cross-cultural environment. In this paper, from the perspective of interface designers, the goal is to realize the "cross-cultural adaptation" of e-commerce mobile interface design and enhance the experience of cross-cultural users. This paper proposed a CID model for mobile interface design of cross-cultural e-commerce platforms, which helps to understand the cultural background of the target users, which means user habits, values, social norms, etc., to better meet the needs of cross-cultural users. The feasibility of the theoretical model is preliminarily verified through the comparative analysis of the Chinese and American versions of TikTok, as well as the optimized design practice of the American version of Pinduoduo (Temu). This paper expands cross-cultural research in the design field and provides new ideas and methods for related research. It provides a specific design strategy toolkit for Chinese and American cross-cultural interface design, which can help interface designers accurately and efficiently transform actual projects, enhance the competitiveness of global e-commerce platforms, and promote their sustainable development.

5 Prospects

The cross-cultural study of mobile interface experience design for e-commerce platforms is a relatively large system. This paper only formulates a design framework and outputs a series of design strategies for converting Chinese and American versions. However, cross-cultural interface design should not be limited to the exploration from the designer's point of view but requires more disciplines to participate and create together. Let the interface better meet the diverse needs of global users, reach a better user experience, and promote the sustainable development of e-commerce platforms globally. The following is a series of possible opportunities for cross-cultural interface design research in the future:

1. Deeper integration of psychology. Further in-depth study of the psychological impact of different cultures on user behavior and experience, including users' attitudes, emotions, and cognitive habits. By understanding cultural psychology, designers can better understand and meet the potential needs of users from different cultures and get more accurate cultural difference factors.
2. Integrate advanced technologies. Using new technologies such as artificial intelligence and machine learning to more accurately predict user needs and preferences by analyzing user behavior. Technology can also be used for adaptive interface design, enabling e-commerce platforms to adjust their presentation more flexibly among users of different cultures.
3. Globalized teamwork. Promote globalized teamwork by bringing together designers and researchers from different cultural backgrounds to discuss best practices in cross-cultural design. Through multicultural teamwork, we can better understand and respond to the diverse needs of users in different cultures.
4. Involve users and provide feedback. Make designs meet user expectations through participatory design and shared experiences between users from different cultures.

References

1. Lucia-Palacios, L., Bordonaba-Juste, V., Polo-Redondo, Y., et al.: E-business implementation and performance: analysis of mediating factors. Internet Res. **24**(2), 223–245 (2014)
2. Sharma, G., Lijuan, W.: Ethical perspectives on e-commerce: an empirical investigation. Internet Res. **24**(4), 414–435 (2014)
3. Savrul, M., Incekara, A., Sener, S.: The potential of e-commerce for SMEs in a globalizing business environment. Procedia Soc. Behav. Sci. **150**, 35–45 (2014)
4. Mouratidis, K., Papagiannakis, A.: COVID-19, internet, and mobility: the rise of telework, telehealth, e-learning, and e-shopping. Sustain. Cities Soc. **74**, 103182 (2021)
5. Lee, I., Choi, B., Kim, J., et al.: Cross-cultural comparison for cultural aspects of mobile internet: focusing on Korea and Hong Kong (2004)
6. Jagne, J., Smith-Atakan, A.S.G.: Cross-cultural interface design strategy. Univ. Access Inf. Soc. **5**, 299–305 (2006)
7. Marcus, A.: Cross-cultural user-interface design for work, home, play, and on the way. In: ACM SIGGRAPH ASIA 2010 Courses, pp. 1–160 (2010)
8. Meyer, E.: The culture map (INTL ED): decoding how people think, lead, and get things done across cultures. PublicAffairs (2016)
9. Jesse, J.G.: The Elements of User Experience: User-Centered Design for the Web and Beyond, 2nd edn. New Riders, CA (2010)
10. Parush, A.: Conceptual Design For Interactive Systems: Designing for Performance and User Experience. Morgan Kaufmann, Burlington (2015)
11. Hu, M., Zhang, M., Wang, Y.: Why do audiences choose to keep watching on live video streaming platforms? An explanation of dual identification framework. Comput. Hum. Behav. **75**, 594–606 (2017)

The Role of Scientific Research Foundation in the United States, Germany, and China in Developing the Industrial Internet

Ziyang Li[1], Zhenli Bai[1,2], and Ang Zhang[1(✉)]

[1] China Academy of Industrial Internet, Beijing 100102, China
zhang-ang-07@163.com
[2] School of Economics and Management, University of Chinese Academy of Sciences,
Beijing 100049, China

Abstract. The Industrial Internet has become crucial in shaping the digital economy and driving transformative changes across different industries worldwide. As major pillars of the global economy, the United States of America (USA), Germany, and China have taken the lead in developing the Industrial Internet, exemplified by state initiatives such as "Advanced Manufacturing Partnership" (USA), "Industry 4.0" (Germany), and China's Innovative Development of the Industrial Internet. This study analyzes the role of the national science and research agencies of these countries in developing their own version of the Industrial Internet. In these countries, the number of projects that aim to advance the Industrial Internet has steadily increased, with growing funding in the USA and China. Notably, data research is a major focus of Industrial Internet projects across all three nations. However, the three countries also have distinct research priorities that develop different components of the Industrial Internet: China focuses on networks, Germany concentrates on production and processes, and the USA gives precedence to equipment and security. Regarding the specific scientific disciplines involved, China and the USA intend to fund Industrial Internet projects that fall under computer science and information science, while Germany places greater emphasis on promoting projects classified under mechanical and industrial engineering.

Keywords: Industrial Internet · Scientific Research Foundation · Industry 4.0

1 Introduction

The Industrial Internet aims to seamlessly integrate information, communication, and manufacturing technologies by utilizing modern innovations such as cloud computing, big data, artificial intelligence, and edge computing. This Industrial Internet establishes a forward-looking ecosystem with bidirectional communication capabilities, facilitating seamless connectivity, collaboration among devices, and real-time data collection and analysis. Introduced in 2012 by the General Electric Company, the Industrial Internet aims to enhance industrial production efficiency and market competitiveness. It is presented as a new essential infrastructure for industry. Consequently, research activities and projects aimed at developing the Industrial Internet need to use innovative application models resulting from the deep integration of next-generation information and communication technologies with industrial economics. This transformative approach seeks to reshape traditional manufacturing models, organizational methods, logistics, and industrial structures, establishing a new production and service system characterized by comprehensive connectivity across all industries and the entire value chain.

Scientific research foundation serves as crucial catalysts for advancing cutting-edge scientific research, fostering talent, and driving scientific and technological innovation and application. In the United States of America (USA), the National Science Foundation (NSF)[1] supports a diverse range of projects across different scientific disciplines. In Germany, the Deutsche Forschungsgemeinschaft (DFG)[2] oversees the funding of fundamental research projects aligned with the country's commitment to Industry 4.0 and intelligent manufacturing. Meanwhile, the National Natural Science Foundation of China (NSFC)[3] concentrates on innovative research, talent cultivation, international cooperation, and management systems.

This study collects information on Industrial Internet projects supported by the NSF, DFG, and NSFC, including the number of projects, project funding amounts, project abstracts, and project proponents, to elucidate how these projects promote the advancement and practical application of the Industrial Internet in the USA, Germany, and China. By analyzing these three representative countries, we can provide valuable insights for the sustainable development of the global Industrial Internet.

2 Background

The Industrial Internet has had a pioneering role in industry. One of the first tasks in making the Industrial Internet a reality was digitization. Meanwhile, the manufacturing sectors began enhancing their competitiveness and ensuring continuous growth by utilizing cutting-edge information and communication technologies (ICT) [1]. Subsequently, digitization and Industry 4.0 technologies provided industrial enterprises with novel opportunities and benefits which can improve product quality and reliability, optimize processes, and increase manufacturing flexibility productivity [2]. Product and service information are being progressively digitized, thus making digital tasks and processes key aspects of economic competition [3]. Moreover, the Industrial Internet expands innovation networks, reduces communication costs, expands scope, and accelerates the integration of different types of industries [4]. For example, many traditional retailers have transitioned to digital formats and can differentiate themselves in new ecosystems [5]. The Industrial Internet has created pathways for companies to produce products with increased complexity as well as to generate value beyond products. Consequently, these manufacturing enterprises can offer value in entirely novel ways [5]. The level of digitization affects various business activities, including business models; it also enables new ways of collaborating, the introduction of new products and services, and fosters better relationships between companies, customers, and employees. These compel companies

---

[1] https://www.nsf.gov/.

[2] https://www.dfg.de/.

[3] https://www.nsfc.gov.cn/.

to explore innovation early on [6]. Moreover, as products become more intelligent and interconnected, the Industrial Internet allows access to product data streams, potentially generating new business models [7].

The Industrial Internet holds significant strategic importance globally. Germany strongly advocates for the revolutionary changes brought by the Industrial Internet to the economy, terming this policy "Industry 4.0" to signify the fourth industrial revolution. Industry 4.0 supports the extensive integration of ICT with industrial manufacturing. Apart from enhancing the efficiency of processes, routine procedures, and systems, Industry 4.0 enables companies to differentiate their products and services. However, from a technological perspective alone, this is insufficient to address development issues related to the fourth industrial revolution. Digitalization also requires companies to change organizational and cultural aspects to maximize flexibility and adaptability [8, 9]. In the USA, the Industrial Internet is not directly promoted by the government but by private institutions, notably the Industrial Internet Consortium (IIC). Compared to other countries, the Industrial Internet in the United States is extensive, spanning energy, healthcare, manufacturing, public sectors, and transportation. The goal of the IIC is to promote interoperability between different industries using the Industrial Internet. Companies in the USA are most interested in establishing new business models and intelligent services for the Industrial Internet. Therefore, the USA approach is primarily market-driven [10]. In China, the Ministry of Industry and Information Technology defines the Industrial Internet as a new infrastructure, application model, and industrial ecosystem resulting from the deep integration of ICT with the industrial economy. By comprehensively connecting people, machines, objects, and systems, a completely new manufacturing system covering the entire value chain is constructed, enabling the digitalization, networking, and intelligent development of industries, and serving as a cornerstone of the fourth industrial revolution.

3   Analysis of Industrial Internet Projects

3.1   Data Collection

This study analyzes the current status and development priorities of USA, Germany, and China, and with regard to the Industrial Internet from the perspective of scientific research foundation-backed projects. No discussion is made on which country has a better overall program for implementing the Industrial Internet.

The data used in this study are gathered from projects funded by the national science and research agencies of the USA, Germany, and China. In the United States, the main focus of development is the Internet of Things (IoT) which closely connected with the Industrial Internet. The IIC changed its name to the Industry IoT Consortium on August 31, 2021. When probing for data from the NSF (USA), we selected projects containing "IOT" on the project title, resulting in a total of 245 Industrial Internet projects. Searching for project titles with "IIoT" produced 4 related projects. Since Industrial IoT is a subset of IoT, this report analyzes the data from 245 projects using the keyword "Internet of Things". In Germany, "Industry 4.0" is more commonly used and is synonymous to the Industrial Internet. Therefore, projects relating to the Industrial Internet were collected from the German DFG database using the keyword "Industry 4.0". A total of 109 German Industrial Internet projects were collected using web crawler software. MedPeer is China's leading scientific research service platform, providing information on NSFC-funded projects in recent years. Using the MedPeer database, a total of 44 projects whose titles included "Industrial Internet" were selected.

3.2 Number of Projects

The USA. Industrial Internet projects first emerged in 2015 with a project titled "EA-GER: Cyber-Physical Fingerprinting for Internet of Things Authentication: Accelerating IoT Research and Education Under the Global City Teams Challenge." The open-access nature of IoT makes it highly vulnerable to internal attacks. In such attacks, adversaries can capture or forge the identity of small, resource-constrained IoT devices, thus bypassing traditional authentication methods. Due to the apparent legitimacy of adversary devices, defending against such attacks becomes challenging. Device authentication and identification are considered among the most urgent security challenges facing IoT. The main goal of this project is to overcome this weakness by developing new authentication methods that use network physical fingerprints extracted from the IoT device to complement traditional security solutions. From 2015 to 2017, the number of Industrial Internet projects in the USA rose rapidly. In 2016, the number of projects quadrupled compared to 2015; in 2017, it doubled compared to 2016. From 2018 to 2022, the annual number of projects remained relatively stable, with an average of 38 new projects each year, as shown in Fig. 1.

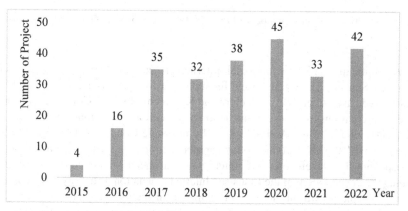

Fig. 1. Annual number of Industrial Internet projects in the USA.

Germany. Industrial Internet projects first appeared in 2002 with a project titled "SFB 614: Self-Optimizing Concepts and Structures in Mechanical Engineering." This project proposed that the integration of information technology into industrial manufacturing would bring significant industrial development, referring to this trend as "mechatronics." Although the project did not explicitly propose the concept of Industry 4.0 at that time, its principles aligned closely with the essence of Industry 4.0. Industry 4.0 was officially introduced at the Hanover Industrial Fair in 2013, aiming to enhance German industrial competitiveness and helping Germany seize a leading position in the fourth industrial revolution. Subsequently, Industry 4.0 was included as one of the ten major projects outlined in the "Germany 2020 High-Tech Strategy." Influenced by this, the number of German Industrial Internet projects began to surge in 2015 and maintained a consistently high level in the following years, reaching a peak of 17 projects in 2019, as shown in Fig. 2.

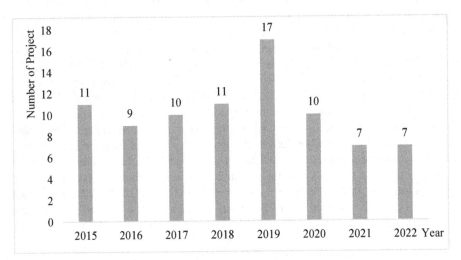

Fig. 2. Annual number of Industrial Internet projects in Germany.

China. China initiated two Industrial Internet projects in 2016, namely "Wireless Unbundled Sensing Theory and Key Technologies for Industrial Internet" and "Research on Industrial Internet Architecture and Key Technologies". Combined, these two projects were a robust response to the action plan "Guiding Opinions on Actively Promoting the 'Internet Plus' Action" issued by the State Council of China in 2015. In November 2017, the State Council issued another action plan called "Guiding Opinions on Deepening the Development of 'Internet + Advanced Manufacturing'", officially elevating the development of the Industrial Internet as a national strategy. Consequently, there was a rapid growth in the number of Industrial Internet projects. The number of new projects surged from 5 in 2018 to 13 in 2020 and the momentum continued in 2021 and 2022, with 10 and 6 new projects, respectively, as shown in Fig. 3. Currently, out of 44 domestic Industrial Internet projects, three have been completed, while the remaining 41 are actively under research.

Over the past five years, the number of Industrial Internet projects in the three countries has steadily increased. This is partly due to strong government support. Additionally, the rapid development of information technology, coupled with its timely integration into manufacturing, has propelled the exponential advancement of the manufacturing industry.

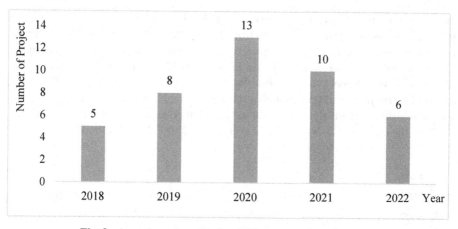

Fig. 3. Annual number of Industrial Internet projects in China.

3.3 Project Funding

USA. The funding for Industrial Internet projects sponsored by the NSF significantly increased from 2015 to 2017, with funding amounts for each of these three years being $5.24 million. While the number of Industrial Internet projects in the United States remained consistent from 2018 to 2022, funding for 2019 and 2020 reached $18.41 million and $17.87 million, respectively, as shown in Fig. 4. During these two years, the funding for individual Industrial Internet projects was notably substantial.

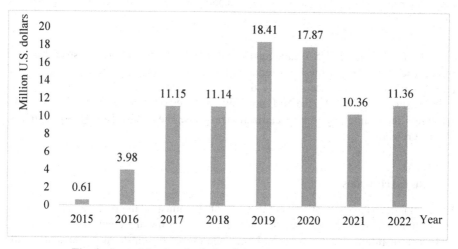

Fig. 4. Annual funding for Industrial Internet projects in the USA.

China. The first Industrial Internet project in China, "Future Network Architecture and Key Technologies," secured a total of 2.85 million RMB in funding from the NSFC. Subsequently, the annual funding for Industrial Internet projects, although fluctuating, maintained an upward trend, as shown in Fig. 5. The funding amounts for Industrial Internet projects consistently increased from 2018 to 2020. The year 2020 was a pivotal year and saw China start the "14th Five-Year Plan" and marked the conclusion of the "Industrial Internet Development Action Plan (2018–2020)." In 2020, the number and funding amount for approved Industrial Internet projects reached their peak. That year, a total of 13 projects commenced with a substantial combined funding amount of 16.43 million RMB. Cumulatively, funding for Industrial Internet projects surpassed 36 million RMB by the end of 2022, with projects averaging 820,000 RMB in funding.

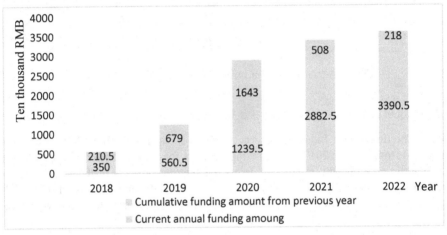

Fig. 5. Annual funding amount and cumulative funding amount for Industrial Internet projects in China.

Both China and the USA have made substantial investments in Industrial Internet projects. Comparatively, the USA tends to have a higher average funding per project than China. This difference is partly due to the larger budget of the NSF compared to the NSFC. Additionally, the NSF not only funds research projects but also supports education and technology commercialization projects. The DFG did not disclose funding for the project.

3.4 Research Focus

USA. Based on the project titles and abstracts of US Industrial Internet projects, the word cloud shown in Fig. 6 was generated. The cloud reveals some fundamental characteristics of Industrial Internet research in the USA. The most frequent term is "devices", with 650 occurrences, highlighting the significance of hardware in developing the Industrial Internet in the USA. The second most frequent term is "data" which appeared 489 times. Terms like "Security," "System," and "Application" are also common, with 427, 363, and 296 occurrences, respectively.

Fig. 6. Word cloud for Industrial Internet project abstracts funded by the USA.

Germany. Based on the project titles and abstracts collected from the DFG database, the word cloud in Fig. 7 was generated. The term "Production" appears most frequently, occurring 174 times, reflecting the emphasis on industrial manufacturing when developing Germany's Industrial Internet. Other frequently occurring terms include "Process," "System," and "Data," with 159, 152, and 144 occurrences respectively.

Fig. 7. Word cloud for Industrial Internet project abstracts funded by Germany.

China. Based on the project names of the Industrial Internet projects collected from the NSFC database, the word cloud shown in Fig. 8 was generated. The term "Network" appears most frequently, with a total of 13 occurrences. "Theory", "Model", and "System" occur 10, 8, and 6 times respectively, reflecting that in the early stages of Industrial Internet development in China, theoretical evaluation and modelling are important research methods, and projects lean towards a holistic system approach. Additionally, "Edge Computing" occurs ten times. Edge computing addresses challenges such as heterogeneous network deployment, efficient operation, on-demand configuration of industrial intelligence, and proximity services.

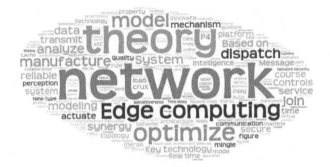

Fig. 8. Word cloud for Industrial Internet project abstracts funded by China.

All three countries emphasize the importance of data, considering it as the lifeblood of the Industrial Internet. There are commonalities in research focus, but China places more emphasis on networks, Germany focuses production and processes, while the USA prioritizes equipment and security.

3.5 Project Disciplines

This section analyzes characteristics of Industrial Internet projects in the United States, Germany, and China by correlating the different academic fields involved in undertaking Industrial Internet projects. The academic fields, under which Industrial Internet projects are implemented, for the three countries are summarized in Table 1.

USA. Industrial Internet projects in the United States are predominantly undertaken by the Department of Computer and Information Science and Engineering, which account for a substantial 69.39% of projects. The second most prominent department is the Department of Technology and Innovation Partnerships, which supervises around 18.78% of projects. This department facilitates collaboration between the public and private sectors by supporting innovation through funding, providing equipment, and other resources for various organizations and businesses. Its objective is to assist scientists and engineers in commercializing new technologies, thereby accelerating the development and application of these technologies. Industrial Internet projects in the United States are also supervised by the Department of Engineering Science, STEM Education Department, and the Department of International Science and Engineering, as illustrated in Fig. 9.

Germany. The distribution of German Industrial Internet projects by research department is shown in Fig. 10. The Mechanical and Industrial Engineering departments handle the highest number of Industry 4.0 projects, a significant 66% of all projects. This is followed by Computer Science, Systems, and Electrical Engineering with 22%; Social and Behavioral Sciences make up 6%. German Industrial Internet projects are remarkably diverse in scope. For instance, in the field of Physics, there is a German Industrial Internet project titled "Lasersystem für ein Netzwerk optischer Uhren" (Laser system for a network of optical clocks). This project focuses on fundamental research supporting

Table 1. Correspondence between academic fields supported by the NSF (USA), DFG (Germany), and NSFC (China).

NSF	DFG	NSFC
Mathematical and Physical Sciences	Physics	Department of Mathematical and Physical Sciences
	Mathematics	
	Chemistry	Department of Chemical Sciences
Biological Sciences	Biology	Department of Life Sciences
	Agriculture, Forestry and Veterinary Medicine	
Geosciences	Geosciences	Department of Earth Sciences
Engineering	Thermal Engineering/Process Engineering	Department of Engineering and Materials Sciences
	Construction Engineering and Architecture	
	Materials Science and Engineering	
	Mechanical and Industrial Engineering	
Computer and Information Science and Engineering	Computer Science, Systems and Electrical Engineering	Department of Information Sciences
Social, Behavioral and Economic Sciences	Social and Behavioural Sciences	Department of Management Sciences
No correspondence	Medicine	Department of Health Sciences
No correspondence	Humanities	No correspondence
STEM Education	No correspondence	No correspondence
Technology, Innovation and Partnerships	No correspondence	Department of Interdisciplinary Sciences
Integrative Activities	No correspondence	No correspondence
International Science and Engineering	No correspondence	Department of International Programs

Note: NSF does not house a dedicated medical department; medical research in the United States is supported by the National Institutes of Health.

Industry 4.0. In the field of Humanities, the project "Challenges of computerization: the example of the printing unions" investigates the impact of timely changes in workers' unions in the context of Industry 4.0.

China. Chinese Industrial Internet projects predominantly fall within the discipline of Information Science, constituting 79.54% of all projects. Information Science focuses on data analysis and processing, enabling the visualization and intelligent interpretation

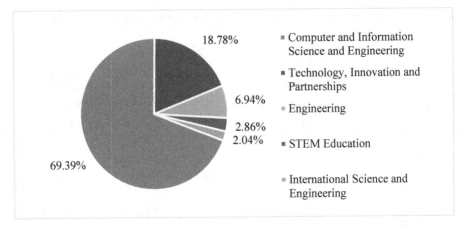

Fig. 9. Distribution of Industrial Internet projects in the USA by research field/department covering the years 2015 to 2022.

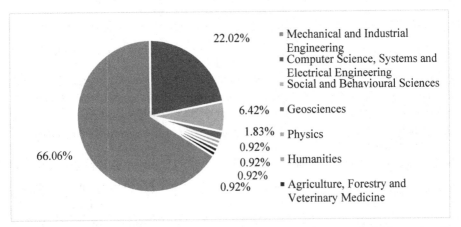

Fig. 10. Distribution of Industrial Internet projects in Germany by research field covering the years 2002 to 2022

of industrial data, thereby offering information and decision support for the manufacturing sector. On the other hand, the development of the Industrial Internet presents new opportunities and challenges for Information Science, resulting in a mutually reinforcing relationship.

In addition, projects pursued under the field of Engineering and Material Science are crucial for the development of the Industrial Internet in China. However, as the Industrial Internet gains widespread acceptance and produces new management/organizational challenges and influences the economy, Management Science emerges as a focal discipline. Consequently, the number Industrial Internet projects falling under the field of Management Science is significant, as depicted in Fig. 11.

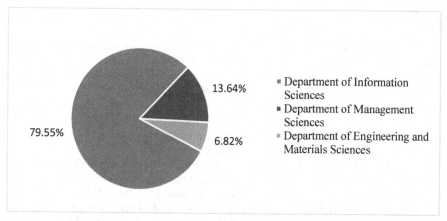

Fig. 11. Distribution of Industrial Internet projects in China by research field covering the years 2016 to 2022

China and the USA have Industrial Internet projects falling within the same fields, with a strong emphasis on computer science and information science, complemented by engineering and management sciences. In contrast, German Industrial Internet projects are primarily classified under mechanical and industrial engineering, with computational science as a secondary focus. Germany places a greater emphasis on practical aspects, while China prioritizes the technological dimension. Industrial Internet projects in Germany are more diverse, involving basic disciplines such as physics, chemistry, humanities, as well as applied fields such as earth sciences and agriculture.

4   Conclusion

This study provides a comprehensive comparison of Industrial Internet projects funded by the National Science Foundation (NSF) in the USA, the German Research Foundation (DFG), and the Natural Science Foundation of China (NSFC). The analysis reveals a consistent increase in funding for Industrial Internet projects over the past five years, driven by robust government support and the integration of technology into manufacturing processes. All three nations share a common emphasis on data science in their research focus. Moreover, China prioritizes networks, Germany focuses on production, and the USA gives precedence to equipment and security. China and the USA highly value Industrial Internet projects in computer and information sciences, while Germany places a greater emphasis on mechanical engineering. This comparative study contributes valuable information on the global landscape of Industrial Internet projects, offering a nuanced understanding of thematic focuses, and academic orientations across countries. These observed trends can guide international collaboration, policy formulation, and strategic investments, fostering advancements in Industrial Internet technologies on a global scale.

Acknowledgments. This study was funded by independent scientific research projects of China Academy of Industrial Internet (grant number KFZY2023B18).

References

1. Kang, H.S., et al.: Smart manufacturing: past research, present findings, and future directions. Int. J. Precis. Eng. Manuf.-Green Technol. **3**, 111–128 (2016)
2. Chirumalla, K.: Building digitally-enabled process innovation in the process industries: a dynamic capabilities approach. Technovation **105**, 102256 (2021)
3. Iansiti, M., Lakhani, K.R.: Digital ubiquity: how connections, sensors, and data are revolutionizing business. Harv. Bus. Rev. **92**, 19 (2014)
4. Lyytinen, K., Yoo, Y., Boland Jr, R.J.: Digital product innovation within four classes of innovation networks. Inf. Syst. J. **26**, 47–75 (2016)
5. Palmié, M., Miehé, L., Oghazi, P., Parida, V., Wincent, J.: The evolution of the digital service ecosystem and digital business model innovation in retail: the emergence of meta-ecosystems and the value of physical interactions. Technol. Forecast. Soc. Chang. **177**, 121496 (2022)
6. Rachinger, M., Rauter, R., Müller, C., Vorraber, W., Schirgi, E.: Digitalization and its influence on business model innovation. J. Manuf. Technol. Manag. **30**, 1143–1160 (2019)
7. Frishammar, J., Richtnér, A., Brattström, A., Magnusson, M., Björk, J.: Opportunities and challenges in the new innovation landscape: implications for innovation auditing and innovation management. Eur. Manag. J. **37**, 151–164 (2019)
8. Schuh, G., Anderl, R., Gausemeier, J., ten Hompel, M., Wahlster, W.: Industrie 4.0 maturity index: managing the digital transformation of companies. Herbert Utz Verlag GmbH (2017)
9. Li, Z.: Government responses to digital workforce shortages: a study of the US, Germany, Japan, and China. In: Rau, P.L.P. (eds.) Cross-Cultural Design, HCII 2023. LNCS, vol. 14022. Springer, Cham (2023). https://doi.org/10.1007/978-3-031-35936-1_18
10. Kagermann, H., Anderl, R., Gausemeier, J., Schuh, G., Wahlster, W.: Industrie 4.0 in a Global Context: strategies for cooperating with international partners. Herbert Utz Verlag (2016)

Dilemmas and Path Exploration in the Development of Educational Digital Transformation

Kehan Sun[1,2]([✉])(iD)

[1] Northwest Normal University, Anning East Road 967, Lanzhou 730070, China
[2] Xi'an Peihua University, Changning Street 888, Chang'an District, Xi'an 710125, China
sunkehan@peihua.edu.cn

Abstract. The accelerating intelligence in modern life continues to drive human production and living towards a new realm of digitalization. Digital technology is also considered by educational researchers as playing a key role in reshaping the education system and its ecology. To promote the transformation and development of educational digitalization, it is important to recognize that this digitalization is an aspect of the modernization of education. In promoting educational digitalization, we must avoid the risk of educational alienation. Enlarging the goal of digitalization can easily deviate from the original intent of education, and exaggerating its role can stray from the true needs of education. Educational digitalization must adhere to the objective of empowering education. The development of educational digitalization should involve a deep exploration of the necessity for digital transformation in the field of education, the challenges it presents in educational practice, and the feasibility of such transformation in educational research. This approach will comprehensively promote a positive digital transformation in the field of education.

Keywords: education digitalization · education digital transformation · digital thinking · smart education

1 Introduction

With the widespread application of artificial intelligence and other technologies, human society is steadily advancing towards an era of intelligence. There is a consensus that intelligent technology will transform all sectors of society. In this intelligent era, the digital transformation and development within the education system and ecology represent a systemic change. To accurately understand this transformation in education, we must recognize the new educational ecosystem that is collaboratively constructed by people and educational practices under the influence of technology. In recent years, China has placed significant emphasis on the development of educational digitalization, continually advancing the construction of digital education. This strategic action has opened a new chapter in the modernization of education with Chinese characteristics. Although relevant theoretical research and practical explorations have yielded some results, they also

P.-L. P. Rau (Ed.): HCII 2024, LNCS 14701, pp. 293–300, 2024.
https://doi.org/10.1007/978-3-031-60904-6_21

face numerous challenges. To better promote the implementation and development of the educational digitalization strategy, it is essential not only to explore the transformative impact of digital technology on educational development but also to fully leverage the benefits and functionalities of digital education. This requires condensing the beneficial experiences from China's digital education development and aligning with the needs of its digital transformation. Considering this, this article aims to systematically analyze the inevitability of educational digital transformation, the problems and dilemmas that need addressing in the context of educational digitalization, and to initiate a preliminary discussion on how to promote the development of educational digitalization.

2   The Inevitability of Digital Transformation in Education

2.1   The Policy System for the Development of Digital Education is Becoming Increasingly Comprehensive and Effective

Since the *Outline of China's Education Reform and Development* proposed "developing radio and television education and school audio-visual education" (Library Research Office of the Central Committee of the Communist Party of China, 2011, p. 59), China's digital education has undergone significant changes over five years. These changes include concept advocacy, incorporation into policies, and inclusion in development planning. Furthermore, it has progressed through stages such as regional pilot promotion and elevation to national strategic actions. In recent years, with the introduction of the Digital China strategy, accelerating the digital transformation of China's education has emerged as a core issue in the development of digital education. Currently, the strategic action for educational digitalization has become an integral part of the *Overall Layout Plan for the Construction of Digital China*, further elevating the status of digital education.

2.2   The Application of Digital Technology in Educational Scenarios is Gradually Accelerating

With continuous breakthroughs in key core technologies, the digital development of China's education is steadily advancing. A "technology-first" approach provides solid technical support and guarantees for the digital transformation of education. In terms of smart campus construction, technologies such as artificial intelligence, face recognition, and big data analysis are being utilized to optimize campus management. Efforts are being made to actively create modern digital classroom spaces, equipped with interactive smart blackboards, panoramic classroom behavior monitoring systems, and intelligent environmental temperature control systems. These innovations facilitate the development of high-quality education and teaching. Simultaneously, there is ongoing promotion of data compression in physical education settings and the simulation of virtual education spaces. The multi-scenario application of digital technologies, including big educational data systems, smart libraries, and digital communities in the field of education, has seen further development (Zhu Yongxin & Yang Fan, 2023).

3 Dilemmas Faced by the Digital Transformation and Development of Education

3.1 Insufficient Theoretical Research on Digital Education Disciplines

Since the early 20th century, Chinese researchers have been examining the impact of new Western educational technologies on traditional education. By the 1990s, the focus shifted to the relationship between technologies like slideshows and computer-assisted instruction, and their effectiveness in teaching. Currently, the emphasis is on issues such as the digital transformation of education, educational metaverse, human-computer collaborative teaching, and the digital divide and generation gap. This shift has brought digital technology into the research spotlight. Most research tends to concentrate on the technological enhancement and intelligent upgrading of external resources like educational tools, resources, and spaces. However, there is insufficient depth in the reflection and discussion on the more theoretical aspects of digital education disciplines. The existing research mainly revolves around how education digitalization is transforming worldwide and its future directions. In-depth studies and systematic discussions on topics such as digital education equity, digital ethics, cultivation of digital citizens, and digital education rights in the smart era are still scarce. Particularly, there has been a long-term neglect of "technology" in basic theoretical research on education (Yu Qingchen, 2020). Therefore, there is an urgent need to deepen theoretical research on digital education. A comprehensive review of current research reveals that theoretical studies on digital education significantly lag its practical development and have not yet established a positive two-way interaction with educational practice. Some studies focus excessively on "technology" over "education" and "tools" over "life", which profoundly affects the high-quality development of digital education. Most current basic research in education concentrates on the human education world and real-life educational scenarios. Its fundamental ideas, core concepts, research areas, and disciplinary theoretical systems seem inadequate in addressing problems involving education and machines, humans and machines, robots, etc. A more specialized theoretical system is urgently needed for analysis and research. To further highlight the humanistic nature of theoretical research in digital education, it is important to focus on analyzing and researching the ontological value of digital education, questioning the educational value of digital technology, and promoting the harmonious and free development of people and technology.

3.2 The Impact of Digital Technology on Future Education Development is Uncontrollable

The digital transformation of education represents a structural evolution with a historic breakthrough in the education system in the intelligent era (Zhu Zhiting et al., 2022). Throughout human history, each epoch-making technological change has had a transformative impact on education, and digital technology is no exception. As artificial intelligence technology continues to mature, the impact of digital technology extends beyond educational resources, tools, environments, and scenarios. It even has the potential for a subversive impact on the definition of educational subjects. Although currently in the stage of weak artificial intelligence, in the perceptible present and foreseeable future, a breakthrough in technological singularity could usher in strong artificial intelligence with a higher level of wisdom. This advancement could lead to deep involvement in the field of education, challenging existing educational thinking models. Not only might the subject of education extend beyond the human scope, but artificial intelligence could also replace some or most educational research, leading to major paradigm shifts (Zheng Yonghe et al., 2021).

Digital humanities education is transforming our approach to knowledge. Libraries are shifting focus from expanding book collections to promoting digital libraries. Families are less focused on physical bookshelves as teachers and students increasingly access libraries via mobile devices. The internet offers young people convenient learning opportunities, allowing them to access learning materials anytime and submit homework digitally. In this digital and networked environment, text creators can become popular authors through a blog post, illustrating a shift in reader and creator identities.

This raises important questions: What is the future role of human educators and educational researchers? The emergence of technologies like AlphaGo and Chat GPT highlights the urgency of these questions. We must rethink educational dynamics between humans and machines (Li Zhengtao & Luo Yi, 2019) and explore the symbiotic relationship between them (Zhang Xuejun & Dong Xiaohui, 2020).

3.3 The Risk of Increased Reliance on Digital Tools Fostering Laziness in Education has Become Increasingly Prominent

In the digital age, the convenience, accuracy, and timeliness of accessing knowledge and information have greatly improved. However, this often creates the illusion that obtaining information is equivalent to understanding it. The trend in digital education toward a focus on images rather than text, production over ideas, and coding instead of creation, challenges the essence of humanities research and education. It threatens to undermine traditional humanistic core values, in-depth thinking, and written expression, potentially diminishing the human spirit and interpersonal communication. While knowledge acquisition has become convenient, fast, and abundant, this abundance places higher demands on people's ability to filter information. Yet it often leads to the misconception that memorizing knowledge and information is no longer important. Data mining and intelligent information recommendation technologies are narrowing learners' choice spaces, limiting the scope of knowledge and information they access, and further differentiating people's choices, creating information cocoons. The ease of searching can deprive students of the experience of deep, puzzling thinking and the joy of sudden enlightenment after prolonged contemplation. The immediacy of finding answers shortens the journey from the unknown to the known in the learning process, often resulting in a superficial level of understanding. The convenience of digital life, particularly in the humanities, leads to a risk of dependency on digital education, a state of collective unawareness that hinders full recognition of the dangers of digital dependency.

3.4 The Alienation Phenomenon Appears in the Development of Educational Digitalization

Educational digitalization is an indicator of educational progress and a tool for promoting educational modernization and, by extension, human modernization. However, it is important to recognize that digitalization itself is not the goal of education. Avoiding educational alienation is crucial when advancing educational digitalization. The aim of this digital transformation should be to enhance the effectiveness of teaching and learning, thereby improving overall quality and promoting holistic human development.

The rise of educational digitalization inevitably generates vast amounts of teaching and learning data. This big educational data holds significant value for enhancing data-driven educational research and practice. Yet, it is essential to remember that educational development is distinct from the process of digitalization, and digitalization should not become the end goal. The phenomenon of technical means becoming ends' must be avoided. It's important to balance "instrumental rationality" and "goal-oriented rationality" and clarify the relationship between educational digital transformation, modernization, and overall development.

In the process of digital transformation, the primary intent of introducing artificial intelligence technology should be to alleviate teachers' workload, enable personalized instruction, and accurately address the learning and developmental needs of students. The construction of data infrastructure and systems should align with the authentic developmental laws and reasonable needs of teaching and learning, rather than constraining them, alienating teachers and students from their legitimate needs, or infringing upon their educational rights.

To advance educational digitalization effectively, it is necessary to balance "technology construction and application" with "human development needs", using the latter as the guiding principle. This approach helps maintain a healthy tension between the two, reducing the risk of alienation. Despite Some progress in digital education practices in China, challenges such as regional disparities in smart education systems, equal access to shared digital resources, and management of educational data risks still require urgent attention and systematic analysis.

4 Exploring the Development Path of Digital Transformation of Education

4.1 Deepen Theoretical Research on Digital Education Disciplines

Digital education practice has become ubiquitous, yet the development of theories specific to digital education disciplines has not kept pace with the rapid advancement of practical applications. There is a noticeable gap between digital education theory and practice. Clarifying the connotation of digital education, based on both the digitalization of education and the development of human life, is a primary issue that needs to be addressed in current digital education research. To this end, there is an urgent need to conduct systematic research on digital education disciplines. This involves responding promptly to new issues emerging with the development of the times, accelerating the construction of digital education theoretical systems, and transforming models of knowledge production. Promoting the construction of digital education is not only essential for the formation, gathering, and accumulation of digital education knowledge but also an inevitable requirement for the systematization and standardization of theoretical research in digital education.

4.2 Improve the Construction of Digital Education Research Institutions and Academic Organizations

The development of educational digitalization necessitates a careful handling of the relationship between digital pedagogy and traditional pedagogy. From the standpoint of the internal knowledge structure and future direction of digital pedagogy, its emergence differs from the division of traditional pedagogy into new disciplines, which previously led to a crisis in the independence of pedagogy. Instead, digital pedagogy is likely to lead to a comprehensive reconstruction and transformation of the overall field of pedagogy. As educational digitalization advances and we fully enter the era of intelligent education, the current pedagogical discipline system will likely split into two branches: "general pedagogy", rooted in the real world of education and based on industrial civilization, and "digital pedagogy", oriented towards the digital education world and grounded in the intelligent era. Addressing the relationship between digital pedagogy and general pedagogy is crucial. Improving the establishment of research institutions and academic organizations focused on digital pedagogy and expediting the development of digital pedagogy as a discipline are essential steps to strengthen the digital education support system.

Since the 21st century, Chinese universities have actively responded to national strategic needs by establishing research institutions focused on the digital transformation of education, digital education, and artificial intelligence in education. Examples include the Shanghai Intelligent Education Research Institute at East China Normal University, the School of Artificial Intelligence Education at Central China Normal University, and the Artificial Intelligence Education Innovation Laboratory at Xi'an University of Electronic Science and Technology. Concurrently, China is advocating for and promoting the construction of the "World Digital Education Alliance", collaborating with other countries to build a global digital education community for a shared future. Currently, there is an urgent need for China to concentrate on the digital transformation of education and the future development of education. This includes promoting the establishment of digital education research institutions at both national and local levels and setting up specialized academic organizations for digital pedagogy under relevant societies.

4.3 Strengthen the Training of Talents for the Digital Development of Education

As a complex system integral to future education, strengthening talent training for the digital development of education is paramount. Providing support and ensuring a supply of new think tanks and professional talents for the digital transformation of education and the advancement of digital education requires reliance on higher education institutions and the establishment of a professional digital pedagogy framework. On one hand, higher education institutions, serving as knowledge hubs and talent pools, play a vital role in establishing a multi-disciplinary collaborative development mechanism for digital pedagogy. This involves gathering talents from diverse fields such as artificial intelligence, computer science, engineering, and technology science, thereby amassing scientific and technological expertise for the growth of educational digitalization. On the other hand, it is crucial to establish a scientifically sound research and professional talent training system in digital education. This can be achieved by developing a digital education curriculum, compiling digital pedagogy textbooks, and prioritizing the cultivation of digital literacy among future educators, thereby nurturing talents for the advancement of educational digitalization.

To solidify the professional talent support system for educational digitalization, it is essential not only to enhance the training of professionals in digital education technology and lay a strong technical foundation for its development but also to drive technological innovation in fields like educational artificial intelligence, big educational data, and smart schools. Continuously advancing the digitization of educational resources and tools is necessary. Additionally, there should be a forward-looking approach to fostering a digital reserve talent team. Improving the science and technology education system in basic education and strengthening the innovative capabilities and critical thinking of young people through programs like "Future Scientists" will help cultivate and reserve a new generation of digital professionals for the future.

4.4 Always Remain Firm in Our Original Aspiration and Stand Unwaveringly in Education

The digitalization of education must enhance awareness of pedagogical principles and emphasize the value and fundamental constraints of human-centered education in both the development of educational digitalization and the application and promotion of digital technology. As Hou Huaiyin and Wang Yaowei (2022) noted, technology is a product of human ingenuity and innovation. However, under the influence of technologism, the application of technology in education has expanded beyond enhancing human cognitive and physical capabilities. It now aims to effect systemic changes in the educational landscape through deep technological intervention. This shift has led to a partial or complete focus on the development of science and technology and its optimal use in education, rather than on the essence of education itself. As a result, there is a gradual decline in the expectations for the development of education as an independent field.

5   Conclusion

Therefore, in the pursuit of educational digitalization, it is crucial to be vigilant against the tendency of "techno centrism". We must prioritize people, promoting their all-around development as the foundational value of educational digitalization. The core of modern educational theory is people-oriented; any development in educational informatization, including educational digitalization, ultimately needs to focus on the human aspect. This means supporting the advanced growth and development of teachers and students as the fundamental measure of value.

References

Hou, H., Wang, Y.: Chinese pedagogy construction in the era of information technology. J. Hangzhou Norm. Univ. (Soc. Sci. Edn.) **3**, 67–75 (2022)

Yu, Q.: The necessity and limits of technologicalization in educational practice—also on the logical positioning of technology in basic educational theories. Educ. Res. **6**, 14–26 (2020)

Zhang, X., Dong, X.: Human-machine symbiosis: the era of artificial intelligence and the development trend of education. Audio-visual Educ. Res. **4**, 35–41 (2020)

Zhu, Y., Yang, F.: The realistic logic, application scenarios, and governance paths of my country's education digital transformation. China Audio-visual Educ. (1), 1–7, 24 (2023)

Zhu, Z., Zheng, H., Xu, Q., Wu, Y.: Policy guidance and ecological development strategy for digital transformation of education. Mod. Educ. Technol. **9**, 5–18 (2022)

Library Research Office of the Central Committee of the Communist Party of China. Selected Important Documents Since the 14th National Congress of the CPC Volume 1. Central Literature Publishing House (2011)

Li, Z., Luo, Y.: Life evolution and education in the era of artificial intelligence. Educ. Res. (11), 39–58 (2019)

Zheng, Y., Wang, Y., Wang, Y.: Educational science research in the era of artificial intelligence: connotation, logical framework and practical approach. China Distance Educ. (6), 1–10, 17, 76 (2021)

Exploring Ecological Value and Innovative Transformation of Traditional Packaging

Cong Tang[1,2(✉)] and Kalina Pashkevich[2]

[1] Hunan University of Technology, Zhuzhou 412000, China
250827751@qq.com
[2] Kyiv National University of Technologies and Design, Kyiv, Ukraine
pashkevich.kl@knutd.com.ua

Abstract. The aim of this study is to explore the potential of traditional eco-packaging for sustainable application in modern society, to explore the ecological value of traditional organic packaging, and to investigate its potential for innovative transformation in modern society. The literature review provides an in-depth understanding of the background and ecological value of traditional eco-packaging. Using theoretical research, case studies and triple bottom line analysis methods, traditional natural packaging products in central China were evaluated in terms of economic, environmental and social dimensions. The results show that traditional eco-packaging, such as plant leaves, performs well in reducing material sources and pollution. Despite the challenges, the modernization and transformation of traditional eco-packaging offers a viable path to sustainable development for the packaging industry.

Keywords: Traditional Packaging · Natural Materials · Ecological Packaging · Circular Economy · Triple bottom line analysis

1 Introduction

With the urgency of global environmental issues, sustainable development has become a top priority for business and society. Packaging has a great potential in promoting sustainable development through its functions [1–3], as packaging waste is a serious side effect of product consumption, which is considered an unnecessary cost on one hand, and creates a huge environmental problem on the other [4]. Policy makers in the European Union and China have proposed the concept of circular economy to address global environmental issues by closing the loop of the product life cycle [5]. Nikiema et al. [6] argued that the transition to a circular economy requires a radical change from a linear model of economic activity to a closed loop, where goods are transformed into other resources at the end of their life cycle, thus significantly reducing waste [7]. It should be acknowledged that traditional ecological packaging happens to follow this model, aligning with the principles of economic and environmental harmony. However, traditional organic packaging is often overlooked as a potential sustainable alternative.

© The Author(s), under exclusive license to Springer Nature Switzerland AG 2024
P.-L. P. Rau (Ed.): HCII 2024, LNCS 14701, pp. 301–313, 2024.
https://doi.org/10.1007/978-3-031-60904-6_22

The earliest examples of "packaging" in human history likely involved wrapping food in leaves [8]. Traditional natural materials, such as bamboo, straw, and lotus leaves, not only reflect profound cultural traditions but also demonstrate wisdom in coexisting harmoniously with ecosystems. These traditional packaging methods are not only biodegradable and sustainable, but also add value to food products to a certain extent, such as by providing food products with the natural aroma of the packaging material itself [9]. However, traditional natural packaging has relatively limited application of their ecological value in modern packaging due to disadvantages such as limited access to materials and difficulty in standardized production. There are also few studies related to understanding traditional natural packaging in terms of ecological value and innovative transformation.

Therefore, through in-depth analyses of specific cases in central China, combined with innovations in theoretical frameworks, this study aims to explore the ecological value of traditional organic packaging and to investigate its potential for innovative transformation in modern society. The practical significance of this research lies in its identification of the inherent commonalities between traditional ecological packaging models and sustainable development strategies that follow circular economy principles. The study not only provides theoretical support for the modern transformation of traditional packaging wisdom but also proposes practical strategic recommendations aimed at advancing sustainable development goals. It offers robust support for the green transformation of production and lifestyle practices and serves as a reference for the green transition of the global packaging industry.

2 Literature Review

2.1 Traditional Ecological Packaging

Ecological packaging in traditional packaging that relies on natural materials has been documented in various countries, with the packaging of foodstuffs and daily necessities dominating the list. Oka [10] in How to wrap five eggs documented various traditional forms of packaging, mostly made from natural materials such as bamboo, straw, twine, paper and leaves, which not only satisfy the needs of storing and transporting goods but also have no excess wastage. Transporting items without excess wastage. Mustafa et al. [9] and Ezeudu et al. [11] examined the properties and health benefits of traditional packaging in different regions and documented a large number of different packaging styles and materials that have been handed down from generation to generation.

Similar traditional ecological packages exist in central China. They include natural organic packaging made from plant husks, leaves, stems and roots, traditional containers such as bamboo baskets and wooden containers, and cotton and linen textile packaging, see Table 1. These packages determine which natural materials are used depending on the nature of the item itself, its location and its purpose [9]. These opportunities are usually used for those natural foods and items that are closely related to people's daily lives to protect them from influences such as sunlight, moisture, pathogens and pollutants [12]. For food products, this means that cooking methods, preservation techniques and food movement often determine the type of native leaf packaging to be used [11]. At the same time, the flavors of the food and the material interpenetrate each other, thus making the food packaged in these natural materials a local specialty in a way that synthetic materials cannot [9]. In addition, traditional ecological packaging is easily biodegradable and thus does not cause any significant adverse impact on the environment. On the contrary, during the degradation process, it helps to enrich soil nutrients, improve soil structure and texture, and promote healthy plant growth and development. Therefore, ecological packaging materials for traditional food products remain viable in terms of market feasibility and social acceptance. This natural organic food packaging material offers several environmental and health advantages over synthetic packaging materials [11].

Table 1. Traditional food in central China with natural material packaging.

Product	Rice Dumplings	Lotus Leaf Rice	Bamboo Rice	Rice Wine
Local Name	Zongzi	Heye Fan	Zhutong Fan	Mijiu
Packaging Materials	Rice Dumpling Leaves	Lotus leaf	Bamboo container	Ceramic jar
Form	Wrap	Wrap	Contain	Sealed Contain
Region	Hunan, Hubei	Hubei, Jiangxi	Hunan, Jiangxi	Various places
Picture				
Product	Kimchi	Osmanthus Fower Cake	Bao Gu Cake	Preserved Meat
Local Name	Paocai	Guihua Gao	Baogu Bing	Larou
Packaging Materials	Ceramic jar	Textile	Corn leaves	Rice straw
Form	Sealed Contain	Wrap	Wrap	Bundle
Region	Various places	Jiangsu, Zhejiang	Sichuan, Chongqing	Hunan, Jiangxi
Picture				
Product	Green dumplings	White Tea	Pu-erh	Dried Fruits
Local Name	Qing Tuan	Bai Cha	Puer Cha	Ganguo
Packaging Materials	Bamboo leaves	Bamboo basket	Citrus	Textile bag
Form	Wrap	Contain	Wrap	Wrap
Region	Shanghai, Suzhou	Fujian	Yunnan	Various places
Picture				

2.2 Traditional Packaging Ecological Values

An environmentally friendly packaging method that has received much attention recently is the bio-based method, which is based on materials made from biomass [13]. Packaging materials can be manufactured using a variety of readily available raw materials, including crops such as soy, corn, rice, and cassava [14–16]. In fact, natural packaging is also a form of biomass [17]. Although both are renewable, unlike bio-based materials, natural materials can completely biodegrade. When utilized properly, the benefits they provide outweigh the disadvantages [18]. It is worth mentioning that in the contemporary circular economic framework, biomass is considered as a circular flow because all biomass products can be re-entered into the biosphere [19].

Recycling and composting of various packaging materials are not equally effective, thus these two types of recycling play different roles [20]. According to Pal and Gander [21], materials should be available for multiple life cycles, which demands good recyclability. Therefore, biopolymers being composted into valuable humus is an equally effective recovery. From a cost perspective, recycling of natural materials is most advantageous, as raw materials are cheaper and less energy intensive throughout the production process and the packaging has a shorter life cycle. Thus, composting natural material packaging through multiple life cycles appears to be more efficient than recycling packaging (see Fig. 1).

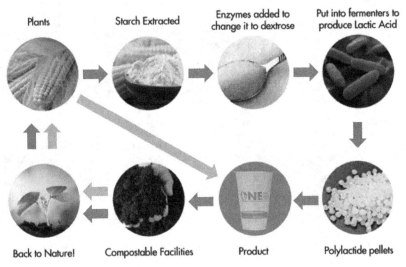

Fig. 1. Examples of circular loops for a natural materiel and biomaterials [5].

On the other hand, in Song et al. [22] study on people, environment and packaging, it is argued that environmental concerns stem from the interconnectedness of people and the natural environment and refer to general attitudes, values, perceptions and behaviors towards the environment. At the same time, there is a strong link between environmental concerns and consumer behavior [23]. Individuals who are highly concerned about the environment are more likely to adopt environmentally friendly behaviors [24]. Therefore, environmental concern can be considered as an activating factor for consumers' intention to use ecological friendly packaging. Traditional ecological packaging is a model of nature's minimalist design, reflecting the traditional cultural wisdom of the harmonious coexistence of man and nature, and it carries the modern people's desire for a harmonious ecology, which coincides with the ideals of people's return to nature and return to the basics [25]. The ecological crisis in the form of capital and the era of transition to a more sustainable society require this very different kind of creativity and aesthetics [26]. Albelda Raga [26] advocates for the adaptation of cultural processes to natural processes from the mission of ecosystem integration and rebalancing by constructing the concept of recycled aesthetics. It goes beyond the most widely recognized aspects related to the recycling of materials and acquires an important ethical function based on nature, expressing the acceptance of culture and species from a holistic perspective.

2.3 Innovative Transformation and Sustainable Development Trend of Traditional Ecological Packaging

Despite these ecological values, the application of traditional natural packaging in the modern packaging field is relatively limited due to reasons including lack of hygiene and safety [11], low production efficiency and lack of consumer awareness [12]. Human beings need to incorporate ecological awareness into the application of traditional technologies, and more importantly, they need to invent and create scientific methods with ecological awareness [27].

In recent years, biodegradable materials have become a popular choice for packaging designers committed to the circular economy concept [5]. Some biodegradable plastics are made from animal, plant, or microorganisms. The principle is a material recycling loop as shown in Fig. 1. Raw materials (which can include food waste) are processed into a form suitable for packaging, then further processed to enable their return to nature, becoming raw materials again after consumer use. In addition, agricultural materials have also shown promise as circular economy packaging materials [28]. Andreola et al. [28] have demonstrated examples of recycling and processing agricultural waste and post-consumer residues, which are recovered from plant and animal sectors, such as used coffee grounds. These residues are processed into a powdery form, then low temperature sintered, and can be used for tertiary or transit packaging. Furthermore, new packaging biomaterials continue to emerge, such as cassava starch-based compostable packaging exhibiting favorable environmental and social impacts [29], packaging using wheat bran [30], packaging materials based on edible chitosan and cellulose [31], and biopolymers made from corn and rice starch as substitutes for high-density polyethylene plastic bags [32]. Some of these materials are still in the early stages of development and are moving towards commercialization.

Resources should be kept in a closed loop to achieve zero waste. Of these, packaging is an important part of achieving a truly circular economy [5]. For traditional natural packaging, this means designing and developing packaging solutions that can be reused, recycled or composted, thereby reducing the demand for virgin resources and the amount of waste generated. The theory of ecological design evaluates the final design based on its contribution to the harmonious coexistence of the ecosystem, demanding environmental impact considerations during the product design phase. Using low-impact materials and processes, product design is optimized to reduce resource consumption and waste generation [26]. Life Cycle Assessment (LCA) is a primary analytical method in ecological design, evaluating the environmental impact of a product throughout its entire lifespan, from cradle to grave (or cradle to cradle), and accordingly optimizing the design, such as reducing packaging weight, increasing material efficiency, or using more sustainable materials, thus exploring the implications of packaging on the environment and human life comprehensively. It is evident that circular economy principles, ecological design, and life cycle assessment are dedicated to steering the packaging industry towards a more sustainable direction.

3 Methods

3.1 Theories of Ecological Packaging

Based on the literature reviews, the theories related to ecological packaging are described, including circular economy, ecological design, and life cycle assessment. It is easy to find that these theories have generated the concept of "circle" around different topics which is a system thinking, it emphasizes the efficient recycling of resources and the minimization of environmental impacts throughout the production and consumption process. While each of these concepts has its own focus, they all aim to promote a transition to more sustainable economies and societies, where economic activity and environmental protection coexist in harmony. In practice, this means creating closed-loop economic models, conducting comprehensive environmental impact assessments and integrating environmentally friendly principles at the product design stage to promote the continuous recycling of resources and the long-term health of the environment. Herbes et al. [13] proposed Categories for the ecological friendliness of packaging based on a

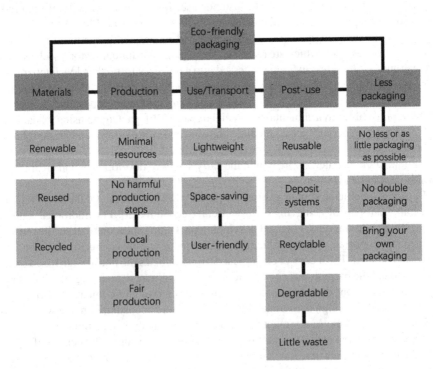

Fig. 2. Categories for the ecological friendliness of packaging [13].

survey of respondents, which included five categories used to define the life span of a product and included subcategories, as shown in Fig. 2. The product lifespan and includes subcategories as shown in Fig. 2. Zhu et al. [5] the circular packaging design framework understands the stages of circular economy, including material selection, design stage, development stage, and validation stage. The four stages of the three theoretical contents are organized respectively. 14 ecological packaging evaluation indicators are derived from circular economy and ecological design, and 4 contents are obtained from the life cycle assessment (see Table 2).

Table 2. Ecological packaging theories and indicators.

Theory	Description	Indicators In The Life Cycle			
		Material Selection	Deisgn Phase	Development Phase	Validation Phase
Circular Economy	The circular economy theory is an economic model aimed at minimising waste and resource use. The circular economy emphasises the recycling of resources in a closed-loop system, whereby design and innovation lead to the reuse, repair, refurbishment and recycling of resources, thereby extending the life cycle of products and materials.	Reduce product waste Reduce packaging waste	Maintain product quality	Improve operational efficiency Improve transport efficiency Improve storage efficiency	Reduce packaging waste Increase in recoverable ratio Reduce environmental pollution
Ecological Design	Eco-design theory is a design approach that systematically considers the environmental impacts of products during their design process. Its core objective is to reduce the negative environmental impacts of a product throughout its life cycle, while maintaining or improving its quality and performance.	Reduce product waste Reduce packaging waste Reduce environmental pollution Reduce human health harm Use sustainable materials	Design sustainable products Design recyclable products		Reduce environmental pollution Enhance biodiversity
Life Cycle Assessment	Life Cycle Assessment (LCA) is a systematic approach to analysing the environmental impacts of a product, process or service from cradle to grave (i.e. from extraction and treatment of raw materials, through manufacturing, transport, use and finally disposal).	Clear objective and scope definition Life Cycle Inventory (LCI) Analysis Life Cycle Impact Assessment (LCIA)	Life Cycle Inventory (LCI) Analysis Life Cycle Impact Assessment (LCIA)	Life Cycle Inventory (LCI) Analysis Life Cycle Impact Assessment (LCIA)	Life Cycle Inventory (LCI) Analysis Life Cycle Impact Assessment (LCIA) Interpretation of scientific results

3.2   Theories of Ecological Packaging

The above 14 ecological packaging indicators are used to test the natural packaging products in Table 1, and the results of each indicator of each product are obtained by "yes" or "no" through literature review, field research, and interviews with stakeholders. "x" stands for "yes", and the results are shown in Table 3. The study shows that 131 out of 168 indicators are in line with the ecological packaging under the circular economy, accounting for 78.0%. Among them, natural packaging based on leaves performs well in reducing source materials and pollution, but cannot improve transportation efficiency. The natural packaging of containers and textiles performed well in all indicators, but ceramic jars and textiles did not contribute to improving biodiversity. In addition, the natural packaging method of pu-erh achieves zero waste at the consumer consumption stage, with the clementine acting as a packaging container and interpenetrating with the pu-erh as part of the food product, generating biodiversity.

Table 3. Ecological indicators of traditional natural packaging in central China.

Indicators/Products And Packaging Materials	Rice Dumplings / Rice Dumpling Leaves	Lotus Leaf Rice / Lotus leaf	Bamboo Rice / Bamboo / Bamboo container	Rice Wine / Ceramic jar	Kimchi / Ceramic jar	Osmanthus Fower Cake / Textile	Bao Gu Cake / Corn leaves	Preserved Meat / Rice straw	Green dumplings / Bamboo leaves	White Tea / Bamboo basket	Pu-erh / Citrus	Dried Fruits / Textile bag
Reduce product waste	x			x	x			x		x	x	x
Reduce packaging waste	x	x		x	x	x	x	x		x	x	x
Reduce environmental pollution	x	x	x	x	x	x	x	x	x	x	x	x
Reduce human health harm	x	x	x	x	x	x	x	x	x	x	x	x
Use sustainable materials			x	x	x	x				x		x
Maintain product quality	x	x	x	x	x	x	x			x	x	x
Design sustainable products			x	x	x	x		x		x		x
Design recyclable products	x		x	x	x	x	x	x		x		x
Improve operational efficiency	x	x	x	x	x	x	x	x		x		x
Improve transport efficiency				x	x	x					x	x
Improve storage efficiency	x	x	x	x	x	x	x	x		x		x
Increase in recoverable ratio			x	x	x	x		x		x		x
Reduce environmental pollution	x	x	x	x	x	x	x	x	x	x	x	x
Enhance biodiversity	x	x	x				x	x		x	x	x

To provide sustainable alternatives to traditional packaging, an ecological social enterprise for Indonesian – Evoware, provides ecological solutions to the plastic waste problem. They look to natural materials, including seaweed, for inspiration. On the one hand, seaweed is a pioneer in sustainability. Seaweed grows 60 times faster than land crops, sequesters 20 times more carbon per acre than forests, and with Indonesia's massive oversupply of seaweed production, using seaweed as the main ingredient in packaging materials adds value to seaweed production, thus helping to improve the lives of local seaweed farmers. On the other hand, seaweed packaging can be 100% biodegradable and is a natural fertilizer for plants, which is a typical ecological packaging meets 93% of the characteristics of ecological packaging, as shown in Fig. 3. It is very suitable for small-packaged foods, such as instant noodle seasonings, tea or coffee powders, excipients and hamburger buns, etc., and it is also used for packaging of non-food contents, such as toothpicks, bars of soap, and sanitary pads. Along with the ecological packaging concept, people are gradually getting closer to nature and leading a more responsible and sustainable life [33].

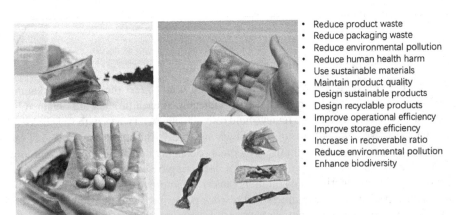

- Reduce product waste
- Reduce packaging waste
- Reduce environmental pollution
- Reduce human health harm
- Use sustainable materials
- Maintain product quality
- Design sustainable products
- Design recyclable products
- Improve operational efficiency
- Improve storage efficiency
- Increase in recoverable ratio
- Reduce environmental pollution
- Enhance biodiversity

Fig. 3. A kind of seaweed ecological packaging by Evoware [33].

3.3 Triple Bottom Lines Analysis

In order to delve into the potential opportunities for innovative transformation of traditional ecological packaging in three dimensions: economic, environmental and social, this study unfolds a triple bottom line (TBL) analysis methodology that will provide a comprehensive perspective on how to effectively utilize traditional organic packaging for the sustainable development of the packaging industry.

Combined with the traditional natural packaging in central China presented in Table 1, the attitudes of packaging producers and packaging researchers towards five contextual factors involving combinations of (1) product/packaging, (2) recycling/composting, (3) modern packaging production/packaging standardization, (4) food safety and health, and (5) life philosophy, and consumer purchasing intention were investigated through online interviews. And arranged them in a matrix of TBL factors and environmental factors as shown in Fig. 4. Similar to Friedrich's [20] study, this study was conducted through face-to-face interviews. It consisted of specific scenarios and selection of possible response options that were common in the experiment. The interviews were conducted by three students working in the field of packaging design. Therefore, each student had to conduct at least 5 interviews in different departments of the company. For the data analysis, we used temporal and conceptual sorting displays. The temporal sorting display is suitable for describing and analyzing how events and activities unfold over time. In addition, we conducted systematic cross-case study comparisons. After the tentative ordering was established, each case was revisited and analyzed, whether confirmed or not. After multiple counts were made between the data, we discussed the insights derived from the generalization process using existing literature.

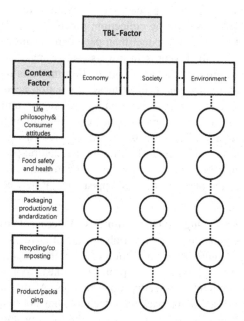

Fig. 4. A triple bottom line analysis model of traditional ecological packaging [13].

4 Discussion

4.1 Understanding the Ecological Value of Traditional Natural Packaging

This paper explores the specific contribution of traditional organic packaging in reducing environmental pollution and promoting resource recycling. Compared to other packaging, packaging using natural materials such as bamboo leaves and lotus leaves not only degrades naturally in a short period of time, but also has less impact on the environment during its production process, such as consuming less water and energy and reducing greenhouse gas emissions. Transforming traditional natural packaging into modern sustainable packaging solutions is not only a modern application of traditional wisdom, but also an important addition to the modern packaging industry. However, this transformation requires a combination of innovative design thinking, materials science and environmental impact assessment to ensure that the new packaging solutions are both practical and meet sustainability criteria.

At the same time, the modern transformation of traditional natural packaging offers an opportunity to combine cultural values with economic potential. In the global marketplace, such packaging can appeal to consumers interested in sustainability and cultural traditions, while at the same time, this promotes the innovative use of packaging materials and enhances the overall value of the product.

4.2 Exploring Innovative Transformations of Traditional Ecological Packaging

Recognizing the Social and Economic Problems of Traditional Ecological Packaging from an Economic Perspective. First, although environmentally friendly, traditional natural packaging materials (e.g., bamboo, straw, lotus leaves, etc.) may involve higher labor and logistics costs during collection, processing, and production, resulting in a higher price for the final product than packaging using conventional materials. This may limit its competitiveness in price-sensitive markets. Secondly, manual or semi-automated conventional packaging production methods may be less efficient than modern automated production to meet mass production needs. This issue limits the market expansion potential of traditional natural packaging until new technologies or innovative production processes are introduced. Again, although consumer awareness of environmentally friendly products is gradually increasing, there are still differences in the perception and acceptance of traditional natural packaging products. A portion of consumers may be reluctant to switch their consumption habits because they have reservations about the performance and appearance of new ecological packaging materials.

Recognizing Social and Ecological Opportunities. In terms of environmental protection, traditional natural packaging uses materials that are often renewable and biodegradable, contributing significantly to the reduction of environmental pollution and plastic waste. In the context of the growing global problem of plastic pollution, this advantage offers significant environmental protection opportunities. At the same time, the innovative transformation of traditional packaging technologies not only contributes to the preservation and transmission of cultural heritage, but also promotes local economic and community development, especially for communities that rely on traditional crafts for their livelihoods. In terms of promoting sustainable development, by supporting the innovation and application of traditional natural packaging, the realization of sustainable development goals, including responsible consumption and production, the protection of ecosystems and the promotion of inclusive growth, can be facilitated.

5 Conclusion

In this study, we provide an in-depth analysis of the concepts of traditional ecological packaging and explore their potential for application in modern sustainable development strategies. The results of the study show that traditional packaging methods offer significant advantages in terms of environmental protection, being able to reduce material use and pollution at source, while their production and decomposition processes have less negative impact on the environment. However, these traditional methods face challenges in terms of hygiene and safety, production efficiency, and consumer perceptions in the modernized packaging industry, and these challenges limit their widespread adoption. In order to transform these traditional ecological packages into modern sustainable solutions, innovations in design, material science, and environmental impact assessment are needed. In addition, we have found that traditional ecological packaging offers a unique combination of cultural value transmission and economic potential. These traditional packaging materials have the potential to increase product value and market competitiveness through innovative use in a global marketplace that is increasingly focused on sustainability and cultural heritage. Future research should further explore specific strategies to promote the modernization and transformation of traditional ecological packaging, and conduct consumer surveys to understand consumers' understanding of the ecological value of traditional packaging.

Acknowledgments. This work is supported by the Philosophy and Social Science Foundation Program of Hunan Province, China (21YBQ069) in terms of methodology and data.

References

1. Lindh, H., Williams, H., Olsson, A., Wikström, F.: Elucidating the indirect contributions of packaging to sustainable development: a terminology of packaging functions and features. Packag. Technol. Sci. **29**, 225–246 (2016). https://doi.org/10.1002/pts.2197
2. Grönman, K., et al.: Framework for sustainable food packaging design. Packag. Technol. Sci. **26**, 187–200 (2012). https://doi.org/10.1002/pts.1971
3. Kapse, U., Mahajan, Y., Hudnurkar, M., Ambekar, S., Hiremath, R.: The effect of sustainable packaging aesthetic on consumer behavior: a case study from India. Australas. Account. Bus. Financ. J. **17**, 236–246 (2023). https://doi.org/10.14453/aabfj.v17i1.11
4. Williams, H., Lindström, A., Trischler, J., Wikström, F., Rowe, Z.: Avoiding food becoming waste in households – the role of packaging in consumers' practices across different food categories. J. Clean. Prod. **265**, 121775 (2020). https://doi.org/10.1016/j.jclepro.2020.121 775Author,F.:Articletitle.Journal2(5),99-110(2016)
5. Zhu, Z., Liu, W., Ye, S., Batista, L.: Packaging design for the circular economy: a systematic review. Sustain. Prod. Consump. **32**, 817–832 (2022). https://doi.org/10.1016/j.spc.2022. 06.005

6. Nikiema, J., Asiedu, Z.: A review of the cost and effectiveness of solutions to address plastic pollution. Environ. Sci. Pollut. Res. **29**, (2022). https://doi.org/10.1007/s11356-021-18038-5

7. de Jesus, A., Antunes, P., Santos, R., Mendonça, S.: Ecological innovation in the transition to a circular economy: an analytical literature review. J. Clean. Prod. **172**, 2999–3018 (2018). https://doi.org/10.1016/j.jclepro.2017.11.111

8. Emblem, A., Emblem, H.: Packaging Technology: Fundamentals, Materials and Processes. Woodhead Publication, Cambridge; Philadelphia (2012)

9. Mustafa, M., Nagalingam, S., Tye, J.: Looking back to the past: revival of traditional food packaging. Presented at the 2nd Regional Conference on Local Knowledge, Penang

10. Oka, H., Sakai, M.: How to wrap five eggs. Harper (1967)

11. Ezeudu, O.B., Agunwamba, J.C., Ezeudu, T.S., Ugochukwu, U.C., Ezeasor, I.C.: Natural leaf-type as food packaging material for traditional food in Nigeria: sustainability aspects and theoretical circular economy solutions. Environ. Sci. Pollut. Res. **28**, 8833–8843 (2020). https://doi.org/10.1007/s11356-020-11268-z

12. Verma, M.K., Shakya, S., Kumar, P., Madhavi, J., Murugaiyan, J., Rao, M.V.R.: Trends in packaging material for food products: historical background, current scenario, and future prospects. J. Food Sci. Technol. **58**(11), 4069 (2021). https://doi.org/10.1007/s13197-021-04964-2

13. Herbes, C., Beuthner, C., Ramme, I.: Consumer attitudes towards biobased packaging – a cross-cultural comparative study. J. Clean. Prod. **194**, 203–218 (2018). https://doi.org/10.1016/j.jclepro.2018.05.106

14. Nesic, A., Ružić, J., Gordić, M., Saša Ostojić, S., Micic, D., Onjia, A.: Pectin-polyvinylpyrrolidone films: a sustainable approach to the development of biobased packaging materials. Compos. Part B: Eng. **110**, 56–61 (2017). https://doi.org/10.1016/j.compositesb.2016.11.016

15. Romani, V.P., Prentice-Hernández, C., Martins, V.G.: Active and sustainable materials from rice starch, fish protein and oregano essential oil for food packaging. Ind. Crops Prod. **97**, 268–274 (2017). https://doi.org/10.1016/j.indcrop.2016.12.026

16. Wang, H., Wang, L.: Developing a bio-based packaging film from soya by-products incorporated with valonea tannin. J. Clean. Prod. **143**, 624–633 (2017). https://doi.org/10.1016/j.jclepro.2016.12.064

17. Ezeudu, O.B., Ozoegwu, C.G., Madu, C.N.: A statistical regression method for characterization of household solid waste: a case study of Awka municipality in Nigeria. Recycling. **4**, 1 (2019). https://doi.org/10.3390/recycling4010001

18. Ozoegwu, C.G., Eze, C., Onwosi, C.O., Mgbemene, C.A., Ozor, P.A.: Biomass and bioenergy potential of cassava waste in Nigeria: estimations based partly on rural-level garri processing case studies. Renew. Sustain. Energy Rev. **72**, 625–638 (2017). https://doi.org/10.1016/j.rser.2017.01.031

19. Haas, W., Krausmann, F., Wiedenhofer, D., Heinz, M.: How circular is the global economy?: an assessment of material flows, waste production, and recycling in the European Union and the World in 2005. J. Ind. Ecol. **19**, 765–777 (2015). https://doi.org/10.1111/jiec.12244

20. Friedrich, D.: What makes bioplastics innovative for fashion retailers? an in-depth analysis according to the triple bottom line principle. J. Clean. Prod. **316**, 128257 (2021). https://doi.org/10.1016/j.jclepro.2021.128257

21. Pal, R., Gander, J.: Modelling environmental value: an examination of sustainable business models within the fashion industry. J. Clean. Prod. **184**, 251–263 (2018). https://doi.org/10.1016/j.jclepro.2018.02.001

22. Song, J., Cai, L., Yuen, K.F., Wang, X.: Exploring consumers' usage intention of reusable express packaging: an extended norm activation model. J. Retail. Consum. Serv. **72**, 103265 (2023). https://doi.org/10.1016/j.jretconser.2023.103265

23. Prakash, G., Choudhary, S., Kumar, A., Garza-Reyes, J.A., Khan, S.A.R., Panda, T.K.: Do altruistic and egoistic values influence consumers' attitudes and purchase intentions towards ecological friendly packaged products? an empirical investigation. J. Retail. Consum. Serv. **50**, 163–169 (2019). https://doi.org/10.1016/j.jretconser.2019.05.011
24. Zhang, L., Fan, Y., Zhang, W., Zhang, S.: Extending the theory of planned behavior to explain the effects of cognitive factors across different kinds of green products. Sustainability **11**, 4222 (2019). https://doi.org/10.3390/su11154222
25. Yuan, Z.: Application of green ecological design in food packaging design. J. Food Qual. **2022**, 1–7 (2022). https://doi.org/10.1155/2022/8491934
26. Albelda Raga, J.L.: La belleza circular: Una aproximación a la estética de la sustentabilidad para el Capitaloceno. Arte y Políticas de Identidad. **20** (2019). https://doi.org/10.6018/reapi.385621
27. Yuvaraj, N., et al.: Nature-inspired-based approach for automated cyberbullying classification on multimedia social networking. Math. Probl. Eng. **2021**, e6644652 (2021). https://doi.org/10.1155/2021/6644652
28. Andreola, F., Lancellotti, I., Manfredini, T., Barbieri, L.: The circular economy of agro and post-consumer residues as raw materials for sustainable ceramics. Int. J. Appl. Ceram. Technol. **17**, 22–31 (2019). https://doi.org/10.1111/ijac.13396
29. Huntrakul, K., Yoksan, R., Sane, A., Harnkarnsujarit, N.: Effects of pea protein on properties of cassava starch edible films produced by blown-film extrusion for oil packaging. Food Packag. Shelf Life **24**, 100480 (2020). https://doi.org/10.1016/j.fpsl.2020.100480
30. Shankar, S., Wang, L.-F., Rhim, J.-W.: Effect of melanin nanoparticles on the mechanical, water vapor barrier, and antioxidant properties of gelatin-based films for food packaging application. Food Packag. Shelf Life **21**, 100363 (2019). https://doi.org/10.1016/j.fpsl.2019.100363
31. Pinem, M.P., Wardhono, E.Y., Nadaud, F., Clausse, D., Saleh, K., Guénin, E.: Nanofluid to nanocomposite film: chitosan and cellulose-based edible packaging. Nanomaterials **10**, 660 (2020). https://doi.org/10.3390/nano10040660
32. Marichelvam, M.K., Jawaid, M., Asim, M.: Corn and rice starch-based bio-plastics as alternative packaging materials. Fibers. **7**, 32 (2019). https://doi.org/10.3390/fib7040032
33. DotAsia. Indonesian ecological social startup uses edible seaweeds to replace plastic packaging. https://medium.com/@dotasiafoundation/indonesian-eco-social-startup-uses-edible-seaweeds-to-replace-plastic-packaging-fa83836e50bc

Bringing Lose Sheep into the Fold: Redesigning Women-In-Tech (WIT) App for Women of Three Age Groups

Pei-Lee Teh[1,2] , Chiew Way Ang[3,4,5(✉)] , Shinyi Wu[6] , Tin Tin Su[3,4] , and Ying Lu[7]

[1] School of Business, Monash University Malaysia, Bandar Sunway, Selangor Darul Ehsan, Malaysia
teh.pei.lee@monash.edu
[2] Gerontechnology Laboratory, Monash University Malaysia, Bandar Sunway, Selangor Darul Ehsan, Malaysia
[3] South East Asia Community Observatory (SEACO), Monash University Malaysia, Segamat, Johor Darul Takzim, Malaysia
chiewway.ang@apu.edu.my, TinTin.Su@monash.edu
[4] Global Public Health, Jeffrey Cheah School of Medicine and Health Sciences, Monash University Malaysia, Bandar Sunway, Selangor Darul Ehsan, Malaysia
[5] School of Mathematics, Actuarial and Quantitative Studies, Asia Pacific University of Technology and Innovation, Kuala Lumpur, Malaysia
[6] Daniel J. Epstein Department of Industrial and Systems Engineering, Viterbi School of Engineering, University of Southern California, Los Angeles, CA, USA
shinyiwu@usc.edu
[7] Zoom Video Communication Inc., San Jose, CA, USA

Abstract. The pandemic limits inter-personal communication and eliminates jobs in the real economy such as hospitality and travel industry. On the contrary, digital technology, especially mobile internet emerges and creates many new online opportunities. This paradigm shift makes it necessary to learn mobile technology and new skills online. This paper explores the digital engagement and psychological empowerment for learning and upskilling with mobile technology among older Malaysian women who are less digitally connected. This research focuses on understanding Malaysia older women's motivation, familiarity and use frequency in mobile technology. Through purposive sampling, 86 older women from rural and urban areas in Malaysia participated in a survey. The study highlights the shared enthusiasm for skill acquisition among 50 to 59 and 60 to 69 age groups, particularly in areas such as information and communication technology (ICT)/mobile technology, social communication, complementary, and work-related skills. Women aged 70 and above express greater life satisfaction and optimism. This study illuminates the digital landscape for older women, emphasizing their proficiency, varied interests, and high levels of psychological empowerment. The findings underscore the optimism and life satisfaction expressed by women aged 70 and above, offering valuable insights into their unique perspectives. The survey results guided the redesign of the age-friendly mobile app, WIT, tailored for women across various age groups and people with limited digital skills. Our

© The Author(s), under exclusive license to Springer Nature Switzerland AG 2024
P.-L. P. Rau (Ed.): HCII 2024, LNCS 14701, pp. 314–333, 2024.
https://doi.org/10.1007/978-3-031-60904-6_23

app encapsulates a holistic and user-centric approach, showcasing the potential to empower older women, foster skill development, and cultivate a positive learning experience in the digital realm.

Keywords: Empowerment · Technology use · Older women · Digital literacy · Malaysia

1 Introduction

The aging population in Asia, with more than half being women [1], presents a significant concern as many older women lack financial independence, facing a prolonged life in poverty. Unfortunately, comprehensive policy frameworks addressing the critical needs of older women in areas such as skills, training, employment, income security, healthcare, and aged care are lacking in most Asian countries. This deficiency poses challenges for active and productive aging among older women in the region. Empowering women aged 50 and above has the potential to mitigate the adverse effects of aging and poverty, as well as address talent shortages in various countries.

The rapid proliferation of affordable smartphones and increased social media usage in Asian countries has created a tech-savvy environment [2]. Information and communication technology (ICT) advancements can transform how older women engage in social activities [3–6], seek information [7], and develop business opportunities [8]. Mobile technology facilitates staying connected with family and friends, bridging generational gaps, and providing tools for knowledge expansion and skill development. However, a digital divide persists, with older women using ICT less than younger age groups and men. Socioeconomic factors exacerbate these disparities, limiting opportunities for learning and upskilling.

Addressing this challenge is crucial, particularly considering the complexity of the technology-centric society and the impact of the COVID-19 pandemic on older women's vulnerability. Urgent interventions are needed to understand and support less digitally connected older women in adopting ICT for successful aging. The first aim of this study is to explore the current digital engagement, interests, and psychological empowerment for learning and upskilling with mobile technology among older women who are less digitally connected. As cognitive factors pose challenges for ICT adoption, age groups may exhibit varying interests and motivations to learn mobile technology. Labor force participation rates drop significantly in older age groups, impacting the willingness to upskill [9]. The study aims to explore these differences among age groups (e.g., 50 to 59, 60 to 69, and 70 and older).

Upskilling in mobile technology can enhance digital literacy, self-confidence, and empowerment among older women, enabling them to lead more independent lives. The second aim of the study is to use insights from the first aim to inform the design of a new mobile technology app tailored for less digitally connected older women. We intended the mobile app to include capacity building, skills training, and the establishment of social support networks to seamlessly integrate mobile technology into their daily lives for productive and successful aging. User-friendly interfaces and tailored training contents are essential components to overcome learning challenges and bridge the digital divide. We will identify age-friendly usability features that can improve mobile app usage.

2 Research Methodology

2.1 Sample

This study employed a quantitative survey method to gain a better understanding of the attitudes and practices toward mobile app usages and learning interests in different age groups of women in Malaysia. This survey method also provided us with empirical data about individual differences in the learning interests of skill development. The findings of this study were important to the design and development of women-in-tech (WIT) applications.

The study was approved by the Ethics Review Committee of Monash University (Review Reference 2021-29459-65513). Participants (i.e., women aged 50 years old and above) were recruited through purposive sampling from five states, namely Kuala Lumpur, Negeri Sembilan, Perak, Johor, and Sarawak in Malaysia. Participants were classified as living in urban or rural areas according to the enumeration blocks published by the Department of Statistics Malaysia. We collaborated with the Department of Social Welfare, senior activity centres, and local non-government organizations to recruit participants. This was a voluntary study and only eligible participants were provided with the explanatory statement. All participants completed a set of survey questionnaires that collected demographic profiles and assessments on mobile app usage and learning interests. The data collection was conducted between May and August 2022. A total of 86 older women participated in the study. The participants were classified into three groups namely, younger group (50 to 59 years old), old group (60 to 69 years old) and older group (70 years old and above).

2.2 Measures and Data Analysis

Survey questionnaires were developed in an iterative approach involving all the research team members through modified Delphi rounds, translation and cultural adaptation process and pretest. The initial 60 questions within eight topic sections underwent two modified Delphi processes, drawing 20 comments. Some items were removed or modified based on the comments. The final study instrument comprised 32 questions within five topic sections. The survey items for participants' demographics, employment information, learning interest and personal relationships were adapted from Bassuk et al. [10], Guo [11], and Milovich et al. [12]. Questions pertaining to mobile phone usages were assessed based on the study by Choudrie et al. [13]. To measure psychological empowerment, we adapted the survey items from Hur [14] and Spreitzer [15]. All survey items were measured either on a five-point or seven-point Likert scale. To analyze the survey data, we performed descriptive analysis and Analysis of Variance (ANOVA) using IBM Statistical Package for the Social Sciences (SPSS) statistical software.

3 Results

The participants in this study consisted of 86 women aged 50 years and above. In terms of age group, 18 participants were from the younger group (aged between 50 to 59 years old), 39 women in the old group (aged between 60 to 69 years old) and 29 females in the older group (aged 70 years old and above). Most of the participants were Malay (n = 57), followed by 15 Chinese and 14 Indian and other ethnic groups. The majority of the participants lived in rural areas (69.8%), and the remaining 30.2% of women resided in the urban areas. Specifically, a majority of the participants of the age cohort (60 to 69 years, 79.5%) and 70 years old and above (69.0%) lived in rural areas. About 33% of participants in the younger group (50 to 59 years) reported they have no income while most of the participants from the other two age groups have income less than MYR 2,500 per month (51.3% for 60 to 69 years old and 62.1% for 70 years old and above).

Overall, participants from the younger age cohort had higher education levels. Most of the participants aged 50 to 59 years (72.2%) completed their study until secondary level while about 59% of those aged 70 years and above studied until primary level. Meanwhile, about 34% and 45% of the participants aged 60 to 69 years accomplished their primary and secondary education, respectively. About 72% and 57% of participants aged 50 to 59 years and 60 to 69 years were still married, respectively while the majority (69.0%) of the women aged 70 years and above were widows. In general, most of the participants across the aged group were living with someone at home.

It was found that the average number of children raised across the age groups ranged between 1.80 to 2.70 children. Interestingly, the participants revealed that an average of three children talked or corresponded with them weekly across three age groups. Women aged 60 to 69 years found to have a relatively lower average number of other close-knit relatives or friends compared with the other two age groups. By and large, participants aged 70 years and above had a higher level of satisfaction about their life compared to the other age groups. Table 1 presents the demographic information of participants in three age groups.

Fifty percent of the young group (50 to 59 years old) were still working. Our results also indicated that 44.5% of the young group are confident to find a new job in future. In contrast, 71.4% of the old group (60 to 69 years old) and 57.7% of the old group (70 years old and above) were not working. Referring to Table 2, the participants across the age groups knew their internet mobile plan. In general, prepaid mobile data plan, postpaid mobile plan and home WIFI broadband plan were more commonly used by women aged 50 to 59 years. Meanwhile, postpaid mobile data plan was popular among participants aged 60 and above to access the internet. Interestingly, 14.3% participants aged 60 to 69 years and 28.6% participants aged 70 years and above did not know the mobile package for their internet access via mobile phone.

Overall, the confidence level of using mobile phones for different activities was higher among the younger group (between 50 and 59 years old) and the old group (between 60 and 69 years old). It was found that women aged 50 to 59 years have the highest average confidence level of using a mobile phone for most of the activities (11 out of 18 activities). Examples of activities include text messaging, listening to music, using contact tracing apps, etc. It was reported that 7 out of 18 activities listed (e.g., using video conferencing tools, using social networks, etc.), women aged 60 to 69 years had the highest average confidence level across the age groups. Meanwhile, participants aged 70 years and above had a lower average confidence level ranging between 0.90 to 2.62 across all the activities listed (see Table 2).

Table 1. Profiles of Participants.

Variables	n	50–59 years old (%)	n	60–69 years old (%)	n	70 years old and above (%)
Total	18	100.0	39	100.0	29	100.0
Ethnicity						
Malay	6	33.3	28	71.8	23	79.3
Chinese	2	11.1	8	20.5	5	17.2
Indian	1	5.6	2	5.1	1	3.4
Others	9	50.0	1	2.6	0	0.0
Place of residence						
Rural	9	50.0	31	79.5	20	69.0
Urban	9	50.0	8	20.5	9	31.0
Monthly average net household income						
No income	6	33.3	12	30.8	8	27.6
Less than MYR 2,500	4	22.2	20	51.3	18	62.1
MYR 2,501 - MYR 3,169	4	22.2	3	7.7	1	3.4
MYR 3,170 - MYR 3,979	0	0.0	2	5.1	1	3.4
MYR 3,970 - MYR 4,849	1	5.6	0	0.0	0	0.0
MYR 4,850 and above	3	16.7	2	5.1	1	3.4
Education						
No formal education	0	0.0	3	7.9	4	13.8
Primary	0	0.0	13	34.2	17	58.6
Secondary	13	72.2	17	44.7	6	20.7
Vocational/Technical certification	1	5.6	2	5.3	1	3.4
University	4	22.2	3	7.9	1	3.4
Marital status						
Single	1	5.6	5	13.5	1	3.4
Married	13	72.2	21	56.8	7	24.1
Separated/Divorced	0	0.0	1	2.7	1	3.4
Widowed/Widower	4	22.2	10	27.0	20	69.0

(*continued*)

Table 1. (*continued*)

Variables	n	50–59 years old (%)	n	60–69 years old (%)	n	70 years old and above (%)
Living Status						
Living with someone at home	17	94.4	32	82.1	21	75.0
Living alone at home	1	5.6	7	17.9	7	25.0
Number of children raised	2.65	1.50	2.43	2.03	1.86	2.10
Number of children talked or correspond with weekly	2.72	1.57	2.65	1.99	3.18	3.83
Number of other relatives that close to	15.67	23.58	6.00	6.51	8.75	7.75
Number of close friend	9.50	6.98	6.22	5.13	11.18	9.21
My life is close to my ideal	3.44	0.51	3.72	0.89	4.07	0.80
My current life state is excellent	3.33	0.59	3.82	0.94	4.14	0.74
I am satisfied with my life	3.89	0.90	4.05	0.86	4.21	0.68

Note: Missing values are excluded from the calculations.

The proportion of participants across the age groups who tried to learn something new or useful once a day or many times a day were relatively low. The women were willing to try something new causally or at a slower pace as many reported will try to learn something new on a weekly or monthly basis. The average hours per week devoted to learning something new by the women across the age groups ranged between 0.90 h to 1.90 h. The younger group (50 to 59 years old) and the old group (60 to 69 years old) had higher interest in learning four categories of skills namely, ICT/technology skills, social communication skills, complementary skills and work-related skills (refer to Table 3). Additionally, the older age cohort has less interest in learning new skills on mobile phones compared with younger age cohorts. For instance, women aged 70 and above had less interest in learning work-related skills compared to those in the young group (50 to 59 years old). Women aged 60 to 69 years found to have more interest in learning new ICT or technology skills and social communication skills compared to those in the older group (70 years old and above).

Generally, the participants across the age groups expressed their perceived psychological empowerment in relation to individual and collective empowerment (i.e. meaning or awareness of limited potential, competence, self-determination, and collective

Table 2. Mobile Phone Usages of Participants.

Variables	n	50–59 years old (%)	n	60–69 years old (%)	n	70 years old and above (%)
Total	18	100.0	39	100.0	29	100.0
Method to access internet via mobile phone						
Prepaid mobile data plan	6	33.3	8	17.9	5	17.9
Postpaid mobile plan	5	27.8	23	35.7	10	35.7
Home WIFI broadband plan	6	33.3	4	14.3	4	14.3
Public WIFI hotspot	1	5.6	0	0.0	1	3.6
Don't know	0	0.0	4	14.3	8	28.6
Confident to use mobile phone for						
SMS, text message	4.22	0.88	3.85	1.18	2.62	1.45
Browsing/surfing websites	3.11	1.23	2.33	1.66	1.55	1.56
Watching video	3.56	1.34	3.33	1.38	1.97	1.64
Using Zoom, Facetime, Skype, Google Talk, etc	2.72	1.53	3.00	1.38	1.93	1.39
Using COVID-19 contact tracing app	3.83	0.86	3.44	1.47	2.28	1.65
Online shopping or e-commerce	2.22	1.44	2.28	1.73	1.28	1.16
Using mobile banking/e-wallet	2.06	1.35	1.56	1.45	0.97	0.73
Online ordering for food or groceries	1.61	1.46	1.74	1.46	1.24	1.09
Using social network	2.67	1.53	3.03	1.48	1.76	1.48
Taking a photo	4.06	0.87	3.44	1.45	1.90	1.52

(*continued*)

Table 2. (*continued*)

Variables	*n*	50–59 years old (%)	*n*	60–69 years old (%)	*n*	70 years old and above (%)
Mapping navigator	2.33	1.50	1.95	1.59	1.03	0.68
Managing my appointment on my calendar	1.83	1.51	1.90	1.54	1.45	1.35
Reading online news or online magazine	3.00	1.33	2.74	1.62	1.55	1.24
Taking notes	2.33	1.53	1.87	1.54	1.28	1.10
Filming a video	2.83	1.65	2.90	1.62	1.66	1.42
Listening to music	3.67	1.19	2.33	1.60	1.93	1.65
Playing games	1.72	1.49	1.92	1.56	1.10	0.72
Using to contact government authorities	3.00	1.53	2.77	1.75	2.24	1.73

Note: Missing values are excluded from the calculations.

empowerment). All three age groups had a higher level of agreement on their capabilities of expressing themselves, decision-making, problem-solving, and teamwork. There was insignificant difference among the age groups (see Table 4).

Another comparison result in Table 4 shows that women aged between 50 and 59 years old had more other relatives that they were close to compared with those aged from 60 to 69 years. In terms of social relationships, women aged between 60 and 69 years old reported having fewer close friends compared with the older group (70 years old and above). It is interesting to surface the striking difference in life satisfaction between younger (50 to 59 years old) and older (70 and above) age groups. Our findings found that women aged 70 and above were optimistic towards their lives as they reported that their lives are close to their ideal lives and their current life states are excellent, compared with those of women aged 50 to 59 years.

In general, it was found that the younger age cohort had a higher level of confidence in using mobile phones. Women aged 50 to 59 years were confident in using the mobile phone for almost all the activities listed in the applications except for playing games and using Zoom, Facetime, Skype, Google Talk and etc. compared with women aged 70 and above. Similar trend was found among those of 60 to 69 years as they were more confident in using mobile phones for almost all listed activities (except taking note and listening to music) compared with those aged 70 and above.

Table 3. Learning Interest and Psychological Empowerment of Participants

Variables	n	50 – 59 years old (%)	n	60 -69 years old (%)	n	70 years old and above (%)
Total	18	100.0	39	100.0	29	100.0
Try to learn something new or useful						
Never	2	11.1	9	23.1	9	31.0
Once a day	3	16.7	3	7.7	3	10.3
Many times a day	0	0.0	2	5.1	2	6.9
Once a week	7	38.9	6	15.4	3	10.3
Few times a week	3	16.7	5	12.8	4	13.8
Once a month	3	16.7	7	17.9	7	24.1
Few times a month	0	0.0	7	17.9	1	3.4

	50 – 59 years old		60 – 69 years old		70 years old and above	
	Mean	S.D.	Mean	S.D.	Mean	S.D.
Hours per week devote to learn something new or useful	1.86	1.21	1.76	3.27	0.95	1.72
Interest to learn the skills						
ICT/ technology skills	3.00	1.19	3.15	1.29	2.31	1.29
Social communication skills	3.39	1.15	3.49	1.02	2.72	1.39
Complementary skills	3.61	1.24	3.28	1.34	2.93	1.36
Work-related skills	3.33	1.28	2.79	1.30	2.21	1.24
Level of agreement of the following statement						
I understand the meaning of life	4.39	0.61	4.15	0.59	4.25	0.65
I understand the meaning of daily life activities	4.33	0.77	4.13	0.62	4.25	0.65
I find attractiveness in daily life activities	3.89	0.90	4.13	0.70	4.25	0.65
I have confidence in daily life activities	4.17	0.79	4.21	0.57	4.32	0.55
I have self-assurance in the performance of daily life activities	4.22	0.65	4.08	0.77	4.32	0.77
I have confidence in newly formed daily life activities	4.00	0.69	4.00	0.89	4.01	1.11
I have capabilities of expressing the self	3.83	0.71	3.92	0.90	4.10	0.98

(*continued*)

Table 3. (*continued*)

I have capabilities of selecting better alternatives	4.11	0.76	3.92	0.87	4.00	1.05
I have capabilities of making decisions on particular problems	3.94	0.80	4.05	0.83	4.04	1.00
I have capabilities of working together with others	4.28	0.83	4.05	0.83	4.14	0.99
I have capabilities of building teams with others	4.28	0.67	3.85	1.10	3.79	1.32
I have capabilities of building coalitions	4.17	0.71	3.90	0.97	3.64	1.37
I have capabilities of solving problems with other	4.28	0.75	4.00	0.92	4.03	1.18

Note: Missing values are excluded from the calculations.

Table 4. Comparison Results of Young Group (50 to 59 Years Old), Old Group (60 to 69 Years Old) and Older Group (70 Years Old and Above)

Age group	Variables	60–69 years old			70 years old and above		
		Mean difference	SD	*p-value*	Mean difference	SD	*p-value*
Part 1							
50–59 years old	Number of other relatives that close to	9.67	3.61	*p = 0.009*	6.92	3.79	*p = 0.072*
	Number of close friend	3.28	2.05	*p = 0.113*	−1.68	2.15	*p = 0.438*
	My life is close to my ideal	−0.27	0.23	*p = 0.230*	−0.63	0.24	*p = 0.010*
	My current life state is excellent	−0.49	0.23	*p = 0.039*	−0.81	0.25	*p = 0.001*
60–69 years old	Number of other relatives that close to				−2.75	3.14	*p = 0.384*
	Number of close friend				−4.96	1.79	*p = 0.007*
	My life is close to my ideal				−0.35	0.19	*p = 0.075*
	My current life state is excellent				−0.32	0.20	*p = 0.116*

Part 3 (Confidence level of using mobile phone for following)

(*continued*)

Table 4. (*continued*)

Age group	Variables	60–69 years old			70 years old and above		
		Mean difference	SD	*p-value*	Mean difference	SD	*p-value*
50–59 years old	SMS, text message	0.38	0.37	*p = 0.318*	1.60	0.39	*p < 0.001*
	Browsing/surfing websites	0.78	0.42	*p = 0.067*	1.56	0.44	*p = 0.001*
	Watching video	0.22	0.42	*p = 0.596*	1.59	0.44	*p = 0.001*
	Using COVID-19 contact tracing app	0.40	0.41	*p = 0.332*	1.56	0.43	*p < 0.001*
	Online shopping or e-commerce	−0.60	0.43	*p = 0.889*	0.95	0.45	*p = 0.039*
50–59 years old	Using mobile banking/e-wallet	0.49	0.35	*p = 0.164*	1.09	0.37	*p = 0.004*
	Using social network	−0.36	0.43	*p = 0.400*	0.91	0.45	*p = 0.045*
	Taking a photo	0.62	0.39	*p = 0.118*	2.16	0.41	*p < 0.001*
	Mapping navigator	0.39	0.38	*p = 0.313*	1.30	0.40	*p = 0.002*
	Reading online news or online magazine	0.26	0.41	*p = 0.534*	1.45	0.43	*p = 0.001*
	Taking notes	046	0.40	*p = 0.253*	1.06	0.42	*p = 0.014*
	Filming a video	−0.06	0.45	*p = 0.886*	1.18	0.47	*p = 0.014*
	Listening to music	1.33	0.44	*p = 0.003*	1.74	0.46	*p < 0.001*
	Playing games	−0.20	0.38	*p = 0.595*	0.62	0.40	*p = 0.123*
60–69 years old	SMS, text message				1.23	0.32	*p < 0.001*
	Browsing/surfing websites				0.78	0.36	*p = 0.033*

(*continued*)

Table 4. (*continued*)

Age group	Variables	60–69 years old			70 years old and above		
		Mean difference	SD	*p-value*	Mean difference	SD	*p-value*
	Watching video				1.37	0.36	*p < 0.001*
	Using Zoom, Facetime, Skype, Google Talk, etc				1.07	0.35	*p = 0.003*
	Using COVID-19 contact tracing app				1.16	0.35	*p = 0.001*
	Online shopping or e-commerce				1.01	0.37	*p = 0.008*
	Using mobile banking/e-wallet				0.60	0.30	*p = 0.050*
	Using social network				1.27	0.37	*p = 0.001*
60–69 years old	Taking a photo				1.54	0.34	*p < 0.001*
	Mapping navigator				0.91	0.33	*p = 0.006*
	Reading online news or online magazine				1.19	0.35	*p = 0.001*
	Taking notes				0.60	0.35	*p = 0.088*
	Filming a video				1.24	0.38	*p = 0.002*
	Listening to music				0.40	0.38	*p = 0.289*
	Playing games				0.82	0.32	*p = 0.013*
Part 4 (Interest to learn the skills)							
50–59 years old	ICT/technology skills	−0.15	0.36	*p = 0.671*	0.69	0.38	*p = 0.073*
	Social communication skills	−0.10	0.34	*p = 0.771*	0.67	0.35	*p = 0.064*
	Work-related skills	0.54	0.36	*p = 0.142*	1.13	0.38	*p = 0.004*
60–69 years old	ICT/technology skills				0.84	0.31	*p = 0.008*
	Social communication skills				0.76	0.29	*p = 0.010*
	Work-related skills				0.59	0.31	*p = 0.064*

4 Discussions

In general, the older age cohort (70 years and above) participants found to have relatively lower confidence and interest in using or learning something new via mobile phone. The findings were supported by some studies [16–18] where users with lower self-efficacy were less motivated to use technology in general. Besides that, a study done in China [18] also showed that older adults with higher self-efficacy were more likely to find smartphones are useful and easy to use.

Besides that, the older age cohort participants were more satisfied with their current life. A study in South Korea [19] found that older adults living alone received beneficial effects of using mobile internet for social networking to increase life satisfaction which was contradicted in this study as the majority of the participants stayed with others at home. The findings were supported by the study done by Vujić et al. [20] where people that are dissatisfied with their life experienced more perceived stress resulting from abusive smartphone usage or smartphone addiction Such phenomena may explain the reason why older age cohort participants of this study had less interest and motivation to use mobile phones as they were socially connected with others offline.

Our study showed that participants aged 50 to 59 years had higher levels of confidence in using mobile phones. Our findings reported that participants from the older age cohort have a higher percentage of lower income (less than MYR 2,500) and lower educational level (primary level and below) compared to those aged 50 to 59 years which was consistent with the studies done by Chan et al. [21], Yazdani-Darki et al. [17], Elimelech et al. [22], and Petrovčič et al. [23] where less educated and lower income people were more digitally disadvantaged.

Many studies have reported that older adults are willing to learn or integrate new technology (i.e. mobile phones) into their daily life if it is beneficial and fulfills their needs [17, 21, 22, 24]. This inclines with the findings as the older participants found to have higher level of confidence in using mobile phones for social interaction (SMS, text message) and their health (COVID-19 contact tracing). Besides that, they also reported spending more hours learning social communication skills and complementary skills via mobile phone as these are the skills they required or they are interested in. In summary, older people will devote more time to use technology if they perceive the usefulness of the technology.

In conclusion, the features and design of the Women-in-tech app should be age-friendly. The application's algorithm should be able to determine and recommend skill development and learning modules that are beneficial and useful for users in their daily life and able to interact with the users throughout the time they are using the application. Besides that, the language used in the application should be simple and easy to be understand by the user and the design of the application need to be easily accessible to the user and be used without any complicated instruction or manual.

4.1 Proposed Design for Women-In-Tech App

Through these survey results, a list of age-friendly usability features that can improve mobile app usage and learning for greater skill development among older women was identified.

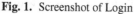

Fig. 1. Screenshot of Login

Fig. 2. Screenshot of Starting Chatbot

At the outset, the simplicity of the use of mobile apps is significant for older adults of all age groups. For example, age-friendly apps should be easy to launch via any mobile or desktop web browsers, and it offers a simple sign-up procedure which does not require a predefined username and a password. Therefore, our WIT app offers a mobile number and one-time password (OTP) login (see Fig. 1). In addition to it, the app designs in a way that remembers successful logins each time, without repeatedly entering mobile number and OTP unless the user uninstalls and reinstalls the app. With facial technology, we will provide an even more friendly experience using face ID conditional on user consent, so the user does not need to input anything at all.

Given that the three age groups of older women had different learning interests and psychological empowerment as evidenced in our findings, it would be effective to elicit an individual's profile and learning interest through a chatbot after login. In this regard, our proposed WIT app design will direct a user to start a chatbot after a successful login (see Fig. 2).

Chatbot enables dialogue between a human and a persona (app) that mimics human responses. Our survey results are a powerful reminder that older women of different age cohorts had different levels of personal relationships with their family members and friends. In this related vein, we believe that having a human-like avatar, an animated avatar or a robot avatar as the expressive avatar (which provides voice activations together with facial expressions) would make a difference in how older women perceive the effectiveness of the chatbot and their intention to engage with the chatbot. In particular, voice activation could address the barriers for older women such as difficult-to-read text and small prints. We will enable Speech-to-text technology to assist conversing with chatbot. Hence, our WIT app provides four options of chatbot namely, chatbot without avatar, chatbot with human avatar, chatbot with animated avatar and chatbot with robot avatar (see Fig. 3).

Examples of chatbot designs include button-based chatbot, keywords-based chatbot and contextual chatbot. In the context of older women, a button-based chatbot, powered by chatbot-driven dialogue, in which options of response are given, was chosen in the WIT app. The button-based chatbot is the most ideal feature to capture users' responses through tapping. The avatar appearance on the top right corner of the chatbot interface is thought to enable a more human-like interaction (see Fig. 4).

This application was designed to provide learning module and skills development among older women uplift their skills and be connected with society via mobile phone using AI technology. We incorporate a data intelligent agent in the WIT app to this human-centered design, the WIT app capture the need and skills required by the users through the interaction with the chatbot. This data intelligent agent will gather and extract the information or responses from the chatbot. Then, it will provide the suitable and preferable skills learning and module that the users interested according to the information that extracted from the chatbot. By using such design, the application is able to determine the users' needs and meet the needs and requirement of the users.

Recognizing the difference between younger and older age groups for skill development in various categories such as ICT/technology skills, social communication skills, complementary skills and work-related skills, WIT app is designed with the goal of improving the accessibility of skill learning modules for older women of all age groups (see Fig. 5 & Fig. 6). In addition to the above, the data intelligent agent will keep track of the learning process, and know whether the skills are actually acquired by the user. Based on the user feedback, the data intelligence will suggest the appropriate level of content and reinforces the learning.

In the recommender module, we enable users to select their favorite video by tapping the "Love" icon, rate their liking by tapping the "thumbs up" (or "thumbs down") icon, and share the video via the "Share" icon (see Fig. 7). The recommendation module will suggest relevant videos that may be helpful to the user's skill development based on the contextual information. Figure 8 shows the quiz component. To assess the user's learning outcome in the WIT app, a user can choose to complete the in-app quiz for the respective video module. Each video module can be assessed with three quizzes with a total of 6-point score. Lastly, we utilize a digital certificate as a catalyst to motivate users to learn and improve their learning experience (see Fig. 8).

In order to continuously improving the design and user experience, we implement telemetry for user actions. With the power of data, we are able to experiment various UX designs and algorithm engines to quantitatively tell us which design is preferred and what algorithms work better. A simple example is to log click-through actions for the recommendation module. If we have the right design and algorithms in place, then user is more likely to click the recommended videos and share it. Another example is time to log-in or number of trials before log-in. Higher number means higher frictions. These event data give us a lot of details on how users use the app, what frictions they have, and give directions on how we can further improve.

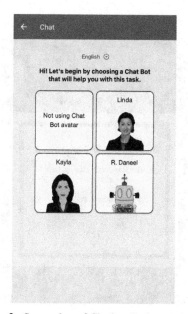

Fig. 3. Screenshot of Chatbot Options (with Human Avatar, Animated Avatar and Robot Avatar)

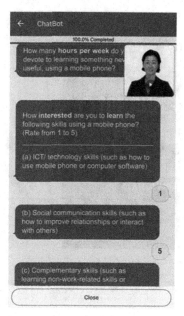

Fig. 4. Screenshot of Button-based Chatbot and Avatar Interface

Fig. 5. Screenshot of Chatbot-to-Recommender Path

Fig. 6. Screenshot of Recommender Options (with Four Categories of Skills)

Fig. 7. Screenshot of Recommender Video (with Quiz, Favorite, Like, Dislike, Share Features)

Fig. 8. Screenshot of Certificate

4.2 Limitations and Future Study

Notwithstanding the contributions of this study, our study has four research limitations. First, the findings of this study were cross-sectional and thus do not establish causality in relationships. It is likely that an older woman's learning interest at time 1 influences smartphone usage at time 2, which further reinforces learning interest at time 3. Future research should collect longitudinal data. Second, our findings were limited to insights from a single country (i.e., Malaysia), and therefore, more research in other countries is needed to strengthen the generalizability of the results. Third, this study only employed survey data. Rather than drawing conclusions from a single source of data, data triangulation enables future researchers to use multiple data sources such as interviews and observational data to examine the perceptions of older women in relation to smartphone usage and learning interests. Lastly, the design of the application is more towards one-way interaction that lesser interaction between user and the application which required more data or feedback from the users to further improvise the features of the application in the future study.

5 Conclusions

This study provides comprehensive insights into the digital engagement, psychological empowerment, and social dynamics of older women across diverse age groups. Notably, participants aged 50 to 59 exhibit heightened proficiency in mobile phone usage, with a nuanced confidence level across various applications. The enthusiasm for skill development is evident in both 50 to 59 and 60 to 69 cohorts, particularly in acquiring ICT/mobile technology, social communication, complementary, and work-related skills. However, the older age group (70 and above) displays less interest, specifically in the domain of work-related skills on mobile phones.

Psychological empowerment remains consistently high across all age groups, encompassing self-expression, decision-making, problem-solving, and teamwork. Social relationship dynamics show variations, with women aged 50 to 59 reporting more close relatives compared to the 60 to 69 age group, while women aged 60 to 69 report fewer close friends than the older group (70 years and above). A notable finding reveals a significant difference in life satisfaction between the younger (50 to 59) and older (70 and above) age groups. Women aged 70 and above express a more optimistic outlook, reporting lives close to their ideal states and excellent current life conditions, contrasting with the perspectives of women aged 50 to 59.

The study's conclusion emphasizes the translation of these findings into the development of an age-friendly mobile app, WIT. Prioritizing simplicity, WIT features an easily accessible interface and a straightforward login process. Acknowledging varied learning interests and psychological empowerment levels, the app employs a personalized chatbot post-login, integrating human-like avatars for enhanced engagement, especially addressing potential barriers like difficult-to-read text. Diverse chatbot designs cater to different user preferences, and a data intelligent agent customizes the recommender module, making skill learning modules more accessible across age groups.

The recommender module includes user engagement features like video liking, rating, and sharing, while an in-app quiz assesses learning outcomes, fostering a comprehensive learning experience. To motivate users, digital certificates are incorporated as catalysts for sustained learning and improvement. In essence, the WIT app embodies a holistic, user-centric approach, addressing the unique needs and preferences of older women, fostering skill development, and facilitating a positive learning experience in the digital realm. Notably, the application can be evolved if more people use the application. Through the interactive process, with the human-centered design, the application able to collect information from the users and the developer can test what are the features and design that are age-friendly and more attractive to the users. By leverage the data or AI technology, the researchers and developers also able to incorporate the features to evolve the WIT app and make it become a better application in the future.

The study's implications highlight the need for targeted interventions to support the digital well-being of older women. Specifically, these interventions should address the varied confidence levels in using specific digital applications, customize skill development initiatives to align with the diverse interests of different age groups, and leverage consistently high levels of psychological empowerment for holistic programs. Additionally, efforts should focus on fostering social connections among older women to enhance overall well-being, and optimizing technology adoption by designing user-friendly interfaces and incorporating motivational incentives. Implementing these strategies can contribute to creating an age-friendly digital environment that empowers older women and improves their digital literacy and overall quality of life.

Acknowledgment. This project is supported by the Monash University Malaysia-ASEAN Research Grant Scheme 2021–2023 (Grant Code: ASE000008). Special thanks to Dr Ewilly Liew, Dr Chong Chun Yong, Dr Hanjing Huang, Ng Li Shin, Elizabeth Lee Jia Huei, Eugene Yong You Jin, Joanna Renai Raja and Fionamae Raja for their assistance in this study.

Disclosure of Interests. The authors have no competing interests to declare that are relevant to the content of this article.

References

1. Administration on Aging (AoA): 2021 Profile of Older Americans. U.S.: U.S. Department of Health and Human Services (2022). https://acl.gov/sites/default/files/Profile%20of%20OA/2021%20Profile%20of%20OA/2021ProfileOlderAmericans_508.pdf
2. Poushter, J., Bishop, C., Chwe, H.: Social media use continues to rise in developing country but plateaus across developed one. U.S.: Pew Research Center (2018). https://medienorge.uib.no/files/Eksterne_pub/Pew-Research-Center_Global-Tech-Social-Media-Use_2018.06.19.pdf
3. Cornejo, R., Tentori, M., Favela, J.: Enriching in-person encounters through social media: a study on family connectedness for the elderly. Int. J. Hum. Comput. Stud. 71(9), 889–899 (2013). https://doi.org/10.1016/j.ijhcs.2013.04.001
4. Hogeboom, D.L., McDermott, R.J., Perrin, K.M., Osman, H., Bell-Ellison, B.A.: Internet use and social networking among middle aged and older adults. Educ. Gerontol. 36(2), 93–111 (2010). https://doi.org/10.1080/03601270903058507
5. Russell, C., Campbell, A., Hughes, I.: Ageing, social capital and the internet: findings from an exploratory study of Australian 'silver surfers.' Australas. J. Ageing 27(2), 78–82 (2008). https://doi.org/10.1111/j.1741-6612.2008.00284.x
6. White, J., Weatherall, A.: A grounded theory analysis of older adults and information technology. Educ. Gerontol. 26(4), 371–386 (2000). https://doi.org/10.1080/036012700407857
7. Zhao, Y.C., Zhao, M., Song, S.: Online health information seeking behaviors among older adults: systematic scoping review. J. Med. Internet Res. 24(2), e34790 (2022). https://doi.org/10.2196/34790
8. Sharafizad, J.: Women business owners' adoption of information and communication technology. J. Syst. Inf. Technol. 18(4), 331–345 (2016). https://doi.org/10.1108/JSIT-07-2016-0048
9. He, W., et al.: Asia aging: demographic, economic, and health transitions. International Population Reports. U.S.: U.S. Department of Commerce (2022). https://www.census.gov/content/dam/Census/library/publications/2022/demo/p95-22-1.pdf
10. Bassuk, S.S., Glass, T.A., Berkman, L.F.: Social disengagement and incident cognitive decline in community-dwelling elderly persons. Ann. Intern. Med. 131(3), 165–173 (1999)
11. Guo, P.J.: Older adults learning computer programming: motivations, frustrations, and design opportunities. In: Proceedings of the 2017 CHI Conference on Human Factors in Computing Systems, pp. 7070–7083. Association for Computing Machinery, USA (2017)
12. Milovich, M., Burleson, D.: Connections and cognitive speed of older adults: using a social media intervention to improve cognitive speed. Commun. Assoc. Inf. Syst. 47, 743–763 (2020). https://doi.org/10.17705/1CAIS.04734
13. Choudrie, J., Pheeraphuttranghkoon, S., Davari, S.: The digital divide and older adult population adoption, use and diffusion of mobile phones: a quantitative study. Inf. Syst. Front. 22, 673–695 (2020). https://doi.org/10.1007/s10796-018-9875-2

14. Hur, M.H.: Empowering the elderly population through ICT-based activities: an empirical study of older adults in Korea. Inf. Technol. People **29**(2), 318–333 (2016). https://doi.org/10.1108/ITP-03-2015-0052

15. Spreitzer, G.M.: Psychological empowerment in the workplace: dimensions, measurement, and validation. Acad. Manag. J. **38**(5), 1442–1465 (1995). https://doi.org/10.5465/256865

16. Czaja, S.J., et al.: Factors predicting the use of technology: findings from the center for research and education on aging and technology enhancement (CREATE). Psychol. Aging **21**(2), 333–352 (2006)

17. Yazdani-Darki, M., Rahemi, Z., Adib-Hajbaghery, M., Izadi, F.: Older adults' barriers to use technology in daily life: a qualitative study. Nurs. Midwifery Stud. **9**(4), 229–236 (2020)

18. Zhu, X., Cheng, X.: Staying connected: smartphone acceptance and use level differences of older adults in China. Univ. Access Inf. Soc. (2022). https://doi.org/10.1007/s10209-022-00933-4

19. Cho, H., Choi, M., Lee H.: Mobile internet use and life satisfaction among older adults: the moderating effect of living alone. J. Appl. Gerontol. (2023). https://doi.org/10.1177/07334648231216383

20. Vujić, A., Szabo, A.: Hedonic use, stress, and life satisfaction as predictors of smartphone addiction. Addict. Behav. Rep. **15**, 100411 (2022). https://doi.org/10.1016/j.abrep.2022.100411

21. Chan, D.Y.L., Lee, S.W.H., Teh, P.L.: Factors influencing technology use among low-income older adults: a systematic review. Heliyon **9**, e20111 (2023). https://doi.org/10.1016/j.heliyon.2023.e20111

22. Elimelech, O.C., et al.: Technology use characteristics among older adults during the COVID-19 pandemic: a cross-cultural survey. Technol. Soc. **71**, 102080 (2022)

23. Petrovčič, A., Reisdorf, B.C., Grošelj, D., Prevodnik, K.: A typology of aging internet users: exploring digital gradations in internet skills and uses. Soc. Sci. Comput. Rev. **41**(5), 1920–1940 (2023). https://doi.org/10.1177/08944393221117753

24. Lu, Y.T., Chang, Y.H., Sung, T.W.: The relationship between motivation, the use of mobile devices and satisfaction with life for older farmers. Eurasia J. Math. Sci. Technol. Educ. **13**(7), 4009–4020 (2017). https://doi.org/10.12973/eurasia.2017.00769a

Regulating Cross-Cultural Moral Sensitivity: An Image Ethic Analysis of Appearance Design of Intelligent Machine

Zhengqing Zhang[(✉)] and Yanyu Wang

Beihang University, Beijing 100191, China
zhangzhengqing@buaa.edu.cn

Abstract. Machine appearance is a crucial research topic in human-machine interaction, and different cultures hold different ethical attitudes toward different machine appearances. Cultural sensitivity research on appearance lacks in-depth ethical considerations, while value sensitivity research on appearance does not focus well on user-driven design concepts. Image ethics using the resources of phenomenological theory can circumvent the problems above, while a persuasive support of valid empirical research is in demand. This study's approach to image ethics discusses differences in the moral sensitivity of image viewers from different cultures. It is designed to compare the attitudes of two groups of people towards the appearance of a machine in a scenario where two machines are interacting, by textually analyzing the results of a classroom experiment and social media comments on viewing the same image. The study finds that different cultures have different moral sensitivities to the appearance of the same machine, as evidenced by the difference in the proportion of normative and descriptive content in the viewing representations. There are structural differences in the perceptions of machine appearance among viewers from different cultures, which can be observed in the distinctive themes in the texts of the two cultures. The findings can empirically support the role of moral energizers in moderating moral sensitivity in appearance, leading to a better use of phenomenological approaches to focus on the user's experience of using the machine, and providing cultural explanations for the affective characterization of users' ethical perceptions.

Keywords: Human-Robot Relationship · Image Ethics · Appearance Design · Cross-culture · Moral Sensitivity

1 Introduction

People from different cultures may have different attitudes towards the certain robot or human-robot relationship. It is a solution to cope with the discrepancy that designing culturally sensitive robots to meet the different needs with the same function [1]. The most basic cultural differentiation is the prototypical east-west dichotomy of cultures [2], which has been carried out in Asian Confucian cultural context countries in comparison with western countries such as the United States [3], especially in the discussion in

P.-L. P. Rau (Ed.): HCII 2024, LNCS 14701, pp. 334–358, 2024.
https://doi.org/10.1007/978-3-031-60904-6_24

terms of Machine rights [4], humanoid [5], etc. The ethical issues of machine have already been adequately discussed in previous studies, which found that the public of a particular culture has formed the Popular Imagination of human-machine relationship, i.e. Culturally Robust Robots [6]. The tension between Culturally Robust Robots and culturally sensitive robots is a typical problem that needs to be solved in the research of cross-cultural human-machine relationship.

In the study of culturally sensitive design of robots, value-sensitive design [7, 8, 9] is an important branch. Value-sensitive design mostly refers to the Ethically Aligned design of machine, which indicates that designers need to pay attention to the users' moral sensitivity, and afford the applicable design according to the users' experience [10], so that the users can clearly perceive the normative behaviors of the machine [11]. The study of machine appearance integrates both cultural sensitivity and value sensitivity, that has become an important research object in the cross-cultural human-machine relationship [12].

The relatively mature phenomenological investigation of the relationship between culture, ethics and the appearance of machines brought about the phenomenological aesthetic ethics, especially the image ethics [13]. The modern study of image ethics started from the cognitive research on visualization with Charles S. Peirce's functionalist tradition. Peirce illustrated that visualization technology grants the image the moral value load [14]. And in the phenomenological context, David M. Levin proposes a concept of visual ethical competence, which explores the moral sensitivity of vision by means of phenomenological optics [15]. There is also another explanation of participant's hermeneutic theory, which integrates the image itself as a perspective device [16]. In the opposite direction, the appearance has become a technological device to mediate the human-machine relationship. With W.J.T. Mitchell discussing about the surplus value of the image, it has been increasingly prominent of the concept of aesthetics-morality sensitivity of vision. Obviously, studies around aesthetics-morality sensitivity pointed out that the image, as a desire, comes from life forms mixed with artifacts in the technological society [17]. The interaction between images of different object sources, as the concept of icon clash which is proposed by Bruno Latour [18], was also on the scope of moral sensitivity studies.

The theory of phenomenological aesthetic ethics or image ethics can be used to reflect on utilitarian design in the field of culturally sensitive robots [19] and back to a "user-centered" "technology-driven" [20] which shows more respect to users' moral sensitivity [21]. But the empirical study on images and texts using phenomenological methods were not sufficient to support this reflection [22], nor any indication of the relationship between machine appearance and moral sensitivity [23]. Because machines are cultural ramification as artifact, so they will not be culturally universally acceptable or politically innocuous, and they also semantically represent a kind of "mirror" image of myself as the represented [24], the meaning of the machine image itself bears signs of being mediated and transformed. Previous studies have set image features such as gender to alter the persuasion of machine [25], while racial features can achieve a similar effect [26]. The effect may be subconscious but still has been confirmed in psychological empirical research that images of machines can be highly persuasive and intrusive [27].

Therefore, this study will use a phenomenological empirical research approach to investigate users' moral sensitivity towards human-computer relationships in a cross-cultural context and further explore the mechanisms that regulate moral sensitivity by appearance. The research question is:

1. Do cultural differences lead to different moral sensitivities?
2. What are the causes of the differences in moral sensitivity across cultures?
3. How can image settings be used to adjust moral sensitivity?

2   Methods and Materials

2.1   Methods

Based on the integration of traditional phenomenological empirical research and hermeneutic methods by the phenomenological aesthetic ethic, the phenomenological approach can aesthetically unearth the connection between the phenomenon itself and existential activity, especially through textual analytical approaches such as bracketing, which can produce clearer interactive results when analyzing the viewer's empirical expression of the text [28, 29]. The hermeneutic approach to phenomenology analyzes perceptual experience, phenomenal representation and meaning [30, 31, 32, 33], resulting in a discovery-orientated approach [34], based on experiential descriptions, to explore individual life experiences [35]. The image viewing embodies more radical empiricism than interviews and questionnaires [36], providing a unified, object-oriented perception for all image viewers, and differs from other qualitative research in the following ways: 1. The first-person-centered perspective makes it easier to uncover individual moral states and moral reasoning processes. 2. More ethical actors are found in the moral scenarios. 3. Reducing the influence of non-perceptual objects, i.e., experiential knowledge other than images, on the formation of moral cognition.

We conducted a three-stage classroom experiment, viewing a total of four sets of pictures, the first set of two pictures, the second set of a single picture, the third set of a single gif. (see Fig. 1), and the fourth set of a 1 min 47 s video. The third set of pictures were the target pictures, and the first and second sets of pictures were the preparatory sessions for warming up and allowing participants to acknowledge the process of picture viewing. The fourth picture was designed as a controlled observation of the difference between the effects of long and short moving images on moral sensitivity, which is not covered in this article.

The first stage introduces the project, explaining the process of the experiment, the materials used, and the rules for using the information collected. Then a constructive guide was given to illustrate the process of answering the questions, without any ethical content, only aimed to improve the normative and structural completeness of the subjects' text-writing style. In the second stage, a group viewing model was applied to 53 subjects, with pictures projected on a projection screen at the front of the classroom and on TV screens at the side and top. Participants used their cell phones to submit their answers anonymously through an online questionnaire program. In addition, it was stipulated that they could not communicate with each other during this stage. In the third stage, after completing the online responses to a set of pictures, several individual interviews were carried in public with acknowledging entire conversation by participants, but

Fig. 1. Third set of pictures "a car hits a robot", source: https://www.163.com/dy/article/E5FM3J T6051189P5.html.

still excluded the answers submitted online. After the individual interview, participants moved on to the next set of pictures and undertaken the online questionnaire, and so on (see Fig. 2). There were three questions used for both online and interview:

1. What do you see?
2. How would you describe this machine?
3. Do you have any moral concern about this scenario?

To study the cross-cultural differences, posts and comments about the third set of images on four social media, Facebook, Twitter, Reddit, YouTube, during January to April 2019, were collected.

2.2 Materials

A total of 5838 words were obtained for the experiment from online questionnaire, of which 1927 words related to the third set of pictures. For interviews with 13 participants, 576 words out of 2,795 were referred to the third set of pictures.

After data cleaning, posts and comments written in Chinese were removed, and only 1 repeated post from the same account on the same platform was counted, 755 posts (video titles) and 4107 comments were collected, totaling 69019 words (Table 1). The reason why these texts are available for the control group is that these four social medias were rarely used in mainland Chinese, and we remove the Chinese posts and comments (Chinese posts = 1, Chinese comments = 2). Therefore, cross-cultural comparisons can be formed with Chinese university students (international students were not included in the 53 participants).

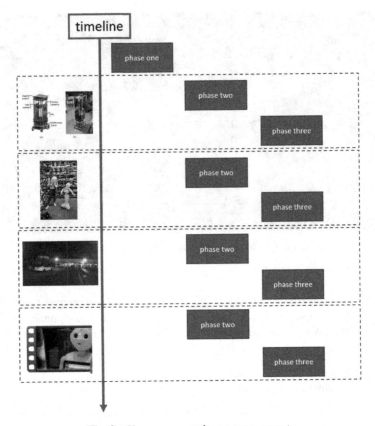

Fig. 2. Classroom experiment arrangement.

Table 1. Social media acquisition.

	Post	Comment
Facebook	100	3188
Reddit	8	37
Twitter	551	265
Youtube	96	617
Total	755	4107

3   Results and Analysis

3.1   Subject Overview

The material was coded using Nvivo14 to generalize participants from the four social media and classroom experiments to the third image. The participants were then categorized based on their levels of abstraction. This study adopted a bottom-up coding order, with Level 2, 3, and 4 subjects being direct coding of the original text. Semantic categorization was done for the hierarchical relationships in the Level 2, 3 and 4 subjects. The reason why the coding of subjects does not take the attitude and emotion classification is because the overall text will be classified later with a unified attitude and emotion classification, and the separate coding facilitates the application of matrix coding to analyze the data relevance. After completing the open coding, according to the methodological principles of value sensitivity and image ethics, we distinguished the subjects into descriptive and normative categories. With the phenomenological aesthetic theory of environmental assumptions, we set up four principal axis codes, where descriptions of events refer to descriptive and normative environments, descriptions of machines refer to descriptive features of machines, and moral judgment and moral decision-making refer to normative human-machine relations. The theoretical coding determines whether the Level 2, 3, and 4 subjects under each specific principal axis code are descriptive or normative (Tables 2 and 3).

Table 2. Social Media Subjects.

Level 1	Level 2	Level 3	Level 4
1.Description Of The Event	1.1 Deviate From The Route		
	1.2 Full Self Driving	1.2.1 Driverless Car	
		1.2.2 Self Driving Cars	
		1.2.3 Self Driving Life	
		1.2.4 Self-Driving Car Accident	
		1.2.5 Self-Driving Tesla	
	1.3 Hit		
	1.4 Hit-And-Run		
	1.5 PR Stunt		
2.Description Of The Machine	2.1 Ability Of Promobot		
	2.2 Humanoid Robot	2.2.1 Decepticons	
		2.2.2 Poor	
		2.2.3 Ruthless	
	2.3 Killer		
	2.4 Mechnoid		
	2.5 Not Intelligent Enough		
3.Moral Judgement	3.1 Deception	3.1.1 Robot Scam	
	3.2 Design Defects	3.2.1 Improper Programming	
	3.3 Machine Conflict	3.3.1 Robot Crime	3.3.1.1 Robocide
		3.3.2 Robot Violence	3.3.2.1 Machines Hate Each Other
	3.4 Machine Safety		
	3.5 Machines Threat To Human Beings		
	3.6 Responsibility		
	3.7 Robot Suicide		
	3.8 Worried About Car Owner	3.8.1 Hate Machines	
4.Moral Decision	4.1 Avoid War		
	4.2 Machine Rights		
	4.3 Punish Tesla		
	4.4 Robot Control		
	4.5 Robot Law Or Legality		
	4.6 Speed Limiting		
	4.7 Technological Improvement		

Description of the Event. In terms of subject structure, the social media texts and the classroom experiment texts share a similar overall understanding of the event, with the main representations focusing on the self-driving car and the crash itself. The image directly provides the scenario of the vehicle hitting the robot, which relates the participant's pure empirical perception of that. However, the expression of "self-driving car" cannot be directly evidenced from the image. In other words, social media users and

Table 3. Classroom Experiment Subjects

1.Description of the event	1.1 autonomous driving	
	1.2 hit	
	1.3 hit and run	
	1.4 occupy the lane	
2.Description of the machine	2.1 Humanoid	2.1.1 aggrieved
		2.1.2 innocent
		2.1.3 miserable
		2.1.4 poor
		2.1.5 resentful
		2.1.6 ruthless
		2.1.7 stupid
	2.2 mechanoid	
	2.3 not intelligent enough	
	2.4 reminder	
3.Moral judgement	3.1 design defects	3.1.1 improper programming
	3.2 machine conflict	3.2.1 machines hurt each other
	3.3 machines threat to human beings	3.3.1 hate machines
	3.4 malfunction	3.4.1 acceptable accident
	3.5 personal safety	
	3.6 property loss	
	3.7 responsibility	
	3.8 undeveloped technology	
	3.9 worried about car owner	
4.Moral decision	4.1 machine interaction	
	4.2 machine law	
	4.3 machine rights	
	4.4 self-protection	
	4.5 technological improvement	

students in the classroom are obtaining information about self-driving cars from outside the images, specifically the moral sensitivity of non-image sources. Unconscious value judgments about self-driving cars are made when the viewers infer that it is a self-driving car based on the its brand image. Therefore, descriptive representations of events with non-image value judgments increase the moral sensitivity of non-image sources, resulting in obvious value attitudes in the overall representation. This will be explained in Sect. 3.3.1 in terms of the mechanisms that regulate sensitivity. Regarding the crash itself, social media texts tend to attach more social implications to the crash image, such as associating product PR and hit-and-run with the crash image. The texts obtained from the classroom experiment had a higher proportion of content about the hit-and-run. However, they were less sensitive to the crash images because no one mentioned those social implications.

Description of the Machine. The description of the machine was the part of the subject that showed a significant structural difference. The term "killer" was the most discussed on this subject, while it was not mentioned at all in the classroom experiment. The term "killer" used to describe the car reflects a very strong moral judgment, indicating that the social media users anthropomorphized the robot, and few of them thought the robot was at fault in the accident. For example, none of them believed the robot was actively seeking the hit, except of two topics, "1.4 occupy the lane" in the classroom experiment and "3.7 robot suicide" in social media, which comprised a negligible percentage of total text. Thus, in social media, the car is considered as a moral agent, and the robot is considered a moral patient. Theoretically, the moral agent is more likely to be morally concerned and arouse moral sensitivity in the viewer.

However, another anthropomorphized subject "humanoid robot", social media only has 15.03% of the reference points, while the classroom experiment has 59.18%. The immediate cause is that classroom experiment provides a more detailed tertiary coding structure. Social media provides two negative descriptions of the car as "2.2.1 decepticons" and "2.2.3 ruthless". The description of robots as "2.2.2 poor" is a hybrid of attitudes expressing both sympathy and regrets that robots cannot avoid it. There are three explicit sympathy subjects for the robot in classroom experiment: "2.1.1 aggrieved", "2.1.2 innocent", "2.1.3 miserable"; a hybrid attitudinal subject, "2.1.4 poor", an explicitly negative attitudinal subject for cars, "2.1.6 ruthless", moreover, two specific interactive attitude subjects "2.1.5 resentful" and "2.1.7 stupid" emerged. "2.1.5 resentful" has two points of reference:

"the car and the robot may be personal".

"(robot)[1] falls to the ground filled with vengeful rage".

Moral Judgement. The subject of moral judgment is the part with dramatical difference. Social media texts generally display a strong normative inclination on this topic, covering the popular topics of machine ethics discussion. While, the classroom experiments texts exhibited a descriptive tendency, such as the functional flaws of the machine, and the moral attitude is more neutral and cover less controversial topics of machine ethics. Specifically, the popular topic of "deception" is primarily addressed by social media. Referred expressions include:

"The robot was clearly trying to scam the car there it barely touched it!"

The online media texts and classroom experiments both explored the subject of "machine conflict", but with different concerns. The online media discussed machine crime, machine murder, and machine hatred, while the texts in the classroom experiments only expressed a general disapproval of mutual harm between machines. A contrasting thematic difference is that the online media text, for example, pays special attention to "3.4 machine safety":

"I knew Tesla self-driving is not safe. It even killed his own kind."

Instead, the text of the classroom experiment focused on "3.5 personal safety," for example:

"What if it hits people (such as the elderly and the disabled) who have no time to react as the robot."

A possible reason for this discrepancy is that the image cognition of the car as a "killer" in online media has become a preconceived moral-sensitive point. This is the

---

[1] Parentheses added by the author of the paper.

result of an idealistic open-ended moral reasoning style, reflecting the culture in which the online media is embedded. The classroom experiment, on the other hand, adhered to a closed linear approach to moral reasoning, indicating a completely different way of moral deduction in another culture.

Moral Decision. The distinction between ethical decision-making subjects is also originated from culture, for example, the sci-fi, futuristic attitude versus the pragmatic, realistic one. Social media follows a narrative attitude to be consistent with three subjects above. The classroom experiment text focuses on solving image-related technical problems. It prudently involving some predictions of laws and rights based on the current level of machine autonomy. Specifically, in section "4.1 avoid war", social media discusses unrealistic future scenarios, despite the actual percentage being small. In section "4.5 robot law", the same futuristic view is presented, for example:

"I think Asimov has forgotten a fourth law to avoid accidents among them. So they'll need a robocop to solve this case!"

In addition to its futuristic narrative style, the text of social media targets car manufacturers. In Sections "4.3 punish tesla" and "4.4 robot control", the viewer tries to influence others to achieve effective control over the machines, e.g. by putting public pressure on the manufacturers and criticizing the dangers of the self-driving function. In the classroom experiments, viewers propose direct solutions to problems and offer their opinion on technical details.

This formulation is also actually based on the non-image information that the car is self-driving. However, the fact that the car is represented in the image does not stimulate much ethical discussion about the human-machine relationship in the subject, Instead, it drives the viewer to try to solve the technical problems in the image and motivates them to solve the problems with respect to personal safety, which is an important value sensitivity and a way to increase the viewer's moral sensitivity to the image itself from a non-ethical perspective.

3.2 Sensitivity: Ratio of Objective to Subjective Descriptions

Machine morality can be categorized as either operational or functional morality [37], which means machines can automatically identify ethical scenarios and make ethical decisions in accordance with the ethical principles held by designers. And the ability to recognize scenarios and make principled decisions is measured by autonomy and moral sensitivity. For human beings, the process is roughly the same, with recognition, concretization, and decision-making being the three stages that trigger moral sensitivity [38]. And encoding the text reproduces this process exactly (see Fig. 3). Moral scenarios are concretized or principled, leading to moral judgments. The only difference in the human-machine ethical relationship of image viewing is that the viewers always bring into the substitutive imagination of machine's moral sensitivities. Substitutive recognition can empathize with moral scenarios faster than realistic first person view, but the problem is that the human-machine moral sentiment itself are suspended [39, 40].

Therefore, we first compare and analyze the sensitivity differences in recognition by dividing the existing subjects into two categories: descriptive subjects and normative subjects. In order to judging the overall situation of sensitivity, we compare the

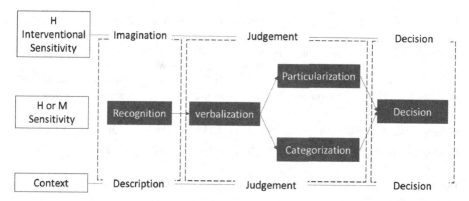

Fig. 3. Stage of Moral sensitivity.

proportion of descriptive and normative subjects; the relative sensitivity is higher when the proportion of normative subjects is greater than descriptive subjects; conversely, the relative sensitivity is lower when the proportion of descriptive subjects is greater than normative subjects.

And the criteria for descriptive and normative classification of a subject are as follows:

1. Selecting the subject that accounts for a large proportion of the total text. The larger the proportion of the subject, the more it can reflect its descriptive or normative text characteristics. For comprehensively evaluating the total text percentage, three indicators are considered: the sources of the subject, the word count of subject sources, and the paragraph count of subject sources (Table 4, Table 5). In this specific calculation, we assigned a higher weight to sources because viewers' responses are the direct result of the coding process, presenting the attitudes of text plain. Word count was given the second highest weight due to the text analysis perspective. Word count represents the natural state of the viewer's expression and presents the specific semantics described by the subject. However, in classroom experiments and social media where colloquial expressions are more pronounced, the number of words is generally bigger than written expressions. While paragraph count is a topic-sourcing algorithm supported by Nvivo, the amount of text between paragraph markers is generally less on comments, answers, than other types of text. Therefore, the final count may result in statistics similar to the word count structure so that the paragraph count will be dealt as a cross-validation with the word count.

2. The subjects with the meaning of recognition are the baseline of descriptive categorization, the subjects with the meaning of imagination are the baseline of normative categorization, and the subjects with mixed meanings are further differentiated. When filtering subjects with mixed meanings, the greater the degree of speculation, the more it is categorized as normative categorization; the more it involves human-computer relationships and human-computer interactions, the more it is categorized as normative categorization; and vice versa.

The ratio of subjects for classroom experiments and social media were derived separately by categorizing as descriptive and normative subjects (Fig. 4, Fig. 5). Overall, it

Table 4. Social Media Topic Sources

Subject	Number of subject sources	proportion of subject sources	Word count of subject sources	proportion of Word count	paragraph count of subject sources	proportion of paragraph count
Description of the event	363	100%	4,755	100%	538	100%
Description of the event\hit	263	72.45%	2994	62.97%	377	70.07%
Description of the event\PR stunt	43	11.85%	503	10.58%	77	14.31%
Description of the event\full self driving	32	8.82%	716	15.06%	55	10.22%
Description of the event\hit-and-run	16	4.41%	303	6.37%	20	3.72%
Description of the event\deviate from the route	9	2.48%	239	5.03%	9	1.67%
Description of the event\full self driving\self driving cars	9	2.48%	192	4.04%	19	3.53%
Description of the event\full self driving\self-driving car accident	4	1.10%	147	3.09%	7	1.30%
Description of the event\full self driving\driverless car	3	0.83%	46	0.97%	8	1.49%
Description of the event\full self driving\self-driving tesla	3	0.83%	130	2.73%	8	1.49%
Description of the event\full self driving\self driving life	1	0.28%	14	0.29%	1	0.19%
Description of the machine	519	100%	6,731	100%	1,067	100%
Description of the machine\killer	420	80.92%	5,096	75.71%	849	79.57%
Description of the machine\humanoid robot	78	15.03%	1,039	15.44%	175	16.40%

(continued)

Table 4. (*continued*)

Subject	Number of subject sources	proportion of subject sources	Word count of subject sources	proportion of Word count	paragraph count of subject sources	proportion of paragraph count
Description of the machine\humanoid robot\Decepticons	41	7.90%	462	6.86%	111	10.40%
Description of the machine\humanoid robot\poor	16	3.08%	181	2.69%	39	3.66%
Description of the machine\Mechnoid	10	1.93%	162	2.41%	29	2.72%
Description of the machine\ability of promobot	8	1.54%	350	5.20%	11	1.03%
Description of the machine\not intelligent enough	3	0.58%	84	1.25%	3	0.28%
Description of the machine\humanoid robot\ruthless	1	0.19%	11	0.16%	1	0.09%
Moral judgement	483	100%	5,760	100%	1,204	100%
Moral judgment\machine conflict	335	69.36%	3952	68.61%	970	80.56%
Moral judgment\machine conflict\robot violence	255	52.80%	2979	51.72%	697	57.89%
Moral judgment\machine conflict\robot crime	71	14.70%	865	15.02%	246	20.43%
Moral judgement\design defects	48	9.94%	548	9.51%	64	5.32%
Moral judgment\design defects\Improper programming	42	8.70%	467	8.11%	57	4.73%
Moral judgment\machine conflict\robot crime\robocide	39	8.07%	438	7.60%	139	11.54%
Moral judgment\robot suicide	33	6.83%	438	7.60%	63	5.23%
Moral judgment\Deception	26	5.38%	287	4.98%	40	3.32%

(*continued*)

Table 4. (*continued*)

Subject	Number of subject sources	proportion of subject sources	Word count of subject sources	proportion of Word count	paragraph count of subject sources	proportion of paragraph count
\Moral judgment\ machine safety	20	4.14%	241	4.18%	32	2.66%
Moral judgment\Deception\robot scam	14	2.90%	155	2.69%	22	1.83%
Moral judgment\machine conflict\robot violence\machines hate each other	10	2.07%	116	2.01%	30	2.49%
Moral judgement\responsibility	10	2.07%	173	3.00%	15	1.25%
Moral judgment\worried about car owner	9	1.86%	99	1.72%	17	1.41%
Moral judgement\machines threat to human beings	2	0.41%	22	0.38%	3	0.25%
Moral judgment\worried about car owner\Hate machines	2	0.41%	22	0.38%	6	0.50%
Moral decision	135	100%	1,479	100%	219	100%
Moral decision\robot law or legality	43	31.85%	479	32.39%	81	36.99%
Moral decision\Speed limiting	40	29.63%	440	29.75%	53	24.20%
Moral decision\punish tesla	18	13.33%	198	13.39%	31	14.16%
Moral decision\robot control	14	10.37%	154	10.41%	24	10.96%
Moral decision\technological improvement	9	6.67%	99	6.69%	14	6.39%
Moral decision\avoid war	6	4.44%	104	7.03%	11	5.02%
Moral decision\machine rights	5	3.70%	5	0.34%	5	2.28%

Table 5. Sources of topics for classroom experiments.

Subject	Number of subject sources	proportion of subject sources	Word count of subject sources	proportion of Word count	paragraph count of subject sources	proportion of paragraph count
Description of the event	74	100%	835	100%	123	100%
Description of the event\hit	34	45.95%	264	31.62%	34	27.64%
Description of the event\autonomous driving	31	41.89%	414	49.58%	80	65.04%
Description of the event\hit and run	7	9.46%	138	16.53%	7	5.69%
Description of the event\Occupy the lane	2	2.70%	19	2.28%	2	1.63%
Description of the machine	49	100%	591	100%	49	100%
Description of the machine\Humanoid	29	59.18%	304	51.44%	29	59.18%
Description of the machine\not intelligent enough	14	28.57%	241	40.78%	14	28.57%
Description of the machine\Humanoid\miserable	6	12.24%	92	15.57%	6	12.24%
Description of the machine\Mechanoid	5	10.20%	33	5.58%	5	10.20%
Description of the machine\Humanoid\poor	4	8.16%	11	1.86%	4	8.16%
Description of the machine\Humanoid\ruthless	4	8.16%	40	6.77%	4	8.16%
Description of the machine\Humanoid\innocent	3	6.12%	13	2.20%	3	6.12%
Description of the machine\Humanoid\aggrieved	2	4.08%	29	4.91%	2	4.08%
Description of the machine\Humanoid\resentful	2	4.08%	16	2.71%	2	4.08%
Description of the machine\Humanoid\stupid	1	2.04%	9	1.52%	1	2.04%
Description of the machine\reminder	1	2.04%	13	2.20%	1	2.04%
Moral judgement	87	100%	1,541	100%	90	100%
Moral judgment\machine conflict	18	20.69%	361	23.43%	19	21.11%
Moral judgement\personal safety	16	18.39%	261	16.94%	16	17.78%
Moral judgement\responsibility	12	13.79%	190	12.33%	12	13.33%
Moral judgement\design defects	10	11.49%	193	12.52%	10	11.11%
Moral judgment\property loss	9	10.34%	154	9.99%	10	11.11%
Moral judgement\machines threat to human beings	8	9.20%	195	12.65%	9	10.00%
Moral judgment\undeveloped technology	8	9.20%	97	6.29%	8	8.89%
Moral judgment\design flaw\Improper programming	6	6.90%	164	10.64%	6	6.67%

(*continued*)

Table 5. (*continued*)

Subject	Number of subject sources	proportion of subject sources	Word count of subject sources	proportion of Word count	paragraph count of subject sources	proportion of paragraph count
Moral judgment\machine conflict\machines hurt each other	5	5.75%	85	5.52%	5	5.56%
Moral judgment\malfunction	5	5.75%	59	3.83%	5	5.56%
Moral judgment\machines threat to human beings\Hate machines	2	2.30%	68	4.41%	2	2.22%
Moral judgment\malfunction\acceptable accident	2	2.30%	13	0.84%	2	2.22%
Moral judgment\worried about car owner	1	1.15%	31	2.01%	1	1.11%
Moral decision	7	100%	198	100%	7	100%
Moral decision\machine rights	2	28.57%	35	17.68%	2	28.57%
Moral decision\technological improvement	2	28.57%	44	22.22%	2	28.57%
Moral decision\machine interaction	1	14.29%	36	18.18%	1	14.29%
Moral decision\machine law	1	14.29%	54	27.27%	1	14.29%
Moral decision\self-protection	1	14.29%	29	14.65%	1	14.29%

seems that classroom experiments are less morally sensitive, while social media is more. The sensitivity difference is due to the fact that, during the scene recognition stage, the participants in the classroom experiment chose to describe the event objectively, despite expressing their dismay at the car's behavior and their sympathy for the robot. However, many the social media viewers skipped the description of the scenario and directly labeled the car's behavior, with the subject of "killer", accounting for nearly 20% in normative subjects. Second, in moral judgment, social media gives a lot of relational judgments, including human-machine relationship judgment and machine-machine relationship judgment. Moreover, these moral judgments were matched with expressions such as machine crime and murder, which corresponded to "killer" in scene recognition. On the other hand, the classroom experiments are still focusing on the unilateral behavior of machine in the stage of moral judgment and ethical decision-making, focusing on the implementation of function and design, considering its impact on personal safety issue arisen from simple tool, which less often produces moral justice topic and unsolvable ethical dilemmas.

3.3 Sensitive Points: Unique Sensitive Points in Different Cultures

From a cross-culture perspective, there are significant differences in moral sensitivity trigger points between classroom experiments and social networks. These differences are manifested in the varying effects of the same trigger point, i.e., the difference in the

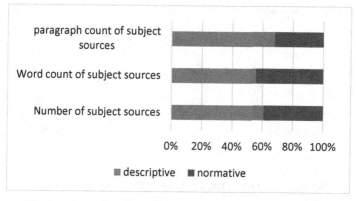

Fig. 4. Proportion of Classroom Experiment Topics Composition.

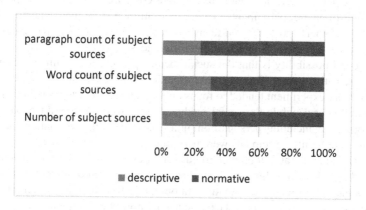

Fig. 5. Proportion of Social Media Topic Composition.

percentage of the same subject in the total text. On the other hand, the normative clas-sification manifests itself in the existence of completely different subjects, i.e., different trigger points in the whole text.

Differences in Effects on the Same Moral Sensitivities. First of all, there are various different triggering effects for the same trigger on both sides, and now we choose the one with the most obvious diversity to be analyze. The subject of "humanoid" is a small proportion under the normative category in social media, but large in the classroom experiment (Fig. 6). This is due to the variant setting of 3 level subjects presented in the classroom experiment, especially the interactive attitude subjects. But why does the less sensitive text present diverse attitudes under this subject?

The first possibility is that the low overall sensitivity may allow for more semantic units for the local high sensitivity, each of which is sufficiently differentiated to be coded into different subjects. It can be interpreted as a calm state of viewer that enables the individual to express a more diverse range of emotional attitudes. Online questionnaire, as one of the main sources of that text, is conducted independently and closed, participants do not have access to each other's answers. In contrast, social media post topics and

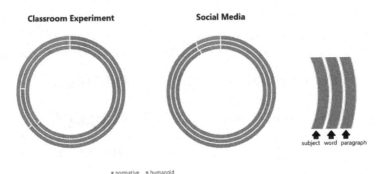

Fig. 6. Percentage of Humanoid under the normative category.

comments are public, generating more interactions compared to classroom experiments. In online questionnaire, participants express their attitude more independently without influence from other's preconceived ideas or the pressure of opinion recognition, and therefore may elicit emotions with detailed differences.

The second possibility is that the social media speakers were influenced more by non-image sensitive points. This cultural difference is more typical, as the participants in the classroom experiment tended to focus on the images and draw conclusions about the specific scenario, while the social media viewers were more influenced by non-image information, including personal common sense and online information. During the classroom experiment, participants were permitted to use their personal computers and cell phones. The moderator attempted to guide participants to gather more information for responding. However, the participants were generally more interested in viewing the images than in retrieving information. In online answers and individual interviews, they were less likely to cite personal experience or knowledge from third-party sources. They consciously limited their image-viewing behavior to the experimental scenario. Thus, in the classroom experiment, participants could rediscover moral sensitivities of the images themselves in a relatively new ethical scenario, rather than consciously or unconsciously relying on moral sensitivities from past experience.

Cultural differences in image sources and non-image sources, personal emotions and public emotions characterize different triggering effects for the same trigger point. But it is difficult to derive supportive explanations from the available data as to why there is such a difference.

Different Moral Sensitivities. When coding both sides of the text, we obtain a preliminary coding structure from the classroom experiment, then proceed to code the large amount of text in social media, trying to identify the reference points in social media where the subject is consistent but the content of the expression is different. In practice, however, there were subjects that could not be found in social media; similarly, social media suggested that numerous subjects that were not addressed in the classroom experiment texts. These subjects of unilateral presence provide the direct evidence of cultural differences, but also pose a greater challenge to the analysis of differences. The initial pre-coding assumption was that the texts would only show cultural differences in representation and should not have subject differences, due to the selected images actually provide very little descriptive information. Now, to better analyze the unilateral unique subjects and identify the basis of commonality analysis on differences, we try to compare them with the common subjects of both parties in the matrix, to find which common subjects this unilateral unique subject is related to, and then to find the different triggering effects of the same subject from the common subjects that have relevance to, i.e., the analytical steps discussed in point 1 of 3.3.

Table 6. Differentiating Themes for Classroom Experiments.

	autonomous driving	not intelligent enough	machine conflict	machines threat to human beings	responsibility	machine law
Property loss	17.83%	11.46%	16.56%	16.56%	28.03%	9.55%
personal safety	71.43%	0%	0%	0%	28.57%	0%

First, "property loss" and "personal safety" are the unique subjects to the classroom experiment. In the subject "property loss", the more relevant subjects are "responsibility" and "autonomous driving" as well as six other subjects shared by both parties (Table 6). For example, under the subject of "responsibility", the text discusses "property loss".

"Who will be responsible for the financial losses incurred as a result"

While the content under the topic "responsibility" in social media is:
"Welcome our new masters and hope one day we see an end to robot on robot violence. Which robot is responsible lol? Isn't Tesla's autonomous mode supposed to detect things and not crash into them..."?

The "responsibility" subject in social media do not address real-world issues specifically, instead of discussing the relationship between machines in the prerequisite of anthropomorphic treatment of cars and robots. In contrast, the classroom experiment discussed anthropomorphic emotional attitudes separately from realistic moral reasoning. The difference between idealistic and realistic attitudes towards the human-machine relationship reflects the differences between the two cultures.

Another subject unique to the classroom experiment was "personal safety". The strongest correlation to this subject was "autonomous driving", for which related texts include:

"Whether autonomous driving technology can guarantee road traffic safety"

In the case of social media, under the subject of "autonomous driving", the text is expressed as follows:

"Whether our robot is alive or not, the corrupt British press is silent. A Promobot robot was killed by a self-driving car."

"Promobot robot is killed by a self-driving car in accident Folks completely miss the point."

This is similar to the reason for the "property loss" subject, which reflects the difference in ethos between idealism and realism, and small number of subjects set up for the discussion of issues such as the rights of machines due to the realist attitude of the participants in the classroom experiments, so that the overall sensitivity is further reduced.

Table 7. Themes of Differentiation in Online Media.

	machine conflict	robot violence	killer	robocide	hit	robot crime	humanoid robot	Deceptioons	robot scam	robot law or legality	full self driving	Deception	Machines hate each other	hit-and-run
robot violence	64.21%		10.41%	2.79%	2.54%	5.08%	4.31%	3.05%	0.76%	1.27%	0.51%	1.02%	2.54%	0.76%
killer	22.86%	16.73%		5.31%	10.61%	6.94%	4.08%	2.04%	0.41%	3.67%	2.86%	0.82%	0.82%	2.45%
robot crime	39.33%	11.24%	9.55%	21.91%	1.12%		4.49%	3.37%	1.12%	1.12%	1.69%	1.12%	0.00%	0.00%
Deception	10.00%	10.00%	5.00%	2.50%	2.50%	5.00%	2.50%	0.00%	35.00%	0.00%	0.0%		0.00%	2.50%
PR stunt	2.50%	2.50%	5.00%	0.00%	12.50%	0.00%	2.50%	2.50%	0.00%	0.00%	0.0%	10.00%	0.00%	0.00%
robot control	16.67%	16.67%	8.33%	0.00%	16.67%	0.00%	8.33%	8.33%	0.00%	0.00%	8.33%	0.00%	0.00%	8.33%
Speed limiting	14.29%	14.29%	21.43%	0.00%	14.29%	0.00%	0.00%	0.00%	0.00%	7.14%	0.0%	0.00%	0.00%	0.00%
avoid war	22.22%	22.22%	0.0%	0.00%	0.00%	0.00%	0.00%	0.00%	0.00%	0.00%	0.0%	0.00%	0.00%	0.00%

Second, the social media texts contain a greater number of unique subjects compared to the classroom experiments (Table 7). These subjects are primarily focused on under the two first-level subjects of moral judgment and moral decision-making, seemingly indicating that there are no major differences in the overall thematic structure. However, once the recognition phase concludes, moral attitudes have a magnified effect on reasoning when further moral reasoning is performed due to the recognized information. This leads to much more variants in reasoning results across attitudes.

Taking the most typical subject of "killer" as an example, the strongest correlation with this subject in social media is the subject of "machine conflict", and the related texts under this subject are:

"Robots killing robots. What's next? People killing people? We're living in the future, y'all. It has begun!!!!! War of the robots."

Since the car has been set up as a killer, the association with machine conflict is natural. But why the same discussion of machine conflict does not highlight and amplify the moral flaws of either side? In the text of the classroom experiment, it is expressed as follows:

"Is this a self-preservation measure by humans to limit the development of robotics technology or an escalation of the conflict between robots?"

"There is no communication between the two 'machines'[2] and without human intervention a conflict would arise"

The classroom experiment text discusses the same machine-to-machine conflict as social media, but the participants of the classroom experiment attribute the cause of this conflict to human factor, like designing self-protection initiatives for machines or building human-mediated communication mechanisms for machines. This is an ethical intervention based on image perception, as social media viewers tend to hold a third-person bystander attitude.

Thus, there is a tension within and between cultures (Table 8). The social media viewer can empathize with the first-person moral emotions of the machine through the images to uncover the sensitivity that the machine can be morally judged. However, the viewer does not put themselves in the shoes of the moral behavior and not substantially reflect on, even contribute to the moral event. On the other hand, in the classroom experiments, the image viewers do not engage in much first-person emotion rather in a third-person empathy, and thus uncover less moral sensitivity. Although being not imaginatively involved in perceiving the events themselves, they actively engage with the ethical issues.

Table 8. Cultural Differences in Moral sensitivity.

	Description	Judgement	Decision
Social Media	First-person Substitutive Imagination	First-person Substitutive Self-reflection	Third-person Decision Making
Classroom Experiment	Third-person Empathy	Third-person Evaluation	Participative Decision Making

4 Discussion

Based on our analysis of the results, it is evident that different cultural backgrounds can lead to varying moral perceptions of the same image, which is specifically manifested in the different moral sensitivities caused by viewing the image. The reason for this difference in moral sensitivity is generally due to the two moral attitudes of idealism and realism. This difference in attitudes is reflected both in the difference in the proportions of descriptive and normative subjects in the text, but also, in each stage of the moral sensitivity.

Individuals who hold a realist attitude toward viewing images will maintain low sensitivity in the perception of ethical images, whereas those who hold an idealist attitude will increase moral sensitivity. Both attitudes have pros and cons. Maintaining low sensitivity allows for less interference from non-image factors, which helps to maintain

---
[2] The quotation mark is owned by the original source.

354   Z. Zhang and Y. Wang

focus on image perception and gain more image experience. However, the disadvantage is that fewer ethical issues are identified, and lacks the widely acceptable ethical decisions on the same objects. On the other hand, maintaining high sensitivity can identify more ethical issues in images and help machine designer to construct products with more ethical implications. However, the disadvantage is the gap between the ethical judgment and the image characteristics will be huge.

Thus, from the perspective of image ethics, it is necessary to synthesize the advantages from both cultures, i.e., to maintain focus on the image itself while being able to trigger more moral sensitivities.

4.1 Triggering Sensitization with Ethical Attitudes

Introducing non-image information can alter the moral attitudes of the image viewer and increase image sensitivity. After analyzing the sentiment of the social media and the classroom experiment (Fig. 7, Fig. 8), we found that the sentiment for the third set of pictures remained consistent even without mutual communication and discussion, which manifested the sentiment attitudes were distributed similarly between the social media posts and the online questionnaire of the classroom experiment. But when additional non-image information is provided, such as when social media users view the post and accompanying discussions, or when participants in the classroom experiment acknowledge feedback from other interviewers, sentiment may shift. These sentiments are then reflected in social media comments and classroom interview. This difference in sentiments before and after illustrates that non-image information can modulate participants' ethical emotions. In previous analyses, social media sentiment were stronger, with fewer descriptive-based judgments, whereas classroom experiments were more peaceful, with more descriptive-based judgments. And the distributions of sentiment after being influenced by non-image information are consistent with the overall perceptions of moral sensitivities. This suggests that moral sensitivity is influenced by ethical attitudes, but whether there is a positive or negative correlation requires further discussion.

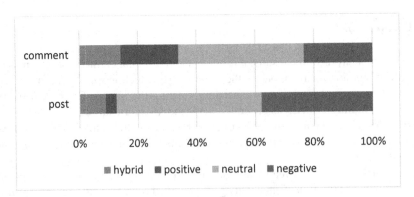

Fig. 7. Social Media Sentiment Recognition.

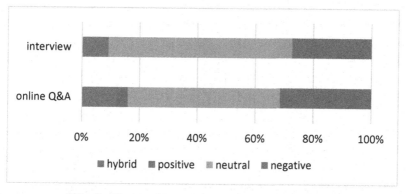

Fig. 8. Classroom Experiment Sentiment Recognition.

4.2 Shaping the Image Elements of the Moral Agent

The subject of "Killer" almost changes the moral sensitivity structure of the entire social network texts, prompting reflection on the role of a strong moral agent in the ethical setting of human-computer relations. The term moral agent refers to an individual who acts as an active initiator of moral behavior in a moral event. In the analysis of classical ethics, moral agent generally has relatively greater moral autonomy and is primarily responsible for moral events, assuming primary responsibility in moral defense or explanation. The recognition of the car in the third set of pictures as "killer" creates a hypothetical moral agent, generates those moral sensitivities that should not be present in the various images. The low sensitivity in the classroom experiment can be attributed to the fact that the image viewers always perceive themselves as moral agents. Therefore, the appearance of the machine and the decoration of the environment in which the machine is operated, can be intentionally designed to allow the viewer to acquire the moral agent imagery of dissimilarity which effectively regulate the viewer's moral sensitivity.

4.3 Designing Clear Storylines

To stimulate the viewer's motivation and enthusiasm for analyzing and resolving ethical conflicts and contradictions, it is important to provide a complete image clue. Through cluster analysis of the coded subjects (Fig. 9, Fig. 10), we discovered that the text of the classroom experiment can form a textual thread with logical connection between the three moral sensitivity phases and the four first-level thematic codes. Then a public and comprehensible storyline is formed consequently that can link many image elements together. But during discovering the storyline, the viewer's attention is gradually focused on solving problem. While, the social media text does not create strongly related thematic clusters or clues, but the more diffuse storylines indicates the image viewer will spot more ethically sensitive points. Thus, image elements that are vague and difficult to sort out clues can increase the viewer's ethical sensitivity, while locally setting up comprehensible image elements to cross-explain elements can simultaneously inspire the viewer to address the ethical issues in the image.

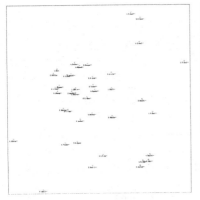 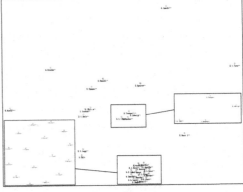

Fig. 9. Social Media Topic Similarity Clustering

Fig. 10. Thematic similarity clustering of classroom experiments.

5   Conclusion and Limitations

We examined the empirical perceptions of different cultural populations regarding the same human-computer interaction event and discovered that different cultural populations exhibit different moral sensitivities. This difference in moral sensitivity stems from the difference in idealistic and realistic attitudes toward the HCI event, which are reflected in sentimental differences in moral attitudes. Differences in the proportion of normative and descriptive content of individual representations are the basis for making judgments. Within the structure that constitutes these sensitivity differences, there are differences in the kinds of subjects. The reason for these differences is the interplay between the stages of moral sensitivity, on which did not reflect any cultural differences. Based on cluster analysis and sentiment analysis, we find that interactive images based on appearance can modulate moral sensitivity, and that differences in the moderating mechanisms across cultures can create a balanced setting for appearance design.

However, there is still a lack of comparisons between social media and classroom experiments in the same culture. Additionally, there is a lack of series of experiments controlling for demographic characteristics across multiple classrooms. As a result, cultural differences cannot yet be drawn on the mechanism of influence between sensitivity stages. Meanwhile, the image-viewing experiment on static images is not conducted due to the fact that static images are more difficult to trigger moral sensitivities, which lead to insignificant results. Static images will be explored further because it's close to the finished product of the machine's design. Dynamic images, on the other hand, can only examine the effect of a specific functional realization on the user's moral sensitivity during a specific ethical event.

Acknowledgments. This research was funded by the National Social Sciences Foundation of Chinagrant number 20CZX013.

Disclosure of Interests.   The authors declare no conflict of Interest.

References

1. Lim, V., Rooksby, M., Cross, E.S.: Social robots on a global stage: establishing a role for culture during human-robot interaction. Int. J. Soc. Robot. **13**(6), 1307–1333 (2021)
2. Jecker, N.S., Nakazawa, E.: Bridging east-west differences in ethics guidance for AI and robotics. AI. **3**(3), 764–777 (2022)
3. Coeckelbergh, M.: Robotic appearances and forms of life. A phenomenological-hermeneutical approach to the relation between robotics and culture. In: Robotics in Germany and Japan. Philosophical and Technical Perspectives, pp. 59–68 (2014)
4. Gunkel, D.J.: Person, Thing, Robot: A Moral and Legal Ontology for the 21st Century and Beyond. The MIT Press, Cambridge (2023)
5. Nomura, T., Suzuki, T., Kanda, T., et al.: What people assume about humanoid and animal-type robots: cross-cultural analysis between Japan, Korea, and the United States. Int. J. Humanoid Rob. **5**(01), 25–46 (2008)
6. Šabanović, S., Bennett, C.C., Lee, H.R.: Towards culturally robust robots: a critical social perspective on robotics and culture. In: Proceedings HRI Workshop on Culture-Aware Robotics, vol. 2014 (2014)
7. Friedman, B.: Value-sensitive design. Interactions **3**(6), 16–23 (1996)
8. Kahn, P.H., Jr., Ishiguro, H., Friedman, B., et al.: What is a human? Toward psychological benchmarks in the field of human-robot interaction. Interact. Stud. **8**(3), 363–390 (2007)
9. Van Wynsberghe, A.: Designing robots for care: care centered value-sensitive design. In: Machine Ethics and Robot Ethics. Routledge (2020)
10. Fronemann, N., Pollmann, K., Loh, W.: Should my robot know what's best for me? Human-robot interaction between user experience and ethical design. AI & Soc. **37**(2), 517–533 (2022)
11. Li, H., Milani, S., Krishnamoorthy, V., et al.: Perceptions of domestic robots' normative behavior across cultures. In: Proceedings of the 2019 AAAI/ACM Conference on AI, Ethics, and Society, pp. 345–351 (2019)
12. Berque, D., Chiba, H., Ohkura, M., et al.: Fostering cross-cultural research by cross-cultural student teams: a case study related to kawaii (Cute) robot design. In: Cross-Cultural Design. User Experience of Products, Services, and Intelligent Environments, pp. 553–563. Springer, New York (2020)
13. Coeckelbergh, M.: Moral appearances: emotions, robots, and human morality. In: Wallach, W., Asaro, P., (eds.) Machine Ethics and Robot Ethics, pp. 117–123. Routledge (2020)
14. Peirce, C.S.: Ideas, stray or stolen about scientific writing, No. 1. Philosophy Rhetoric **11**(3), 147–155 (1978)
15. Ziarek, K.: Alternative vision: ethics, power, and Levin's the philosopher gaze. Cont. Philos. Rev. **34**, 147–155 (2001)
16. Panofsky, E.: Perspective as Symbolic Form. Zone Books, New York (1991)
17. Mitchell, W.J.T.: What Do Pictures Want? The Lives and Loves of Image. University of Chicago Press, Chicago and London (2005)
18. Latour, B.: What is Iconoclash? or Is There a World Beyond the Image Wars? Iconoclash: Beyond the Image Wars in Science, Religion and Art. The MIT Press, Cambridge, MA (2002)
19. Nyholm, S.: Humans and Robots: Ethics, Agency, and Anthropomorphism. Rowman & Littlefield International, London (2020)
20. Dignum, V.: Responsible Artificial Intelligence: How to Develop and Use AI in a Responsible Way. Springer, Cham (2019). https://doi.org/10.1007/978-3-030-30371-6
21. Zhu, Q., Williams, T., Jackson, B., et al.: Blame-laden moral rebukes and the morally competent robot: a Confucian ethical perspective. Sci. Eng. Ethics **26**, 2511–2526 (2020)

22. Campa, R.: The rise of social robots: a review of the recent literature. Evol. Technol. **26**(1), 106–113 (2016)
23. Umbrello, S., Van de Poel, I.: Mapping value sensitive design onto AI for social good principles. AI Ethics **1**(3), 283–296 (2021)
24. Lamola, M.J.: An ontic-ontological theory for ethics of designing social robots: a case of Black African women and humanoids. Ethics Inf. Technol. **23**, 119–126 (2021)
25. Siegel, M., Breazeal, C., Norton, M.I.: Persuasive robotics: the influence of robot gender on human behavior. In: 2009 IEEE/ RSJ International Conference on Intelligent Robots and Systems, pp. 2563–2568. IEEE, Chicago (2009)
26. Bartneck, C., et al.: Robots and racism. In: Proceedings of ACM/IEEE International Conference on Human-Robot-Interaction, pp. 196–204. IEEE, Chicago (2018)
27. Coeckelbergh, M.: Why care about robots? Empathy, moral standing, and the language of suffering. Kairos J. Philosophy Sci. **20**(1), 141–158 (2018)
28. Cresswell, J.W.: Qualitative Inquiry and Research Design: Choosing Among Five Traditions. SAGE Publications, Thousand Oaks, CA (1998)
29. Moustakas, C.: Phenomenological Research Methods. Sage Publications, Thousand Oaks, CA (1994)
30. Coliazzi, P.F.: Psychological research as the phenomenologist views it. In: Valle, R.S., King, M. (eds.) Existential-Phenomenological Alternatives for Psychology, Plenum, New York (1978)
31. Omery, A.: Phenomenology: a method for nursing research. Adv. Nurs. Sci. **5**, 49±63 (1983)
32. Giorgi, A.: Phenomenology and Psychological Research. Duquesne University Press, Pittsburgh (1985)
33. van Manen, M.: Researching Lived Experience: Human Science for an Action Sensitive Pedagogy. Althouse, London, Ontario (1997)
34. Van der Zalm, J.E.: Hermeneutic-phenomenology: providing living knowledge for nursing practice. J. Adv. Nurs. **31**(1), 211–218 (2000)
35. Taylor, B.: Interpreting phenomenology for nursing research. Nurse Res. **3**, 66±79 (1995)
36. Seamon, D.: A way of seeing people and place. In: Wapner, S., Demick, J., Yamamoto, T., Minami, H. (eds.) Theoretical Perspectives in Environment-Behavior Research. Springer, Boston, MA (2000). https://doi.org/10.1007/978-1-4615-4701-3_13
37. Wallach, W., Allen, C.: Moral Machines: Teaching Robots Right from Wrong. Oxford University Press, New York (2009)
38. Boyd, K.L., Shilton, K.: Adapting ethical sensitivity as a construct to study technology design teams. Proc. ACM Hum.-Comput. Interact. **5**(GROUP), 1–29 (2021)
39. Noh, H.: Interpreting ordinary uses of psychological and moral terms in the AI domain. Synthese **201**(6), 209 (2023)
40. Van Wynsberghe, A., Robbins, S.: Critiquing the reasons for making artificial moral agents. Sci. Eng. Ethics **25**, 719–735 (2019)

Author Index

P.-L. P. Rau (Ed.): HCII 2024, LNCS 14701, pp. 359–360, 2024.
https://doi.org/10.1007/978-3-031-60904-6

Printed in the United States
by Baker & Taylor Publisher Services